The Divine Comedy
The Vision or, Hell, Purgatory, and Paradise
of Dante Alighieri
The Cary Edition
Translated by the Rev. H. F. Cary, A.M.
This Edition Edited by Anthony Uyl

Ingersoll, Ontario, Canada 2025

The Divine Comedy

The Divine Comedy
The Vision or, Hell, Purgatory, and Paradise of Dante Alighieri
The Cary Edition
Translated by the Rev. H. F. Cary, A.M.
This Edition Edited by Anthony Uyl

The text of *The Divine Comedy: The Vision or, Hell, Purgatory, and Paradise The Cary Edition* is all protected under Copyright ©2025 Devoted Publishing. The covers, background, layout and Devoted Publishing logo are Copyright ©2025 Devoted Publishing. This edition is published by Devoted Publishing a division of 2165467 Ontario Inc.

Contact us at: devotedpub@hotmail.com
X (Formerly Twitter): @AnthonyDevPub

Published in Ingersoll, Ontario, Canada 2025.

ISBN: 978-1-77356-534-7

Table of Contents

- PREFACE by the TRANSLATOR 5
- HELL 6
  - CANTO I 6
  - CANTO II 8
  - CANTO III 11
  - CANTO IV 14
  - CANTO V 17
  - CANTO VI 20
  - CANTO VII 22
  - CANTO VIII 25
  - CANTO IX 28
  - CANTO X 30
  - CANTO XI 33
  - CANTO XII 36
  - CANTO XIII 39
  - CANTO XIV 42
  - CANTO XV 45
  - CANTO XVI 47
  - CANTO XVII 50
  - CANTO XVIII 53
  - CANTO XIX 55
  - CANTO XX 58
  - CANTO XXI 61
  - CANTO XXII 64
  - CANTO XXIII 67
  - CANTO XXIV 70
  - CANTO XXV 73
  - CANTO XXVI 76
  - CANTO XXVII 79
  - CANTO XXVIII 81
  - CANTO XXIX 84
  - CANTO XXX 87
  - CANTO XXXI 90
  - CANTO XXXII 93
  - CANTO XXXIII 96
  - CANTO XXXIV 99
- NOTES TO HELL 102
- PURGATORY 136
  - CANTO I 136
  - CANTO II 139
  - CANTO III 141
  - CANTO IV 144
  - CANTO V 147
  - CANTO VI 150
  - CANTO VII 153
  - CANTO VIII 156
  - CANTO IX 158
  - CANTO X 161
  - CANTO XI 164
  - CANTO XII 167
  - CANTO XIII 169
  - CANTO XIV 172
  - CANTO XV 176
  - CANTO XVI 179
  - CANTO XVII 182
  - CANTO XVIII 184
  - CANTO XIX 187
  - CANTO XX 190
  - CANTO XXI 193
  - CANTO XXII 196
  - CANTO XXIII 199
  - CANTO XXIV 202
  - CANTO XXV 205
  - CANTO XXVI 208
  - CANTO XXVII 211
  - CANTO XXVIII 214
  - CANTO XXIX 217
  - CANTO XXX 220
  - CANTO XXXI 223
  - CANTO XXXII 226

The Divine Comedy

- CANTO XXXIII 229
- NOTES TO PURGATORY 233
- PARADISE 260
  - CANTO I 260
  - CANTO II 263
  - CANTO III 266
  - CANTO IV 268
  - CANTO V 271
  - CANTO VI 274
  - CANTO VII 277
  - CANTO VIII 280
  - CANTO IX 283
  - CANTO X 286
  - CANTO XI 289
  - CANTO XII 291
  - CANTO XIII 294
  - CANTO XIV 297
  - CANTO XV 300
  - CANTO XVI 303
  - CANTO XVII 306
  - CANTO XVIII 309
  - CANTO XIX 311
  - CANTO XX 314
  - CANTO XXI 317
  - CANTO XXII 320
  - CANTO XXIII 323
  - CANTO XXIV 326
  - CANTO XXV 329
  - CANTO XXVI 332
  - CANTO XXVII 335
  - CANTO XXVIII 338
  - CANTO XXIX 340
  - CANTO XXX 343
  - CANTO XXXI 346
  - CANTO XXXII 349
  - CANTO XXXIII 352
- NOTES TO PARADISE 356
- A CHRONOLOGICAL VIEW OF THE AGE OF DANTE 393

PREFACE by the TRANSLATOR

In the years 1805 and 1806, I published the first part of the following translation, with the text of the original.

Since that period, two impressions of the whole of the Divina Commedia, in Italian, have made their appearance in this country.

It is not necessary that I should add a third: and I am induced to hope that the Poem, even in the present version of it, may not be without interest for the mere English reader.

The translation of the second and third parts, "The Purgatory" and "The Paradise," was begun long before the first, and as early as the year 1797; but, owing to many interruptions, not concluded till the summer before last.

On a retrospect of the time and exertions that have been thus employed, I do not regard those hours as the least happy of my

life, during which (to use the eloquent language of Mr. Coleridge) "my individual recollections have been suspended, and lulled to sleep amid the music of nobler thoughts;"

nor that study as misapplied, which has familiarized me with one of the sublimest efforts of the human invention.

To those, who shall be at the trouble of examining into the degree of accuracy with which the task has been executed, I may be allowed to suggest, that their judgment should not be formed on a comparison with any single text of my Author; since, in more instances than I have noticed, I have had to make my choice out of a variety of readings and interpretations, presented by different editions and commentators.

In one or two of those editions is to be found the title of "The Vision," which I have adopted, as more conformable to the genius of our language than that of "The Divine Comedy."

Dante himself, I believe, termed it simply "The Comedy;" in the first place, because the style was of the middle kind:

and in the next, because the story (if story it may be called) ends happily.

Instead of a Life of my Author, I have subjoined, in chronological order, a view not only of the principal events which befell him, but of the chief public occurrences that happened in his time:

concerning both of which the reader may obtain further information, by turning to the passages referred to in the Poem and Notes.

January, 1814

HELL

CANTO I

IN the midway of this our mortal life,
I found me in a gloomy wood, astray
Gone from the path direct: and e'en to tell
It were no easy task, how savage wild
That forest, how robust and rough its growth,
Which to remember only, my dismay
Renews, in bitterness not far from death.
Yet to discourse of what there good befell,
All else will I relate discover'd there.
How first I enter'd it I scarce can say,
Such sleepy dullness in that instant weigh'd
My senses down, when the true path I left,
But when a mountain's foot I reach'd, where clos'd
The valley, that had pierc'd my heart with dread,
I look'd aloft, and saw his shoulders broad
Already vested with that planet's beam,
Who leads all wanderers safe through every way.
    Then was a little respite to the fear,
That in my heart's recesses deep had lain,
All of that night, so pitifully pass'd:
And as a man, with difficult short breath,
Forespent with toiling, 'scap'd from sea to shore,
Turns to the perilous wide waste, and stands
At gaze; e'en so my spirit, that yet fail'd
Struggling with terror, turn'd to view the straits,
That none hath pass'd and liv'd. My weary frame
After short pause recomforted, again
I journey'd on over that lonely steep,
The hinder foot still firmer. Scarce the ascent
Began, when, lo! a panther, nimble, light,
And cover'd with a speckled skin, appear'd,
Nor, when it saw me, vanish'd, rather strove
To check my onward going; that ofttimes
With purpose to retrace my steps I turn'd.
    The hour was morning's prime, and on his way
Aloft the sun ascended with those stars,
That with him rose, when Love divine first mov'd
Those its fair works: so that with joyous hope
All things conspir'd to fill me, the gay skin

Dante Alighieri

Of that swift animal, the matin dawn
And the sweet season. Soon that joy was chas'd,
And by new dread succeeded, when in view
A lion came, 'gainst me, as it appear'd,
With his head held aloft and hunger-mad,
That e'en the air was fear-struck. A she-wolf
Was at his heels, who in her leanness seem'd
Full of all wants, and many a land hath made
Disconsolate ere now. She with such fear
O'erwhelmed me, at the sight of her appall'd,
That of the height all hope I lost. As one,
Who with his gain elated, sees the time
When all unwares is gone, he inwardly
Mourns with heart-griping anguish; such was I,
Haunted by that fell beast, never at peace,
Who coming o'er against me, by degrees
Impell'd me where the sun in silence rests.
    While to the lower space with backward step
I fell, my ken discern'd the form one of one,
Whose voice seem'd faint through long disuse of speech.
When him in that great desert I espied,
"Have mercy on me!" cried I out aloud,
"Spirit! or living man! what e'er thou be!"
    He answer'd: "Now not man, man once I was,
And born of Lombard parents, Mantuana both
By country, when the power of Julius yet
Was scarcely firm. At Rome my life was past
Beneath the mild Augustus, in the time
Of fabled deities and false. A bard
Was I, and made Anchises' upright son
The subject of my song, who came from Troy,
When the flames prey'd on Ilium's haughty towers.
But thou, say wherefore to such perils past
Return'st thou? wherefore not this pleasant mount
Ascendest, cause and source of all delight?"
"And art thou then that Virgil, that well-spring,
From which such copious floods of eloquence
Have issued?" I with front abash'd replied.
"Glory and light of all the tuneful train!
May it avail me that I long with zeal
Have sought thy volume, and with love immense
Have conn'd it o'er. My master thou and guide!
Thou he from whom alone I have deriv'd
That style, which for its beauty into fame
Exalts me. See the beast, from whom I fled.
O save me from her, thou illustrious sage!
For every vein and pulse throughout my frame
She hath made tremble." He, soon as he saw
That I was weeping, answer'd, "Thou must needs
Another way pursue, if thou wouldst 'scape

From out that savage wilderness. This beast,
At whom thou criest, her way will suffer none
To pass, and no less hindrance makes than death:
So bad and so accursed in her kind,
That never sated is her ravenous will,
Still after food more craving than before.
To many an animal in wedlock vile
She fastens, and shall yet to many more,
Until that greyhound come, who shall destroy
Her with sharp pain. He will not life support
By earth nor its base metals, but by love,
Wisdom, and virtue, and his land shall be
The land 'twixt either Feltro. In his might
Shall safety to Italia's plains arise,
For whose fair realm, Camilla, virgin pure,
Nisus, Euryalus, and Turnus fell.
He with incessant chase through every town
Shall worry, until he to hell at length
Restore her, thence by envy first let loose.
I for thy profit pond'ring now devise,
That thou mayst follow me, and I thy guide
Will lead thee hence through an eternal space,
Where thou shalt hear despairing shrieks, and see
Spirits of old tormented, who invoke
A second death; and those next view, who dwell
Content in fire, for that they hope to come,
Whene'er the time may be, among the blest,
Into whose regions if thou then desire
T' ascend, a spirit worthier then I
Must lead thee, in whose charge, when I depart,
Thou shalt be left: for that Almighty King,
Who reigns above, a rebel to his law,
Adjudges me, and therefore hath decreed,
That to his city none through me should come.
He in all parts hath sway; there rules, there holds
His citadel and throne. O happy those,
Whom there he chooses!" I to him in few:
"Bard! by that God, whom thou didst not adore,
I do beseech thee (that this ill and worse
I may escape) to lead me, where thou saidst,
That I Saint Peter's gate may view, and those
Who as thou tell'st, are in such dismal plight."
 Onward he mov'd, I close his steps pursu'd.

CANTO II

NOW was the day departing, and the air,
Imbrown'd with shadows, from their toils releas'd
All animals on earth; and I alone

Dante Alighieri

Prepar'd myself the conflict to sustain,
Both of sad pity, and that perilous road,
Which my unerring memory shall retrace.
    O Muses! O high genius! now vouchsafe
Your aid! O mind! that all I saw hast kept
Safe in a written record, here thy worth
And eminent endowments come to proof.
    I thus began: "Bard! thou who art my guide,
Consider well, if virtue be in me
Sufficient, ere to this high enterprise
Thou trust me. Thou hast told that Silvius' sire,
Yet cloth'd in corruptible flesh, among
Th' immortal tribes had entrance, and was there
Sensible present. Yet if heaven's great Lord,
Almighty foe to ill, such favour shew'd,
In contemplation of the high effect,
Both what and who from him should issue forth,
It seems in reason's judgment well deserv'd:
Sith he of Rome, and of Rome's empire wide,
In heaven's empyreal height was chosen sire:
Both which, if truth be spoken, were ordain'd
And 'stablish'd for the holy place, where sits
Who to great Peter's sacred chair succeeds.
He from this journey, in thy song renown'd,
Learn'd things, that to his victory gave rise
And to the papal robe. In after-times
The chosen vessel also travel'd there,
To bring us back assurance in that faith,
Which is the entrance to salvation's way.
But I, why should I there presume? or who
Permits it? not, Aeneas I nor Paul.
Myself I deem not worthy, and none else
Will deem me. I, if on this voyage then
I venture, fear it will in folly end.
Thou, who art wise, better my meaning know'st,
Than I can speak." As one, who unresolves
What he hath late resolv'd, and with new thoughts
Changes his purpose, from his first intent
Remov'd; e'en such was I on that dun coast,
Wasting in thought my enterprise, at first
So eagerly embrac'd. "If right thy words
I scan," replied that shade magnanimous,
"Thy soul is by vile fear assail'd, which oft
So overcasts a man, that he recoils
From noblest resolution, like a beast
At some false semblance in the twilight gloom.
That from this terror thou mayst free thyself,
I will instruct thee why I came, and what
I heard in that same instant, when for thee
Grief touch'd me first. I was among the tribe,

The Divine Comedy

Who rest suspended, when a dame, so blest
And lovely, I besought her to command,
Call'd me; her eyes were brighter than the star
Of day; and she with gentle voice and soft
Angelically tun'd her speech address'd:
"O courteous shade of Mantua! thou whose fame
Yet lives, and shall live long as nature lasts!
A friend, not of my fortune but myself,
On the wide desert in his road has met
Hindrance so great, that he through fear has turn'd.
Now much I dread lest he past help have stray'd,
And I be ris'n too late for his relief,
From what in heaven of him I heard. Speed now,
And by thy eloquent persuasive tongue,
And by all means for his deliverance meet,
Assist him. So to me will comfort spring.
I who now bid thee on this errand forth
Am Beatrice; from a place I come

    (Note: Beatrice. I use this word, as it is pronounced in the Italian, as consisting of four syllables, of which the third is a long one.)

Revisited with joy. Love brought me thence,
Who prompts my speech. When in my Master's sight
I stand, thy praise to him I oft will tell."
    She then was silent, and I thus began:
"O Lady! by whose influence alone,
Mankind excels whatever is contain'd
Within that heaven which hath the smallest orb,
So thy command delights me, that to obey,
If it were done already, would seem late.
No need hast thou farther to speak thy will;
Yet tell the reason, why thou art not loth
To leave that ample space, where to return
Thou burnest, for this centre here beneath."
    She then: "Since thou so deeply wouldst inquire,
I will instruct thee briefly, why no dread
Hinders my entrance here. Those things alone
Are to be fear'd, whence evil may proceed,
None else, for none are terrible beside.
I am so fram'd by God, thanks to his grace!
That any suff'rance of your misery
Touches me not, nor flame of that fierce fire
Assails me. In high heaven a blessed dame
Besides, who mourns with such effectual grief
That hindrance, which I send thee to remove,
That God's stern judgment to her will inclines.
To Lucia calling, her she thus bespake:
"Now doth thy faithful servant need thy aid
And I commend him to thee." At her word

Dante Alighieri

Sped Lucia, of all cruelty the foe,
And coming to the place, where I abode
Seated with Rachel, her of ancient days,
She thus address'd me: "Thou true praise of God!
Beatrice! why is not thy succour lent
To him, who so much lov'd thee, as to leave
For thy sake all the multitude admires?
Dost thou not hear how pitiful his wail,
Nor mark the death, which in the torrent flood,
Swoln mightier than a sea, him struggling holds?"
Ne'er among men did any with such speed
Haste to their profit, flee from their annoy,
As when these words were spoken, I came here,
Down from my blessed seat, trusting the force
Of thy pure eloquence, which thee, and all
Who well have mark'd it, into honour brings."
    "When she had ended, her bright beaming eyes
Tearful she turn'd aside; whereat I felt
Redoubled zeal to serve thee. As she will'd,
Thus am I come: I sav'd thee from the beast,
Who thy near way across the goodly mount
Prevented. What is this comes o'er thee then?
Why, why dost thou hang back? why in thy breast
Harbour vile fear? why hast not courage there
And noble daring? Since three maids so blest
Thy safety plan, e'en in the court of heaven;
And so much certain good my words forebode."
    As florets, by the frosty air of night
Bent down and clos'd, when day has blanch'd their leaves,
Rise all unfolded on their spiry stems;
So was my fainting vigour new restor'd,
And to my heart such kindly courage ran,
That I as one undaunted soon replied:
"O full of pity she, who undertook
My succour! and thou kind who didst perform
So soon her true behest! With such desire
Thou hast dispos'd me to renew my voyage,
That my first purpose fully is resum'd.
Lead on: one only will is in us both.
Thou art my guide, my master thou, and lord."
    So spake I; and when he had onward mov'd,
I enter'd on the deep and woody way.

CANTO III

"THROUGH me you pass into the city of woe:
Through me you pass into eternal pain:
Through me among the people lost for aye.
Justice the founder of my fabric mov'd:

The Divine Comedy

To rear me was the task of power divine,
Supremest wisdom, and primeval love.
Before me things create were none, save things
Eternal, and eternal I endure.
All hope abandon ye who enter here."
    Such characters in colour dim I mark'd
Over a portal's lofty arch inscrib'd:
Whereat I thus: "Master, these words import
Hard meaning." He as one prepar'd replied:
"Here thou must all distrust behind thee leave;
Here be vile fear extinguish'd. We are come
Where I have told thee we shall see the souls
To misery doom'd, who intellectual good
Have lost." And when his hand he had stretch'd forth
To mine, with pleasant looks, whence I was cheer'd,
Into that secret place he led me on.
    Here sighs with lamentations and loud moans
Resounded through the air pierc'd by no star,
That e'en I wept at entering. Various tongues,
Horrible languages, outcries of woe,
Accents of anger, voices deep and hoarse,
With hands together smote that swell'd the sounds,
Made up a tumult, that for ever whirls
Round through that air with solid darkness stain'd,
Like to the sand that in the whirlwind flies.
    I then, with error yet encompass'd, cried:
"O master! What is this I hear? What race
Are these, who seem so overcome with woe?"
    He thus to me: "This miserable fate
Suffer the wretched souls of those, who liv'd
Without or praise or blame, with that ill band
Of angels mix'd, who nor rebellious prov'd
Nor yet were true to God, but for themselves
Were only. From his bounds Heaven drove them forth,
Not to impair his lustre, nor the depth
Of Hell receives them, lest th' accursed tribe
Should glory thence with exultation vain."
    I then: "Master! what doth aggrieve them thus,
That they lament so loud?" He straight replied:
"That will I tell thee briefly. These of death
No hope may entertain: and their blind life
So meanly passes, that all other lots
They envy. Fame of them the world hath none,
Nor suffers; mercy and justice scorn them both.
Speak not of them, but look, and pass them by."
    And I, who straightway look'd, beheld a flag,
Which whirling ran around so rapidly,
That it no pause obtain'd: and following came
Such a long train of spirits, I should ne'er
Have thought, that death so many had despoil'd.

Dante Alighieri

    When some of these I recogniz'd, I saw
And knew the shade of him, who to base fear
Yielding, abjur'd his high estate. Forthwith
I understood for certain this the tribe
Of those ill spirits both to God displeasing
And to his foes. These wretches, who ne'er lived,
Went on in nakedness, and sorely stung
By wasps and hornets, which bedew'd their cheeks
With blood, that mix'd with tears dropp'd to their feet,
And by disgustful worms was gather'd there.
    Then looking farther onwards I beheld
A throng upon the shore of a great stream:
Whereat I thus: "Sir! grant me now to know
Whom here we view, and whence impell'd they seem
So eager to pass o'er, as I discern
Through the blear light?" He thus to me in few:
"This shalt thou know, soon as our steps arrive
Beside the woeful tide of Acheron."
    Then with eyes downward cast and fill'd with shame,
Fearing my words offensive to his ear,
Till we had reach'd the river, I from speech
Abstain'd. And lo! toward us in a bark
Comes on an old man hoary white with eld,
Crying, "Woe to you wicked spirits! hope not
Ever to see the sky again. I come
To take you to the other shore across,
Into eternal darkness, there to dwell
In fierce heat and in ice. And thou, who there
Standest, live spirit! get thee hence, and leave
These who are dead." But soon as he beheld
I left them not, "By other way," said he,
"By other haven shalt thou come to shore,
Not by this passage; thee a nimbler boat
Must carry." Then to him thus spake my guide:
"Charon! thyself torment not: so 't is will'd,
Where will and power are one: ask thou no more."
    Straightway in silence fell the shaggy cheeks
Of him the boatman o'er the livid lake,
Around whose eyes glar'd wheeling flames. Meanwhile
Those spirits, faint and naked, color chang'd,
And gnash'd their teeth, soon as the cruel words
They heard. God and their parents they blasphem'd,
The human kind, the place, the time, and seed
That did engender them and give them birth.
    Then all together sorely wailing drew
To the curs'd strand, that every man must pass
Who fears not God. Charon, demoniac form,
With eyes of burning coal, collects them all,
Beck'ning, and each, that lingers, with his oar
Strikes. As fall off the light autumnal leaves,

One still another following, till the bough
Strews all its honours on the earth beneath;
E'en in like manner Adam's evil brood
Cast themselves one by one down from the shore,
Each at a beck, as falcon at his call.
  Thus go they over through the umber'd wave,
And ever they on the opposing bank
Be landed, on this side another throng
Still gathers. "Son," thus spake the courteous guide,
"Those, who die subject to the wrath of God,
All here together come from every clime,
And to o'erpass the river are not loth:
For so heaven's justice goads them on, that fear
Is turn'd into desire. Hence ne'er hath past
Good spirit. If of thee Charon complain,
Now mayst thou know the import of his words."
  This said, the gloomy region trembling shook
So terribly, that yet with clammy dews
Fear chills my brow. The sad earth gave a blast,
That, lightening, shot forth a vermilion flame,
Which all my senses conquer'd quite, and I
Down dropp'd, as one with sudden slumber seiz'd.

CANTO IV

BROKE the deep slumber in my brain a crash
Of heavy thunder, that I shook myself,
As one by main force rous'd. Risen upright,
My rested eyes I mov'd around, and search'd
With fixed ken to know what place it was,
Wherein I stood. For certain on the brink
I found me of the lamentable vale,
The dread abyss, that joins a thund'rous sound
Of plaints innumerable. Dark and deep,
And thick with clouds o'erspread, mine eye in vain
Explor'd its bottom, nor could aught discern.
  "Now let us to the blind world there beneath
Descend;" the bard began all pale of look:
"I go the first, and thou shalt follow next."
  Then I his alter'd hue perceiving, thus:
"How may I speed, if thou yieldest to dread,
Who still art wont to comfort me in doubt?"
  He then: "The anguish of that race below
With pity stains my cheek, which thou for fear
Mistakest. Let us on. Our length of way
Urges to haste." Onward, this said, he mov'd;
And ent'ring led me with him on the bounds
Of the first circle, that surrounds th' abyss.
Here, as mine ear could note, no plaint was heard

Dante Alighieri

Except of sighs, that made th' eternal air
Tremble, not caus'd by tortures, but from grief
Felt by those multitudes, many and vast,
Of men, women, and infants. Then to me
The gentle guide: "Inquir'st thou not what spirits
Are these, which thou beholdest? Ere thou pass
Farther, I would thou know, that these of sin
Were blameless; and if aught they merited,
It profits not, since baptism was not theirs,
The portal to thy faith. If they before
The Gospel liv'd, they serv'd not God aright;
And among such am I. For these defects,
And for no other evil, we are lost;
Only so far afflicted, that we live
Desiring without hope." So grief assail'd
My heart at hearing this, for well I knew
Suspended in that Limbo many a soul
Of mighty worth. "O tell me, sire rever'd!
Tell me, my master!" I began through wish
Of full assurance in that holy faith,
Which vanquishes all error; "say, did e'er
Any, or through his own or other's merit,
Come forth from thence, whom afterward was blest?"

    Piercing the secret purport of my speech,
He answer'd: "I was new to that estate,
When I beheld a puissant one arrive
Amongst us, with victorious trophy crown'd.
He forth the shade of our first parent drew,
Abel his child, and Noah righteous man,
Of Moses lawgiver for faith approv'd,
Of patriarch Abraham, and David king,
Israel with his sire and with his sons,
Nor without Rachel whom so hard he won,
And others many more, whom he to bliss
Exalted. Before these, be thou assur'd,
No spirit of human kind was ever sav'd."

    We, while he spake, ceas'd not our onward road,
Still passing through the wood; for so I name
Those spirits thick beset. We were not far
On this side from the summit, when I kenn'd
A flame, that o'er the darken'd hemisphere
Prevailing shin'd. Yet we a little space
Were distant, not so far but I in part
Discover'd, that a tribe in honour high
That place possess'd. "O thou, who every art
And science valu'st! who are these, that boast
Such honour, separate from all the rest?"

    He answer'd: "The renown of their great names
That echoes through your world above, acquires
Favour in heaven, which holds them thus advanc'd."

The Divine Comedy

Meantime a voice I heard: "Honour the bard
Sublime! his shade returns that left us late!"
No sooner ceas'd the sound, than I beheld
Four mighty spirits toward us bend their steps,
Of semblance neither sorrowful nor glad.
    When thus my master kind began: "Mark him,
Who in his right hand bears that falchion keen,
The other three preceding, as their lord.
This is that Homer, of all bards supreme:
Flaccus the next in satire's vein excelling;
The third is Naso; Lucan is the last.
Because they all that appellation own,
With which the voice singly accosted me,
Honouring they greet me thus, and well they judge."
    So I beheld united the bright school
Of him the monarch of sublimest song,
That o'er the others like an eagle soars.
When they together short discourse had held,
They turn'd to me, with salutation kind
Beck'ning me; at the which my master smil'd:
Nor was this all; but greater honour still
They gave me, for they made me of their tribe;
And I was sixth amid so learn'd a band.
    Far as the luminous beacon on we pass'd
Speaking of matters, then befitting well
To speak, now fitter left untold. At foot
Of a magnificent castle we arriv'd,
Seven times with lofty walls begirt, and round
Defended by a pleasant stream. O'er this
As o'er dry land we pass'd. Next through seven gates
I with those sages enter'd, and we came
Into a mead with lively verdure fresh.
    There dwelt a race, who slow their eyes around
Majestically mov'd, and in their port
Bore eminent authority; they spake
Seldom, but all their words were tuneful sweet.
    We to one side retir'd, into a place
Open and bright and lofty, whence each one
Stood manifest to view. Incontinent
There on the green enamel of the plain
Were shown me the great spirits, by whose sight
I am exalted in my own esteem.
    Electra there I saw accompanied
By many, among whom Hector I knew,
Anchises' pious son, and with hawk's eye
Caesar all arm'd, and by Camilla there
Penthesilea. On the other side
Old King Latinus, seated by his child
Lavinia, and that Brutus I beheld,
Who Tarquin chas'd, Lucretia, Cato's wife

Dante Alighieri

Marcia, with Julia and Cornelia there;
And sole apart retir'd, the Soldan fierce.
    Then when a little more I rais'd my brow,
I spied the master of the sapient throng,
Seated amid the philosophic train.
Him all admire, all pay him rev'rence due.
There Socrates and Plato both I mark'd,
Nearest to him in rank; Democritus,
Who sets the world at chance, Diogenes,
With Heraclitus, and Empedocles,
And Anaxagoras, and Thales sage,
Zeno, and Dioscorides well read
In nature's secret lore. Orpheus I mark'd
And Linus, Tully and moral Seneca,
Euclid and Ptolemy, Hippocrates,
Galenus, Avicen, and him who made
That commentary vast, Averroes.
    Of all to speak at full were vain attempt;
For my wide theme so urges, that ofttimes
My words fall short of what bechanc'd. In two
The six associates part. Another way
My sage guide leads me, from that air serene,
Into a climate ever vex'd with storms:
And to a part I come where no light shines.

CANTO V

FROM the first circle I descended thus
Down to the second, which, a lesser space
Embracing, so much more of grief contains
Provoking bitter moans. There, Minos stands
Grinning with ghastly feature: he, of all
Who enter, strict examining the crimes,
Gives sentence, and dismisses them beneath,
According as he foldeth him around:
For when before him comes th' ill fated soul,
It all confesses; and that judge severe
Of sins, considering what place in hell
Suits the transgression, with his tail so oft
Himself encircles, as degrees beneath
He dooms it to descend. Before him stand
Always a num'rous throng; and in his turn
Each one to judgment passing, speaks, and hears
His fate, thence downward to his dwelling hurl'd.
    "O thou! who to this residence of woe
Approachest?" when he saw me coming, cried
Minos, relinquishing his dread employ,
"Look how thou enter here; beware in whom
Thou place thy trust; let not the entrance broad

The Divine Comedy

Deceive thee to thy harm." To him my guide:
"Wherefore exclaimest? Hinder not his way
By destiny appointed; so 'tis will'd
Where will and power are one. Ask thou no more."
     Now 'gin the rueful wailings to be heard.
Now am I come where many a plaining voice
Smites on mine ear. Into a place I came
Where light was silent all. Bellowing there groan'd
A noise as of a sea in tempest torn
By warring winds. The stormy blast of hell
With restless fury drives the spirits on
Whirl'd round and dash'd amain with sore annoy.
When they arrive before the ruinous sweep,
There shrieks are heard, there lamentations, moans,
And blasphemies 'gainst the good Power in heaven.
     I understood that to this torment sad
The carnal sinners are condemn'd, in whom
Reason by lust is sway'd. As in large troops
And multitudinous, when winter reigns,
The starlings on their wings are borne abroad;
So bears the tyrannous gust those evil souls.
On this side and on that, above, below,
It drives them: hope of rest to solace them
Is none, nor e'en of milder pang. As cranes,
Chanting their dol'rous notes, traverse the sky,
Stretch'd out in long array: so I beheld
Spirits, who came loud wailing, hurried on
By their dire doom. Then I: "Instructor! who
Are these, by the black air so scourg'd?"--" The first
'Mong those, of whom thou question'st," he replied,
"O'er many tongues was empress. She in vice
Of luxury was so shameless, that she made
Liking be lawful by promulg'd decree,
To clear the blame she had herself incurr'd.
This is Semiramis, of whom 'tis writ,
That she succeeded Ninus her espous'd;
And held the land, which now the Soldan rules.
The next in amorous fury slew herself,
And to Sicheus' ashes broke her faith:
Then follows Cleopatra, lustful queen."
     There mark'd I Helen, for whose sake so long
The time was fraught with evil; there the great
Achilles, who with love fought to the end.
Paris I saw, and Tristan; and beside
A thousand more he show'd me, and by name
Pointed them out, whom love bereav'd of life.
     When I had heard my sage instructor name
Those dames and knights of antique days, o'erpower'd
By pity, well-nigh in amaze my mind
Was lost; and I began: "Bard! willingly

Dante Alighieri

I would address those two together coming,
Which seem so light before the wind." He thus:
"Note thou, when nearer they to us approach.
Then by that love which carries them along,
Entreat; and they will come." Soon as the wind
Sway'd them toward us, I thus fram'd my speech:
"O wearied spirits! come, and hold discourse
With us, if by none else restrain'd." As doves
By fond desire invited, on wide wings
And firm, to their sweet nest returning home,
Cleave the air, wafted by their will along;
Thus issu'd from that troop, where Dido ranks,
They through the ill air speeding; with such force
My cry prevail'd by strong affection urg'd.

   "O gracious creature and benign! who go'st
Visiting, through this element obscure,
Us, who the world with bloody stain imbru'd;
If for a friend the King of all we own'd,
Our pray'r to him should for thy peace arise,
Since thou hast pity on our evil plight.
()f whatsoe'er to hear or to discourse
It pleases thee, that will we hear, of that
Freely with thee discourse, while e'er the wind,
As now, is mute. The land, that gave me birth,
Is situate on the coast, where Po descends
To rest in ocean with his sequent streams.

   "Love, that in gentle heart is quickly learnt,
Entangled him by that fair form, from me
Ta'en in such cruel sort, as grieves me still:
Love, that denial takes from none belov'd,
Caught me with pleasing him so passing well,
That, as thou see'st, he yet deserts me not.
Love brought us to one death: Caina waits
The soul, who spilt our life." Such were their words;
At hearing which downward I bent my looks,
And held them there so long, that the bard cried:
"What art thou pond'ring?" I in answer thus:
"Alas! by what sweet thoughts, what fond desire
Must they at length to that ill pass have reach'd!"

   Then turning, I to them my speech address'd.
And thus began: "Francesca! your sad fate
Even to tears my grief and pity moves.
But tell me; in the time of your sweet sighs,
By what, and how love granted, that ye knew
Your yet uncertain wishes?" She replied:
"No greater grief than to remember days
Of joy, when mis'ry is at hand! That kens
Thy learn'd instructor. Yet so eagerly
If thou art bent to know the primal root,
From whence our love gat being, I will do,

As one, who weeps and tells his tale. One day
For our delight we read of Lancelot,
How him love thrall'd. Alone we were, and no
Suspicion near us. Ofttimes by that reading
Our eyes were drawn together, and the hue
Fled from our alter'd cheek. But at one point
Alone we fell. When of that smile we read,
The wished smile, rapturously kiss'd
By one so deep in love, then he, who ne'er
From me shall separate, at once my lips
All trembling kiss'd. The book and writer both
Were love's purveyors. In its leaves that day
We read no more." While thus one spirit spake,
The other wail'd so sorely, that heartstruck
I through compassion fainting, seem'd not far
From death, and like a corpse fell to the ground.

CANTO VI

MY sense reviving, that erewhile had droop'd
With pity for the kindred shades, whence grief
O'ercame me wholly, straight around I see
New torments, new tormented souls, which way
Soe'er I move, or turn, or bend my sight.
In the third circle I arrive, of show'rs
Ceaseless, accursed, heavy, and cold, unchang'd
For ever, both in kind and in degree.
Large hail, discolour'd water, sleety flaw
Through the dun midnight air stream'd down amain:
Stank all the land whereon that tempest fell.
    Cerberus, cruel monster, fierce and strange,
Through his wide threefold throat barks as a dog
Over the multitude immers'd beneath.
His eyes glare crimson, black his unctuous beard,
His belly large, and claw'd the hands, with which
He tears the spirits, flays them, and their limbs
Piecemeal disparts. Howling there spread, as curs,
Under the rainy deluge, with one side
The other screening, oft they roll them round,
A wretched, godless crew. When that great worm
Descried us, savage Cerberus, he op'd
His jaws, and the fangs show'd us; not a limb
Of him but trembled. Then my guide, his palms
Expanding on the ground, thence filled with earth
Rais'd them, and cast it in his ravenous maw.
E'en as a dog, that yelling bays for food
His keeper, when the morsel comes, lets fall
His fury, bent alone with eager haste
To swallow it; so dropp'd the loathsome cheeks

Dante Alighieri

Of demon Cerberus, who thund'ring stuns
The spirits, that they for deafness wish in vain.
    We, o'er the shades thrown prostrate by the brunt
Of the heavy tempest passing, set our feet
Upon their emptiness, that substance seem'd.
    They all along the earth extended lay
Save one, that sudden rais'd himself to sit,
Soon as that way he saw us pass. "O thou!"
He cried, "who through the infernal shades art led,
Own, if again thou know'st me. Thou wast fram'd
Or ere my frame was broken." I replied:
"The anguish thou endur'st perchance so takes
Thy form from my remembrance, that it seems
As if I saw thee never. But inform
Me who thou art, that in a place so sad
Art set, and in such torment, that although
Other be greater, more disgustful none
Can be imagin'd." He in answer thus:
"Thy city heap'd with envy to the brim,
Ay that the measure overflows its bounds,
Held me in brighter days. Ye citizens
Were wont to name me Ciacco. For the sin
Of glutt'ny, damned vice, beneath this rain,
E'en as thou see'st, I with fatigue am worn;
Nor I sole spirit in this woe: all these
Have by like crime incurr'd like punishment."
    No more he said, and I my speech resum'd:
"Ciacco! thy dire affliction grieves me much,
Even to tears. But tell me, if thou know'st,
What shall at length befall the citizens
Of the divided city; whether any just one
Inhabit there: and tell me of the cause,
Whence jarring discord hath assail'd it thus?"
    He then: "After long striving they will come
To blood; and the wild party from the woods
Will chase the other with much injury forth.
Then it behoves, that this must fall, within
Three solar circles; and the other rise
By borrow'd force of one, who under shore
Now rests. It shall a long space hold aloof
Its forehead, keeping under heavy weight
The other oppress'd, indignant at the load,
And grieving sore. The just are two in number,
But they neglected. Av'rice, envy, pride,
Three fatal sparks, have set the hearts of all
On fire." Here ceas'd the lamentable sound;
And I continu'd thus: "Still would I learn
More from thee, farther parley still entreat.
Of Farinata and Tegghiaio say,
They who so well deserv'd, of Giacopo,

Arrigo, Mosca, and the rest, who bent
Their minds on working good. Oh! tell me where
They bide, and to their knowledge let me come.
For I am press'd with keen desire to hear,
If heaven's sweet cup or poisonous drug of hell
Be to their lip assign'd."   He answer'd straight:
"These are yet blacker spirits. Various crimes
Have sunk them deeper in the dark abyss.
If thou so far descendest, thou mayst see them.
But to the pleasant world when thou return'st,
Of me make mention, I entreat thee, there.
No more I tell thee, answer thee no more."
      This said, his fixed eyes he turn'd askance,
A little ey'd me, then bent down his head,
And 'midst his blind companions with it fell.
      When thus my guide: "No more his bed he leaves,
Ere the last angel-trumpet blow. The Power
Adverse to these shall then in glory come,
Each one forthwith to his sad tomb repair,
Resume his fleshly vesture and his form,
And hear the eternal doom re-echoing rend
The vault." So pass'd we through that mixture foul
Of spirits and rain, with tardy steps; meanwhile
Touching, though slightly, on the life to come.
For thus I question'd: "Shall these tortures, Sir!
When the great sentence passes, be increas'd,
Or mitigated, or as now severe?"
      He then: "Consult thy knowledge; that decides
That as each thing to more perfection grows,
It feels more sensibly both good and pain.
Though ne'er to true perfection may arrive
This race accurs'd, yet nearer then than now
They shall approach it." Compassing that path
Circuitous we journeyed, and discourse
Much more than I relate between us pass'd:
Till at the point, where the steps led below,
Arriv'd, there Plutus, the great foe, we found.

CANTO VII

"AH me! O Satan! Satan!" loud exclaim'd
Plutus, in accent hoarse of wild alarm:
And the kind sage, whom no event surpris'd,
To comfort me thus spake: "Let not thy fear
Harm thee, for power in him, be sure, is none
To hinder down this rock thy safe descent."
Then to that sworn lip turning, " Peace!" he cried,
"Curs'd wolf! thy fury inward on thyself
Prey, and consume thee! Through the dark profound

Dante Alighieri

Not without cause he passes. So 't is will'd
On high, there where the great Archangel pour'd
Heav'n's vengeance on the first adulterer proud."
     As sails full spread and bellying with the wind
Drop suddenly collaps'd, if the mast split;
So to the ground down dropp'd the cruel fiend.
     Thus we, descending to the fourth steep ledge,
Gain'd on the dismal shore, that all the woe
Hems in of all the universe. Ah me!
Almighty Justice! in what store thou heap'st
New pains, new troubles, as I here beheld!
Wherefore doth fault of ours bring us to this?
     E'en as a billow, on Charybdis rising,
Against encounter'd billow dashing breaks;
Such is the dance this wretched race must lead,
Whom more than elsewhere numerous here I found,
From one side and the other, with loud voice,
Both roll'd on weights by main forge of their breasts,
Then smote together, and each one forthwith
Roll'd them back voluble, turning again,
Exclaiming these, "Why holdest thou so fast?"
Those answering, "And why castest thou away?"
So still repeating their despiteful song,
They to the opposite point on either hand
Travers'd the horrid circle: then arriv'd,
Both turn'd them round, and through the middle space
Conflicting met again. At sight whereof
I, stung with grief, thus spake: "O say, my guide!
What race is this? Were these, whose heads are shorn,
On our left hand, all sep'rate to the church?"
     He straight replied: "In their first life these all
In mind were so distorted, that they made,
According to due measure, of their wealth,
No use. This clearly from their words collect,
Which they howl forth, at each extremity
Arriving of the circle, where their crime
Contrary' in kind disparts them. To the church
Were separate those, that with no hairy cowls
Are crown'd, both Popes and Cardinals, o'er whom
Av'rice dominion absolute maintains."
     I then: "Mid such as these some needs must be,
Whom I shall recognize, that with the blot
Of these foul sins were stain'd." He answering thus:
"Vain thought conceiv'st thou. That ignoble life,
Which made them vile before, now makes them dark,
And to all knowledge indiscernible.
Forever they shall meet in this rude shock:
These from the tomb with clenched grasp shall rise,
Those with close-shaven locks. That ill they gave,
And ill they kept, hath of the beauteous world

Depriv'd, and set them at this strife, which needs
No labour'd phrase of mine to set if off.
Now may'st thou see, my son! how brief, how vain,
The goods committed into fortune's hands,
For which the human race keep such a coil!
Not all the gold, that is beneath the moon,
Or ever hath been, of these toil-worn souls
Might purchase rest for one." I thus rejoin'd:

"My guide! of thee this also would I learn;
This fortune, that thou speak'st of, what it is,
Whose talons grasp the blessings of the world?"

He thus: "O beings blind! what ignorance
Besets you? Now my judgment hear and mark.
He, whose transcendent wisdom passes all,
The heavens creating, gave them ruling powers
To guide them, so that each part shines to each,
Their light in equal distribution pour'd.
By similar appointment he ordain'd
Over the world's bright images to rule.
Superintendence of a guiding hand
And general minister, which at due time
May change the empty vantages of life
From race to race, from one to other's blood,
Beyond prevention of man's wisest care:
Wherefore one nation rises into sway,
Another languishes, e'en as her will
Decrees, from us conceal'd, as in the grass
The serpent train. Against her nought avails
Your utmost wisdom. She with foresight plans,
Judges, and carries on her reign, as theirs
The other powers divine. Her changes know
Nore intermission: by necessity
She is made swift, so frequent come who claim
Succession in her favours. This is she,
So execrated e'en by those, whose debt
To her is rather praise; they wrongfully
With blame requite her, and with evil word;
But she is blessed, and for that recks not:
Amidst the other primal beings glad
Rolls on her sphere, and in her bliss exults.
Now on our way pass we, to heavier woe
Descending: for each star is falling now,
That mounted at our entrance, and forbids
Too long our tarrying." We the circle cross'd
To the next steep, arriving at a well,
That boiling pours itself down to a foss
Sluic'd from its source. Far murkier was the wave
Than sablest grain: and we in company
Of the' inky waters, journeying by their side,
Enter'd, though by a different track, beneath.

Into a lake, the Stygian nam'd, expands
The dismal stream, when it hath reach'd the foot
Of the grey wither'd cliffs. Intent I stood
To gaze, and in the marish sunk descried
A miry tribe, all naked, and with looks
Betok'ning rage. They with their hands alone
Struck not, but with the head, the breast, the feet,
Cutting each other piecemeal with their fangs.

      The good instructor spake; "Now seest thou, son!
The souls of those, whom anger overcame.
This too for certain know, that underneath
The water dwells a multitude, whose sighs
Into these bubbles make the surface heave,
As thine eye tells thee wheresoe'er it turn.
Fix'd in the slime they say: "Sad once were we
In the sweet air made gladsome by the sun,
Carrying a foul and lazy mist within:
Now in these murky settlings are we sad."
Such dolorous strain they gurgle in their throats.
But word distinct can utter none." Our route
Thus compass'd we, a segment widely stretch'd
Between the dry embankment, and the core
Of the loath'd pool, turning meanwhile our eyes
Downward on those who gulp'd its muddy lees;
Nor stopp'd, till to a tower's low base we came.

CANTO VIII

MY theme pursuing, I relate that ere
We reach'd the lofty turret's base, our eyes
Its height ascended, where two cressets hung
We mark'd, and from afar another light
Return the signal, so remote, that scarce
The eye could catch its beam. I turning round
To the deep source of knowledge, thus inquir'd:
"Say what this means? and what that other light
In answer set? what agency doth this?"

      "There on the filthy waters," he replied,
"E'en now what next awaits us mayst thou see,
If the marsh-gender'd fog conceal it not."

      Never was arrow from the cord dismiss'd,
That ran its way so nimbly through the air,
As a small bark, that through the waves I spied
Toward us coming, under the sole sway
Of one that ferried it, who cried aloud:
"Art thou arriv'd, fell spirit?"--"Phlegyas, Phlegyas,
This time thou criest in vain," my lord replied;
"No longer shalt thou have us, but while o'er
The slimy pool we pass." As one who hears

Of some great wrong he hath sustain'd, whereat
Inly he pines; so Phlegyas inly pin'd
In his fierce ire. My guide descending stepp'd
Into the skiff, and bade me enter next
Close at his side; nor till my entrance seem'd
The vessel freighted. Soon as both embark'd,
Cutting the waves, goes on the ancient prow,
More deeply than with others it is wont.

    While we our course o'er the dead channel held.
One drench'd in mire before me came, and said;
"Who art thou, that thou comest ere thine hour?"

    I answer'd: "Though I come, I tarry not;
But who art thou, that art become so foul?"

    "One, as thou seest, who mourn: " he straight replied.

    To which I thus: " In mourning and in woe,
Curs'd spirit! tarry thou. I know thee well,
E'en thus in filth disguis'd." Then stretch'd he forth
Hands to the bark; whereof my teacher sage
Aware, thrusting him back: "Away! down there
To the' other dogs!" then, with his arms my neck
Encircling, kiss'd my cheek, and spake: "O soul
Justly disdainful! blest was she in whom
Thou was conceiv'd! He in the world was one
For arrogance noted; to his memory
No virtue lends its lustre; even so
Here is his shadow furious. There above
How many now hold themselves mighty kings
Who here like swine shall wallow in the mire,
Leaving behind them horrible dispraise!"

    I then: "Master! him fain would I behold
Whelm'd in these dregs, before we quit the lake."

    He thus: "Or ever to thy view the shore
Be offer'd, satisfied shall be that wish,
Which well deserves completion." Scarce his words
Were ended, when I saw the miry tribes
Set on him with such violence, that yet
For that render I thanks to God and praise
"To Filippo Argenti:" cried they all:
And on himself the moody Florentine
Turn'd his avenging fangs. Him here we left,
Nor speak I of him more. But on mine ear
Sudden a sound of lamentation smote,
Whereat mine eye unbarr'd I sent abroad.

    And thus the good instructor: "Now, my son!
Draws near the city, that of Dis is nam'd,
With its grave denizens, a mighty throng."

    I thus: "The minarets already, Sir!
There certes in the valley I descry,
Gleaming vermilion, as if they from fire
Had issu'd." He replied: "Eternal fire,

Dante Alighieri

That inward burns, shows them with ruddy flame
Illum'd; as in this nether hell thou seest."
    We came within the fosses deep, that moat
This region comfortless. The walls appear'd
As they were fram'd of iron. We had made
Wide circuit, ere a place we reach'd, where loud
The mariner cried vehement: "Go forth!
The' entrance is here!" Upon the gates I spied
More than a thousand, who of old from heaven
Were hurl'd. With ireful gestures, "Who is this,"
They cried, "that without death first felt, goes through
The regions of the dead?" My sapient guide
Made sign that he for secret parley wish'd;
Whereat their angry scorn abating, thus
They spake: "Come thou alone; and let him go
Who hath so hardily enter'd this realm.
Alone return he by his witless way;
If well he know it, let him prove. For thee,
Here shalt thou tarry, who through clime so dark
Hast been his escort." Now bethink thee, reader!
What cheer was mine at sound of those curs'd words.
I did believe I never should return.
    "O my lov'd guide! who more than seven times
Security hast render'd me, and drawn
From peril deep, whereto I stood expos'd,
Desert me not," I cried, "in this extreme.
And if our onward going be denied,
Together trace we back our steps with speed."
    My liege, who thither had conducted me,
Replied: "Fear not: for of our passage none
Hath power to disappoint us, by such high
Authority permitted. But do thou
Expect me here; meanwhile thy wearied spirit
Comfort, and feed with kindly hope, assur'd
I will not leave thee in this lower world."
    This said, departs the sire benevolent,
And quits me. Hesitating I remain
At war 'twixt will and will not in my thoughts.
    I could not hear what terms he offer'd them,
But they conferr'd not long, for all at once
To trial fled within. Clos'd were the gates
By those our adversaries on the breast
Of my liege lord: excluded he return'd
To me with tardy steps. Upon the ground
His eyes were bent, and from his brow eras'd
All confidence, while thus with sighs he spake:
"Who hath denied me these abodes of woe?"
Then thus to me: "That I am anger'd, think
No ground of terror: in this trial I
Shall vanquish, use what arts they may within

For hindrance. This their insolence, not new,
Erewhile at gate less secret they display'd,
Which still is without bolt; upon its arch
Thou saw'st the deadly scroll: and even now
On this side of its entrance, down the steep,
Passing the circles, unescorted, comes
One whose strong might can open us this land."

CANTO IX

THE hue, which coward dread on my pale cheeks
Imprinted, when I saw my guide turn back,
Chas'd that from his which newly they had worn,
And inwardly restrain'd it. He, as one
Who listens, stood attentive: for his eye
Not far could lead him through the sable air,
And the thick-gath'ring cloud. "It yet behooves
We win this fight"--thus he began--" if not--
Such aid to us is offer'd. --Oh, how long
Me seems it, ere the promis'd help arrive!"
      I noted, how the sequel of his words
Clok'd their beginning; for the last he spake
Agreed not with the first. But not the less
My fear was at his saying; sith I drew
To import worse perchance, than that he held,
His mutilated speech. "Doth ever any
Into this rueful concave's extreme depth
Descend, out of the first degree, whose pain
Is deprivation merely of sweet hope?"
      Thus I inquiring. "Rarely," he replied,
"It chances, that among us any makes
This journey, which I wend. Erewhile 'tis true
Once came I here beneath, conjur'd by fell
Erictho, sorceress, who compell'd the shades
Back to their bodies. No long space my flesh
Was naked of me, when within these walls
She made me enter, to draw forth a spirit
From out of Judas' circle. Lowest place
Is that of all, obscurest, and remov'd
Farthest from heav'n's all-circling orb. The road
Full well I know: thou therefore rest secure.
That lake, the noisome stench exhaling, round
The city' of grief encompasses, which now
We may not enter without rage." Yet more
He added: but I hold it not in mind,
For that mine eye toward the lofty tower
Had drawn me wholly, to its burning top.
Where in an instant I beheld uprisen
At once three hellish furies stain'd with blood:

Dante Alighieri

In limb and motion feminine they seem'd;
Around them greenest hydras twisting roll'd
Their volumes; adders and cerastes crept
Instead of hair, and their fierce temples bound.
    He knowing well the miserable hags
Who tend the queen of endless woe, thus spake:
"Mark thou each dire Erinnys. To the left
This is Megaera; on the right hand she,
Who wails, Alecto; and Tisiphone
I' th' midst." This said, in silence he remain'd
Their breast they each one clawing tore; themselves
Smote with their palms, and such shrill clamour rais'd,
That to the bard I clung, suspicion-bound.
"Hasten Medusa: so to adamant
Him shall we change;" all looking down exclaim'd.
"E'en when by Theseus' might assail'd, we took
No ill revenge." "Turn thyself round, and keep
Thy count'nance hid; for if the Gorgon dire
Be shown, and thou shouldst view it, thy return
Upwards would be for ever lost." This said,
Himself my gentle master turn'd me round,
Nor trusted he my hands, but with his own
He also hid me. Ye of intellect
Sound and entire, mark well the lore conceal'd
Under close texture of the mystic strain!
    And now there came o'er the perturbed waves
Loud-crashing, terrible, a sound that made
Either shore tremble, as if of a wind
Impetuous, from conflicting vapours sprung,
That 'gainst some forest driving all its might,
Plucks off the branches, beats them down and hurls
Afar; then onward passing proudly sweeps
Its whirlwind rage, while beasts and shepherds fly.
    Mine eyes he loos'd, and spake: "And now direct
Thy visual nerve along that ancient foam,
There, thickest where the smoke ascends." As frogs
Before their foe the serpent, through the wave
Ply swiftly all, till at the ground each one
Lies on a heap; more than a thousand spirits
Destroy'd, so saw I fleeing before one
Who pass'd with unwet feet the Stygian sound.
He, from his face removing the gross air,
Oft his left hand forth stretch'd, and seem'd alone
By that annoyance wearied. I perceiv'd
That he was sent from heav'n, and to my guide
Turn'd me, who signal made that I should stand
Quiet, and bend to him. Ah me! how full
Of noble anger seem'd he! To the gate
He came, and with his wand touch'd it, whereat
Open without impediment it flew.

The Divine Comedy

"Outcasts of heav'n! O abject race and scorn'd!"
Began he on the horrid grunsel standing,
"Whence doth this wild excess of insolence
Lodge in you? wherefore kick you 'gainst that will
Ne'er frustrate of its end, and which so oft
Hath laid on you enforcement of your pangs?
What profits at the fays to but the horn?
Your Cerberus, if ye remember, hence
Bears still, peel'd of their hair, his throat and maw."

This said, he turn'd back o'er the filthy way,
And syllable to us spake none, but wore
The semblance of a man by other care
Beset, and keenly press'd, than thought of him
Who in his presence stands. Then we our steps
Toward that territory mov'd, secure
After the hallow'd words. We unoppos'd
There enter'd; and my mind eager to learn
What state a fortress like to that might hold,
I soon as enter'd throw mine eye around,
And see on every part wide-stretching space
Replete with bitter pain and torment ill.

As where Rhone stagnates on the plains of Arles,
Or as at Pola, near Quarnaro's gulf,
That closes Italy and laves her bounds,
The place is all thick spread with sepulchres;
So was it here, save what in horror here
Excell'd: for 'midst the graves were scattered flames,
Wherewith intensely all throughout they burn'd,
That iron for no craft there hotter needs.

Their lids all hung suspended, and beneath
From them forth issu'd lamentable moans,
Such as the sad and tortur'd well might raise.

I thus: "Master! say who are these, interr'd
Within these vaults, of whom distinct we hear
The dolorous sighs?" He answer thus return'd:

"The arch-heretics are here, accompanied
By every sect their followers; and much more,
Than thou believest, tombs are freighted: like
With like is buried; and the monuments
Are different in degrees of heat. "This said,
He to the right hand turning, on we pass'd
Betwixt the afflicted and the ramparts high.

CANTO X

NOW by a secret pathway we proceed,
Between the walls, that hem the region round,
And the tormented souls: my master first,
I close behind his steps. "Virtue supreme!"

Dante Alighieri

I thus began; "who through these ample orbs
In circuit lead'st me, even as thou will'st,
Speak thou, and satisfy my wish. May those,
Who lie within these sepulchres, be seen?
Already all the lids are rais'd, and none
O'er them keeps watch." He thus in answer spake
"They shall be closed all, what-time they here
From Josaphat return'd shall come, and bring
Their bodies, which above they now have left.
The cemetery on this part obtain
With Epicurus all his followers,
Who with the body make the spirit die.
Here therefore satisfaction shall be soon
Both to the question ask'd, and to the wish,
Which thou conceal'st in silence." I replied:
"I keep not, guide belov'd! from thee my heart
Secreted, but to shun vain length of words,
A lesson erewhile taught me by thyself."

    "O Tuscan! thou who through the city of fire
Alive art passing, so discreet of speech!
Here please thee stay awhile. Thy utterance
Declares the place of thy nativity
To be that noble land, with which perchance
I too severely dealt." Sudden that sound
Forth issu'd from a vault, whereat in fear
I somewhat closer to my leader's side
Approaching, he thus spake: "What dost thou? Turn.
Lo, Farinata, there! who hath himself
Uplifted: from his girdle upwards all
Expos'd behold him." On his face was mine
Already fix'd; his breast and forehead there
Erecting, seem'd as in high scorn he held
E'en hell. Between the sepulchres to him
My guide thrust me with fearless hands and prompt,
This warning added: "See thy words be clear!"

    He, soon as there I stood at the tomb's foot,
Ey'd me a space, then in disdainful mood
Address'd me: "Say, what ancestors were thine?"

    I, willing to obey him, straight reveal'd
The whole, nor kept back aught: whence he, his brow
Somewhat uplifting, cried: "Fiercely were they
Adverse to me, my party, and the blood
From whence I sprang: twice therefore I abroad
Scatter'd them." "Though driv'n out, yet they each time
From all parts," answer'd I, "return'd; an art
Which yours have shown, they are not skill'd to learn."

    Then, peering forth from the unclosed jaw,
Rose from his side a shade, high as the chin,
Leaning, methought, upon its knees uprais'd.
It look'd around, as eager to explore

The Divine Comedy

If there were other with me; but perceiving
That fond imagination quench'd, with tears
Thus spake: "If thou through this blind prison go'st,
Led by thy lofty genius and profound,
Where is my son? and wherefore not with thee?"

    I straight replied: "Not of myself I come,
By him, who there expects me, through this clime
Conducted, whom perchance Guido thy son
Had in contempt." Already had his words
And mode of punishment read me his name,
Whence I so fully answer'd. He at once
Exclaim'd, up starting, "How! said'st thou he HAD?
No longer lives he? Strikes not on his eye
The blessed daylight?" Then of some delay
I made ere my reply aware, down fell
Supine, not after forth appear'd he more.

    Meanwhile the other, great of soul, near whom
I yet was station'd, chang'd not count'nance stern,
Nor mov'd the neck, nor bent his ribbed side.
"And if," continuing the first discourse,
"They in this art," he cried, "small skill have shown,
That doth torment me more e'en than this bed.
But not yet fifty times shall be relum'd
Her aspect, who reigns here Queen of this realm,
Ere thou shalt know the full weight of that art.
So to the pleasant world mayst thou return,
As thou shalt tell me, why in all their laws,
Against my kin this people is so fell?"

    "The slaughter and great havoc," I replied,
"That colour'd Arbia's flood with crimson stain--
To these impute, that in our hallow'd dome
Such orisons ascend." Sighing he shook
The head, then thus resum'd: "In that affray
I stood not singly, nor without just cause
Assuredly should with the rest have stirr'd;
But singly there I stood, when by consent
Of all, Florence had to the ground been raz'd,
The one who openly forbad the deed."

    "So may thy lineage find at last repose,"
I thus adjur'd him, "as thou solve this knot,
Which now involves my mind. If right I hear,
Ye seem to view beforehand, that which time
Leads with him, of the present uninform'd."

    "We view, as one who hath an evil sight,"
He answer'd, "plainly, objects far remote:
So much of his large spendour yet imparts
The' Almighty Ruler; but when they approach
Or actually exist, our intellect
Then wholly fails, nor of your human state
Except what others bring us know we aught.

Hence therefore mayst thou understand, that all
Our knowledge in that instant shall expire,
When on futurity the portals close."
      Then conscious of my fault, and by remorse
Smitten, I added thus: "Now shalt thou say
To him there fallen, that his offspring still
Is to the living join'd; and bid him know,
That if from answer silent I abstain'd,
'Twas that my thought was occupied intent
Upon that error, which thy help hath solv'd."
      But now my master summoning me back
I heard, and with more eager haste besought
The spirit to inform me, who with him
Partook his lot. He answer thus return'd:
      "More than a thousand with me here are laid
Within is Frederick, second of that name,
And the Lord Cardinal, and of the rest
I speak not." He, this said, from sight withdrew.
But I my steps towards the ancient bard
Reverting, ruminated on the words
Betokening me such ill. Onward he mov'd,
And thus in going question'd: "Whence the' amaze
That holds thy senses wrapt?" I satisfied
The' inquiry, and the sage enjoin'd me straight:
"Let thy safe memory store what thou hast heard
To thee importing harm; and note thou this,"
With his rais'd finger bidding me take heed,
      "When thou shalt stand before her gracious beam,
Whose bright eye all surveys, she of thy life
The future tenour will to thee unfold."
      Forthwith he to the left hand turn'd his feet:
We left the wall, and tow'rds the middle space
Went by a path, that to a valley strikes;
Which e'en thus high exhal'd its noisome steam.

CANTO XI

UPON the utmost verge of a high bank,
By craggy rocks environ'd round, we came,
Where woes beneath more cruel yet were stow'd:
And here to shun the horrible excess
Of fetid exhalation, upward cast
From the profound abyss, behind the lid
Of a great monument we stood retir'd,
Whereon this scroll I mark'd: "I have in charge
Pope Anastasius, whom Photinus drew
From the right path.--Ere our descent behooves
We make delay, that somewhat first the sense,
To the dire breath accustom'd, afterward

Regard it not." My master thus; to whom
Answering I spake: "Some compensation find
That the time past not wholly lost." He then:
"Lo! how my thoughts e'en to thy wishes tend!
My son! within these rocks," he thus began,
"Are three close circles in gradation plac'd,
As these which now thou leav'st. Each one is full
Of spirits accurs'd; but that the sight alone
Hereafter may suffice thee, listen how
And for what cause in durance they abide.

    "Of all malicious act abhorr'd in heaven,
The end is injury; and all such end
Either by force or fraud works other's woe
But fraud, because of man peculiar evil,
To God is more displeasing; and beneath
The fraudulent are therefore doom'd to' endure
Severer pang. The violent occupy
All the first circle; and because to force
Three persons are obnoxious, in three rounds
Hach within other sep'rate is it fram'd.
To God, his neighbour, and himself, by man
Force may be offer'd; to himself I say
And his possessions, as thou soon shalt hear
At full. Death, violent death, and painful wounds
Upon his neighbour he inflicts; and wastes
By devastation, pillage, and the flames,
His substance. Slayers, and each one that smites
In malice, plund'rers, and all robbers, hence
The torment undergo of the first round
In different herds. Man can do violence
To himself and his own blessings: and for this
He in the second round must aye deplore
With unavailing penitence his crime,
Whoe'er deprives himself of life and light,
In reckless lavishment his talent wastes,
And sorrows there where he should dwell in joy.
To God may force be offer'd, in the heart
Denying and blaspheming his high power,
And nature with her kindly law contemning.
And thence the inmost round marks with its seal
Sodom and Cahors, and all such as speak
Contemptuously' of the Godhead in their hearts.

    "Fraud, that in every conscience leaves a sting,
May be by man employ'd on one, whose trust
He wins, or on another who withholds
Strict confidence. Seems as the latter way
Broke but the bond of love which Nature makes.
Whence in the second circle have their nest
Dissimulation, witchcraft, flatteries,
Theft, falsehood, simony, all who seduce

Dante Alighieri

To lust, or set their honesty at pawn,
With such vile scum as these. The other way
Forgets both Nature's general love, and that
Which thereto added afterwards gives birth
To special faith. Whence in the lesser circle,
Point of the universe, dread seat of Dis,
The traitor is eternally consum'd."

    I thus: "Instructor, clearly thy discourse
Proceeds, distinguishing the hideous chasm
And its inhabitants with skill exact.
But tell me this: they of the dull, fat pool,
Whom the rain beats, or whom the tempest drives,
Or who with tongues so fierce conflicting meet,
Wherefore within the city fire-illum'd
Are not these punish'd, if God's wrath be on them?
And if it be not, wherefore in such guise
Are they condemned?" He answer thus return'd:
"Wherefore in dotage wanders thus thy mind,
Not so accustom'd? or what other thoughts
Possess it? Dwell not in thy memory
The words, wherein thy ethic page describes
Three dispositions adverse to Heav'n's will,
Incont'nence, malice, and mad brutishness,
And how incontinence the least offends
God, and least guilt incurs? If well thou note
This judgment, and remember who they are,
Without these walls to vain repentance doom'd,
Thou shalt discern why they apart are plac'd
From these fell spirits, and less wreakful pours
Justice divine on them its vengeance down."

    "O Sun! who healest all imperfect sight,
Thou so content'st me, when thou solv'st my doubt,
That ignorance not less than knowledge charms.
Yet somewhat turn thee back," I in these words
Continu'd, "where thou saidst, that usury
Offends celestial Goodness; and this knot
Perplex'd unravel." He thus made reply:
"Philosophy, to an attentive ear,
Clearly points out, not in one part alone,
How imitative nature takes her course
From the celestial mind and from its art:
And where her laws the Stagyrite unfolds,
Not many leaves scann'd o'er, observing well
Thou shalt discover, that your art on her
Obsequious follows, as the learner treads
In his instructor's step, so that your art
Deserves the name of second in descent
From God. These two, if thou recall to mind
Creation's holy book, from the beginning
Were the right source of life and excellence

The Divine Comedy

To human kind. But in another path
The usurer walks; and Nature in herself
And in her follower thus he sets at nought,
Placing elsewhere his hope. But follow now
My steps on forward journey bent; for now
The Pisces play with undulating glance
Along the' horizon, and the Wain lies all
O'er the north-west; and onward there a space
Is our steep passage down the rocky height."

CANTO XII

THE place where to descend the precipice
We came, was rough as Alp, and on its verge
Such object lay, as every eye would shun.
    As is that ruin, which Adice's stream
On this side Trento struck, should'ring the wave,
Or loos'd by earthquake or for lack of prop;
For from the mountain's summit, whence it mov'd
To the low level, so the headlong rock
Is shiver'd, that some passage it might give
To him who from above would pass; e'en such
Into the chasm was that descent: and there
At point of the disparted ridge lay stretch'd
The infamy of Crete, detested brood
Of the feign'd heifer: and at sight of us
It gnaw'd itself, as one with rage distract.
To him my guide exclaim'd: "Perchance thou deem'st
The King of Athens here, who, in the world
Above, thy death contriv'd. Monster! avaunt!
He comes not tutor'd by thy sister's art,
But to behold your torments is he come."
    Like to a bull, that with impetuous spring
Darts, at the moment when the fatal blow
Hath struck him, but unable to proceed
Plunges on either side; so saw I plunge
The Minotaur; whereat the sage exclaim'd:
"Run to the passage! while he storms, 't is well
That thou descend." Thus down our road we took
Through those dilapidated crags, that oft
Mov'd underneath my feet, to weight like theirs
Unus'd. I pond'ring went, and thus he spake:
    "Perhaps thy thoughts are of this ruin'd steep,
Guarded by the brute violence, which I
Have vanquish'd now. Know then, that when I erst
Hither descended to the nether hell,
This rock was not yet fallen. But past doubt
(If well I mark) not long ere He arrived,
Who carried off from Dis the mighty spoil

Dante Alighieri

Of the highest circle, then through all its bounds
Such trembling seiz'd the deep concave and foul,
I thought the universe was thrill'd with love,
Whereby, there are who deem, the world hath oft
Been into chaos turn'd: and in that point,
Here, and elsewhere, that old rock toppled down.
But fix thine eyes beneath: the river of blood
Approaches, in the which all those are steep'd,
Who have by violence injur'd." O blind lust!
O foolish wrath! who so dost goad us on
In the brief life, and in the eternal then
Thus miserably o'erwhelm us. I beheld
An ample foss, that in a bow was bent,
As circling all the plain; for so my guide
Had told. Between it and the rampart's base
On trail ran Centaurs, with keen arrows arm'd,
As to the chase they on the earth were wont.
    At seeing us descend they each one stood;
And issuing from the troop, three sped with bows
And missile weapons chosen first; of whom
One cried from far: "Say to what pain ye come
Condemn'd, who down this steep have journied? Speak
From whence ye stand, or else the bow I draw."
    To whom my guide: "Our answer shall be made
To Chiron, there, when nearer him we come.
Ill was thy mind, thus ever quick and rash."
    Then me he touch'd, and spake: "Nessus is this,
Who for the fair Deianira died,
And wrought himself revenge for his own fate.
He in the midst, that on his breast looks down,
Is the great Chiron who Achilles nurs'd;
That other Pholus, prone to wrath." Around
The foss these go by thousands, aiming shafts
At whatsoever spirit dares emerge
From out the blood, more than his guilt allows.
    We to those beasts, that rapid strode along,
Drew near, when Chiron took an arrow forth,
And with the notch push'd back his shaggy beard
To the cheek-bone, then his great mouth to view
Exposing, to his fellows thus exclaim'd:
"Are ye aware, that he who comes behind
Moves what he touches? The feet of the dead
Are not so wont." My trusty guide, who now
Stood near his breast, where the two natures join,
Thus made reply: "He is indeed alive,
And solitary so must needs by me
Be shown the gloomy vale, thereto induc'd
By strict necessity, not by delight.
She left her joyful harpings in the sky,
Who this new office to my care consign'd.

37

The Divine Comedy

He is no robber, no dark spirit I.
But by that virtue, which empowers my step
To treat so wild a path, grant us, I pray,
One of thy band, whom we may trust secure,
Who to the ford may lead us, and convey
Across, him mounted on his back; for he
Is not a spirit that may walk the air."

    Then on his right breast turning, Chiron thus
To Nessus spake: "Return, and be their guide.
And if ye chance to cross another troop,
Command them keep aloof." Onward we mov'd,
The faithful escort by our side, along
The border of the crimson-seething flood,
Whence from those steep'd within loud shrieks arose.

    Some there I mark'd, as high as to their brow
Immers'd, of whom the mighty Centaur thus:
"These are the souls of tyrants, who were given
To blood and rapine. Here they wail aloud
Their merciless wrongs. Here Alexander dwells,
And Dionysius fell, who many a year
Of woe wrought for fair Sicily. That brow
Whereon the hair so jetty clust'ring hangs,
Is Azzolino; that with flaxen locks
Obizzo' of Este, in the world destroy'd
By his foul step-son." To the bard rever'd
I turned me round, and thus he spake; "Let him
Be to thee now first leader, me but next
To him in rank." Then farther on a space
The Centaur paus'd, near some, who at the throat
Were extant from the wave; and showing us
A spirit by itself apart retir'd,
Exclaim'd: "He in God's bosom smote the heart,
Which yet is honour'd on the bank of Thames."

    A race I next espied, who held the head,
And even all the bust above the stream.
'Midst these I many a face remember'd well.
Thus shallow more and more the blood became,
So that at last it but imbru'd the feet;
And there our passage lay athwart the foss.

    "As ever on this side the boiling wave
Thou seest diminishing," the Centaur said,
"So on the other, be thou well assur'd,
It lower still and lower sinks its bed,
Till in that part it reuniting join,
Where 't is the lot of tyranny to mourn.
There Heav'n's stern justice lays chastising hand
On Attila, who was the scourge of earth,
On Sextus, and on Pyrrhus, and extracts
Tears ever by the seething flood unlock'd
From the Rinieri, of Corneto this,

Pazzo the other nam'd, who fill'd the ways
With violence and war." This said, he turn'd,
And quitting us, alone repass'd the ford.

CANTO XIII

ERE Nessus yet had reach'd the other bank,
We enter'd on a forest, where no track
Of steps had worn a way. Not verdant there
The foliage, but of dusky hue; not light
The boughs and tapering, but with knares deform'd
And matted thick: fruits there were none, but thorns
Instead, with venom fill'd. Less sharp than these,
Less intricate the brakes, wherein abide
Those animals, that hate the cultur'd fields,
Betwixt Corneto and Cecina's stream.
    Here the brute Harpies make their nest, the same
Who from the Strophades the Trojan band
Drove with dire boding of their future woe.
Broad are their pennons, of the human form
Their neck and count'nance, arm'd with talons keen
The feet, and the huge belly fledge with wings
These sit and wail on the drear mystic wood.
    The kind instructor in these words began:
"Ere farther thou proceed, know thou art now
I' th' second round, and shalt be, till thou come
Upon the horrid sand: look therefore well
Around thee, and such things thou shalt behold,
As would my speech discredit." On all sides
I heard sad plainings breathe, and none could see
From whom they might have issu'd. In amaze
Fast bound I stood. He, as it seem'd, believ'd,
That I had thought so many voices came
From some amid those thickets close conceal'd,
And thus his speech resum'd: "If thou lop off
A single twig from one of those ill plants,
The thought thou hast conceiv'd shall vanish quite."
    Thereat a little stretching forth my hand,
From a great wilding gather'd I a branch,
And straight the trunk exclaim'd: "Why pluck'st thou me?"
Then as the dark blood trickled down its side,
These words it added: "Wherefore tear'st me thus?
Is there no touch of mercy in thy breast?
Men once were we, that now are rooted here.
Thy hand might well have spar'd us, had we been
The souls of serpents." As a brand yet green,
That burning at one end from the' other sends
A groaning sound, and hisses with the wind
That forces out its way, so burst at once,

Forth from the broken splinter words and blood.
    I, letting fall the bough, remain'd as one
Assail'd by terror, and the sage replied:
"If he, O injur'd spirit! could have believ'd
What he hath seen but in my verse describ'd,
He never against thee had stretch'd his hand.
But I, because the thing surpass'd belief,
Prompted him to this deed, which even now
Myself I rue. But tell me, who thou wast;
That, for this wrong to do thee some amends,
In the upper world (for thither to return
Is granted him) thy fame he may revive."
    "That pleasant word of thine," the trunk replied
"Hath so inveigled me, that I from speech
Cannot refrain, wherein if I indulge
A little longer, in the snare detain'd,
Count it not grievous. I it was, who held
Both keys to Frederick's heart, and turn'd the wards,
Opening and shutting, with a skill so sweet,
That besides me, into his inmost breast
Scarce any other could admittance find.
The faith I bore to my high charge was such,
It cost me the life-blood that warm'd my veins.
The harlot, who ne'er turn'd her gloating eyes
From Caesar's household, common vice and pest
Of courts, 'gainst me inflam'd the minds of all;
And to Augustus they so spread the flame,
That my glad honours chang'd to bitter woes.
My soul, disdainful and disgusted, sought
Refuge in death from scorn, and I became,
Just as I was, unjust toward myself.
By the new roots, which fix this stem, I swear,
That never faith I broke to my liege lord,
Who merited such honour; and of you,
If any to the world indeed return,
Clear he from wrong my memory, that lies
Yet prostrate under envy's cruel blow."
    First somewhat pausing, till the mournful words
Were ended, then to me the bard began:
"Lose not the time; but speak and of him ask,
If more thou wish to learn." Whence I replied:
"Question thou him again of whatsoe'er
Will, as thou think'st, content me; for no power
Have I to ask, such pity' is at my heart."
    He thus resum'd; "So may he do for thee
Freely what thou entreatest, as thou yet
Be pleas'd, imprison'd Spirit! to declare,
How in these gnarled joints the soul is tied;
And whether any ever from such frame
Be loosen'd, if thou canst, that also tell."

Dante Alighieri

     Thereat the trunk breath'd hard, and the wind soon
Chang'd into sounds articulate like these;
     Briefly ye shall be answer'd. When departs
The fierce soul from the body, by itself
Thence torn asunder, to the seventh gulf
By Minos doom'd, into the wood it falls,
No place assign'd, but wheresoever chance
Hurls it, there sprouting, as a grain of spelt,
It rises to a sapling, growing thence
A savage plant. The Harpies, on its leaves
Then feeding, cause both pain and for the pain
A vent to grief. We, as the rest, shall come
For our own spoils, yet not so that with them
We may again be clad; for what a man
Takes from himself it is not just he have.
Here we perforce shall drag them; and throughout
The dismal glade our bodies shall be hung,
Each on the wild thorn of his wretched shade."
     Attentive yet to listen to the trunk
We stood, expecting farther speech, when us
A noise surpris'd, as when a man perceives
The wild boar and the hunt approach his place
Of station'd watch, who of the beasts and boughs
Loud rustling round him hears. And lo! there came
Two naked, torn with briers, in headlong flight,
That they before them broke each fan o' th' wood.
"Haste now," the foremost cried, "now haste thee death!"
The' other, as seem'd, impatient of delay
Exclaiming, "Lano! not so bent for speed
Thy sinews, in the lists of Toppo's field."
And then, for that perchance no longer breath
Suffic'd him, of himself and of a bush
One group he made. Behind them was the wood
Full of black female mastiffs, gaunt and fleet,
As greyhounds that have newly slipp'd the leash.
On him, who squatted down, they stuck their fangs,
And having rent him piecemeal bore away
The tortur'd limbs. My guide then seiz'd my hand,
And led me to the thicket, which in vain
Mourn'd through its bleeding wounds: "O Giacomo
Of Sant' Andrea! what avails it thee,"
It cried, "that of me thou hast made thy screen?
For thy ill life what blame on me recoils?"
     When o'er it he had paus'd, my master spake:
"Say who wast thou, that at so many points
Breath'st out with blood thy lamentable speech?"
     He answer'd: "Oh, ye spirits: arriv'd in time
To spy the shameful havoc, that from me
My leaves hath sever'd thus, gather them up,
And at the foot of their sad parent-tree

The Divine Comedy

Carefully lay them. In that city' I dwelt,
Who for the Baptist her first patron chang'd,
Whence he for this shall cease not with his art
To work her woe: and if there still remain'd not
On Arno's passage some faint glimpse of him,
Those citizens, who rear'd once more her walls
Upon the ashes left by Attila,
Had labour'd without profit of their toil.
I slung the fatal noose from my own roof."

CANTO XIV

SOON as the charity of native land
Wrought in my bosom, I the scatter'd leaves
Collected, and to him restor'd, who now
Was hoarse with utt'rance. To the limit thence
We came, which from the third the second round
Divides, and where of justice is display'd
Contrivance horrible. Things then first seen
Clearlier to manifest, I tell how next
A plain we reach'd, that from its sterile bed
Each plant repell'd. The mournful wood waves round
Its garland on all sides, as round the wood
Spreads the sad foss. There, on the very edge,
Our steps we stay'd. It was an area wide
Of arid sand and thick, resembling most
The soil that erst by Cato's foot was trod.
    Vengeance of Heav'n! Oh! how shouldst thou be fear'd
By all, who read what here my eyes beheld!
    Of naked spirits many a flock I saw,
All weeping piteously, to different laws
Subjected: for on the' earth some lay supine,
Some crouching close were seated, others pac'd
Incessantly around; the latter tribe,
More numerous, those fewer who beneath
The torment lay, but louder in their grief.
    O'er all the sand fell slowly wafting down
Dilated flakes of fire, as flakes of snow
On Alpine summit, when the wind is hush'd.
As in the torrid Indian clime, the son
Of Ammon saw upon his warrior band
Descending, solid flames, that to the ground
Came down: whence he bethought him with his troop
To trample on the soil; for easier thus
The vapour was extinguish'd, while alone;
So fell the eternal fiery flood, wherewith
The marble glow'd underneath, as under stove
The viands, doubly to augment the pain.
Unceasing was the play of wretched hands,

Dante Alighieri

Now this, now that way glancing, to shake off
The heat, still falling fresh. I thus began:
"Instructor! thou who all things overcom'st,
Except the hardy demons, that rush'd forth
To stop our entrance at the gate, say who
Is yon huge spirit, that, as seems, heeds not
The burning, but lies writhen in proud scorn,
As by the sultry tempest immatur'd?"

    Straight he himself, who was aware I ask'd
My guide of him, exclaim'd: "Such as I was
When living, dead such now I am. If Jove
Weary his workman out, from whom in ire
He snatch'd the lightnings, that at my last day
Transfix'd me, if the rest be weary out
At their black smithy labouring by turns
In Mongibello, while he cries aloud;
"Help, help, good Mulciber!" as erst he cried
In the Phlegraean warfare, and the bolts
Launch he full aim'd at me with all his might,
He never should enjoy a sweet revenge."

    Then thus my guide, in accent higher rais'd
Than I before had heard him: "Capaneus!
Thou art more punish'd, in that this thy pride
Lives yet unquench'd: no torrent, save thy rage,
Were to thy fury pain proportion'd full."

    Next turning round to me with milder lip
He spake: "This of the seven kings was one,
Who girt the Theban walls with siege, and held,
As still he seems to hold, God in disdain,
And sets his high omnipotence at nought.
But, as I told him, his despiteful mood
Is ornament well suits the breast that wears it.
Follow me now; and look thou set not yet
Thy foot in the hot sand, but to the wood
Keep ever close." Silently on we pass'd
To where there gushes from the forest's bound
A little brook, whose crimson'd wave yet lifts
My hair with horror. As the rill, that runs
From Bulicame, to be portion'd out
Among the sinful women; so ran this
Down through the sand, its bottom and each bank
Stone-built, and either margin at its side,
Whereon I straight perceiv'd our passage lay.

    "Of all that I have shown thee, since that gate
We enter'd first, whose threshold is to none
Denied, nought else so worthy of regard,
As is this river, has thine eye discern'd,
O'er which the flaming volley all is quench'd."

    So spake my guide; and I him thence besought,
That having giv'n me appetite to know,

The food he too would give, that hunger crav'd.
    "In midst of ocean," forthwith he began,
"A desolate country lies, which Crete is nam'd,
Under whose monarch in old times the world
Liv'd pure and chaste. A mountain rises there,
Call'd Ida, joyous once with leaves and streams,
Deserted now like a forbidden thing.
It was the spot which Rhea, Saturn's spouse,
Chose for the secret cradle of her son;
And better to conceal him, drown'd in shouts
His infant cries. Within the mount, upright
An ancient form there stands and huge, that turns
His shoulders towards Damiata, and at Rome
As in his mirror looks. Of finest gold
His head is shap'd, pure silver are the breast
And arms; thence to the middle is of brass.
And downward all beneath well-temper'd steel,
Save the right foot of potter's clay, on which
Than on the other more erect he stands,
Each part except the gold, is rent throughout;
And from the fissure tears distil, which join'd
Penetrate to that cave. They in their course
Thus far precipitated down the rock
Form Acheron, and Styx, and Phlegethon;
Then by this straiten'd channel passing hence
Beneath, e'en to the lowest depth of all,
Form there Cocytus, of whose lake (thyself
Shall see it) I here give thee no account."
    Then I to him: "If from our world this sluice
Be thus deriv'd; wherefore to us but now
Appears it at this edge?" He straight replied:
"The place, thou know'st, is round; and though great part
Thou have already pass'd, still to the left
Descending to the nethermost, not yet
Hast thou the circuit made of the whole orb.
Wherefore if aught of new to us appear,
It needs not bring up wonder in thy looks."
    Then I again inquir'd: "Where flow the streams
Of Phlegethon and Lethe? for of one
Thou tell'st not, and the other of that shower,
Thou say'st, is form'd." He answer thus return'd:
"Doubtless thy questions all well pleas'd I hear.
Yet the red seething wave might have resolv'd
One thou proposest. Lethe thou shalt see,
But not within this hollow, in the place,
Whither to lave themselves the spirits go,
Whose blame hath been by penitence remov'd."
He added: "Time is now we quit the wood.
Look thou my steps pursue: the margins give
Safe passage, unimpeded by the flames;

For over them all vapour is extinct."

CANTO XV

One of the solid margins bears us now
Envelop'd in the mist, that from the stream
Arising, hovers o'er, and saves from fire
Both piers and water. As the Flemings rear
Their mound, 'twixt Ghent and Bruges, to chase back
The ocean, fearing his tumultuous tide
That drives toward them, or the Paduans theirs
Along the Brenta, to defend their towns
And castles, ere the genial warmth be felt
On Chiarentana's top; such were the mounds,
So fram'd, though not in height or bulk to these
Made equal, by the master, whosoe'er
He was, that rais'd them here. We from the wood
Were not so far remov'd, that turning round
I might not have discern'd it, when we met
A troop of spirits, who came beside the pier.

    They each one ey'd us, as at eventide
One eyes another under a new moon,
And toward us sharpen'd their sight as keen,
As an old tailor at his needle's eye.

    Thus narrowly explor'd by all the tribe,
I was agniz'd of one, who by the skirt
Caught me, and cried, "What wonder have we here!"

    And I, when he to me outstretch'd his arm,
Intently fix'd my ken on his parch'd looks,
That although smirch'd with fire, they hinder'd not
But I remember'd him; and towards his face
My hand inclining, answer'd: "Sir! Brunetto!
And art thou here?" He thus to me: "My son!
Oh let it not displease thee, if Brunetto
Latini but a little space with thee
Turn back, and leave his fellows to proceed."

    I thus to him replied: "Much as I can,
I thereto pray thee; and if thou be willing,
That I here seat me with thee, I consent;
His leave, with whom I journey, first obtain'd."

    "O son!" said he, " whoever of this throng
One instant stops, lies then a hundred years,
No fan to ventilate him, when the fire
Smites sorest. Pass thou therefore on. I close
Will at thy garments walk, and then rejoin
My troop, who go mourning their endless doom."

    I dar'd not from the path descend to tread
On equal ground with him, but held my head
Bent down, as one who walks in reverent guise.

The Divine Comedy

    "What chance or destiny," thus be began,
"Ere the last day conducts thee here below?
And who is this, that shows to thee the way?"

    "There up aloft," I answer'd, "in the life
Serene, I wander'd in a valley lost,
Before mine age had to its fullness reach'd.
But yester-morn I left it: then once more
Into that vale returning, him I met;
And by this path homeward he leads me back."

    "If thou," he answer'd, "follow but thy star,
Thou canst not miss at last a glorious haven:
Unless in fairer days my judgment err'd.
And if my fate so early had not chanc'd,
Seeing the heav'ns thus bounteous to thee, I
Had gladly giv'n thee comfort in thy work.
But that ungrateful and malignant race,
Who in old times came down from Fesole,
Ay and still smack of their rough mountain-flint,
Will for thy good deeds shew thee enmity.
Nor wonder; for amongst ill-savour'd crabs
It suits not the sweet fig-tree lay her fruit.
Old fame reports them in the world for blind,
Covetous, envious, proud. Look to it well:
Take heed thou cleanse thee of their ways. For thee
Thy fortune hath such honour in reserve,
That thou by either party shalt be crav'd
With hunger keen: but be the fresh herb far
From the goat's tooth. The herd of Fesole
May of themselves make litter, not touch the plant,
If any such yet spring on their rank bed,
In which the holy seed revives, transmitted
From those true Romans, who still there remain'd,
When it was made the nest of so much ill."

    "Were all my wish fulfill'd," I straight replied,
"Thou from the confines of man's nature yet
Hadst not been driven forth; for in my mind
Is fix'd, and now strikes full upon my heart
The dear, benign, paternal image, such
As thine was, when so lately thou didst teach me
The way for man to win eternity;
And how I priz'd the lesson, it behooves,
That, long as life endures, my tongue should speak,
What of my fate thou tell'st, that write I down:
And with another text to comment on
For her I keep it, the celestial dame,
Who will know all, if I to her arrive.
This only would I have thee clearly note:
That so my conscience have no plea against me;
Do fortune as she list, I stand prepar'd.
Not new or strange such earnest to mine ear.

Dante Alighieri

Speed fortune then her wheel, as likes her best,
The clown his mattock; all things have their course."
     Thereat my sapient guide upon his right
Turn'd himself back, then look'd at me and spake:
"He listens to good purpose who takes note."
     I not the less still on my way proceed,
Discoursing with Brunetto, and inquire
Who are most known and chief among his tribe.
     "To know of some is well;" thus he replied,
"But of the rest silence may best beseem.
Time would not serve us for report so long.
In brief I tell thee, that all these were clerks,
Men of great learning and no less renown,
By one same sin polluted in the world.
With them is Priscian, and Accorso's son
Francesco herds among that wretched throng:
And, if the wish of so impure a blotch
Possess'd thee, him thou also might'st have seen,
Who by the servants' servant was transferr'd
From Arno's seat to Bacchiglione, where
His ill-strain'd nerves he left. I more would add,
But must from farther speech and onward way
Alike desist, for yonder I behold
A mist new-risen on the sandy plain.
A company, with whom I may not sort,
Approaches. I commend my TREASURE to thee,
Wherein I yet survive; my sole request."
     This said he turn'd, and seem'd as one of those,
Who o'er Verona's champain try their speed
For the green mantle, and of them he seem'd,
Not he who loses but who gains the prize.

CANTO XVI

NOW came I where the water's din was heard,
As down it fell into the other round,
Resounding like the hum of swarming bees:
When forth together issu'd from a troop,
That pass'd beneath the fierce tormenting storm,
Three spirits, running swift. They towards us came,
And each one cried aloud, "Oh do thou stay!
Whom by the fashion of thy garb we deem
To be some inmate of our evil land."
     Ah me! what wounds I mark'd upon their limbs,
Recent and old, inflicted by the flames!
E'en the remembrance of them grieves me yet.
     Attentive to their cry my teacher paus'd,
And turn'd to me his visage, and then spake;
"Wait now! our courtesy these merit well:

And were 't not for the nature of the place,
Whence glide the fiery darts, I should have said,
That haste had better suited thee than them."
    They, when we stopp'd, resum'd their ancient wail,
And soon as they had reach'd us, all the three
Whirl'd round together in one restless wheel.
As naked champions, smear'd with slippery oil,
Are wont intent to watch their place of hold
And vantage, ere in closer strife they meet;
Thus each one, as he wheel'd, his countenance
At me directed, so that opposite
The neck mov'd ever to the twinkling feet.
    "If misery of this drear wilderness,"
Thus one began, "added to our sad cheer
And destitute, do call forth scorn on us
And our entreaties, let our great renown
Incline thee to inform us who thou art,
That dost imprint with living feet unharm'd
The soil of Hell. He, in whose track thou see'st
My steps pursuing, naked though he be
And reft of all, was of more high estate
Than thou believest; grandchild of the chaste
Gualdrada, him they Guidoguerra call'd,
Who in his lifetime many a noble act
Achiev'd, both by his wisdom and his sword.
The other, next to me that beats the sand,
Is Aldobrandi, name deserving well,
In the' upper world, of honour; and myself
Who in this torment do partake with them,
Am Rusticucci, whom, past doubt, my wife
Of savage temper, more than aught beside
Hath to this evil brought." If from the fire
I had been shelter'd, down amidst them straight
I then had cast me, nor my guide, I deem,
Would have restrain'd my going; but that fear
Of the dire burning vanquish'd the desire,
Which made me eager of their wish'd embrace.
    I then began: "Not scorn, but grief much more,
Such as long time alone can cure, your doom
Fix'd deep within me, soon as this my lord
Spake words, whose tenour taught me to expect
That such a race, as ye are, was at hand.
I am a countryman of yours, who still
Affectionate have utter'd, and have heard
Your deeds and names renown'd. Leaving the gall
For the sweet fruit I go, that a sure guide
Hath promis'd to me. But behooves, that far
As to the centre first I downward tend."
    "So may long space thy spirit guide thy limbs,"
He answer straight return'd; "and so thy fame

Dante Alighieri

Shine bright, when thou art gone; as thou shalt tell,
If courtesy and valour, as they wont,
Dwell in our city, or have vanish'd clean?
For one amidst us late condemn'd to wail,
Borsiere, yonder walking with his peers,
Grieves us no little by the news he brings."

"An upstart multitude and sudden gains,
Pride and excess, O Florence! have in thee
Engender'd, so that now in tears thou mourn'st!"
Thus cried I with my face uprais'd, and they
All three, who for an answer took my words,
Look'd at each other, as men look when truth
Comes to their ear. "If thou at other times,"
They all at once rejoin'd, "so easily
Satisfy those, who question, happy thou,
Gifted with words, so apt to speak thy thought!
Wherefore if thou escape this darksome clime,
Returning to behold the radiant stars,
When thou with pleasure shalt retrace the past,
See that of us thou speak among mankind."

This said, they broke the circle, and so swift
Fled, that as pinions seem'd their nimble feet.

Not in so short a time might one have said
"Amen," as they had vanish'd. Straight my guide
Pursu'd his track. I follow'd; and small space
Had we pass'd onward, when the water's sound
Was now so near at hand, that we had scarce
Heard one another's speech for the loud din.

E'en as the river, that holds on its course
Unmingled, from the mount of Vesulo,
On the left side of Apennine, toward
The east, which Acquacheta higher up
They call, ere it descend into the vale,
At Forli by that name no longer known,
Rebellows o'er Saint Benedict, roll'd on
From the' Alpine summit down a precipice,
Where space enough to lodge a thousand spreads;
Thus downward from a craggy steep we found,
That this dark wave resounded, roaring loud,
So that the ear its clamour soon had stunn'd.

I had a cord that brac'd my girdle round,
Wherewith I erst had thought fast bound to take
The painted leopard. This when I had all
Unloosen'd from me (so my master bade)
I gather'd up, and stretch'd it forth to him.
Then to the right he turn'd, and from the brink
Standing few paces distant, cast it down
Into the deep abyss. "And somewhat strange,"
Thus to myself I spake, "signal so strange
Betokens, which my guide with earnest eye

Thus follows." Ah! what caution must men use
With those who look not at the deed alone,
But spy into the thoughts with subtle skill!
     "Quickly shall come," he said, "what I expect,
Thine eye discover quickly, that whereof
Thy thought is dreaming." Ever to that truth,
Which but the semblance of a falsehood wears,
A man, if possible, should bar his lip;
Since, although blameless, he incurs reproach.
But silence here were vain; and by these notes
Which now I sing, reader! I swear to thee,
So may they favour find to latest times!
That through the gross and murky air I spied
A shape come swimming up, that might have quell'd
The stoutest heart with wonder, in such guise
As one returns, who hath been down to loose
An anchor grappled fast against some rock,
Or to aught else that in the salt wave lies,
Who upward springing close draws in his feet.

CANTO XVII

"LO! the fell monster with the deadly sting!
Who passes mountains, breaks through fenced walls
And firm embattled spears, and with his filth
Taints all the world!" Thus me my guide address'd,
And beckon'd him, that he should come to shore,
Near to the stony causeway's utmost edge.
     Forthwith that image vile of fraud appear'd,
His head and upper part expos'd on land,
But laid not on the shore his bestial train.
His face the semblance of a just man's wore,
So kind and gracious was its outward cheer;
The rest was serpent all: two shaggy claws
Reach'd to the armpits, and the back and breast,
And either side, were painted o'er with nodes
And orbits. Colours variegated more
Nor Turks nor Tartars e'er on cloth of state
With interchangeable embroidery wove,
Nor spread Arachne o'er her curious loom.
As ofttimes a light skiff, moor'd to the shore,
Stands part in water, part upon the land;
Or, as where dwells the greedy German boor,
The beaver settles watching for his prey;
So on the rim, that fenc'd the sand with rock,
Sat perch'd the fiend of evil. In the void
Glancing, his tail upturn'd its venomous fork,
With sting like scorpion's arm'd. Then thus my guide:
"Now need our way must turn few steps apart,

Dante Alighieri

Far as to that ill beast, who couches there."
    Thereat toward the right our downward course
We shap'd, and, better to escape the flame
And burning marle, ten paces on the verge
Proceeded. Soon as we to him arrive,
A little further on mine eye beholds
A tribe of spirits, seated on the sand
Near the wide chasm. Forthwith my master spake:
"That to the full thy knowledge may extend
Of all this round contains, go now, and mark
The mien these wear: but hold not long discourse.
Till thou returnest, I with him meantime
Will parley, that to us he may vouchsafe
The aid of his strong shoulders." Thus alone
Yet forward on the' extremity I pac'd
Of that seventh circle, where the mournful tribe
Were seated. At the eyes forth gush'd their pangs.
Against the vapours and the torrid soil
Alternately their shifting hands they plied.
Thus use the dogs in summer still to ply
Their jaws and feet by turns, when bitten sore
By gnats, or flies, or gadflies swarming round.
    Noting the visages of some, who lay
Beneath the pelting of that dolorous fire,
One of them all I knew not; but perceiv'd,
That pendent from his neck each bore a pouch
With colours and with emblems various mark'd,
On which it seem'd as if their eye did feed.
    And when amongst them looking round I came,
A yellow purse I saw with azure wrought,
That wore a lion's countenance and port.
Then still my sight pursuing its career,
Another I beheld, than blood more red.
A goose display of whiter wing than curd.
And one, who bore a fat and azure swine
Pictur'd on his white scrip, addressed me thus:
"What dost thou in this deep? Go now and know,
Since yet thou livest, that my neighbour here
Vitaliano on my left shall sit.
A Paduan with these Florentines am I.
Ofttimes they thunder in mine ears, exclaiming
"O haste that noble knight! he who the pouch
With the three beaks will bring!" This said, he writh'd
The mouth, and loll'd the tongue out, like an ox
That licks his nostrils. I, lest longer stay
He ill might brook, who bade me stay not long,
Backward my steps from those sad spirits turn'd.
    My guide already seated on the haunch
Of the fierce animal I found; and thus
He me encourag'd. "Be thou stout; be bold.

The Divine Comedy

Down such a steep flight must we now descend!
Mount thou before: for that no power the tail
May have to harm thee, I will be i' th' midst."

    As one, who hath an ague fit so near,
His nails already are turn'd blue, and he
Quivers all o'er, if he but eye the shade;
Such was my cheer at hearing of his words.
But shame soon interpos'd her threat, who makes
The servant bold in presence of his lord.

    I settled me upon those shoulders huge,
And would have said, but that the words to aid
My purpose came not, "Look thou clasp me firm!"

    But he whose succour then not first I prov'd,
Soon as I mounted, in his arms aloft,
Embracing, held me up, and thus he spake:
"Geryon! now move thee! be thy wheeling gyres
Of ample circuit, easy thy descent.
Think on th' unusual burden thou sustain'st."

    As a small vessel, back'ning out from land,
Her station quits; so thence the monster loos'd,
And when he felt himself at large, turn'd round
There where the breast had been, his forked tail.
Thus, like an eel, outstretch'd at length he steer'd,
Gath'ring the air up with retractile claws.

    Not greater was the dread when Phaeton
The reins let drop at random, whence high heaven,
Whereof signs yet appear, was wrapt in flames;
Nor when ill-fated Icarus perceiv'd,
By liquefaction of the scalded wax,
The trusted pennons loosen'd from his loins,
His sire exclaiming loud, "Ill way thou keep'st!"
Than was my dread, when round me on each part
The air I view'd, and other object none
Save the fell beast. He slowly sailing, wheels
His downward motion, unobserv'd of me,
But that the wind, arising to my face,
Breathes on me from below. Now on our right
I heard the cataract beneath us leap
With hideous crash; whence bending down to' explore,
New terror I conceiv'd at the steep plunge:
For flames I saw, and wailings smote mine ear:
So that all trembling close I crouch'd my limbs,
And then distinguish'd, unperceiv'd before,
By the dread torments that on every side
Drew nearer, how our downward course we wound.

    As falcon, that hath long been on the wing,
But lure nor bird hath seen, while in despair
The falconer cries, "Ah me! thou stoop'st to earth!"
Wearied descends, and swiftly down the sky
In many an orbit wheels, then lighting sits

At distance from his lord in angry mood;
So Geryon lighting places us on foot
Low down at base of the deep-furrow'd rock,
And, of his burden there discharg'd, forthwith
Sprang forward, like an arrow from the string.

CANTO XVIII

THERE is a place within the depths of hell
Call'd Malebolge, all of rock dark-stain'd
With hue ferruginous, e'en as the steep
That round it circling winds. Right in the midst
Of that abominable region, yawns
A spacious gulf profound, whereof the frame
Due time shall tell. The circle, that remains,
Throughout its round, between the gulf and base
Of the high craggy banks, successive forms
Ten trenches, in its hollow bottom sunk.

    As where to guard the walls, full many a foss
Begirds some stately castle, sure defence
Affording to the space within, so here
Were model'd these; and as like fortresses
E'en from their threshold to the brink without,
Are flank'd with bridges; from the rock's low base
Thus flinty paths advanc'd, that 'cross the moles
And dikes, struck onward far as to the gulf,
That in one bound collected cuts them off.
Such was the place, wherein we found ourselves
From Geryon's back dislodg'd. The bard to left
Held on his way, and I behind him mov'd.

    On our right hand new misery I saw,
New pains, new executioners of wrath,
That swarming peopled the first chasm. Below
Were naked sinners. Hitherward they came,
Meeting our faces from the middle point,
With us beyond but with a larger stride.
E'en thus the Romans, when the year returns
Of Jubilee, with better speed to rid
The thronging multitudes, their means devise
For such as pass the bridge; that on one side
All front toward the castle, and approach
Saint Peter's fane, on th' other towards the mount.

    Each divers way along the grisly rock,
Horn'd demons I beheld, with lashes huge,
That on their back unmercifully smote.
Ah! how they made them bound at the first stripe!
None for the second waited nor the third.

    Meantime as on I pass'd, one met my sight
Whom soon as view'd; "Of him," cried I, "not yet

The Divine Comedy

Mine eye hath had his fill." With fixed gaze
I therefore scann'd him. Straight the teacher kind
Paus'd with me, and consented I should walk
Backward a space, and the tormented spirit,
Who thought to hide him, bent his visage down.
But it avail'd him nought; for I exclaim'd:
"Thou who dost cast thy eye upon the ground,
Unless thy features do belie thee much,
Venedico art thou. But what brings thee
Into this bitter seas'ning? " He replied:
"Unwillingly I answer to thy words.
But thy clear speech, that to my mind recalls
The world I once inhabited, constrains me.
Know then 'twas I who led fair Ghisola
To do the Marquis' will, however fame
The shameful tale have bruited. Nor alone
Bologna hither sendeth me to mourn
Rather with us the place is so o'erthrong'd
That not so many tongues this day are taught,
Betwixt the Reno and Savena's stream,
To answer SIPA in their country's phrase.
And if of that securer proof thou need,
Remember but our craving thirst for gold."

    Him speaking thus, a demon with his thong
Struck, and exclaim'd, "Away! corrupter! here
Women are none for sale." Forthwith I join'd
My escort, and few paces thence we came
To where a rock forth issued from the bank.
That easily ascended, to the right
Upon its splinter turning, we depart
From those eternal barriers. When arriv'd,
Where underneath the gaping arch lets pass
The scourged souls: "Pause here," the teacher said,
"And let these others miserable, now
Strike on thy ken, faces not yet beheld,
For that together they with us have walk'd."

    From the old bridge we ey'd the pack, who came
From th' other side towards us, like the rest,
Excoriate from the lash. My gentle guide,
By me unquestion'd, thus his speech resum'd:
"Behold that lofty shade, who this way tends,
And seems too woe-begone to drop a tear.
How yet the regal aspect he retains!
Jason is he, whose skill and prowess won
The ram from Colchos. To the Lemnian isle
His passage thither led him, when those bold
And pitiless women had slain all their males.
There he with tokens and fair witching words
Hypsipyle beguil'd, a virgin young,
Who first had all the rest herself beguil'd.

Impregnated he left her there forlorn.
Such is the guilt condemns him to this pain.
Here too Medea's inj'ries are avenged.
All bear him company, who like deceit
To his have practis'd. And thus much to know
Of the first vale suffice thee, and of those
Whom its keen torments urge." Now had we come
Where, crossing the next pier, the straighten'd path
Bestrides its shoulders to another arch.

    Hence in the second chasm we heard the ghosts,
Who jibber in low melancholy sounds,
With wide-stretch'd nostrils snort, and on themselves
Smite with their palms. Upon the banks a scurf
From the foul steam condens'd, encrusting hung,
That held sharp combat with the sight and smell.

    So hollow is the depth, that from no part,
Save on the summit of the rocky span,
Could I distinguish aught. Thus far we came;
And thence I saw, within the foss below,
A crowd immers'd in ordure, that appear'd
Draff of the human body. There beneath
Searching with eye inquisitive, I mark'd
One with his head so grim'd, 't were hard to deem,
If he were clerk or layman. Loud he cried:
"Why greedily thus bendest more on me,
Than on these other filthy ones, thy ken?"

    "Because if true my mem'ry," I replied,
"I heretofore have seen thee with dry locks,
And thou Alessio art of Lucca sprung.
Therefore than all the rest I scan thee more."

    Then beating on his brain these words he spake:
"Me thus low down my flatteries have sunk,
Wherewith I ne'er enough could glut my tongue."

    My leader thus: "A little further stretch
Thy face, that thou the visage well mayst note
Of that besotted, sluttish courtezan,
Who there doth rend her with defiled nails,
Now crouching down, now risen on her feet.
Thais is this, the harlot, whose false lip
Answer'd her doting paramour that ask'd,
'Thankest me much!'--'Say rather wondrously,'
And seeing this here satiate be our view."

CANTO XIX

WOE to thee, Simon Magus! woe to you,
His wretched followers! who the things of God,
Which should be wedded unto goodness, them,
Rapacious as ye are, do prostitute

The Divine Comedy

For gold and silver in adultery!
Now must the trumpet sound for you, since yours
Is the third chasm. Upon the following vault
We now had mounted, where the rock impends
Directly o'er the centre of the foss.

    Wisdom Supreme! how wonderful the art,
Which thou dost manifest in heaven, in earth,
And in the evil world, how just a meed
Allotting by thy virtue unto all!

    I saw the livid stone, throughout the sides
And in its bottom full of apertures,
All equal in their width, and circular each,
Nor ample less nor larger they appear'd
Than in Saint John's fair dome of me belov'd
Those fram'd to hold the pure baptismal streams,
One of the which I brake, some few years past,
To save a whelming infant; and be this
A seal to undeceive whoever doubts
The motive of my deed. From out the mouth
Of every one, emerg'd a sinner's feet
And of the legs high upward as the calf
The rest beneath was hid. On either foot
The soles were burning, whence the flexile joints
Glanc'd with such violent motion, as had snapt
Asunder cords or twisted withs. As flame,
Feeding on unctuous matter, glides along
The surface, scarcely touching where it moves;
So here, from heel to point, glided the flames.

    "Master! say who is he, than all the rest
Glancing in fiercer agony, on whom
A ruddier flame doth prey?" I thus inquir'd.

    "If thou be willing," he replied, "that I
Carry thee down, where least the slope bank falls,
He of himself shall tell thee and his wrongs."

    I then: "As pleases thee to me is best.
Thou art my lord; and know'st that ne'er I quit
Thy will: what silence hides that knowest thou."
Thereat on the fourth pier we came, we turn'd,
And on our left descended to the depth,
A narrow strait and perforated close.
Nor from his side my leader set me down,
Till to his orifice he brought, whose limb
Quiv'ring express'd his pang. "Whoe'er thou art,
Sad spirit! thus revers'd, and as a stake
Driv'n in the soil!" I in these words began,
"If thou be able, utter forth thy voice."

    There stood I like the friar, that doth shrive
A wretch for murder doom'd, who e'en when fix'd,
Calleth him back, whence death awhile delays.

Dante Alighieri

     He shouted: "Ha! already standest there?
Already standest there, O Boniface!
By many a year the writing play'd me false.
So early dost thou surfeit with the wealth,
For which thou fearedst not in guile to take
The lovely lady, and then mangle her?"
     I felt as those who, piercing not the drift
Of answer made them, stand as if expos'd
In mockery, nor know what to reply,
When Virgil thus admonish'd: "Tell him quick,
I am not he, not he, whom thou believ'st."
     And I, as was enjoin'd me, straight replied.
     That heard, the spirit all did wrench his feet,
And sighing next in woeful accent spake:
"What then of me requirest?" If to know
So much imports thee, who I am, that thou
Hast therefore down the bank descended, learn
That in the mighty mantle I was rob'd,
And of a she-bear was indeed the son,
So eager to advance my whelps, that there
My having in my purse above I stow'd,
And here myself. Under my head are dragg'd
The rest, my predecessors in the guilt
Of simony. Stretch'd at their length they lie
Along an opening in the rock. 'Midst them
I also low shall fall, soon as he comes,
For whom I took thee, when so hastily
I question'd. But already longer time
Hath pass'd, since my souls kindled, and I thus
Upturn'd have stood, than is his doom to stand
Planted with fiery feet. For after him,
One yet of deeds more ugly shall arrive,
From forth the west, a shepherd without law,
Fated to cover both his form and mine.
He a new Jason shall be call'd, of whom
In Maccabees we read; and favour such
As to that priest his king indulgent show'd,
Shall be of France's monarch shown to him."
     I know not if I here too far presum'd,
But in this strain I answer'd: "Tell me now,
What treasures from St. Peter at the first
Our Lord demanded, when he put the keys
Into his charge? Surely he ask'd no more
But, Follow me! Nor Peter nor the rest
Or gold or silver of Matthias took,
When lots were cast upon the forfeit place
Of the condemned soul. Abide thou then;
Thy punishment of right is merited:
And look thou well to that ill-gotten coin,
Which against Charles thy hardihood inspir'd.

If reverence of the keys restrain'd me not,
Which thou in happier time didst hold, I yet
Severer speech might use. Your avarice
O'ercasts the world with mourning, under foot
Treading the good, and raising bad men up.
Of shepherds, like to you, th' Evangelist
Was ware, when her, who sits upon the waves,
With kings in filthy whoredom he beheld,
She who with seven heads tower'd at her birth,
And from ten horns her proof of glory drew,
Long as her spouse in virtue took delight.
Of gold and silver ye have made your god,
Diff'ring wherein from the idolater,
But he that worships one, a hundred ye?
Ah, Constantine! to how much ill gave birth,
Not thy conversion, but that plenteous dower,
Which the first wealthy Father gain'd from thee!"

    Meanwhile, as thus I sung, he, whether wrath
Or conscience smote him, violent upsprang
Spinning on either sole. I do believe
My teacher well was pleas'd, with so compos'd
A lip, he listen'd ever to the sound
Of the true words I utter'd. In both arms
He caught, and to his bosom lifting me
Upward retrac'd the way of his descent.

    Nor weary of his weight he press'd me close,
Till to the summit of the rock we came,
Our passage from the fourth to the fifth pier.
His cherish'd burden there gently he plac'd
Upon the rugged rock and steep, a path
Not easy for the clamb'ring goat to mount.

    Thence to my view another vale appear'd

CANTO XX

AND now the verse proceeds to torments new,
Fit argument of this the twentieth strain
Of the first song, whose awful theme records
The spirits whelm'd in woe. Earnest I look'd
Into the depth, that open'd to my view,
Moisten'd with tears of anguish, and beheld
A tribe, that came along the hollow vale,
In silence weeping: such their step as walk
Quires chanting solemn litanies on earth.

    As on them more direct mine eye descends,
Each wondrously seem'd to be revers'd
At the neck-bone, so that the countenance
Was from the reins averted: and because
None might before him look, they were compell'd

Dante Alighieri

To' advance with backward gait. Thus one perhaps
Hath been by force of palsy clean transpos'd,
But I ne'er saw it nor believe it so.
     Now, reader! think within thyself, so God
Fruit of thy reading give thee! how I long
Could keep my visage dry, when I beheld
Near me our form distorted in such guise,
That on the hinder parts fall'n from the face
The tears down-streaming roll'd. Against a rock
I leant and wept, so that my guide exclaim'd:
"What, and art thou too witless as the rest?
Here pity most doth show herself alive,
When she is dead. What guilt exceedeth his,
Who with Heaven's judgment in his passion strives?
Raise up thy head, raise up, and see the man,
Before whose eyes earth gap'd in Thebes, when all
Cried out, 'Amphiaraus, whither rushest?
'Why leavest thou the war?' He not the less
Fell ruining far as to Minos down,
Whose grapple none eludes. Lo! how he makes
The breast his shoulders, and who once too far
Before him wish'd to see, now backward looks,
And treads reverse his path. Tiresias note,
Who semblance chang'd, when woman he became
Of male, through every limb transform'd, and then
Once more behov'd him with his rod to strike
The two entwining serpents, ere the plumes,
That mark'd the better sex, might shoot again.
     "Aruns, with rere his belly facing, comes.
On Luni's mountains 'midst the marbles white,
Where delves Carrara's hind, who wons beneath,
A cavern was his dwelling, whence the stars
And main-sea wide in boundless view he held.
     "The next, whose loosen'd tresses overspread
Her bosom, which thou seest not (for each hair
On that side grows) was Manto, she who search'd
Through many regions, and at length her seat
Fix'd in my native land, whence a short space
My words detain thy audience. When her sire
From life departed, and in servitude
The city dedicate to Bacchus mourn'd,
Long time she went a wand'rer through the world.
Aloft in Italy's delightful land
A lake there lies, at foot of that proud Alp,
That o'er the Tyrol locks Germania in,
Its name Benacus, which a thousand rills,
Methinks, and more, water between the vale
Camonica and Garda and the height
Of Apennine remote. There is a spot
At midway of that lake, where he who bears

The Divine Comedy

Of Trento's flock the past'ral staff, with him
Of Brescia, and the Veronese, might each
Passing that way his benediction give.
A garrison of goodly site and strong
Peschiera stands, to awe with front oppos'd
The Bergamese and Brescian, whence the shore
More slope each way descends. There, whatsoev'er
Benacus' bosom holds not, tumbling o'er
Down falls, and winds a river flood beneath
Through the green pastures. Soon as in his course
The steam makes head, Benacus then no more
They call the name, but Mincius, till at last
Reaching Governo into Po he falls.
Not far his course hath run, when a wide flat
It finds, which overstretchmg as a marsh
It covers, pestilent in summer oft.
Hence journeying, the savage maiden saw
'Midst of the fen a territory waste
And naked of inhabitants. To shun
All human converse, here she with her slaves
Plying her arts remain'd, and liv'd, and left
Her body tenantless. Thenceforth the tribes,
Who round were scatter'd, gath'ring to that place
Assembled; for its strength was great, enclos'd
On all parts by the fen. On those dead bones
They rear'd themselves a city, for her sake,
Calling it Mantua, who first chose the spot,
Nor ask'd another omen for the name,
Wherein more numerous the people dwelt,
Ere Casalodi's madness by deceit
Was wrong'd of Pinamonte. If thou hear
Henceforth another origin assign'd
Of that my country, I forewarn thee now,
That falsehood none beguile thee of the truth."

    I answer'd: "Teacher, I conclude thy words
So certain, that all else shall be to me
As embers lacking life. But now of these,
Who here proceed, instruct me, if thou see
Any that merit more especial note.
For thereon is my mind alone intent."

    He straight replied: "That spirit, from whose cheek
The beard sweeps o'er his shoulders brown, what time
Graecia was emptied of her males, that scarce
The cradles were supplied, the seer was he
In Aulis, who with Calchas gave the sign
When first to cut the cable. Him they nam'd
Eurypilus: so sings my tragic strain,
In which majestic measure well thou know'st,
Who know'st it all. That other, round the loins
So slender of his shape, was Michael Scot,

Practis'd in ev'ry slight of magic wile.
    "Guido Bonatti see: Asdente mark,
Who now were willing, he had tended still
The thread and cordwain; and too late repents.

    "See next the wretches, who the needle left,
The shuttle and the spindle, and became
Diviners: baneful witcheries they wrought
With images and herbs. But onward now:
For now doth Cain with fork of thorns confine
On either hemisphere, touching the wave
Beneath the towers of Seville. Yesternight
The moon was round. Thou mayst remember well:
For she good service did thee in the gloom
Of the deep wood." This said, both onward mov'd.

CANTO XXI

THUS we from bridge to bridge, with other talk,
The which my drama cares not to rehearse,
Pass'd on; and to the summit reaching, stood
To view another gap, within the round
Of Malebolge, other bootless pangs.
    Marvelous darkness shadow'd o'er the place.
    In the Venetians' arsenal as boils
Through wintry months tenacious pitch, to smear
Their unsound vessels; for th' inclement time
Sea-faring men restrains, and in that while
His bark one builds anew, another stops
The ribs of his, that hath made many a voyage;
One hammers at the prow, one at the poop;
This shapeth oars, that other cables twirls,
The mizen one repairs and main-sail rent
So not by force of fire but art divine
Boil'd here a glutinous thick mass, that round
Lim'd all the shore beneath. I that beheld,
But therein nought distinguish'd, save the surge,
Rais'd by the boiling, in one mighty swell
Heave, and by turns subsiding and fall. While there
I fix'd my ken below, "Mark! mark!" my guide
Exclaiming, drew me towards him from the place,
Wherein I stood. I turn'd myself as one,
Impatient to behold that which beheld
He needs must shun, whom sudden fear unmans,
That he his flight delays not for the view.
Behind me I discern'd a devil black,
That running, up advanc'd along the rock.
Ah! what fierce cruelty his look bespake!
In act how bitter did he seem, with wings
Buoyant outstretch'd and feet of nimblest tread!

The Divine Comedy

His shoulder proudly eminent and sharp
Was with a sinner charg'd; by either haunch
He held him, the foot's sinew griping fast.
    "Ye of our bridge!" he cried, "keen-talon'd fiends!
Lo! one of Santa Zita's elders! Him
Whelm ye beneath, while I return for more.
That land hath store of such. All men are there,
Except Bonturo, barterers: of 'no'
For lucre there an 'aye' is quickly made."
    Him dashing down, o'er the rough rock he turn'd,
Nor ever after thief a mastiff loos'd
Sped with like eager haste. That other sank
And forthwith writing to the surface rose.
But those dark demons, shrouded by the bridge,
Cried "Here the hallow'd visage saves not: here
Is other swimming than in Serchio's wave.
Wherefore if thou desire we rend thee not,
Take heed thou mount not o'er the pitch." This said,
They grappled him with more than hundred hooks,
And shouted: "Cover'd thou must sport thee here;
So, if thou canst, in secret mayst thou filch."
E'en thus the cook bestirs him, with his grooms,
To thrust the flesh into the caldron down
With flesh-hooks, that it float not on the top.
    Me then my guide bespake: "Lest they descry,
That thou art here, behind a craggy rock
Bend low and screen thee; and whate'er of force
Be offer'd me, or insult, fear thou not:
For I am well advis'd, who have been erst
In the like fray." Beyond the bridge's head
Therewith he pass'd, and reaching the sixth pier,
Behov'd him then a forehead terror-proof.
    With storm and fury, as when dogs rush forth
Upon the poor man's back, who suddenly
From whence he standeth makes his suit; so rush'd
Those from beneath the arch, and against him
Their weapons all they pointed. He aloud:
"Be none of you outrageous: ere your time
Dare seize me, come forth from amongst you one,
Who having heard my words, decide he then
If he shall tear these limbs." They shouted loud,
"Go, Malacoda!" Whereat one advanc'd,
The others standing firm, and as he came,
"What may this turn avail him?" he exclaim'd.
    "Believ'st thou, Malacoda! I had come
Thus far from all your skirmishing secure,"
My teacher answered, "without will divine
And destiny propitious? Pass we then
For so Heaven's pleasure is, that I should lead
Another through this savage wilderness."

Dante Alighieri

    Forthwith so fell his pride, that he let drop
The instrument of torture at his feet,
And to the rest exclaim'd: "We have no power
To strike him." Then to me my guide: "O thou!
Who on the bridge among the crags dost sit
Low crouching, safely now to me return."
    I rose, and towards him moved with speed: the fiends
Meantime all forward drew: me terror seiz'd
Lest they should break the compact they had made.
Thus issuing from Caprona, once I saw
Th' infantry dreading, lest his covenant
The foe should break; so close he hemm'd them round.
    I to my leader's side adher'd, mine eyes
With fixt and motionless observance bent
On their unkindly visage. They their hooks
Protruding, one the other thus bespake:
"Wilt thou I touch him on the hip?" To whom
Was answer'd: "Even so; nor miss thy aim."
    But he, who was in conf'rence with my guide,
Turn'd rapid round, and thus the demon spake:
"Stay, stay thee, Scarmiglione!" Then to us
He added: "Further footing to your step
This rock affords not, shiver'd to the base
Of the sixth arch. But would you still proceed,
Up by this cavern go: not distant far,
Another rock will yield you passage safe.
Yesterday, later by five hours than now,
Twelve hundred threescore years and six had fill'd
The circuit of their course, since here the way
Was broken. Thitherward I straight dispatch
Certain of these my scouts, who shall espy
If any on the surface bask. With them
Go ye: for ye shall find them nothing fell.
Come Alichino forth," with that he cried,
"And Calcabrina, and Cagnazzo thou!
The troop of ten let Barbariccia lead.
With Libicocco Draghinazzo haste,
Fang'd Ciriatto, Grafflacane fierce,
And Farfarello, and mad Rubicant.
Search ye around the bubbling tar. For these,
In safety lead them, where the other crag
Uninterrupted traverses the dens."
    I then: "O master! what a sight is there!
Ah! without escort, journey we alone,
Which, if thou know the way, I covet not.
Unless thy prudence fail thee, dost not mark
How they do gnarl upon us, and their scowl
Threatens us present tortures?" He replied:
"I charge thee fear not: let them, as they will,
Gnarl on: 't is but in token of their spite

Against the souls, who mourn in torment steep'd."
    To leftward o'er the pier they turn'd; but each
Had first between his teeth prest close the tongue,
Toward their leader for a signal looking,
Which he with sound obscene triumphant gave.

CANTO XXII

IT hath been heretofore my chance to see
Horsemen with martial order shifting camp,
To onset sallying, or in muster rang'd,
Or in retreat sometimes outstretch'd for flight;
Light-armed squadrons and fleet foragers
Scouring thy plains, Arezzo! have I seen,
And clashing tournaments, and tilting jousts,
Now with the sound of trumpets, now of bells,
Tabors, or signals made from castled heights,
And with inventions multiform, our own,
Or introduc'd from foreign land; but ne'er
To such a strange recorder I beheld,
In evolution moving, horse nor foot,
Nor ship, that tack'd by sign from land or star.
    With the ten demons on our way we went;
Ah fearful company! but in the church
With saints, with gluttons at the tavern's mess.
    Still earnest on the pitch I gaz'd, to mark
All things whate'er the chasm contain'd, and those
Who burn'd within. As dolphins, that, in sign
To mariners, heave high their arched backs,
That thence forewarn'd they may advise to save
Their threaten'd vessels; so, at intervals,
To ease the pain his back some sinner show'd,
Then hid more nimbly than the lightning glance.
    E'en as the frogs, that of a wat'ry moat
Stand at the brink, with the jaws only out,
Their feet and of the trunk all else concealed,
Thus on each part the sinners stood, but soon
As Barbariccia was at hand, so they
Drew back under the wave. I saw, and yet
My heart doth stagger, one, that waited thus,
As it befalls that oft one frog remains,
While the next springs away: and Graffiacan,
Who of the fiends was nearest, grappling seiz'd
His clotted locks, and dragg'd him sprawling up,
That he appear'd to me an otter. Each
Already by their names I knew, so well
When they were chosen, I observ'd, and mark'd
How one the other call'd. "O Rubicant!
See that his hide thou with thy talons flay,"

Dante Alighieri

Shouted together all the cursed crew.
    Then I: "Inform thee, master! if thou may,
What wretched soul is this, on whom their hand
His foes have laid." My leader to his side
Approach'd, and whence he came inquir'd, to whom
Was answer'd thus: "Born in Navarre's domain
My mother plac'd me in a lord's retinue,
For she had borne me to a losel vile,
A spendthrift of his substance and himself.
The good king Thibault after that I serv'd,
To peculating here my thoughts were turn'd,
Whereof I give account in this dire heat."
    Straight Ciriatto, from whose mouth a tusk
Issued on either side, as from a boar,
Ript him with one of these. 'Twixt evil claws
The mouse had fall'n: but Barbariccia cried,
Seizing him with both arms: "Stand thou apart,
While I do fix him on my prong transpierc'd."
Then added, turning to my guide his face,
"Inquire of him, if more thou wish to learn,
Ere he again be rent." My leader thus:
"Then tell us of the partners in thy guilt;
Knowest thou any sprung of Latian land
Under the tar?"--"I parted," he replied,
"But now from one, who sojourn'd not far thence;
So were I under shelter now with him!
Nor hook nor talon then should scare me more."--.
    "Too long we suffer," Libicocco cried,
Then, darting forth a prong, seiz'd on his arm,
And mangled bore away the sinewy part.
Him Draghinazzo by his thighs beneath
Would next have caught, whence angrily their chief,
Turning on all sides round, with threat'ning brow
Restrain'd them. When their strife a little ceas'd,
Of him, who yet was gazing on his wound,
My teacher thus without delay inquir'd:
"Who was the spirit, from whom by evil hap
Parting, as thou has told, thou cam'st to shore?"--
    "It was the friar Gomita," he rejoin'd,
"He of Gallura, vessel of all guile,
Who had his master's enemies in hand,
And us'd them so that they commend him well.
Money he took, and them at large dismiss'd.
So he reports: and in each other charge
Committed to his keeping, play'd the part
Of barterer to the height: with him doth herd
The chief of Logodoro, Michel Zanche.
Sardinia is a theme, whereof their tongue
Is never weary. Out! alas! behold
That other, how he grins! More would I say,

65

But tremble lest he mean to maul me sore."
    Their captain then to Farfarello turning,
Who roll'd his moony eyes in act to strike,
Rebuk'd him thus: "Off! cursed bird! Avaunt!"--
    "If ye desire to see or hear," he thus
Quaking with dread resum'd, "or Tuscan spirits
Or Lombard, I will cause them to appear.
Meantime let these ill talons bate their fury,
So that no vengeance they may fear from them,
And I, remaining in this self-same place,
Will for myself but one, make sev'n appear,
When my shrill whistle shall be heard; for so
Our custom is to call each other up."
    Cagnazzo at that word deriding grinn'd,
Then wagg'd the head and spake: "Hear his device,
Mischievous as he is, to plunge him down."
    Whereto he thus, who fail'd not in rich store
Of nice-wove toils; " Mischief forsooth extreme,
Meant only to procure myself more woe!"
    No longer Alichino then refrain'd,
But thus, the rest gainsaying, him bespake:
"If thou do cast thee down, I not on foot
Will chase thee, but above the pitch will beat
My plumes. Quit we the vantage ground, and let
The bank be as a shield, that we may see
If singly thou prevail against us all."
    Now, reader, of new sport expect to hear!
    They each one turn'd his eyes to the' other shore,
He first, who was the hardest to persuade.
The spirit of Navarre chose well his time,
Planted his feet on land, and at one leap
Escaping disappointed their resolve.
    Them quick resentment stung, but him the most,
Who was the cause of failure; in pursuit
He therefore sped, exclaiming; "Thou art caught."
    But little it avail'd: terror outstripp'd
His following flight: the other plung'd beneath,
And he with upward pinion rais'd his breast:
E'en thus the water-fowl, when she perceives
The falcon near, dives instant down, while he
Enrag'd and spent retires. That mockery
In Calcabrina fury stirr'd, who flew
After him, with desire of strife inflam'd;
And, for the barterer had 'scap'd, so turn'd
His talons on his comrade. O'er the dyke
In grapple close they join'd; but the' other prov'd
A goshawk able to rend well his foe;
And in the boiling lake both fell. The heat
Was umpire soon between them, but in vain
To lift themselves they strove, so fast were glued

Dante Alighieri

Their pennons. Barbariccia, as the rest,
That chance lamenting, four in flight dispatch'd
From the' other coast, with all their weapons arm'd.
They, to their post on each side speedily
Descending, stretch'd their hooks toward the fiends,
Who flounder'd, inly burning from their scars:
And we departing left them to that broil.

CANTO XXIII

IN silence and in solitude we went,
One first, the other following his steps,
As minor friars journeying on their road.
      The present fray had turn'd my thoughts to muse
Upon old Aesop's fable, where he told
What fate unto the mouse and frog befell.
For language hath not sounds more like in sense,
Than are these chances, if the origin
And end of each be heedfully compar'd.
And as one thought bursts from another forth,
So afterward from that another sprang,
Which added doubly to my former fear.
For thus I reason'd: "These through us have been
So foil'd, with loss and mock'ry so complete,
As needs must sting them sore. If anger then
Be to their evil will conjoin'd, more fell
They shall pursue us, than the savage hound
Snatches the leveret, panting 'twixt his jaws."
      Already I perceiv'd my hair stand all
On end with terror, and look'd eager back.
      "Teacher," I thus began, "if speedily
Thyself and me thou hide not, much I dread
Those evil talons. Even now behind
They urge us: quick imagination works
So forcibly, that I already feel them."
      He answer'd: "Were I form'd of leaded glass,
I should not sooner draw unto myself
Thy outward image, than I now imprint
That from within. This moment came thy thoughts
Presented before mine, with similar act
And count'nance similar, so that from both
I one design have fram'd. If the right coast
Incline so much, that we may thence descend
Into the other chasm, we shall escape
Secure from this imagined pursuit."
      He had not spoke his purpose to the end,
When I from far beheld them with spread wings
Approach to take us. Suddenly my guide
Caught me, ev'n as a mother that from sleep

Is by the noise arous'd, and near her sees
The climbing fires, who snatches up her babe
And flies ne'er pausing, careful more of him
Than of herself, that but a single vest
Clings round her limbs. Down from the jutting beach
Supine he cast him, to that pendent rock,
Which closes on one part the other chasm.

    Never ran water with such hurrying pace
Adown the tube to turn a landmill's wheel,
When nearest it approaches to the spokes,
As then along that edge my master ran,
Carrying me in his bosom, as a child,
Not a companion. Scarcely had his feet
Reach'd to the lowest of the bed beneath,
When over us the steep they reach'd; but fear
In him was none; for that high Providence,
Which plac'd them ministers of the fifth foss,
Power of departing thence took from them all.

    There in the depth we saw a painted tribe,
Who pac'd with tardy steps around, and wept,
Faint in appearance and o'ercome with toil.
Caps had they on, with hoods, that fell low down
Before their eyes, in fashion like to those
Worn by the monks in Cologne. Their outside
Was overlaid with gold, dazzling to view,
But leaden all within, and of such weight,
That Frederick's compar'd to these were straw.
Oh, everlasting wearisome attire!

    We yet once more with them together turn'd
To leftward, on their dismal moan intent.
But by the weight oppress'd, so slowly came
The fainting people, that our company
Was chang'd at every movement of the step.

    Whence I my guide address'd: "See that thou find
Some spirit, whose name may by his deeds be known,
And to that end look round thee as thou go'st."

    Then one, who understood the Tuscan voice,
Cried after us aloud: "Hold in your feet,
Ye who so swiftly speed through the dusk air.
Perchance from me thou shalt obtain thy wish."

    Whereat my leader, turning, me bespake:
"Pause, and then onward at their pace proceed."

    I staid, and saw two Spirits in whose look
Impatient eagerness of mind was mark'd
To overtake me; but the load they bare
And narrow path retarded their approach.

    Soon as arriv'd, they with an eye askance
Perus'd me, but spake not: then turning each
To other thus conferring said: "This one
Seems, by the action of his throat, alive.

Dante Alighieri

And, be they dead, what privilege allows
They walk unmantled by the cumbrous stole?"
    Then thus to me: "Tuscan, who visitest
The college of the mourning hypocrites,
Disdain not to instruct us who thou art."
    "By Arno's pleasant stream," I thus replied,
"In the great city I was bred and grew,
And wear the body I have ever worn.
but who are ye, from whom such mighty grief,
As now I witness, courseth down your cheeks?
What torment breaks forth in this bitter woe?"
"Our bonnets gleaming bright with orange hue,"
One of them answer'd, "are so leaden gross,
That with their weight they make the balances
To crack beneath them. Joyous friars we were,
Bologna's natives, Catalano I,
He Loderingo nam'd, and by thy land
Together taken, as men used to take
A single and indifferent arbiter,
To reconcile their strifes. How there we sped,
Gardingo's vicinage can best declare."
    "O friars!" I began, "your miseries--"
But there brake off, for one had caught my eye,
Fix'd to a cross with three stakes on the ground:
He, when he saw me, writh'd himself, throughout
Distorted, ruffling with deep sighs his beard.
And Catalano, who thereof was 'ware,
Thus spake: "That pierced spirit, whom intent
Thou view'st, was he who gave the Pharisees
Counsel, that it were fitting for one man
To suffer for the people. He doth lie
Transverse; nor any passes, but him first
Behoves make feeling trial how each weighs.
In straits like this along the foss are plac'd
The father of his consort, and the rest
Partakers in that council, seed of ill
And sorrow to the Jews." I noted then,
How Virgil gaz'd with wonder upon him,
Thus abjectly extended on the cross
In banishment eternal. To the friar
He next his words address'd: "We pray ye tell,
If so be lawful, whether on our right
Lies any opening in the rock, whereby
We both may issue hence, without constraint
On the dark angels, that compell'd they come
To lead us from this depth." He thus replied:
"Nearer than thou dost hope, there is a rock
From the next circle moving, which o'ersteps
Each vale of horror, save that here his cope
Is shatter'd. By the ruin ye may mount:

For on the side it slants, and most the height
Rises below." With head bent down awhile
My leader stood, then spake: "He warn'd us ill,
Who yonder hangs the sinners on his hook."

    To whom the friar: At Bologna erst
I many vices of the devil heard,
Among the rest was said, 'He is a liar,
And the father of lies!'" When he had spoke,
My leader with large strides proceeded on,
Somewhat disturb'd with anger in his look.

    I therefore left the spirits heavy laden,
And following, his beloved footsteps mark'd.

CANTO XXIV

IN the year's early nonage, when the sun
Tempers his tresses in Aquarius' urn,
And now towards equal day the nights recede,
When as the rime upon the earth puts on
Her dazzling sister's image, but not long
Her milder sway endures, then riseth up
The village hind, whom fails his wintry store,
And looking out beholds the plain around
All whiten'd, whence impatiently he smites
His thighs, and to his hut returning in,
There paces to and fro, wailing his lot,
As a discomfited and helpless man;
Then comes he forth again, and feels new hope
Spring in his bosom, finding e'en thus soon
The world hath chang'd its count'nance, grasps his crook,
And forth to pasture drives his little flock:
So me my guide dishearten'd when I saw
His troubled forehead, and so speedily
That ill was cur'd; for at the fallen bridge
Arriving, towards me with a look as sweet,
He turn'd him back, as that I first beheld
At the steep mountain's foot. Regarding well
The ruin, and some counsel first maintain'd
With his own thought, he open'd wide his arm
And took me up. As one, who, while he works,
Computes his labour's issue, that he seems
Still to foresee the' effect, so lifting me
Up to the summit of one peak, he fix'd
His eye upon another. "Grapple that,"
Said he, "but first make proof, if it be such
As will sustain thee." For one capp'd with lead
This were no journey. Scarcely he, though light,
And I, though onward push'd from crag to crag,
Could mount. And if the precinct of this coast

Dante Alighieri

Were not less ample than the last, for him
I know not, but my strength had surely fail'd.
But Malebolge all toward the mouth
Inclining of the nethermost abyss,
The site of every valley hence requires,
That one side upward slope, the other fall.

    At length the point of our descent we reach'd
From the last flag: soon as to that arriv'd,
So was the breath exhausted from my lungs,
I could no further, but did seat me there.

    "Now needs thy best of man;" so spake my guide:
"For not on downy plumes, nor under shade
Of canopy reposing, fame is won,
Without which whosoe'er consumes his days
Leaveth such vestige of himself on earth,
As smoke in air or foam upon the wave.
Thou therefore rise: vanish thy weariness
By the mind's effort, in each struggle form'd
To vanquish, if she suffer not the weight
Of her corporeal frame to crush her down.
A longer ladder yet remains to scale.
From these to have escap'd sufficeth not.
If well thou note me, profit by my words."

    I straightway rose, and show'd myself less spent
Than I in truth did feel me. "On," I cried,
"For I am stout and fearless." Up the rock
Our way we held, more rugged than before,
Narrower and steeper far to climb. From talk
I ceas'd not, as we journey'd, so to seem
Least faint; whereat a voice from the other foss
Did issue forth, for utt'rance suited ill.
Though on the arch that crosses there I stood,
What were the words I knew not, but who spake
Seem'd mov'd in anger. Down I stoop'd to look,
But my quick eye might reach not to the depth
For shrouding darkness; wherefore thus I spake:
"To the next circle, Teacher, bend thy steps,
And from the wall dismount we; for as hence
I hear and understand not, so I see
Beneath, and naught discern."--"I answer not,"
Said he, "but by the deed. To fair request
Silent performance maketh best return."

    We from the bridge's head descended, where
To the eighth mound it joins, and then the chasm
Opening to view, I saw a crowd within
Of serpents terrible, so strange of shape
And hideous, that remembrance in my veins
Yet shrinks the vital current. Of her sands
Let Lybia vaunt no more: if Jaculus,
Pareas and Chelyder be her brood,

Cenchris and Amphisboena, plagues so dire
Or in such numbers swarming ne'er she shew'd,
Not with all Ethiopia, and whate'er
Above the Erythraean sea is spawn'd.
    Amid this dread exuberance of woe
Ran naked spirits wing'd with horrid fear,
Nor hope had they of crevice where to hide,
Or heliotrope to charm them out of view.
With serpents were their hands behind them bound,
Which through their reins infix'd the tail and head
Twisted in folds before. And lo! on one
Near to our side, darted an adder up,
And, where the neck is on the shoulders tied,
Transpierc'd him. Far more quickly than e'er pen
Wrote O or I, he kindled, burn'd, and chang'd
To ashes, all pour'd out upon the earth.
When there dissolv'd he lay, the dust again
Uproll'd spontaneous, and the self-same form
Instant resumed. So mighty sages tell,
The' Arabian Phoenix, when five hundred years
Have well nigh circled, dies, and springs forthwith
Renascent. Blade nor herb throughout his life
He tastes, but tears of frankincense alone
And odorous amomum: swaths of nard
And myrrh his funeral shroud. As one that falls,
He knows not how, by force demoniac dragg'd
To earth, or through obstruction fettering up
In chains invisible the powers of man,
Who, risen from his trance, gazeth around,
Bewilder'd with the monstrous agony
He hath endur'd, and wildly staring sighs;
So stood aghast the sinner when he rose.
    Oh! how severe God's judgment, that deals out
Such blows in stormy vengeance! Who he was
My teacher next inquir'd, and thus in few
He answer'd: "Vanni Fucci am I call'd,
Not long since rained down from Tuscany
To this dire gullet. Me the beastial life
And not the human pleas'd, mule that I was,
Who in Pistoia found my worthy den."
    I then to Virgil: "Bid him stir not hence,
And ask what crime did thrust him hither: once
A man I knew him choleric and bloody."
    The sinner heard and feign'd not, but towards me
His mind directing and his face, wherein
Was dismal shame depictur'd, thus he spake:
"It grieves me more to have been caught by thee
In this sad plight, which thou beholdest, than
When I was taken from the other life.
I have no power permitted to deny

Dante Alighieri

What thou inquirest." I am doom'd thus low
To dwell, for that the sacristy by me
Was rifled of its goodly ornaments,
And with the guilt another falsely charged.
But that thou mayst not joy to see me thus,
So as thou e'er shalt 'scape this darksome realm
Open thine ears and hear what I forebode.
Reft of the Neri first Pistoia pines,
Then Florence changeth citizens and laws.
From Valdimagra, drawn by wrathful Mars,
A vapour rises, wrapt in turbid mists,
And sharp and eager driveth on the storm
With arrowy hurtling o'er Piceno's field,
Whence suddenly the cloud shall burst, and strike
Each helpless Bianco prostrate to the ground.
This have I told, that grief may rend thy heart."

CANTO XXV

WHEN he had spoke, the sinner rais'd his hands
Pointed in mockery, and cried: "Take them, God!
I level them at thee!" From that day forth
The serpents were my friends; for round his neck
One of then rolling twisted, as it said,
"Be silent, tongue!" Another to his arms
Upgliding, tied them, riveting itself
So close, it took from them the power to move.
    Pistoia! Ah Pistoia! why dost doubt
To turn thee into ashes, cumb'ring earth
No longer, since in evil act so far
Thou hast outdone thy seed? I did not mark,
Through all the gloomy circles of the' abyss,
Spirit, that swell'd so proudly 'gainst his God,
Not him, who headlong fell from Thebes. He fled,
Nor utter'd more; and after him there came
A centaur full of fury, shouting, "Where
Where is the caitiff?" On Maremma's marsh
Swarm not the serpent tribe, as on his haunch
They swarm'd, to where the human face begins.
Behind his head upon the shoulders lay,
With open wings, a dragon breathing fire
On whomsoe'er he met. To me my guide:
"Cacus is this, who underneath the rock
Of Aventine spread oft a lake of blood.
He, from his brethren parted, here must tread
A different journey, for his fraudful theft
Of the great herd, that near him stall'd; whence found
His felon deeds their end, beneath the mace
Of stout Alcides, that perchance laid on

The Divine Comedy

A hundred blows, and not the tenth was felt."
    While yet he spake, the centaur sped away:
And under us three spirits came, of whom
Nor I nor he was ware, till they exclaim'd;
"Say who are ye?" We then brake off discourse,
Intent on these alone. I knew them not;
But, as it chanceth oft, befell, that one
Had need to name another. "Where," said he,
"Doth Cianfa lurk?" I, for a sign my guide
Should stand attentive, plac'd against my lips
The finger lifted. If, O reader! now
Thou be not apt to credit what I tell,
No marvel; for myself do scarce allow
The witness of mine eyes. But as I looked
Toward them, lo! a serpent with six feet
Springs forth on one, and fastens full upon him:
His midmost grasp'd the belly, a forefoot
Seiz'd on each arm (while deep in either cheek
He flesh'd his fangs); the hinder on the thighs
Were spread, 'twixt which the tail inserted curl'd
Upon the reins behind. Ivy ne'er clasp'd
A dodder'd oak, as round the other's limbs
The hideous monster intertwin'd his own.
Then, as they both had been of burning wax,
Each melted into other, mingling hues,
That which was either now was seen no more.
Thus up the shrinking paper, ere it burns,
A brown tint glides, not turning yet to black,
And the clean white expires. The other two
Look'd on exclaiming: "Ah, how dost thou change,
Agnello! See! Thou art nor double now,
Nor only one." The two heads now became
One, and two figures blended in one form
Appear'd, where both were lost. Of the four lengths
Two arms were made: the belly and the chest
The thighs and legs into such members chang'd,
As never eye hath seen. Of former shape
All trace was vanish'd. Two yet neither seem'd
That image miscreate, and so pass'd on
With tardy steps. As underneath the scourge
Of the fierce dog-star, that lays bare the fields,
Shifting from brake to brake, the lizard seems
A flash of lightning, if he thwart the road,
So toward th' entrails of the other two
Approaching seem'd, an adder all on fire,
As the dark pepper-grain, livid and swart.
In that part, whence our life is nourish'd first,
One he transpierc'd; then down before him fell
Stretch'd out. The pierced spirit look'd on him
But spake not; yea stood motionless and yawn'd,

Dante Alighieri

As if by sleep or fev'rous fit assail'd.
He ey'd the serpent, and the serpent him.
One from the wound, the other from the mouth
Breath'd a thick smoke, whose vap'ry columns join'd.
     Lucan in mute attention now may hear,
Nor thy disastrous fate, Sabellus! tell,
Nor shine, Nasidius! Ovid now be mute.
What if in warbling fiction he record
Cadmus and Arethusa, to a snake
Him chang'd, and her into a fountain clear,
I envy not; for never face to face
Two natures thus transmuted did he sing,
Wherein both shapes were ready to assume
The other's substance. They in mutual guise
So answer'd, that the serpent split his train
Divided to a fork, and the pierc'd spirit
Drew close his steps together, legs and thighs
Compacted, that no sign of juncture soon
Was visible: the tail disparted took
The figure which the spirit lost, its skin
Soft'ning, his indurated to a rind.
The shoulders next I mark'd, that ent'ring join'd
The monster's arm-pits, whose two shorter feet
So lengthen'd, as the other's dwindling shrunk.
The feet behind then twisting up became
That part that man conceals, which in the wretch
Was cleft in twain. While both the shadowy smoke
With a new colour veils, and generates
Th' excrescent pile on one, peeling it off
From th' other body, lo! upon his feet
One upright rose, and prone the other fell.
Not yet their glaring and malignant lamps
Were shifted, though each feature chang'd beneath.
Of him who stood erect, the mounting face
Retreated towards the temples, and what there
Superfluous matter came, shot out in ears
From the smooth cheeks, the rest, not backward dragg'd,
Of its excess did shape the nose; and swell'd
Into due size protuberant the lips.
He, on the earth who lay, meanwhile extends
His sharpen'd visage, and draws down the ears
Into the head, as doth the slug his horns.
His tongue continuous before and apt
For utt'rance, severs; and the other's fork
Closing unites. That done the smoke was laid.
The soul, transform'd into the brute, glides off,
Hissing along the vale, and after him
The other talking sputters; but soon turn'd
His new-grown shoulders on him, and in few
Thus to another spake: "Along this path

Crawling, as I have done, speed Buoso now!"
    So saw I fluctuate in successive change
Th' unsteady ballast of the seventh hold:
And here if aught my tongue have swerv'd, events
So strange may be its warrant. O'er mine eyes
Confusion hung, and on my thoughts amaze.
    Yet 'scap'd they not so covertly, but well
I mark'd Sciancato: he alone it was
Of the three first that came, who chang'd not: thou,
The other's fate, Gaville, still dost rue.

CANTO XXVI

FLORENCE exult! for thou so mightily
Hast thriven, that o'er land and sea thy wings
Thou beatest, and thy name spreads over hell!
Among the plund'rers such the three I found
Thy citizens, whence shame to me thy son,
And no proud honour to thyself redounds.
    But if our minds, when dreaming near the dawn,
Are of the truth presageful, thou ere long
Shalt feel what Prato, (not to say the rest)
Would fain might come upon thee; and that chance
Were in good time, if it befell thee now.
Would so it were, since it must needs befall!
For as time wears me, I shall grieve the more.
    We from the depth departed; and my guide
Remounting scal'd the flinty steps, which late
We downward trac'd, and drew me up the steep.
Pursuing thus our solitary way
Among the crags and splinters of the rock,
Sped not our feet without the help of hands.
    Then sorrow seiz'd me, which e'en now revives,
As my thought turns again to what I saw,
And, more than I am wont, I rein and curb
The powers of nature in me, lest they run
Where Virtue guides not; that if aught of good
My gentle star, or something better gave me,
I envy not myself the precious boon.
    As in that season, when the sun least veils
His face that lightens all, what time the fly
Gives way to the shrill gnat, the peasant then
Upon some cliff reclin'd, beneath him sees
Fire-flies innumerous spangling o'er the vale,
Vineyard or tilth, where his day-labour lies:
With flames so numberless throughout its space
Shone the eighth chasm, apparent, when the depth
Was to my view expos'd. As he, whose wrongs
The bears aveng'd, at its departure saw

Dante Alighieri

Elijah's chariot, when the steeds erect
Rais'd their steep flight for heav'n; his eyes meanwhile,
Straining pursu'd them, till the flame alone
Upsoaring like a misty speck he kenn'd;
E'en thus along the gulf moves every flame,
A sinner so enfolded close in each,
That none exhibits token of the theft.

    Upon the bridge I forward bent to look,
And grasp'd a flinty mass, or else had fall'n,
Though push'd not from the height. The guide, who mark d
How I did gaze attentive, thus began:
"Within these ardours are the spirits, each
Swath'd in confining fire."--"Master, thy word,"
I answer'd, "hath assur'd me; yet I deem'd
Already of the truth, already wish'd
To ask thee, who is in yon fire, that comes
So parted at the summit, as it seem'd
Ascending from that funeral pile, where lay
The Theban brothers?" He replied: "Within
Ulysses there and Diomede endure
Their penal tortures, thus to vengeance now
Together hasting, as erewhile to wrath.
These in the flame with ceaseless groans deplore
The ambush of the horse, that open'd wide
A portal for that goodly seed to pass,
Which sow'd imperial Rome; nor less the guile
Lament they, whence of her Achilles 'reft
Deidamia yet in death complains.
And there is rued the stratagem, that Troy
Of her Palladium spoil'd."--"If they have power
Of utt'rance from within these sparks," said I,
"O master! think my prayer a thousand fold
In repetition urg'd, that thou vouchsafe
To pause, till here the horned flame arrive.
See, how toward it with desire I bend."

    He thus: "Thy prayer is worthy of much praise,
And I accept it therefore: but do thou
Thy tongue refrain: to question them be mine,
For I divine thy wish: and they perchance,
For they were Greeks, might shun discourse with thee."

    When there the flame had come, where time and place
Seem'd fitting to my guide, he thus began:
"O ye, who dwell two spirits in one fire!
If living I of you did merit aught,
Whate'er the measure were of that desert,
When in the world my lofty strain I pour'd,
Move ye not on, till one of you unfold
In what clime death o'ertook him self-destroy'd."

    Of the old flame forthwith the greater horn
Began to roll, murmuring, as a fire

The Divine Comedy

That labours with the wind, then to and fro
Wagging the top, as a tongue uttering sounds,
Threw out its voice, and spake: "When I escap'd
From Circe, who beyond a circling year
Had held me near Caieta, by her charms,
Ere thus Aeneas yet had nam'd the shore,
Nor fondness for my son, nor reverence
Of my old father, nor return of love,
That should have crown'd Penelope with joy,
Could overcome in me the zeal I had
T' explore the world, and search the ways of life,
Man's evil and his virtue. Forth I sail'd
Into the deep illimitable main,
With but one bark, and the small faithful band
That yet cleav'd to me. As Iberia far,
Far as Morocco either shore I saw,
And the Sardinian and each isle beside
Which round that ocean bathes. Tardy with age
Were I and my companions, when we came
To the strait pass, where Hercules ordain'd
The bound'ries not to be o'erstepp'd by man.
The walls of Seville to my right I left,
On the' other hand already Ceuta past.
"O brothers!" I began, "who to the west
Through perils without number now have reach'd,
To this the short remaining watch, that yet
Our senses have to wake, refuse not proof
Of the unpeopled world, following the track
Of Phoebus. Call to mind from whence we sprang:
Ye were not form'd to live the life of brutes
But virtue to pursue and knowledge high.
With these few words I sharpen'd for the voyage
The mind of my associates, that I then
Could scarcely have withheld them. To the dawn
Our poop we turn'd, and for the witless flight
Made our oars wings, still gaining on the left.
Each star of the' other pole night now beheld,
And ours so low, that from the ocean-floor
It rose not. Five times re-illum'd, as oft
Vanish'd the light from underneath the moon
Since the deep way we enter'd, when from far
Appear'd a mountain dim, loftiest methought
Of all I e'er beheld. Joy seiz'd us straight,
But soon to mourning changed. From the new land
A whirlwind sprung, and at her foremost side
Did strike the vessel. Thrice it whirl'd her round
With all the waves, the fourth time lifted up
The poop, and sank the prow: so fate decreed:
And over us the booming billow clos'd."

Dante Alighieri

CANTO XXVII

NOW upward rose the flame, and still'd its light
To speak no more, and now pass'd on with leave
From the mild poet gain'd, when following came
Another, from whose top a sound confus'd,
Forth issuing, drew our eyes that way to look.

    As the Sicilian bull, that rightfully
His cries first echoed, who had shap'd its mould,
Did so rebellow, with the voice of him
Tormented, that the brazen monster seem'd
Pierc'd through with pain; thus while no way they found
Nor avenue immediate through the flame,
Into its language turn'd the dismal words:
But soon as they had won their passage forth,
Up from the point, which vibrating obey'd
Their motion at the tongue, these sounds we heard:
"O thou! to whom I now direct my voice!
That lately didst exclaim in Lombard phrase,

    Depart thou, I solicit thee no more,'
Though somewhat tardy I perchance arrive
Let it not irk thee here to pause awhile,
And with me parley: lo! it irks not me
And yet I burn. If but e'en now thou fall
into this blind world, from that pleasant land
Of Latium, whence I draw my sum of guilt,
Tell me if those, who in Romagna dwell,
Have peace or war. For of the mountains there
Was I, betwixt Urbino and the height,
Whence Tyber first unlocks his mighty flood."

    Leaning I listen'd yet with heedful ear,
When, as he touch'd my side, the leader thus:
"Speak thou: he is a Latian." My reply
Was ready, and I spake without delay:

    "O spirit! who art hidden here below!
Never was thy Romagna without war
In her proud tyrants' bosoms, nor is now:
But open war there left I none. The state,
Ravenna hath maintain'd this many a year,
Is steadfast. There Polenta's eagle broods,
And in his broad circumference of plume
O'ershadows Cervia. The green talons grasp
The land, that stood erewhile the proof so long,
And pil'd in bloody heap the host of France.

    "The' old mastiff of Verruchio and the young,
That tore Montagna in their wrath, still make,
Where they are wont, an augre of their fangs.

    "Lamone's city and Santerno's range
Under the lion of the snowy lair.

The Divine Comedy

Inconstant partisan! that changeth sides,
Or ever summer yields to winter's frost.
And she, whose flank is wash'd of Savio's wave,
As 'twixt the level and the steep she lies,
Lives so 'twixt tyrant power and liberty.

    "Now tell us, I entreat thee, who art thou?
Be not more hard than others. In the world,
So may thy name still rear its forehead high."

    Then roar'd awhile the fire, its sharpen'd point
On either side wav'd, and thus breath'd at last:
"If I did think, my answer were to one,
Who ever could return unto the world,
This flame should rest unshaken. But since ne'er,
If true be told me, any from this depth
Has found his upward way, I answer thee,
Nor fear lest infamy record the words.

    "A man of arms at first, I cloth'd me then
In good Saint Francis' girdle, hoping so
T' have made amends. And certainly my hope
Had fail'd not, but that he, whom curses light on,
The' high priest again seduc'd me into sin.
And how and wherefore listen while I tell.
Long as this spirit mov'd the bones and pulp
My mother gave me, less my deeds bespake
The nature of the lion than the fox.
All ways of winding subtlety I knew,
And with such art conducted, that the sound
Reach'd the world's limit. Soon as to that part
Of life I found me come, when each behoves
To lower sails and gather in the lines;
That which before had pleased me then I rued,
And to repentance and confession turn'd;
Wretch that I was! and well it had bested me!
The chief of the new Pharisees meantime,
Waging his warfare near the Lateran,
Not with the Saracens or Jews (his foes
All Christians were, nor against Acre one
Had fought, nor traffic'd in the Soldan's land),
He his great charge nor sacred ministry
In himself, rev'renc'd, nor in me that cord,
Which us'd to mark with leanness whom it girded.
As in Socrate, Constantine besought
To cure his leprosy Sylvester's aid,
So me to cure the fever of his pride
This man besought: my counsel to that end
He ask'd: and I was silent: for his words
Seem'd drunken: but forthwith he thus resum'd:
"From thy heart banish fear: of all offence
I hitherto absolve thee. In return,
Teach me my purpose so to execute,

That Penestrino cumber earth no more.
Heav'n, as thou knowest, I have power to shut
And open: and the keys are therefore twain,
The which my predecessor meanly priz'd."
      Then, yielding to the forceful arguments,
Of silence as more perilous I deem'd,
And answer'd: "Father! since thou washest me
Clear of that guilt wherein I now must fall,
Large promise with performance scant, be sure,
Shall make thee triumph in thy lofty seat."
      "When I was number'd with the dead, then came
Saint Francis for me; but a cherub dark
He met, who cried: "'Wrong me not; he is mine,
And must below to join the wretched crew,
For the deceitful counsel which he gave.
E'er since I watch'd him, hov'ring at his hair,
No power can the impenitent absolve;
Nor to repent and will at once consist,
By contradiction absolute forbid."
Oh mis'ry! how I shook myself, when he
Seiz'd me, and cried, "Thou haply thought'st me not
A disputant in logic so exact."
To Minos down he bore me, and the judge
Twin'd eight times round his callous back the tail,
Which biting with excess of rage, he spake:
"This is a guilty soul, that in the fire
Must vanish.' Hence perdition-doom'd I rove
A prey to rankling sorrow in this garb."
      When he had thus fulfill'd his words, the flame
In dolour parted, beating to and fro,
And writhing its sharp horn. We onward went,
I and my leader, up along the rock,
Far as another arch, that overhangs
The foss, wherein the penalty is paid
Of those, who load them with committed sin.

CANTO XXVIII

WHO, e'en in words unfetter'd, might at full
Tell of the wounds and blood that now I saw,
Though he repeated oft the tale? No tongue
So vast a theme could equal, speech and thought
Both impotent alike. If in one band
Collected, stood the people all, who e'er
Pour'd on Apulia's happy soil their blood,
Slain by the Trojans, and in that long war
When of the rings the measur'd booty made
A pile so high, as Rome's historian writes
Who errs not, with the multitude, that felt

The Divine Comedy

The grinding force of Guiscard's Norman steel,
And those the rest, whose bones are gather'd yet
At Ceperano, there where treachery
Branded th' Apulian name, or where beyond
Thy walls, O Tagliacozzo, without arms
The old Alardo conquer'd; and his limbs
One were to show transpierc'd, another his
Clean lopt away; a spectacle like this
Were but a thing of nought, to the' hideous sight
Of the ninth chasm. A rundlet, that hath lost
Its middle or side stave, gapes not so wide,
As one I mark'd, torn from the chin throughout
Down to the hinder passage: 'twixt the legs
Dangling his entrails hung, the midriff lay
Open to view, and wretched ventricle,
That turns th' englutted aliment to dross.

    Whilst eagerly I fix on him my gaze,
He ey'd me, with his hands laid his breast bare,
And cried; "Now mark how I do rip me! lo!
How is Mohammed mangled! before me
Walks Ali weeping, from the chin his face
Cleft to the forelock; and the others all
Whom here thou seest, while they liv'd, did sow
Scandal and schism, and therefore thus are rent.
A fiend is here behind, who with his sword
Hacks us thus cruelly, slivering again
Each of this ream, when we have compast round
The dismal way, for first our gashes close
Ere we repass before him. But say who
Art thou, that standest musing on the rock,
Haply so lingering to delay the pain
Sentenc'd upon thy crimes?"--"Him death not yet,"
My guide rejoin'd, "hath overta'en, nor sin
Conducts to torment; but, that he may make
Full trial of your state, I who am dead
Must through the depths of hell, from orb to orb,
Conduct him. Trust my words, for they are true."

    More than a hundred spirits, when that they heard,
Stood in the foss to mark me, through amazed,
Forgetful of their pangs. "Thou, who perchance
Shalt shortly view the sun, this warning thou
Bear to Dolcino: bid him, if he wish not
Here soon to follow me, that with good store
Of food he arm him, lest impris'ning snows
Yield him a victim to Novara's power,
No easy conquest else." With foot uprais'd
For stepping, spake Mohammed, on the ground
Then fix'd it to depart. Another shade,
Pierc'd in the throat, his nostrils mutilate
E'en from beneath the eyebrows, and one ear

Dante Alighieri

Lopt off, who with the rest through wonder stood
Gazing, before the rest advanc'd, and bar'd
His wind-pipe, that without was all o'ersmear'd
With crimson stain. "O thou!" said 'he, "whom sin
Condemns not, and whom erst (unless too near
Resemblance do deceive me) I aloft
Have seen on Latian ground, call thou to mind
Piero of Medicina, if again
Returning, thou behold'st the pleasant land
That from Vercelli slopes to Mercabo;
And there instruct the twain, whom Fano boasts
Her worthiest sons, Guido and Angelo,
That if 't is giv'n us here to scan aright
The future, they out of life's tenement
Shall be cast forth, and whelm'd under the waves
Near to Cattolica, through perfidy
Of a fell tyrant. 'Twixt the Cyprian isle
And Balearic, ne'er hath Neptune seen
An injury so foul, by pirates done
Or Argive crew of old. That one-ey'd traitor
(Whose realm there is a spirit here were fain
His eye had still lack'd sight of) them shall bring
To confrence with him, then so shape his end,
That they shall need not 'gainst Focara's wind
Offer up vow nor pray'r." I answering thus:

    "Declare, as thou dost wish that I above
May carry tidings of thee, who is he,
In whom that sight doth wake such sad remembrance?"

    Forthwith he laid his hand on the cheek-bone
Of one, his fellow-spirit, and his jaws
Expanding, cried: "Lo! this is he I wot of;
He speaks not for himself: the outcast this
Who overwhelm'd the doubt in Caesar's mind,
Affirming that delay to men prepar'd
Was ever harmful. "Oh how terrified
Methought was Curio, from whose throat was cut
The tongue, which spake that hardy word. Then one
Maim'd of each hand, uplifted in the gloom
The bleeding stumps, that they with gory spots
Sullied his face, and cried: "'Remember thee
Of Mosca, too, I who, alas! exclaim'd,
'The deed once done there is an end,' that prov'd
A seed of sorrow to the Tuscan race."

    I added: "Ay, and death to thine own tribe."

    Whence heaping woe on woe he hurried off,
As one grief stung to madness. But I there
Still linger'd to behold the troop, and saw
Things, such as I may fear without more proof
To tell of, but that conscience makes me firm,
The boon companion, who her strong breast-plate

Buckles on him, that feels no guilt within
And bids him on and fear not. Without doubt
I saw, and yet it seems to pass before me,
A headless trunk, that even as the rest
Of the sad flock pac'd onward. By the hair
It bore the sever'd member, lantern-wise
Pendent in hand, which look'd at us and said,
"Woe's me!" The spirit lighted thus himself,
And two there were in one, and one in two.
How that may be he knows who ordereth so.

    When at the bridge's foot direct he stood,
His arm aloft he rear'd, thrusting the head
Full in our view, that nearer we might hear
The words, which thus it utter'd: "Now behold
This grievous torment, thou, who breathing go'st
To spy the dead; behold if any else
Be terrible as this. And that on earth
Thou mayst bear tidings of me, know that I
Am Bertrand, he of Born, who gave King John
The counsel mischievous. Father and son
I set at mutual war. For Absalom
And David more did not Ahitophel,
Spurring them on maliciously to strife.
For parting those so closely knit, my brain
Parted, alas! I carry from its source,
That in this trunk inhabits. Thus the law
Of retribution fiercely works in me."

CANTO XXIX

SO were mine eyes inebriate with view
Of the vast multitude, whom various wounds
Disfigur'd, that they long'd to stay and weep.

    But Virgil rous'd me: "What yet gazest on?
Wherefore doth fasten yet thy sight below
Among the maim'd and miserable shades?
Thou hast not shewn in any chasm beside
This weakness. Know, if thou wouldst number them
That two and twenty miles the valley winds
Its circuit, and already is the moon
Beneath our feet: the time permitted now
Is short, and more not seen remains to see."

    "If thou," I straight replied, "hadst weigh'd the cause
For which I look'd, thou hadst perchance excus'd
The tarrying still." My leader part pursu'd
His way, the while I follow'd, answering him,
And adding thus: "Within that cave I deem,
Whereon so fixedly I held my ken,
There is a spirit dwells, one of my blood,

Dante Alighieri

Wailing the crime that costs him now so dear."
    Then spake my master: "Let thy soul no more
Afflict itself for him. Direct elsewhere
Its thought, and leave him. At the bridge's foot
I mark'd how he did point with menacing look
At thee, and heard him by the others nam'd
Geri of Bello. Thou so wholly then
Wert busied with his spirit, who once rul'd
The towers of Hautefort, that thou lookedst not
That way, ere he was gone."--"O guide belov'd!
His violent death yet unaveng'd," said I,
"By any, who are partners in his shame,
Made him contemptuous: therefore, as I think,
He pass'd me speechless by; and doing so
Hath made me more compassionate his fate."
    So we discours'd to where the rock first show'd
The other valley, had more light been there,
E'en to the lowest depth. Soon as we came
O'er the last cloister in the dismal rounds
Of Malebolge, and the brotherhood
Were to our view expos'd, then many a dart
Of sore lament assail'd me, headed all
With points of thrilling pity, that I clos'd
Both ears against the volley with mine hands.
    As were the torment, if each lazar-house
Of Valdichiana, in the sultry time
'Twixt July and September, with the isle
Sardinia and Maremma's pestilent fen,
Had heap'd their maladies all in one foss
Together; such was here the torment: dire
The stench, as issuing steams from fester'd limbs.
    We on the utmost shore of the long rock
Descended still to leftward. Then my sight
Was livelier to explore the depth, wherein
The minister of the most mighty Lord,
All-searching Justice, dooms to punishment
The forgers noted on her dread record.
    More rueful was it not methinks to see
The nation in Aegina droop, what time
Each living thing, e'en to the little worm,
All fell, so full of malice was the air
(And afterward, as bards of yore have told,
The ancient people were restor'd anew
From seed of emmets) than was here to see
The spirits, that languish'd through the murky vale
Up-pil'd on many a stack. Confus'd they lay,
One o'er the belly, o'er the shoulders one
Roll'd of another; sideling crawl'd a third
Along the dismal pathway. Step by step
We journey'd on, in silence looking round

The Divine Comedy

And list'ning those diseas'd, who strove in vain
To lift their forms. Then two I mark'd, that sat
Propp'd 'gainst each other, as two brazen pans
Set to retain the heat. From head to foot,
A tetter bark'd them round. Nor saw I e'er
Groom currying so fast, for whom his lord
Impatient waited, or himself perchance
Tir'd with long watching, as of these each one
Plied quickly his keen nails, through furiousness
Of ne'er abated pruriency. The crust
Came drawn from underneath in flakes, like scales
Scrap'd from the bream or fish of broader mail.

   "O thou, who with thy fingers rendest off
Thy coat of proof," thus spake my guide to one,
"And sometimes makest tearing pincers of them,
Tell me if any born of Latian land
Be among these within: so may thy nails
Serve thee for everlasting to this toil."

   "Both are of Latium," weeping he replied,
"Whom tortur'd thus thou seest: but who art thou
That hast inquir'd of us?" To whom my guide:
"One that descend with this man, who yet lives,
From rock to rock, and show him hell's abyss."

   Then started they asunder, and each turn'd
Trembling toward us, with the rest, whose ear
Those words redounding struck. To me my liege
Address'd him: "Speak to them whate'er thou list."

   And I therewith began: "So may no time
Filch your remembrance from the thoughts of men
In th' upper world, but after many suns
Survive it, as ye tell me, who ye are,
And of what race ye come. Your punishment,
Unseemly and disgustful in its kind,
Deter you not from opening thus much to me."

   "Arezzo was my dwelling," answer'd one,
"And me Albero of Sienna brought
To die by fire; but that, for which I died,
Leads me not here. True is in sport I told him,
That I had learn'd to wing my flight in air.
And he admiring much, as he was void
Of wisdom, will'd me to declare to him
The secret of mine art: and only hence,
Because I made him not a Daedalus,
Prevail'd on one suppos'd his sire to burn me.
But Minos to this chasm last of the ten,
For that I practis'd alchemy on earth,
Has doom'd me. Him no subterfuge eludes."

   Then to the bard I spake: "Was ever race
Light as Sienna's? Sure not France herself
Can show a tribe so frivolous and vain."

Dante Alighieri

    The other leprous spirit heard my words,
And thus return'd: "Be Stricca from this charge
Exempted, he who knew so temp'rately
To lay out fortune's gifts; and Niccolo
Who first the spice's costly luxury
Discover'd in that garden, where such seed
Roots deepest in the soil: and be that troop
Exempted, with whom Caccia of Asciano
Lavish'd his vineyards and wide-spreading woods,
And his rare wisdom Abbagliato show'd
A spectacle for all. That thou mayst know
Who seconds thee against the Siennese
Thus gladly, bend this way thy sharpen'd sight,
That well my face may answer to thy ken;
So shalt thou see I am Capocchio's ghost,
Who forg'd transmuted metals by the power
Of alchemy; and if I scan thee right,
Thus needs must well remember how I aped
Creative nature by my subtle art."

CANTO XXX

WHAT time resentment burn'd in Juno's breast
For Semele against the Theban blood,
As more than once in dire mischance was rued,
Such fatal frenzy seiz'd on Athamas,
That he his spouse beholding with a babe
Laden on either arm, "Spread out," he cried,
"The meshes, that I take the lioness
And the young lions at the pass: "then forth
Stretch'd he his merciless talons, grasping one,
One helpless innocent, Learchus nam'd,
Whom swinging down he dash'd upon a rock,
And with her other burden self-destroy'd
The hapless mother plung'd: and when the pride
Of all-presuming Troy fell from its height,
By fortune overwhelm'd, and the old king
With his realm perish'd, then did Hecuba,
A wretch forlorn and captive, when she saw
Polyxena first slaughter'd, and her son,
Her Polydorus, on the wild sea-beach
Next met the mourner's view, then reft of sense
Did she run barking even as a dog;
Such mighty power had grief to wrench her soul.
Bet ne'er the Furies or of Thebes or Troy
With such fell cruelty were seen, their goads
Infixing in the limbs of man or beast,
As now two pale and naked ghost I saw
That gnarling wildly scamper'd, like the swine

Excluded from his stye. One reach'd Capocchio,
And in the neck-joint sticking deep his fangs,
Dragg'd him, that o'er the solid pavement rubb'd
His belly stretch'd out prone. The other shape,
He of Arezzo, there left trembling, spake;
"That sprite of air is Schicchi; in like mood
Of random mischief vent he still his spite."

      To whom I answ'ring: "Oh! as thou dost hope,
The other may not flesh its jaws on thee,
Be patient to inform us, who it is,
Ere it speed hence."--" That is the ancient soul
Of wretched Myrrha," he replied, "who burn'd
With most unholy flame for her own sire,
And a false shape assuming, so perform'd
The deed of sin; e'en as the other there,
That onward passes, dar'd to counterfeit
Donati's features, to feign'd testament
The seal affixing, that himself might gain,
For his own share, the lady of the herd."

      When vanish'd the two furious shades, on whom
Mine eye was held, I turn'd it back to view
The other cursed spirits. One I saw
In fashion like a lute, had but the groin
Been sever'd, where it meets the forked part.
Swoln dropsy, disproportioning the limbs
With ill-converted moisture, that the paunch
Suits not the visage, open'd wide his lips
Gasping as in the hectic man for drought,
One towards the chin, the other upward curl'd.

      "O ye, who in this world of misery,
Wherefore I know not, are exempt from pain,"
Thus he began, "attentively regard
Adamo's woe. When living, full supply
Ne'er lack'd me of what most I coveted;
One drop of water now, alas! I crave.
The rills, that glitter down the grassy slopes
Of Casentino, making fresh and soft
The banks whereby they glide to Arno's stream,
Stand ever in my view; and not in vain;
For more the pictur'd semblance dries me up,
Much more than the disease, which makes the flesh
Desert these shrivel'd cheeks. So from the place,
Where I transgress'd, stern justice urging me,
Takes means to quicken more my lab'ring sighs.
There is Romena, where I falsified
The metal with the Baptist's form imprest,
For which on earth I left my body burnt.
But if I here might see the sorrowing soul
Of Guido, Alessandro, or their brother,
For Branda's limpid spring I would not change

Dante Alighieri

The welcome sight. One is e'en now within,
If truly the mad spirits tell, that round
Are wand'ring. But wherein besteads me that?
My limbs are fetter'd. Were I but so light,
That I each hundred years might move one inch,
I had set forth already on this path,
Seeking him out amidst the shapeless crew,
Although eleven miles it wind, not more
Than half of one across. They brought me down
Among this tribe; induc'd by them I stamp'd
The florens with three carats of alloy."

    "Who are that abject pair," I next inquir'd,
"That closely bounding thee upon thy right
Lie smoking, like a band in winter steep'd
In the chill stream?"--"When to this gulf I dropt,"
He answer'd, "here I found them; since that hour
They have not turn'd, nor ever shall, I ween,
Till time hath run his course. One is that dame
The false accuser of the Hebrew youth;
Sinon the other, that false Greek from Troy.
Sharp fever drains the reeky moistness out,
In such a cloud upsteam'd." When that he heard,
One, gall'd perchance to be so darkly nam'd,
With clench'd hand smote him on the braced paunch,
That like a drum resounded: but forthwith
Adamo smote him on the face, the blow
Returning with his arm, that seem'd as hard.

    "Though my o'erweighty limbs have ta'en from me
The power to move," said he, "I have an arm
At liberty for such employ." To whom
Was answer'd: "When thou wentest to the fire,
Thou hadst it not so ready at command,
Then readier when it coin'd th' impostor gold."

    And thus the dropsied: "Ay, now speak'st thou true.
But there thou gav'st not such true testimony,
When thou wast question'd of the truth, at Troy."

    "If I spake false, thou falsely stamp'dst the coin,"
Said Sinon; "I am here but for one fault,
And thou for more than any imp beside."

    "Remember," he replied, "O perjur'd one,
The horse remember, that did teem with death,
And all the world be witness to thy guilt."

    "To thine," return'd the Greek, "witness the thirst
Whence thy tongue cracks, witness the fluid mound,
Rear'd by thy belly up before thine eyes,
A mass corrupt." To whom the coiner thus:
"Thy mouth gapes wide as ever to let pass
Its evil saying. Me if thirst assails,
Yet I am stuff'd with moisture. Thou art parch'd,
Pains rack thy head, no urging would'st thou need

89

To make thee lap Narcissus' mirror up."
    I was all fix'd to listen, when my guide
Admonish'd: "Now beware: a little more.
And I do quarrel with thee." I perceiv'd
How angrily he spake, and towards him turn'd
With shame so poignant, as remember'd yet
Confounds me. As a man that dreams of harm
Befall'n him, dreaming wishes it a dream,
And that which is, desires as if it were not,
Such then was I, who wanting power to speak
Wish'd to excuse myself, and all the while
Excus'd me, though unweeting that I did.
    "More grievous fault than thine has been, less shame,"
My master cried, "might expiate. Therefore cast
All sorrow from thy soul; and if again
Chance bring thee, where like conference is held,
Think I am ever at thy side. To hear
Such wrangling is a joy for vulgar minds."

CANTO XXXI

THE very tongue, whose keen reproof before
Had wounded me, that either cheek was stain'd,
Now minister'd my cure. So have I heard,
Achilles and his father's javelin caus'd
Pain first, and then the boon of health restor'd.
    Turning our back upon the vale of woe,
W cross'd th' encircled mound in silence. There
Was twilight dim, that far long the gloom
Mine eye advanc'd not: but I heard a horn
Sounded aloud. The peal it blew had made
The thunder feeble. Following its course
The adverse way, my strained eyes were bent
On that one spot. So terrible a blast
Orlando blew not, when that dismal rout
O'erthrew the host of Charlemagne, and quench'd
His saintly warfare. Thitherward not long
My head was rais'd, when many lofty towers
Methought I spied. "Master," said I, "what land
Is this?" He answer'd straight: "Too long a space
Of intervening darkness has thine eye
To traverse: thou hast therefore widely err'd
In thy imagining. Thither arriv'd
Thou well shalt see, how distance can delude
The sense. A little therefore urge thee on."
    Then tenderly he caught me by the hand;
"Yet know," said he, "ere farther we advance,
That it less strange may seem, these are not towers,
But giants. In the pit they stand immers'd,

Dante Alighieri

Each from his navel downward, round the bank."
    As when a fog disperseth gradually,
Our vision traces what the mist involves
Condens'd in air; so piercing through the gross
And gloomy atmosphere, as more and more
We near'd toward the brink, mine error fled,
And fear came o'er me. As with circling round
Of turrets, Montereggion crowns his walls,
E'en thus the shore, encompassing th' abyss,
Was turreted with giants, half their length
Uprearing, horrible, whom Jove from heav'n
Yet threatens, when his mutt'ring thunder rolls.
    Of one already I descried the face,
Shoulders, and breast, and of the belly huge
Great part, and both arms down along his ribs.
    All-teeming nature, when her plastic hand
Left framing of these monsters, did display
Past doubt her wisdom, taking from mad War
Such slaves to do his bidding; and if she
Repent her not of th' elephant and whale,
Who ponders well confesses her therein
Wiser and more discreet; for when brute force
And evil will are back'd with subtlety,
Resistance none avails. His visage seem'd
In length and bulk, as doth the pine, that tops
Saint Peter's Roman fane; and th' other bones
Of like proportion, so that from above
The bank, which girdled him below, such height
Arose his stature, that three Friezelanders
Had striv'n in vain to reach but to his hair.
Full thirty ample palms was he expos'd
Downward from whence a man his garments loops.
"Raphel bai ameth sabi almi,"
So shouted his fierce lips, which sweeter hymns
Became not; and my guide address'd him thus:
"O senseless spirit! let thy horn for thee
Interpret: therewith vent thy rage, if rage
Or other passion wring thee. Search thy neck,
There shalt thou find the belt that binds it on.
Wild spirit! lo, upon thy mighty breast
Where hangs the baldrick!" Then to me he spake:
"He doth accuse himself. Nimrod is this,
Through whose ill counsel in the world no more
One tongue prevails. But pass we on, nor waste
Our words; for so each language is to him,
As his to others, understood by none."
    Then to the leftward turning sped we forth,
And at a sling's throw found another shade
Far fiercer and more huge. I cannot say
What master hand had girt him; but he held

The Divine Comedy

Behind the right arm fetter'd, and before
The other with a chain, that fasten'd him
From the neck down, and five times round his form
Apparent met the wreathed links. "This proud one
Would of his strength against almighty Jove
Make trial," said my guide; "whence he is thus
Requited: Ephialtes him they call.
Great was his prowess, when the giants brought
Fear on the gods: those arms, which then he piled,
Now moves he never." Forthwith I return'd:
"Fain would I, if 't were possible, mine eyes
Of Briareus immeasurable gain'd
Experience next." He answer'd: "Thou shalt see
Not far from hence Antaeus, who both speaks
And is unfetter'd, who shall place us there
Where guilt is at its depth. Far onward stands
Whom thou wouldst fain behold, in chains, and made
Like to this spirit, save that in his looks
More fell he seems." By violent earthquake rock'd
Ne'er shook a tow'r, so reeling to its base,
As Ephialtes. More than ever then
I dreaded death, nor than the terror more
Had needed, if I had not seen the cords
That held him fast. We, straightway journeying on,
Came to Antaeus, who five ells complete
Without the head, forth issued from the cave.

    "O thou, who in the fortunate vale, that made
Great Scipio heir of glory, when his sword
Drove back the troop of Hannibal in flight,
Who thence of old didst carry for thy spoil
An hundred lions; and if thou hadst fought
In the high conflict on thy brethren's side,
Seems as men yet believ'd, that through thine arm
The sons of earth had conquer'd, now vouchsafe
To place us down beneath, where numbing cold
Locks up Cocytus. Force not that we crave
Or Tityus' help or Typhon's. Here is one
Can give what in this realm ye covet. Stoop
Therefore, nor scornfully distort thy lip.
He in the upper world can yet bestow
Renown on thee, for he doth live, and looks
For life yet longer, if before the time
Grace call him not unto herself." Thus spake
The teacher. He in haste forth stretch'd his hands,
And caught my guide. Alcides whilom felt
That grapple straighten'd score. Soon as my guide
Had felt it, he bespake me thus: "This way
That I may clasp thee;" then so caught me up,
That we were both one burden. As appears
The tower of Carisenda, from beneath

Where it doth lean, if chance a passing cloud
So sail across, that opposite it hangs,
Such then Antaeus seem'd, as at mine ease
I mark'd him stooping. I were fain at times
T' have pass'd another way. Yet in th' abyss,
That Lucifer with Judas low ingulfs,
Lightly he plac'd us; nor there leaning stay'd,
But rose as in a bark the stately mast.

CANTO XXXII

COULD I command rough rhimes and hoarse, to suit
That hole of sorrow, o'er which ev'ry rock
His firm abutment rears, then might the vein
Of fancy rise full springing: but not mine
Such measures, and with falt'ring awe I touch
The mighty theme; for to describe the depth
Of all the universe, is no emprize
To jest with, and demands a tongue not us'd
To infant babbling. But let them assist
My song, the tuneful maidens, by whose aid
Amphion wall'd in Thebes, so with the truth
My speech shall best accord. Oh ill-starr'd folk,
Beyond all others wretched! who abide
In such a mansion, as scarce thought finds words
To speak of, better had ye here on earth
Been flocks or mountain goats. As down we stood
In the dark pit beneath the giants' feet,
But lower far than they, and I did gaze
Still on the lofty battlement, a voice
Bespoke me thus: "Look how thou walkest. Take
Good heed, thy soles do tread not on the heads
Of thy poor brethren." Thereupon I turn'd,
And saw before and underneath my feet
A lake, whose frozen surface liker seem'd
To glass than water. Not so thick a veil
In winter e'er hath Austrian Danube spread
O'er his still course, nor Tanais far remote
Under the chilling sky. Roll'd o'er that mass
Had Tabernich or Pietrapana fall'n,
Not e'en its rim had creak'd. As peeps the frog
Croaking above the wave, what time in dreams
The village gleaner oft pursues her toil,
So, to where modest shame appears, thus low
Blue pinch'd and shrin'd in ice the spirits stood,
Moving their teeth in shrill note like the stork.
His face each downward held; their mouth the cold,
Their eyes express'd the dolour of their heart.

The Divine Comedy

    A space I look'd around, then at my feet
Saw two so strictly join'd, that of their head
The very hairs were mingled. "Tell me ye,
Whose bosoms thus together press," said I,
"Who are ye?" At that sound their necks they bent,
And when their looks were lifted up to me,
Straightway their eyes, before all moist within,
Distill'd upon their lips, and the frost bound
The tears betwixt those orbs and held them there.
Plank unto plank hath never cramp clos'd up
So stoutly. Whence like two enraged goats
They clash'd together; them such fury seiz'd.

    And one, from whom the cold both ears had reft,
Exclaim'd, still looking downward: "Why on us
Dost speculate so long? If thou wouldst know
Who are these two, the valley, whence his wave
Bisenzio slopes, did for its master own
Their sire Alberto, and next him themselves.
They from one body issued; and throughout
Caina thou mayst search, nor find a shade
More worthy in congealment to be fix'd,
Not him, whose breast and shadow Arthur's land
At that one blow dissever'd, not Focaccia,
No not this spirit, whose o'erjutting head
Obstructs my onward view: he bore the name
Of Mascheroni: Tuscan if thou be,
Well knowest who he was: and to cut short
All further question, in my form behold
What once was Camiccione. I await
Carlino here my kinsman, whose deep guilt
Shall wash out mine." A thousand visages
Then mark'd I, which the keen and eager cold
Had shap'd into a doggish grin; whence creeps
A shiv'ring horror o'er me, at the thought
Of those frore shallows. While we journey'd on
Toward the middle, at whose point unites
All heavy substance, and I trembling went
Through that eternal chillness, I know not
If will it were or destiny, or chance,
But, passing 'midst the heads, my foot did strike
With violent blow against the face of one.

    "Wherefore dost bruise me?" weeping, he exclaim'd,
"Unless thy errand be some fresh revenge
For Montaperto, wherefore troublest me?"

    I thus: "Instructor, now await me here,
That I through him may rid me of my doubt.
Thenceforth what haste thou wilt." The teacher paus'd,
And to that shade I spake, who bitterly
Still curs'd me in his wrath. "What art thou, speak,
That railest thus on others?" He replied:

Dante Alighieri

"Now who art thou, that smiting others' cheeks
Through Antenora roamest, with such force
As were past suff'rance, wert thou living still?"
    "And I am living, to thy joy perchance,"
Was my reply, "if fame be dear to thee,
That with the rest I may thy name enrol."
    "The contrary of what I covet most,"
Said he, "thou tender'st: hence; nor vex me more.
Ill knowest thou to flatter in this vale."
    Then seizing on his hinder scalp, I cried:
"Name thee, or not a hair shall tarry here."
    "Rend all away," he answer'd, "yet for that
I will not tell nor show thee who I am,
Though at my head thou pluck a thousand times."
    Now I had grasp'd his tresses, and stript off
More than one tuft, he barking, with his eyes
Drawn in and downward, when another cried,
"What ails thee, Bocca? Sound not loud enough
Thy chatt'ring teeth, but thou must bark outright?
What devil wrings thee?"--" Now," said I, "be dumb,
Accursed traitor! to thy shame of thee
True tidings will I bear."--" Off," he replied,
"Tell what thou list; but as thou escape from hence
To speak of him whose tongue hath been so glib,
Forget not: here he wails the Frenchman's gold.
'Him of Duera,' thou canst say, 'I mark'd,
Where the starv'd sinners pine.' If thou be ask'd
What other shade was with them, at thy side
Is Beccaria, whose red gorge distain'd
The biting axe of Florence. Farther on,
If I misdeem not, Soldanieri bides,
With Ganellon, and Tribaldello, him
Who op'd Faenza when the people slept."
    We now had left him, passing on our way,
When I beheld two spirits by the ice
Pent in one hollow, that the head of one
Was cowl unto the other; and as bread
Is raven'd up through hunger, th' uppermost
Did so apply his fangs to th' other's brain,
Where the spine joins it. Not more furiously
On Menalippus' temples Tydeus gnaw'd,
Than on that skull and on its garbage he.
    "O thou who show'st so beastly sign of hate
'Gainst him thou prey'st on, let me hear," said I
"The cause, on such condition, that if right
Warrant thy grievance, knowing who ye are,
And what the colour of his sinning was,
I may repay thee in the world above,
If that, wherewith I speak be moist so long."

The Divine Comedy
CANTO XXXIII

HIS jaws uplifting from their fell repast,
That sinner wip'd them on the hairs o' th' head,
Which he behind had mangled, then began:
"Thy will obeying, I call up afresh
Sorrow past cure, which but to think of wrings
My heart, or ere I tell on't. But if words,
That I may utter, shall prove seed to bear
Fruit of eternal infamy to him,
The traitor whom I gnaw at, thou at once
Shalt see me speak and weep. Who thou mayst be
I know not, nor how here below art come:
But Florentine thou seemest of a truth,
When I do hear thee. Know I was on earth
Count Ugolino, and th' Archbishop he
Ruggieri. Why I neighbour him so close,
Now list. That through effect of his ill thoughts
In him my trust reposing, I was ta'en
And after murder'd, need is not I tell.
What therefore thou canst not have heard, that is,
How cruel was the murder, shalt thou hear,
And know if he have wrong'd me. A small grate
Within that mew, which for my sake the name
Of famine bears, where others yet must pine,
Already through its opening sev'ral moons
Had shown me, when I slept the evil sleep,
That from the future tore the curtain off.
This one, methought, as master of the sport,
Rode forth to chase the gaunt wolf and his whelps
Unto the mountain, which forbids the sight
Of Lucca to the Pisan. With lean brachs
Inquisitive and keen, before him rang'd
Lanfranchi with Sismondi and Gualandi.
After short course the father and the sons
Seem'd tir'd and lagging, and methought I saw
The sharp tusks gore their sides. When I awoke
Before the dawn, amid their sleep I heard
My sons (for they were with me) weep and ask
For bread. Right cruel art thou, if no pang
Thou feel at thinking what my heart foretold;
And if not now, why use thy tears to flow?
Now had they waken'd; and the hour drew near
When they were wont to bring us food; the mind
Of each misgave him through his dream, and I
Heard, at its outlet underneath lock'd up
The' horrible tower: whence uttering not a word
I look'd upon the visage of my sons.
I wept not: so all stone I felt within.

Dante Alighieri

They wept: and one, my little Anslem, cried:
"Thou lookest so! Father what ails thee?" Yet
I shed no tear, nor answer'd all that day
Nor the next night, until another sun
Came out upon the world. When a faint beam
Had to our doleful prison made its way,
And in four countenances I descry'd
The image of my own, on either hand
Through agony I bit, and they who thought
I did it through desire of feeding, rose
O' th' sudden, and cried, 'Father, we should grieve
Far less, if thou wouldst eat of us: thou gav'st
These weeds of miserable flesh we wear,
And do thou strip them off from us again.'
Then, not to make them sadder, I kept down
My spirit in stillness. That day and the next
We all were silent. Ah, obdurate earth!
Why open'dst not upon us? When we came
To the fourth day, then Geddo at my feet
Outstretch'd did fling him, crying, 'Hast no help
For me, my father!' "There he died, and e'en
Plainly as thou seest me, saw I the three
Fall one by one 'twixt the fifth day and sixth:
Whence I betook me now grown blind to grope
Over them all, and for three days aloud
Call'd on them who were dead. Then fasting got
The mastery of grief." Thus having spoke,
Once more upon the wretched skull his teeth
He fasten'd, like a mastiff's 'gainst the bone
Firm and unyielding. Oh thou Pisa! shame
Of all the people, who their dwelling make
In that fair region, where th' Italian voice
Is heard, since that thy neighbours are so slack
To punish, from their deep foundations rise
Capraia and Gorgona, and dam up
The mouth of Arno, that each soul in thee
May perish in the waters! What if fame
Reported that thy castles were betray'd
By Ugolino, yet no right hadst thou
To stretch his children on the rack. For them,
Brigata, Ugaccione, and the pair
Of gentle ones, of whom my song hath told,
Their tender years, thou modern Thebes! did make
Uncapable of guilt. Onward we pass'd,
Where others skarf'd in rugged folds of ice
Not on their feet were turn'd, but each revers'd

    There very weeping suffers not to weep;
For at their eyes grief seeking passage finds
Impediment, and rolling inward turns
For increase of sharp anguish: the first tears

Hang cluster'd, and like crystal vizors show,
Under the socket brimming all the cup.
    Now though the cold had from my face dislodg'd
Each feeling, as 't were callous, yet me seem'd
Some breath of wind I felt. "Whence cometh this,"
Said I, "my master? Is not here below
All vapour quench'd?"--"'Thou shalt be speedily,"
He answer'd, "where thine eye shall tell thee whence
The cause descrying of this airy shower."
    Then cried out one in the chill crust who mourn'd:
"O souls so cruel! that the farthest post
Hath been assign'd you, from this face remove
The harden'd veil, that I may vent the grief
Impregnate at my heart, some little space
Ere it congeal again!" I thus replied:
"Say who thou wast, if thou wouldst have mine aid;
And if I extricate thee not, far down
As to the lowest ice may I descend!"
    "The friar Alberigo," answered he,
"Am I, who from the evil garden pluck'd
Its fruitage, and am here repaid, the date
More luscious for my fig."--"Hah!" I exclaim'd,
"Art thou too dead!"--"How in the world aloft
It fareth with my body," answer'd he,
"I am right ignorant. Such privilege
Hath Ptolomea, that ofttimes the soul
Drops hither, ere by Atropos divorc'd.
And that thou mayst wipe out more willingly
The glazed tear-drops that o'erlay mine eyes,
Know that the soul, that moment she betrays,
As I did, yields her body to a fiend
Who after moves and governs it at will,
Till all its time be rounded; headlong she
Falls to this cistern. And perchance above
Doth yet appear the body of a ghost,
Who here behind me winters. Him thou know'st,
If thou but newly art arriv'd below.
The years are many that have pass'd away,
Since to this fastness Branca Doria came."
    "Now," answer'd I, "methinks thou mockest me,
For Branca Doria never yet hath died,
But doth all natural functions of a man,
Eats, drinks, and sleeps, and putteth raiment on."
    He thus: "Not yet unto that upper foss
By th' evil talons guarded, where the pitch
Tenacious boils, had Michael Zanche reach'd,
When this one left a demon in his stead
In his own body, and of one his kin,
Who with him treachery wrought. But now put forth
Thy hand, and ope mine eyes." I op'd them not.

Ill manners were best courtesy to him.
    Ah Genoese! men perverse in every way,
With every foulness stain'd, why from the earth
Are ye not cancel'd? Such an one of yours
I with Romagna's darkest spirit found,
As for his doings even now in soul
Is in Cocytus plung'd, and yet doth seem
In body still alive upon the earth.

CANTO XXXIV

"THE banners of Hell's Monarch do come forth
Towards us; therefore look," so spake my guide,
"If thou discern him." As, when breathes a cloud
Heavy and dense, or when the shades of night
Fall on our hemisphere, seems view'd from far
A windmill, which the blast stirs briskly round,
Such was the fabric then methought I saw,
    To shield me from the wind, forthwith I drew
Behind my guide: no covert else was there.
    Now came I (and with fear I bid my strain
Record the marvel) where the souls were all
Whelm'd underneath, transparent, as through glass
Pellucid the frail stem. Some prone were laid,
Others stood upright, this upon the soles,
That on his head, a third with face to feet
Arch'd like a bow. When to the point we came,
Whereat my guide was pleas'd that I should see
The creature eminent in beauty once,
He from before me stepp'd and made me pause.
    "Lo!" he exclaim'd, "lo Dis! and lo the place,
Where thou hast need to arm thy heart with strength."
    How frozen and how faint I then became,
Ask me not, reader! for I write it not,
Since words would fail to tell thee of my state.
I was not dead nor living. Think thyself
If quick conception work in thee at all,
How I did feel. That emperor, who sways
The realm of sorrow, at mid breast from th' ice
Stood forth; and I in stature am more like
A giant, than the giants are in his arms.
Mark now how great that whole must be, which suits
With such a part. If he were beautiful
As he is hideous now, and yet did dare
To scowl upon his Maker, well from him
May all our mis'ry flow. Oh what a sight!
How passing strange it seem'd, when I did spy
Upon his head three faces: one in front
Of hue vermilion, th' other two with this

Midway each shoulder join'd and at the crest;
The right 'twixt wan and yellow seem'd: the left
To look on, such as come from whence old Nile
Stoops to the lowlands. Under each shot forth
Two mighty wings, enormous as became
A bird so vast. Sails never such I saw
Outstretch'd on the wide sea. No plumes had they,
But were in texture like a bat, and these
He flapp'd i' th' air, that from him issued still
Three winds, wherewith Cocytus to its depth
Was frozen. At six eyes he wept: the tears
Adown three chins distill'd with bloody foam.
At every mouth his teeth a sinner champ'd
Bruis'd as with pond'rous engine, so that three
Were in this guise tormented. But far more
Than from that gnawing, was the foremost pang'd
By the fierce rending, whence ofttimes the back
Was stript of all its skin. "That upper spirit,
Who hath worse punishment," so spake my guide,
"Is Judas, he that hath his head within
And plies the feet without. Of th' other two,
Whose heads are under, from the murky jaw
Who hangs, is Brutus: lo! how he doth writhe
And speaks not! Th' other Cassius, that appears
So large of limb. But night now re-ascends,
And it is time for parting. All is seen."

 I clipp'd him round the neck, for so he bade;
And noting time and place, he, when the wings
Enough were op'd, caught fast the shaggy sides,
And down from pile to pile descending stepp'd
Between the thick fell and the jagged ice.

 Soon as he reach'd the point, whereat the thigh
Upon the swelling of the haunches turns,
My leader there with pain and struggling hard
Turn'd round his head, where his feet stood before,
And grappled at the fell, as one who mounts,
That into hell methought we turn'd again.

 "Expect that by such stairs as these," thus spake
The teacher, panting like a man forespent,
"We must depart from evil so extreme."
Then at a rocky opening issued forth,
And plac'd me on a brink to sit, next join'd
With wary step my side. I rais'd mine eyes,
Believing that I Lucifer should see
Where he was lately left, but saw him now
With legs held upward. Let the grosser sort,
Who see not what the point was I had pass'd,
Bethink them if sore toil oppress'd me then.

 "Arise," my master cried, "upon thy feet.
"The way is long, and much uncouth the road;

Dante Alighieri

And now within one hour and half of noon
The sun returns." It was no palace-hall
Lofty and luminous wherein we stood,
But natural dungeon where ill footing was
And scant supply of light. "Ere from th' abyss
I sep'rate," thus when risen I began,
"My guide! vouchsafe few words to set me free
From error's thralldom. Where is now the ice?
How standeth he in posture thus revers'd?
And how from eve to morn in space so brief
Hath the sun made his transit?" He in few
Thus answering spake: "Thou deemest thou art still
On th' other side the centre, where I grasp'd
Th' abhorred worm, that boreth through the world.
Thou wast on th' other side, so long as I
Descended; when I turn'd, thou didst o'erpass
That point, to which from ev'ry part is dragg'd
All heavy substance. Thou art now arriv'd
Under the hemisphere opposed to that,
Which the great continent doth overspread,
And underneath whose canopy expir'd
The Man, that was born sinless, and so liv'd.
Thy feet are planted on the smallest sphere,
Whose other aspect is Judecca. Morn
Here rises, when there evening sets: and he,
Whose shaggy pile was scal'd, yet standeth fix'd,
As at the first. On this part he fell down
From heav'n; and th' earth, here prominent before,
Through fear of him did veil her with the sea,
And to our hemisphere retir'd. Perchance
To shun him was the vacant space left here
By what of firm land on this side appears,
That sprang aloof." There is a place beneath,
From Belzebub as distant, as extends
The vaulted tomb, discover'd not by sight,
But by the sound of brooklet, that descends
This way along the hollow of a rock,
Which, as it winds with no precipitous course,
The wave hath eaten. By that hidden way
My guide and I did enter, to return
To the fair world: and heedless of repose
We climbed, he first, I following his steps,
Till on our view the beautiful lights of heav'n
Dawn, through a circular opening in the cave:
Thus issuing we again beheld the stars.

NOTES TO HELL

CANTO I

Verse 1. In the midway.] That the era of the Poem is intended by these words to be fixed to the thirty fifth year of the poet's age, A.D. 1300, will appear more plainly in Canto XXI. where that date is explicitly marked.

v. 16. That planet's beam.] The sun.

v. 29. The hinder foot.] It is to be remembered, that in ascending a hill the weight of the body rests on the hinder foot.

v. 30. A panther.] Pleasure or luxury.

v. 36. With those stars.] The sun was in Aries, in which sign he supposes it to have begun its course at the creation.

v. 43. A lion.] Pride or ambition.

v. 45. A she wolf.] Avarice.

v. 56. Where the sun in silence rests.] Hence Milton appears to have taken his idea in the Samson Agonistes:

    The sun to me is dark
        And silent as the moon, &c

The same metaphor will recur, Canto V. v. 29.

    Into a place I came
   Where light was silent all.

v. 65. When the power of Julius.] This is explained by the commentators to mean "Although it was rather late with respect to my birth before Julius Caesar assumed the supreme authority, and made himself perpetual dictator."

v. 98. That greyhound.] This passage is intended as an eulogium on the liberal spirit of his Veronese patron Can Grande della Scala.

v. 102. 'Twixt either Feltro.] Verona, the country of Can della Scala, is situated between Feltro, a city in the Marca Trivigiana, and Monte Feltro, a city in the territory of Urbino.

v. 103. Italia's plains.] "Umile Italia," from Virgil, Aen lib. iii. 522.
   Humilemque videmus
  Italiam.

v. 115. Content in fire.] The spirits in Purgatory.

v. 118. A spirit worthier.] Beatrice, who conducts the Poet through Paradise.

v. 130. Saint Peter's gate.] The gate of Purgatory, which the Poet feigns to be guarded by an angel placed on that station by St. Peter.

CANTO II

v. 1. Now was the day.] A compendium of Virgil's description Aen. lib. iv 522. Nox erat, &c. Compare Apollonius Rhodius, lib iii. 744, and lib. iv. 1058

v. 8. O mind.]
   O thought that write all that I met,

And in the tresorie it set
Of my braine, now shall men see
If any virtue in thee be.
> Chaucer. Temple of Fame, b. ii. v.18

v. 14. Silvius'sire.] Aeneas.

v. 30. The chosen vessel.] St.Paul, Acts, c. ix. v. 15. "But the Lord said unto him, Go thy way; for he is a chosen vessel unto me."

v. 46. Thy soul.] L'anima tua e da viltate offesa. So in Berni, Orl Inn.lib. iii. c. i. st. 53.
> Se l'alma avete offesa da viltate.

v. 64. Who rest suspended.] The spirits in Limbo, neither admitted to a state of glory nor doomed to punishment.

v. 61. A friend not of my fortune, but myself.] Se non fortunae sed hominibus solere esse amicum. Cornelii Nepotis Attici Vitae, c. ix.

v. 78. Whatever is contain'd.] Every other thing comprised within the lunar heaven, which, being the lowest of all, has the smallest circle.

v. 93. A blessed dame.] The divine mercy.

v. 97. Lucia.] The enlightening grace of heaven.

v. 124. Three maids.] The divine mercy, Lucia, and Beatrice.

v. 127. As florets.] This simile is well translated by Chaucer--
> But right as floures through the cold of night
> Iclosed, stoupen in her stalkes lowe,
> Redressen hem agen the sunne bright,
> And speden in her kinde course by rowe, &c.
>> Troilus and Creseide, b.ii.

It has been imitated by many others, among whom see Berni, Orl.Inn. lib. 1. c. xii. st. 86. Marino, Adone, c. xvii. st. 63. and Sor. "Donna vestita di nero." and Spenser's Faery Queen, b.4. c. xii. st. 34. and b. 6 c. ii. st. 35.

CANTO III

v. 5.   Power divine
Supremest wisdom, and primeval love.] The three persons of the blessed Trinity.

v. 9. all hope abandoned.] Lasciate ogni speranza voi ch'entrate. So Berni, Orl. Inn. lib. i. c. 8. st. 53.
> Lascia pur della vita ogni speranza.

v. 29. Like to the sand.]
> Unnumber'd as the sands
> Of Barca or Cyrene's torrid soil
> Levied to side with warring winds, and poise
> Their lighter wings.
>> Milton, P. L. ii. 908.

v. 40. Lest th' accursed tribe.] Lest the rebellious angels should exult at seeing those who were neutral and therefore less guilty, condemned to the same punishment with themselves.

v. 50. A flag.]

The Divine Comedy

>All the grisly legions that troop
>Under the sooty flag of Acheron
>>Milton. Comus.

v. 56. Who to base fear
Yielding, abjur'd his high estate.] This is commonly understood of Celestine the Fifth, who abdicated the papal power in 1294. Venturi mentions a work written by Innocenzio Barcellini, of the Celestine order, and printed in Milan in 1701, In which an attempt is made to put a different interpretation on this passage.

v. 70. through the blear light.]
>Lo fioco lume

So Filicaja, canz. vi. st. 12.
>Qual fioco lume.

v. 77. An old man.]
>Portitor has horrendus aquas et flumina servat
>Terribili squalore Charon, cui plurima mento
>Canities inculta jacet; stant lumina flamma.
>>Virg. 7. Aen. lib. vi. 2.

v. 82. In fierce heat and in ice.]
>>The delighted spirit
>To bathe in fiery floods or to reside
>In thrilling regions of thick ribbed ice.
>>Shakesp. Measure for Measure, a. iii.s.1.

Compare Milton, P. L. b. ii. 600.

v. 92. The livid lake.] Vada livida.
>>Virg. Aen. lib. vi. 320
>>Totius ut Lacus putidaeque paludis
>Lividissima, maximeque est profunda vorago.
>>Catullus. xviii. 10.

v. 102. With eyes of burning coal.]
>His looks were dreadful, and his fiery eyes
>Like two great beacons glared bright and wide.
>>Spenser. F.Q. b. vi. c. vii.st. 42

v. 104. As fall off the light of autumnal leaves.]
>Quam multa in silvis autumul frigore primo
>Lapsa cadunt folia.
>>Virg. Aen. lib. vi. 309

Compare Apoll. Rhod. lib. iv. 214.

CANTO IV

v. 8. A thund'rous sound.] Imitated, as Mr. Thyer has remarked, by Milton, P. L. b. viii. 242.
>>But long ere our approaching heard
>Noise, other, than the sound of dance or song
>Torment, and loud lament, and furious rage.

v. 50. a puissant one.] Our Saviour.

v. 75.   Honour the bard
    Sublime.]
    Onorate l'altissimo poeta.
So Chiabrera, Canz. Eroiche. 32.
    Onorando l'altissimo poeta.
    v. 79. Of semblance neither sorrowful nor glad.]
    She nas to sober ne to glad.
            Chaucer's Dream.
    v. 90. The Monarch of sublimest song.] Homer.
    v. 100. Fitter left untold.]
    Che'l tacere e bello,
So our Poet, in Canzone 14.
    La vide in parte che'l tacere e bello,
Ruccellai, Le Api, 789.
    Ch'a dire e brutto ed a tacerlo e bello
And Bembo,
    "Vie pui bello e il tacerle, che il favellarne."
            Gli. Asol. lib. 1.
    v. 117. Electra.] The daughter of Atlas, and mother of Dardanus the founder of Troy. See Virg. Aen. b. viii. 134. as referred to by Dante in treatise "De Monarchia," lib. ii. "Electra, scilicet, nata magni nombris regis Atlantis, ut de ambobus testimonium reddit poeta noster in octavo ubi Aeneas ad Avandrum sic ait
    "Dardanus Iliacae," &c.
    v. 125. Julia.] The daughter of Julius Caesar, and wife of Pompey.
    v. 126. The Soldan fierce.] Saladin or Salaheddin, the rival of Richard coeur de lion. See D'Herbelot, Bibl. Orient. and Knolles's Hist. of the Turks p. 57 to 73 and the Life of Saladin, by Bohao'edin Ebn Shedad, published by Albert Schultens, with a Latin translation. He is introduced by Petrarch in the Triumph of Fame, c. ii
    v. 128. The master of the sapient throng.]
    Maestro di color che sanno.
Aristotle--Petrarch assigns the first place to Plato. See Triumph of Fame, c. iii.
Pulci, in his Morgante Maggiore, c. xviii. says,
    Tu se'il maestro di color che sanno.
    v. 132.   Democritus
    Who sets the world at chance.]
Democritus, who maintained the world to have been formed by the fortuitous concourse of atoms.
    v. 140. Avicen.] See D'Herbelot Bibl. Orient. article Sina. He died in 1050. Pulci here again imitates our poet:
    Avicenna quel che il sentimento
    Intese di Aristotile e i segreti,
    Averrois che fece il gran comento.
            Morg. Mag. c. xxv.
    v. 140.   Him who made That commentary vast, Averroes.]
Averroes, called by the Arabians Roschd, translated and commented the works of Aristotle. According to Tiraboschi (storia della Lett. Ital. t. v. 1. ii. c. ii. sect. 4.) he was the source of modern philosophical impiety. The critic quotes some

passages from Petrarch (Senil. 1. v. ep. iii. et. Oper. v. ii. p. 1143) to show how strongly such sentiments prevailed in the time of that poet, by whom they were held in horror and detestation He adds, that this fanatic admirer of Aristotle translated his writings with that felicity, which might be expected from one who did not know a syllable of Greek, and who was therefore compelled to avail himself of the unfaithful Arabic versions. D'Herbelot, on the other hand, informs us, that "Averroes was the first who translated Aristotle from Greek into Arabic, before the Jews had made their translation: and that we had for a long time no other text of Aristotle, except that of the Latin translation, which was made from this Arabic version of this great philosopher (Averroes), who afterwards added to it a very ample commentary, of which Thomas Aquinas, and the other scholastic writers, availed themselves, before the Greek originals of Aristotle and his commentators were known to us in Europe." According to D'Herbelot, he died in 1198: but Tiraboschi places that event about 1206.

CANTO V

v. 5. Grinning with ghastly feature.] Hence Milton:
Death
Grinn'd horrible a ghastly smile.
P. L. b. ii. 845.
v. 46. As cranes.] This simile is imitated by Lorenzo de Medici, in his Ambra, a poem, first published by Mr. Roscoe, in the Appendix to his Life of Lorenzo.
Marking the tracts of air, the clamorous cranes
Wheel their due flight in varied ranks descried:
And each with outstretch'd neck his rank maintains
In marshal'd order through th' ethereal void.
Roscoe, v. i. c. v. p. 257. 4to edit.
Compare Homer. Il. iii. 3. Virgil. Aeneid. 1 x. 264, and Ruccellai, Le Api, 942, and Dante's Purgatory, Canto XXIV. 63.
v. 96. The land.] Ravenna.
v. 99 Love, that in gentle heart is quickly learnt.]
Amor, Ch' al cor gentil ratto s'apprende.
A line taken by Marino, Adone, c. cxli. st. 251.
v. 102. Love, that denial takes from none belov'd.]
Amor, ch' a null' amato amar perdona.
So Boccacio, in his Filocopo. l.1.
Amore mal non perdono l'amore a nullo amato.
And Pulci, in the Morgante Maggiore, c. iv.
E perche amor mal volontier perdona,
Che non sia al fin sempre amato chi ama.
Indeed many of the Italian poets have repeated this verse.
v. 105. Caina.] The place to which murderers are doomed.
v. 113. Francesca.] Francesca, daughter of Guido da Polenta, lord of Ravenna, was given by her father in marriage to Lanciotto, son of Malatesta, lord of Rimini, a man of extraordinary courage, but deformed in his person. His brother Paolo, who unhappily possessed those graces which the husband of Francesca wanted, engaged her affections; and being taken in adultery, they were both put to death by the enraged Lanciotto. See Notes to Canto XXVII. v.

43 The whole of this passage is alluded to by Petrarch, in his Triumph of Love c. iii.

    v. 118.
      No greater grief than to remember days
      Of joy,xwhen mis'ry is at hand!]
Imitated by Marino:
      Che non ha doglia il misero maggiore
      Che ricordar la giola entro il dolore.
          Adone, c. xiv. st. 100
And by Fortiguerra:
      Rimembrare il ben perduto
      Fa piu meschino lo presente stato.
          Ricciardetto, c. xi. st. 83.
The original perhaps was in Boetius de Consol. Philosoph. "In omni adversitate fortunae infelicissimum genus est infortunii fuisse felicem et non esse." 1. 2. pr. 4

    v. 124. Lancelot.] One of the Knights of the Round Table, and the lover of Ginevra, or Guinever, celebrated in romance. The incident alluded to seems to have made a strong impression on the imagination of Dante, who introduces it again, less happily, in the Paradise, Canto XVI.

    v. 128. At one point.]
      Questo quel punto fu, che sol mi vinse.
          Tasso, Il Torrismondo, a. i. s. 3.

    v. 136. And like a corpse fell to the ground]
      E caddi, come corpo morto cade.
So Pulci:
      E cadde come morto in terra cade.
Morgante Maggoire, c. xxii

CANTO VI

    v. 1. My sense reviving.]
      Al tornar della mente, che si chiuse
      Dinanzi alla pieta de' duo cognati.
Berni has made a sportive application of these lines, in his Orl. Inn. l. iii. c. viii. st. 1.

    v. 21. That great worm.] So in Canto XXXIV Lucifer is called
      Th' abhorred worm, that boreth through the world.
Ariosto has imitated Dante:
      Ch' al gran verme infernal mette la briglia,
      E che di lui come a lei par dispone.
          Orl. Fur. c. xlvi. st. 76.

    v. 52. Ciacco.] So called from his inordinate appetite: Ciacco, in Italian, signifying a pig. The real name of this glutton has not been transmitted to us. He is introduced in Boccaccio's Decameron, Giorn. ix. Nov. 8.

    v. 61. The divided city.] The city of Florence, divided into the Bianchi and Neri factions.

    v. 65. The wild party from the woods.] So called, because it was headed by Veri de' Cerchi, whose family had lately come into the city from Acone, and the woody country of the Val di Nievole.

v. 66. The other.] The opposite parts of the Neri, at the head of which was Corso Donati.

v. 67. This must fall.] The Bianchi.

v. 69.   Of one, who under shore
   Now rests.]
Charles of Valois, by whose means the Neri were replaced.

v. 73. The just are two in number.] Who these two were, the commentators are not agreed.

v. 79. Of Farinata and Tegghiaio.] See Canto X. and Notes, and Canto XVI, and Notes.

v. 80. Giacopo.] Giacopo Rusticucci. See Canto XVI, and Notes.

v. 81. Arrigo, Mosca.] Of Arrigo, who is said by the commentators to have been of the noble family of the Fifanti, no mention afterwards occurs. Mosca degli Uberti is introduced in Canto XXVIII. v.

v. 108. Consult thy knowledge.] We are referred to the following passage in St. Augustin:--"Cum fiet resurrectio carnis, et bonorum gaudia et malorum tormenta majora erunt. "--At the resurrection of the flesh, both the happiness of the good and the torments of the wicked will be increased."

CANTO VII

v. 1. Ah me! O Satan! Satan!] Pape Satan, Pape Satan, aleppe. Pape is said by the commentators to be the same as the Latin word papae! "strange!" Of aleppe they do not give a more satisfactory account.

See the Life of Benvenuto Cellini, translated by Dr. Nugent, v. ii. b. iii c. vii. p 113, where he mentions "having heard the words Paix, paix, Satan! allez, paix! in the court of justice at Paris. I recollected what Dante said, when he with his master Virgil entered the gates of hell: for Dante, and Giotto the painter, were together in France, and visited Paris with particular attention, where the court of justice may be considered as hell. Hence it is that Dante, who was likewise perfect master of the French, made use of that expression, and I have often been surprised that it was never understood in that sense."

v. 12. The first adulterer proud.] Satan.

v. 22. E'en as a billow.]
   As when two billows in the Irish sowndes
   Forcibly driven with contrarie tides
   Do meet together, each aback rebounds
   With roaring rage, and dashing on all sides,
   That filleth all the sea with foam, divides
   The doubtful current into divers waves.
           Spenser, F.Q. b. iv. c. 1. st. 42.

v. 48. Popes and cardinals.] Ariosto, having personified Avarice as a strange and hideous monster, says of her--
   Peggio facea nella Romana corte
   Che v'avea uccisi Cardinali e Papi.
           Orl. Fur. c. xxvi. st. 32.
   Worse did she in the court of Rome, for there
   She had slain Popes and Cardinals.

v. 91. By necessity.] This sentiment called forth the reprehension of Cecco d'Ascoli, in his Acerba, l. 1. c. i.

In cio peccasti, O Fiorentin poeta, &c.
Herein, O bard of Florence, didst thou err
Laying it down that fortune's largesses
Are fated to their goal. Fortune is none,
That reason cannot conquer. Mark thou, Dante,
If any argument may gainsay this.

CANTO VIII

v. 18. Phlegyas.] Phlegyas, who was so incensed against Apollo for having violated his daughter Coronis, that he set fire to the temple of that deity, by whose vengeance he was cast into Tartarus. See Virg. Aen. l. vi. 618.

v. 59. Filippo Argenti.] Boccaccio tells us, "he was a man remarkable for the large proportions and extraordinary vigor of his bodily frame, and the extreme waywardness and irascibility of his temper." Decam. g. ix. n. 8.

v. 66. The city, that of Dis is nam'd.] So Ariosto. Orl. Fur. c. xl. st. 32

v. 94. Seven times.] The commentators, says Venturi, perplex themselves with the inquiry what seven perils these were from which Dante had been delivered by Virgil. Reckoning the beasts in the first Canto as one of them, and adding Charon, Minos, Cerberus, Plutus, Phlegyas and Filippo Argenti, as so many others, we shall have the number, and if this be not satisfactory, we may suppose a determinate to have been put for an indeterminate number.

v. 109. At war 'twixt will and will not.]
   Che si, e no nel capo mi tenzona.
So Boccaccio, Ninf. Fiesol. st. 233.
   Il si e il no nel capo gli contende.
The words I have adopted as a translation, are Shakespeare's,
Measure for Measure. a. ii. s. 1.

v. 122. This their insolence, not new.] Virgil assures our poet, that these evil spirits had formerly shown the same insolence when our Savior descended into hell. They attempted to prevent him from entering at the gate, over which Dante had read the fatal inscription. "That gate which," says the Roman poet, "an angel has just passed, by whose aid we shall overcome this opposition, and gain admittance into the city."

CANTO IX

v. 1. The hue.] Virgil, perceiving that Dante was pale with fear, restrained those outward tokens of displeasure which his own countenance had betrayed.

v. 23. Erictho.] Erictho, a Thessalian sorceress, according to Lucan, Pharsal. l. vi. was employed by Sextus, son of Pompey the Great, to conjure up a spirit, who should inform him of the issue of the civil wars between his father and Caesar.

v. 25.   No long space my flesh
   Was naked of me.]
   Quae corpus complexa animae tam fortis inane.
          Ovid. Met. l. xiii f. 2
Dante appears to have fallen into a strange anachronism. Virgil's death did not happen till long after this period.

v. 42. Adders and cerastes.]

The Divine Comedy

>Vipereum crinem vittis innexa cruentis.
>>Virg. Aen. l. vi. 281.
>--spinaque vagi torquente cerastae
>>. . . et torrida dipsas
>Et gravis in geminum vergens eaput amphisbaena.
>>Lucan. Pharsal. l. ix. 719.

So Milton:
>Scorpion and asp, and amphisbaena dire,
>Cerastes horn'd, hydrus and elops drear,
>And dipsas.
>>P. L. b. x. 524.

v. 67. A wind.] Imitated by Berni, Orl. Inn. l. 1. e. ii. st. 6.

v. 83. With his wand.]
>She with her rod did softly smite the raile
>Which straight flew ope.
>>Spenser. F. Q. b. iv. c. iii. st. 46.

v. 96. What profits at the fays to but the horn.] "Of what avail can it be to offer violence to impassive beings?"

v. 97. Your Cerberus.] Cerberus is feigned to have been dragged by Hercules, bound with a three fold chain, of which, says the angel, he still bears the marks.

v. 111. The plains of Arles.] In Provence. See Ariosto, Orl. Fur. c. xxxix. st. 72

v. 112. At Pola.] A city of Istria, situated near the gulf of Quarnaro, in the Adriatic sea.

CANTO X

v. 12. Josaphat.] It seems to have been a common opinion among the Jews, as well as among many Christians, that the general judgment will be held in the valley of Josaphat, or Jehoshaphat: "I will also gather all nations, and will bring them down into the valley of Jehoshaphat, and will plead with them there for my people, and for my heritage Israel, whom they have scattered among the nations, and parted my land." Joel, iii. 2.

v. 32. Farinata.] Farinata degli Uberti, a noble Florentine, was the leader of the Ghibelline faction, when they obtained a signal victory over the Guelfi at Montaperto, near the river Arbia. Macchiavelli calls him "a man of exalted soul, and great military talents." Hist. of Flor. b. ii.

v. 52. A shade.] The spirit of Cavalcante Cavalcanti, a noble Florentine, of the Guelph party.

v. 59. My son.] Guido, the son of Cavalcante Cavalcanti; "he whom I call the first of my friends," says Dante in his Vita Nuova, where the commencement of their friendship is related. >From the character given of him by contemporary writers his temper was well formed to assimilate with that of our poet. "He was," according to G. Villani, l. viii. c. 41. "of a philosophical and elegant mind, if he had not been too delicate and fastidious." And Dino Compagni terms him "a young and noble knight, brave and courteous, but of a lofty scornful spirit, much addicted to solitude and study." Muratori. Rer. Ital. Script t. 9 l. 1. p. 481. He died, either in exile at Serrazana, or soon after his return to Florence, December 1300, during the spring of which year the action of this poem is supposed to be passing.

    v. 62.   Guido thy son Had in contempt.] Guido Cavalcanti, being more given to philosophy than poetry, was perhaps no great admirer of Virgil. Some poetical compositions by Guido are, however, still extant; and his reputation for skill in the art was such as to eclipse that of his predecessor and namesake Guido Guinicelli, as we shall see in the Purgatory, Canto XI. His "Canzone sopra il Terreno Amore" was thought worthy of being illustrated by numerous and ample commentaries. Crescimbeni Ist. della Volg. Poes. l. v.

For a playful sonnet which Dante addressed to him, and a spirited translation of it, see Hayley's Essay on Epic Poetry, Notes to Ep. iii.

    v. 66. Saidst thou he had?] In Aeschylus, the shade of Darius is represented as inquiring with similar anxiety after the fate of his son Xerxes.

[GREEK HERE]

Atossa: Xerxes astonish'd, desolate, alone--
Ghost of Dar: How will this end? Nay, pause not. Is he safe?
        The Persians. Potter's Translation.

    v. 77. Not yet fifty times.] "Not fifty months shall be passed, before thou shalt learn, by woeful experience, the difficulty of returning from banishment to thy native city"

    v.83. The slaughter.] "By means of Farinata degli Uberti, the Guelfi were conquered by the army of King Manfredi, near the river Arbia, with so great a slaughter, that those who escaped from that defeat took refuge not in Florence, which city they considered as lost to them, but in Lucca." Macchiavelli. Hist. of Flor. b 2.

    v. 86. Such orisons.] This appears to allude to certain prayers which were offered up in the churches of Florence, for deliverance from the hostile attempts of the Uberti.

    v. 90. Singly there I stood.] Guido Novello assembled a council of the Ghibellini at Empoli where it was agreed by all, that, in order to maintain the ascendancy of the Ghibelline party in Tuscany, it was necessary to destroy Florence, which could serve only (the people of that city beingvGuelfi) to enable the party attached to the church to recover its strength. This cruel sentence, passed upon so noble a city, met with no opposition from any of its citizens or friends, except Farinata degli Uberti, who openly and without reserve forbade the measure, affirming that he had endured so many hardships, and encountered so many dangers, with no other view than that of being able to pass his days in his own country. Macchiavelli. Hist. of Flor. b. 2.

    v. 103. My fault.] Dante felt remorse for not having returned an immediate answer to the inquiry of Cavalcante, from which delay he was led to believe that his son Guido was no longer living.

    v. 120. Frederick.] The Emperor Frederick the Second, who died in 1250. See Notes to Canto XIII.

    v. 121. The Lord Cardinal.] Ottaviano Ubaldini, a Florentine, made Cardinal in 1245, and deceased about 1273. On account of his great influence, he was generally known by the appellation of "the Cardinal." It is reported of him that he declared, if there were any such thing as a human soul, he had lost his for the Ghibellini.

    v. 132. Her gracious beam.] Beatrice.

The Divine Comedy
CANTO XI

    v. 9. Pope Anastasius.] The commentators are not agreed concerning the identity of the person, who is here mentioned as a follower of the heretical Photinus. By some he is supposed to have been Anastasius the Second, by others, the Fourth of that name; while a third set, jealous of the integrity of the papal faith, contend that our poet has confounded him with Anastasius 1. Emperor of the East.

    v. 17. My son.] The remainder of the present Canto may be considered as a syllabus of the whole of this part of the poem.

    v. 48. And sorrows.] This fine moral, that not to enjoy our being is to be ungrateful to the Author of it, is well expressed in Spenser, F. Q. b. iv. c. viii. st. 15.

> For he whose daies in wilful woe are worne
> The grace of his Creator doth despise,
> That will not use his gifts for thankless

nigardise.

    v. 53. Cahors.] A city in Guienne, much frequented by usurers

    v. 83. Thy ethic page.] He refers to Aristotle's Ethics.
[GREEK HERE]
"In the next place, entering, on another division of the subject,
let it be defined. that respecting morals there are three sorts
of things to be avoided, malice, incontinence, and brutishness."

    v. 104. Her laws.] Aristotle's Physics. [GREEK HERE] "Art imitates nature." --See the Coltivazione of Alamanni, l. i.

    -I'arte umana, &c.

    v. 111. Creation's holy book.] Genesis, c. iii. v. 19. "In the sweat of thy face shalt thou eat bread."

    v. 119. The wain.] The constellation Bootes, or Charles's wain.

CANTO XII

    v. 17. The king of Athens.] Theseus, who was enabled, by the instructions of Ariadne, the sister of the Minotaur, to destroy that monster.

    v. 21. Like to a bull.] [GREEK HERE] Homer Il. xvii 522

> As when some vig'rous youth with sharpen'd axe
> A pastur'd bullock smites behind the horns
> And hews the muscle through; he, at the stroke
> Springs forth and falls.
>   Cowper's Translation.

    v. 36. He arriv'd.] Our Saviour, who, according to Dante, when he ascended from hell, carried with him the souls of the patriarchs, and other just men, out of the first circle. See Canto IV.

    v. 96. Nessus.] Our poet was probably induced, by the following line in Ovid, to assign to Nessus the task of conducting them over the ford:

> Nessus edit membrisque valens scitusque vadorum.
> Metam, l. ix.

And Ovid's authority was Sophocles, who says of this Centaur--
[GREEK HERE] Trach.570

> He in his arms, Evenus' stream

Deep flowing, bore the passenger for hire
Without or sail or billow cleaving oar.

v. 110. Ezzolino.] Ezzolino, or Azzolino di Romano, a most cruel tyrant in the Marca Trivigiana, Lord of Padua, Vicenza, Verona, and Brescia, who died in 1260. His atrocities form the subject of a Latin tragedy, called Eccerinis, by Albertino Mussato, of Padua, the contemporary of Dante, and the most elegant writer of Latin verse of that age. See also the Paradise, Canto IX. Berni Orl. Inn. l ii c. xxv. st. 50. Ariosto. Orl. Fur. c. iii. st. 33. and Tassoni Secchia Rapita, c. viii. st 11.

v. 111. Obizzo' of Este.] Marquis of Ferrara and of the Marca d'Ancona, was murdered by his own son (whom, for the most unnatural act Dante calls his step-son), for the sake of the treasures which his rapacity had amassed. See Ariosto. Orl. Fur. c. iii. st 32. He died in 1293 according to Gibbon. Ant. of the House of Brunswick. Posth. Works, v. ii. 4to.

v. 119. He.] "Henrie, the brother of this Edmund, and son to the foresaid king of Almaine (Richard, brother of Henry III. of England) as he returned from Affrike, where he had been with Prince Edward, was slain at Viterbo in Italy (whither he was come about business which he had to do with the Pope) by the hand of Guy de Montfort, the son of Simon de Montfort, Earl of Leicester, in revenge of the same Simon's death. The murther was committed afore the high altar, as the same Henrie kneeled there to hear divine service." A.D. 1272, Holinshed's chronicles p 275. See also Giov. Villani Hist. I. vii. c. 40.

v. 135. On Sextus and on Pyrrhus.] Sextus either the son of Tarquin the Proud, or of Pompey the Great: or as Vellutelli conjectures, Sextus Claudius Nero, and Pyrrhus king of Epirus.

v. 137.
The Rinieri, of Corneto this,
Pazzo the other named.]
Two noted marauders, by whose depredations the public ways in Italy were infested. The latter was of the noble family of Pazzi in Florence.

CANTO XIII

v. 10. Betwixt Corneto and Cecina's stream.] A wild and woody tract of country, abounding in deer, goats, and wild boars. Cecina is a river not far to the south of Leghorn, Corneto, a small city on the same coast in the patrimony of the church.

v. 12. The Strophades.] See Virg. Aen. l. iii. 210.

v. 14. Broad are their pennons.] From Virg. Aen. l. iii. 216.

v. 48. In my verse described.] The commentators explain this, "If he could have believed, in consequence of my assurances alone, that of which he hath now had ocular proof, he would not have stretched forth his hand against thee." But I am of opinion that Dante makes Virgil allude to his own story of Polydorus in the third book of the Aeneid.

v. 56. That pleasant word of thine.] "Since you have inveigled me to speak my holding forth so gratifying an expectation, let it not displease you if I am as it were detained in the snare you have spread for me, so as to be somewhat prolix in my answer."

v. 60. I it was.] Pietro delle Vigne, a native of Capua, who, from a low condition, raised himself by his eloquence and legal knowledge to the office of Chancellor to the Emperor Frederick II. whose confidence in him was such, that his influence in the empire became unbounded. The courtiers, envious of his exalted situation, contrived, by means of forged letters, to make Frederick believe that he held a secret and traitorous intercourse with the Pope, who was then at enmity with the Emperor. In consequence of this supposed crime he was cruelly condemned by his too credulous sovereign to lose his eyes, and, being driven to despair by his unmerited calamity and disgrace, he put an end to his life by dashing out his brains against the walls of a church, in the year 1245. Both Frederick and Pietro delle Vigne composed verses in the Sicilian dialect which are yet extant.

v. 67. The harlot.] Envy. Chaucer alludes to this in the Prologue to the Legende of Good women.

> Envie is lavender to the court alway,
> For she ne parteth neither night ne day
> Out of the house of Cesar; thus saith Dant.

v. 119. Each fan o' th' wood.] Hence perhaps Milton:

> Leaves and fuming rills, Aurora's fan.
> P. L. b. v. 6.

v. 122. Lano.] Lano, a Siennese, who, being reduced by prodigality to a state of extreme want, found his existence no longer supportable; and, having been sent by his countrymen on a military expedition, to assist the Florentine against the Aretini, took that opportunity of exposing himself to certain death, in the engagement which took place at Toppo near Arezzo. See G. Villani, Hist. l. 7. c. cxix.

v. 133. O Giocomo
Of Sant' Andrea!]

Jacopo da Sant' Andrea, a Paduan, who, having wasted his property in the most wanton acts of profusion, killed himself in despair. v. 144. In that City.] "I was an inhabitant of Florence, that city which changed her first patron Mars for St. John the Baptist, for which reason the vengeance of the deity thus slighted will never be appeased: and, if some remains of his status were not still visible on the bridge over the Arno, she would have been already leveled to the ground; and thus the citizens, who raised her again from the ashes to which Attila had reduced her, would have labored in vain." See Paradise, Canto XVI. 44.

The relic of antiquity to which the superstition of Florence attached so high an importance, was carried away by a flood, that destroyed the bridge on which it stood, in the year 1337, but without the ill effects that were apprehended from the loss of their fancied Palladium.

v. 152. I slung the fatal noose.] We are not informed who this suicide was.

CANTO XIV

v. 15. By Cato's foot.] See Lucan, Phars, l. 9.

v. 26. Dilated flakes of fire.] Compare Tasso. G. L. c. x. st. 61.

v. 28. As, in the torrid Indian clime.] Landino refers to Albertus Magnus for the circumstance here alluded to.

v. 53. In Mongibello.]
   More hot than Aetn' or flaming Mongibell.
      Spenser, F. Q. b. ii. c. ix. st. 29.
See Virg. Aen. 1. viii. 416. and Berni. Orl. Inn 1. i. c. xvi. st. 21. It would be endless to refer to parallel passages in the Greek writers.

v. 64. This of the seven kings was one.] Compare Aesch. Seven Chiefs, 425. Euripides, Phoen. 1179 and Statius. Theb. l. x. 821.

v. 76. Bulicame.] A warm medicinal spring near Viterbo, the waters of which, as Landino and Vellutelli affirm, passed by a place of ill fame. Venturi, with less probability, conjectures that Dante would imply, that it was the scene of much licentious merriment among those who frequented its baths.

v. 91. Under whose monarch.]
   Credo pudicitiam Saturno rege moratam
   In terris.
      Juv. Satir. vi.

v. 102. His head.] Daniel, ch. ii. 32, 33.

v. 133. Whither.] On the other side of Purgatory.

CANTO XV

v. 10. Chiarentana.] A part of the Alps where the Brenta rises, which river is much swoln as soon as the snow begins to dissolve on the mountains.

v. 28. Brunetto.] "Ser Brunetto, a Florentine, the secretary or chancellor of the city, and Dante's preceptor, hath left us a work so little read, that both the subject of it and the language of it have been mistaken. It is in the French spoken in the reign of St. Louis, under the title of Tresor, and contains a species of philosophical course of lectures divided into theory and practice, or, as he expresses it, "un enchaussement des choses divines et humaines," &c. Sir R. Clayton's Translation of Tenhove's Memoirs of the Medici, vol. i. ch. ii. p. 104. The Tresor has never been printed in the original language. There is a fine manuscript of it in the British Museum, with an illuminated portrait of Brunetto in his study prefixed. Mus. Brit. MSS. 17, E. 1. Tesor. It is divided into four books, the first, on Cosmogony and Theology, the second, a translation of Aristotle's Ethics; the third on Virtues and Vices; the fourth, on Rhetoric. For an interesting memoir relating to this work, see Hist. de l'Acad. des Inscriptions, tom. vii. 296. His Tesoretto, one of the earliest productions of Italian poetry, is a curious work, not unlike the writings of Chaucer in style and numbers, though Bembo remarks, that his pupil, however largely he had stolen from it, could not have much enriched himself. As it is perhaps but little known, I will here add a slight sketch of it.

Brunetto describes himself as returning from an embassy to the King of Spain, on which he had been sent by the Guelph party from Florence. On the plain of Roncesvalles he meets a scholar on a bay mule, who tells him that the Guelfi are driven out of the city with great loss.

Struck with grief at these mournful tidings, and musing with his head bent downwards, he loses his road, and wanders into a wood. Here Nature, whose figure is described with sublimity, appears, and discloses to him the secrets of her operations. After this he wanders into a desert; but at length proceeds on his way, under the protection of a banner, with which Nature had furnished him, till on the third day he finds himself in a large pleasant champaign, where are assembled many emperors, kings, and sages. It is the habitation of Virtue and her daughters, the four Cardinal Virtues. Here Brunetto sees also Courtesy, Bounty, Loyalty, and Prowess, and hears the instructions they give to a knight, which occupy about a fourth part of the poem. Leaving this territory, he passes over valleys, mountains, woods, forests, and bridges, till he arrives in a beautiful valley covered with flowers on all sides, and the richest in the world; but which was continually shifting its appearance from a round figure to a square, from obscurity to light, and from populousness to solitude. This is the region of Pleasure, or Cupid, who is accompanied by four ladies, Love, Hope, Fear, and Desire. In one part of it he meets with Ovid, and is instructed by him how to conquer the passion of love, and to escape from that place. After his escape he makes his confession to a friar, and then returns to the forest of visions: and ascending a mountain, he meets with Ptolemy, a venerable old man. Here the narrative breaks off. The poem ends, as it began, with an address to Rustico di Filippo, on whom he lavishes every sort of praise.

It has been observed, that Dante derived the idea of opening his poem by describing himself as lost in a wood, from the Tesoretto of his master. I know not whether it has been remarked, that the crime of usury is branded by both these poets as offensive to God and Nature: or that the sin for which Brunetto is condemned by his pupil, is mentioned in the Tesoretto with great horror. Dante's twenty-fifth sonnet is a jocose one, addressed to Brunetto. He died in 1295.

v. 62. Who in old times came down from Fesole.] See G. Villani Hist. l. iv. c. 5. and Macchiavelli Hist. of Flor. b. ii.

v. 89. With another text.] He refers to the prediction of Farinata, in Canto X.

v. 110. Priscian.] There is no reason to believe, as the commentators observe that the grammarian of this name was stained with the vice imputed to him; and we must therefore suppose that Dante puts the individual for the species, and implies the frequency of the crime among those who abused the opportunities which the education of youth afforded them, to so abominable a purpose.

v. 111. Francesco.] Son of Accorso, a Florentine, celebrated for his skill in jurisprudence, and commonly known by the name of Accursius.

v. 113. Him.] Andrea de' Mozzi, who, that his scandalous life might be less exposed to observation, was translated either by Nicholas III, or Boniface VIII from the see of Florence to that of Vicenza, through which passes the river Baccchiglione. At the latter of these places he died.

v. 114. The servants' servant.] Servo de' servi. So Ariosto, Sat. 3.
      Degli servi
  Io sia il gran servo.

v. 124. I commend my Treasure to thee.] Brunetto's great work, the Tresor.
Sieti raccomandato 'l mio Tesoro.
So Giusto de' Conti, in his Bella Mano, Son. "Occhi:"
    Siavi raccommandato il mio Tesoro.

CANTO XVI

v. 38. Gualdrada.] Gualdrada was the daughter of Bellincione Berti, of whom mention is made in the Paradise, Canto XV, and XVI. He was of the family of Ravignani, a branch of the Adimari.

The Emperor Otho IV. being at a festival in Florence, where Gualdrada was present, was struck with her beauty; and inquiring who she was, was answered by Bellincione, that she was the daughter of one who, if it was his Majesty's pleasure, would make her admit the honour of his salute. On overhearing this, she arose from her seat, and blushing, in an animated tone of voice, desired her father that he would not be so liberal in his offers, for that no man should ever be allowed that freedom, except him who should be her lawful husband. The Emperor was not less delighted by her resolute modesty than he had before been by the loveliness of her person, and calling to him Guido, one of his barons, gave her to him in marriage, at the same time raising him to the rank of a count, and bestowing on her the whole of Casentino, and a part of the territory of Romagna, as her portion. Two sons were the offspring of this union, Guglielmo and Ruggieri, the latter of whom was father of Guidoguerra, a man of great military skill and prowess who, at the head of four hundred Florentines of the Guelph party, was signally instrumental to the victory obtained at Benevento by Charles of Anjou, over Manfredi, King of Naples, in 1265. One of the consequences of this victory was the expulsion of the Ghibellini, and the re-establishment of the Guelfi at Florence.

v. 39. Many a noble act.] Compare Tasso, G. L. c. i. st. 1.

v. 42. Aldobrandiu] Tegghiaio Aldobrandi was of the noble family of Adimari, and much esteemed for his military talents. He endeavored to dissuade the Florentines from the attack, which they meditated against the Siennese, and the rejection of his counsel occasioned the memorable defeat, which the former sustained at Montaperto, and the consequent banishment of the Guelfi from Florence.

v. 45. Rusticucci.] Giacopo Rusticucci, a Florentine, remarkable for his opulence and the generosity of his spirit.

v. 70. Borsiere.] Guglielmo Borsiere, another Florentine, whom Boccaccio, in a story which he relates of him, terms "a man of courteous and elegant manners, and of great readiness in conversation." Dec. Giorn. i. Nov. 8.

v. 84. When thou with pleasure shalt retrace the past.]
  Quando ti giovera dicere io fui.
So Tasso, G. L. c. xv. st. 38.
  Quando mi giovera narrar altrui
  Le novita vedute, e dire; io fui.

v. 121. Ever to that truth.] This memorable apophthegm is repeated by Luigi Pulci and Trissino.

  Sempre a quel ver, ch' ha faccia di menzogna
  E piu senno tacer la lingua cheta
  Che spesso senza colpa fa vergogna.
    Morgante. Magg. c. xxiv.
    La verita, che par mensogna
  Si dovrebbe tacer dall' uom ch'e saggio.
    Italia. Lib. C. xvi.

The Divine Comedy
CANTO XVII

v. 1. The fell monster.] Fraud.

v. 53. A pouch.] A purse, whereon the armorial bearings of each were emblazoned. According to Landino, our poet implies that the usurer can pretend to no other honour, than such as he derives from his purse and his family.

v. 57. A yellow purse.] The arms of the Gianfigliazzi of Florence.

v. 60. Another.] Those of the Ubbriachi, another Florentine family of high distinction.

v. 62. A fat and azure swine.] The arms of the Scrovigni a noble family of Padua.

v. 66. Vitaliano.] Vitaliano del Dente, a Paduan.

v. 69. That noble knight.] Giovanni Bujamonti, a Florentine usurer, the most infamous of his time.

CANTO XVIII

v. 28. With us beyond.] Beyond the middle point they tended the same way with us, but their pace was quicker than ours.

v. 29. E'en thus the Romans.] In the year 1300, Pope Boniface VIII., to remedy the inconvenience occasioned by the press of people who were passing over the bridge of St. Angelo during the time of the Jubilee, caused it to be divided length wise by a partition, and ordered, that all those who were going to St. Peter's should keep one side, and those returning the other.

v. 50. Venedico.] Venedico Caccianimico, a Bolognese, who prevailed on his sister Ghisola to prostitute herself to Obizzo da Este, Marquis of Ferrara, whom we have seen among the tyrants, Canto XII.

v. 62. To answer Sipa.] He denotes Bologna by its situation between the rivers Savena to the east, and Reno to the west of that city; and by a peculiarity of dialect, the use of the affirmative sipa instead of si.

v. 90. Hypsipyle.] See Appolonius Rhodius, l. i. and Valerius Flaccus l.ii. Hypsipyle deceived the other women by concealing her father Thoas, when they had agreed to put all their males to death.

v. 120. Alessio.] Alessio, of an ancient and considerable family in Lucca, called the Interminei.

v. 130. Thais.] He alludes to that passage in the Eunuchus of Terence where Thraso asks if Thais was obliged to him for the present he had sent her, and Gnatho replies, that she had expressed her obligation in the most forcible terms.

T. Magnas vero agere gratias Thais mihi?
G. Ingentes.
    Eun. a. iii. s. i.

CANTO XIX

v. 18. Saint John's fair dome.] The apertures in the rock were of the same dimensions as the fonts of St. John the Baptist at Florence, one of which, Dante says he had broken, to rescue a child that was playing near and fell in. He intimates that the motive of his breaking the font had been maliciously represented by his enemies.

v. 55. O Boniface!] The spirit mistakes Dante for Boniface VIII. who was then alive, and who he did not expect would have arrived so soon, in consequence, as it should seem, of a prophecy, which predicted the death of that Pope at a later period. Boniface died in 1303.

v. 58. In guile.] "Thou didst presume to arrive by fraudulent means at the papal power, and afterwards to abuse it."

v. 71. In the mighty mantle I was rob'd.] Nicholas III, of the Orsini family, whom the poet therefore calls "figliuol dell' orsa," "son of the she-bear." He died in 1281.

v. 86. From forth the west, a shepherd without law.] Bertrand de Got Archbishop of Bordeaux, who succeeded to the pontificate in 1305, and assumed the title of Clement V. He transferred the holy see to Avignon in 1308 (where it remained till 1376), and died in 1314.

v. 88. A new Jason.] See Maccabees, b. ii. c. iv. 7,8.

v. 97. Nor Peter.] Acts of the Apostles, c.i. 26.

v. 100. The condemned soul.] Judas.

v. 103. Against Charles.] Nicholas III. was enraged against Charles I, King of Sicily, because he rejected with scorn a proposition made by that Pope for an alliance between their families. See G. Villani, Hist. l. vii. c. liv.

v. 109. Th' Evangelist.] Rev. c. xvii. 1, 2, 3. Compare Petrarch. Opera fol. ed. Basil. 1551. Epist. sine titulo liber. ep. xvi. p. 729.

v. 118. Ah, Constantine.] He alludes to the pretended gift of the Lateran by Constantine to Silvester, of which Dante himself seems to imply a doubt, in his treatise "De Monarchia." - "Ergo scindere Imperium, Imperatori non licet. Si ergo aliquae, dignitates per Constantinum essent alienatae, (ut dicunt) ab Imperio," &c. l. iii. The gift is by Ariosto very humorously placed in the moon, among the things lost or abused on earth.

    Di varj fiori, &c.
        O. F. c. xxxiv. st. 80.

Milton has translated both this passage and that in the text. Prose works, vol. i. p. 11. ed. 1753.

CANTO XX

v. 11. Revers'd.] Compare Spenser, F. Q. b. i. c. viii. st. 31

v. 30. Before whose eyes.] Amphiaraus, one of the seven kings who besieged Thebes. He is said to have been swallowed up by an opening of the earth. See Lidgate's Storie of Thebes, Part III where it is told how the "Bishop Amphiaraus" fell down to hell.

    And thus the devill for his outrages,
    Like his desert payed him his wages.

A different reason for his being doomed thus to perish is assigned by Pindar.
[GREEK HERE]
        Nem ix.

> For thee, Amphiaraus, earth,
> By Jove's all-riving thunder cleft
> Her mighty bosom open'd wide,
> Thee and thy plunging steeds to hide,
> Or ever on thy back the spear
> Of Periclymenus impress'd
> A wound to shame thy warlike breast
> For struck with panic fear
> The gods' own children flee.

v. 37. Tiresias.]
> Duo magnorum viridi coeuntia sylva
> Corpora serpentum baculi violaverat ictu, &c.
> > Ovid. Met. iii.

v. 43. Aruns.] Aruns is said to have dwelt in the mountains of Luni (from whence that territory is still called Lunigiana), above Carrara, celebrated for its marble. Lucan. Phars. l. i. 575. So Boccaccio in the Fiammetta, l. iii. "Quale Arunte," &c.

"Like Aruns, who amidst the white marbles of Luni, contemplated the celestial bodies and their motions."

v. 50. Manto.] The daughter of Tiresias of Thebes, a city dedicated to Bacchus. From Manto Mantua, the country of Virgil derives its name. The Poet proceeds to describe the situation of that place.

v. 61. Between the vale.] The lake Benacus, now called the Lago di Garda, though here said to lie between Garda, Val Camonica, and the Apennine, is, however, very distant from the latter two

v. 63. There is a spot.] Prato di Fame, where the dioceses of Trento, Verona, and Brescia met.

v. 69. Peschiera.] A garrison situated to the south of the lake, where it empties itself and forms the Mincius.

v. 94. Casalodi's madness.] Alberto da Casalodi, who had got possession of Mantua, was persuaded by Pinamonte Buonacossi, that he might ingratiate himself with the people by banishing to their own castles the nobles, who were obnoxious to them. No sooner was this done, than Pinamonte put himself at the head of the populace, drove out Casalodi and his adherents, and obtained the sovereignty for himself.

v. 111. So sings my tragic strain.]
> Suspensi Eurypilum scitatum oracula Phoebi
> Mittimus.
> > Virg. Aeneid. ii. 14.

v. 115. Michael Scot.] Sir Michael Scott, of Balwearie, astrologer to the Emperor Frederick II. lived in the thirteenth century. For further particulars relating to this singular man, see Warton's History of English Poetry, vol. i. diss. ii. and sect. ix. p 292, and the Notes to Mr. Scott's "Lay of the Last Minstrel," a poem in which a happy use is made of the traditions that are still current in North Britain concerning him. He is mentioned by G. Villani. Hist. l. x. c. cv. and cxli. and l. xii. c. xviii. and by Boccaccio, Dec. Giorn. viii. Nov. 9.

v. 116. Guido Bonatti.] An astrologer of Forli, on whose skill Guido da Montefeltro, lord of that place, so much relied, that he is reported never to have gone into battle, except in the hour recommended to him as fortunate by Bonatti.

Landino and Vellutello, speak of a book, which he composed on the subject of his art.

v. 116. Asdente.] A shoemaker at Parma, who deserted his business to practice the arts of divination.

v. 123. Cain with fork of thorns.] By Cain and the thorns, or what is still vulgarly called the Man in the Moon, the Poet denotes that luminary. The same superstition is alluded to in the Paradise, Canto II. 52. The curious reader may consult Brand on Popular Antiquities, 4to. 1813. vol. ii. p. 476.

CANTO XXI

v. 7. In the Venetians' arsenal.] Compare Ruccellai, Le Api, 165, and Dryden's Annus Mirabilis, st. 146, &c.

v. 37. One of Santa Zita's elders.] The elders or chief magistrates of Lucca, where Santa Zita was held in especial veneration. The name of this sinner is supposed to have been Martino Botaio.

v. 40. Except Bonturo, barterers.] This is said ironically of Bonturo de' Dati. By barterers are meant peculators, of every description; all who traffic the interests of the public for their own private advantage.

v. 48. Is other swimming than in Serchio's wave.]
    Qui si nuota altrimenti che nel Serchio.
Serchio is the river that flows by Lucca. So Pulci, Morg. Mag. c. xxiv.
    Qui si nuota nel sangue, e non nel Serchio.

v. 92. From Caprona.] The surrender of the castle of Caprona to the combined forces of Florence and Lucca, on condition that the garrison should march out in safety, to which event Dante was a witness, took place in 1290. See G. Villani, Hist. l. vii. c. 136.

v. 109. Yesterday.] This passage fixes the era of Dante's descent at Good Friday, in the year 1300 (34 years from our blessed Lord's incarnation being added to 1266), and at the thirty-fifth year of our poet's age. See Canto I. v. 1.

The awful event alluded to, the Evangelists inform us, happened "at the ninth hour," that is, our sixth, when "the rocks were rent," and the convulsion, according to Dante, was felt even in the depths in Hell. See Canto XII. 38.

CANTO XXII

v. 16. In the church.] This proverb is repeated by Pulci, Morg. Magg. c. xvii.

v. 47. Born in Navarre's domain.] The name of this peculator is said to have been Ciampolo.

v. 51. The good king Thibault.] "Thibault I. king of Navarre, died on the 8th of June, 1233, as much to be commended for the desire he showed of aiding the war in the Holy Land, as reprehensible and faulty for his design of oppressing the rights and privileges of the church, on which account it is said that the whole kingdom was under an interdict for the space of three entire years. Thibault undoubtedly merits praise, as for his other endowments, so especially for his cultivation of the liberal arts, his exercise and knowledge of music and poetry in which he much excelled, that he was accustomed to compose verses and sing them to the viol, and to exhibit his poetical compositions publicly in his palace, that they might be criticized by all." Mariana, History of Spain, b. xiii. c. 9.

    An account of Thibault, and two of his songs, with what were probably the original melodies, may be seen in Dr. Burney's History of Music, v. ii. c. iv. His poems, which are in the French language, were edited by M. l'Eveque de la Ravalliere. Paris. 1742. 2 vol. 12mo. Dante twice quotes one of his verses in the Treatise de Vulg. Eloq. l. i. c. ix. and l. ii. c. v. and refers to him again, l. ii. c. vi.

    From "the good king Thibault" are descended the good, but more unfortunate monarch, Louis XVI. of France, and consequently the present legitimate sovereign of that realm. See Henault, Abrege Chron. 1252, 2, 4.

    v. 80. The friar Gomita.] He was entrusted by Nino de' Visconti with the government of Gallura, one of the four jurisdictions into which Sardinia was divided. Having his master's enemies in his power, he took a bribe from them, and allowed them to escape. Mention of Nino will recur in the Notes to Canto XXXIII. and in the Purgatory, Canto VIII.

    v. 88. Michel Zanche.] The president of Logodoro, another of the four Sardinian jurisdictions. See Canto XXXIII.

CANTO XXIII

    v. 5. Aesop's fable.] The fable of the frog, who offered to carry the mouse across a ditch, with the intention of drowning him when both were carried off by a kite. It is not among those Greek Fables which go under the name of Aesop.

    v. 63. Monks in Cologne.] They wore their cowls unusually large.

    v. 66. Frederick's.] The Emperor Frederick II. is said to have punished those who were guilty of high treason, by wrapping them up in lead, and casting them into a furnace.

    v. 101. Our bonnets gleaming bright with orange hue.] It is observed by Venturi, that the word "rance" does not here signify "rancid or disgustful," as it is explained by the old commentators, but "orange-coloured," in which sense it occurs in the Purgatory, Canto II. 9.

    v. 104. Joyous friars.] "Those who ruled the city of Florence on the part of the Ghibillines, perceiving this discontent and murmuring, which they were fearful might produce a rebellion against themselves, in order to satisfy the people, made choice of two knights, Frati Godenti (joyous friars) of Bologna, on whom they conferred the chief power in Florence. One named M. Catalano de' Malavolti, the other M. Loderingo di Liandolo; one an adherent of the Guelph, the other of the Ghibelline party. It is to be remarked, that the Joyous Friars were called Knights of St. Mary, and became knights on taking that habit: their robes were white, the mantle sable, and the arms a white field and red cross with two stars. Their office was to defend widows and orphans; they were to act as mediators; they had internal regulations like other religious bodies. The above-mentioned M. Loderingo was the founder of that order. But it was not long before they too well deserved the appellation given them, and were found to be more bent on enjoying themselves than on any other subject. These two friars were called in by the Florentines, and had a residence assigned them in the palace belonging to the people over against the Abbey. Such was the dependence placed on the character of their order that it was expected they would be impartial, and would save the commonwealth any unnecessary expense; instead of which, though inclined to opposite parties, they secretly and hypocritically concurred in promoting their own advantage rather than the public good." G. Villani, b. vii. c.13. This happened in 1266.

v. 110. Gardingo's vicinage.] The name of that part of the city which was inhabited by the powerful Ghibelline family of Uberti, and destroyed under the partial and iniquitous administration of Catalano and Loderingo.

v. 117. That pierced spirit.] Caiaphas.

v. 124. The father of his consort.] Annas, father-in-law to Caiaphas.

v. 146. He is a liar.] John, c. viii. 44. Dante had perhaps heard this text from one of the pulpits in Bologna.

CANTO XXIV

v. 1. In the year's early nonage.] "At the latter part of January, when the sun enters into Aquarius, and the equinox is drawing near, when the hoar-frosts in the morning often wear the appearance of snow but are melted by the rising sun."

v. 51. Vanquish thy weariness.]
>   Quin corpus onustum
> Hesternis vitiis animum quoque praegravat una,
> Atque affigit humi divinae particulam aurae.
>   Hor. Sat. ii. l. ii. 78.

v. 82. Of her sands.] Compare Lucan, Phars. l. ix. 703.

v. 92. Heliotrope.] The occult properties of this stone are described by Solinus, c. xl, and by Boccaccio, in his humorous tale of Calandrino. Decam. G. viii. N. 3.

In Chiabrera's Ruggiero, Scaltrimento begs of Sofia, who is sending him on a perilous errand, to lend him the heliotrope.

> In mia man fida
> L'elitropia, per cui possa involarmi
> Secondo il mio talento agli occhi altrui.
>   c. vi.

> Trust to my hand the heliotrope, by which
> I may at will from others' eyes conceal me

Compare Ariosto, Il Negromante, a. 3. s. 3. Pulci, Morg. Magg. c xxv. and Fortiguerra, Ricciardetto, c. x. st. 17.
Gower in his Confessio Amantis, lib. vii, enumerates it among the jewels in the diadem of the sun.

> Jaspis and helitropius.

v. 104. The Arabian phoenix.] This is translated from Ovid, Metam. l. xv.
> Una est quae reparat, seque ipsa reseminat ales, &c.

See also Petrarch, Canzone:
"Qual piu," &c.

v. 120. Vanni Fucci.] He is said to have been an illegitimate offspring of the family of Lazari in Pistoia, and, having robbed the sacristy of the church of St. James in that city, to have charged Vanni della Nona with the sacrilege, in consequence of which accusation the latter suffered death.

The Divine Comedy

   v. 142. Pistoia.] "In May 1301, the Bianchi party, of Pistoia, with the assistance and favor of the Bianchi who ruled Florence, drove out the Neri party from the former place, destroying their houses, Palaces and farms." Giov. Villani, Hist. l. viii. e xliv.

   v. 144. From Valdimagra.] The commentators explain this prophetical threat to allude to the victory obtained by the Marquis Marcello Malaspina of Valdimagra (a tract of country now called the Lunigiana) who put himself at the head of the Neri and defeated their opponents the Bianchi, in the Campo Piceno near Pistoia, soon after the occurrence related in the preceding note.

   Of this engagement I find no mention in Villani. Currado Malaspina is introduced in the eighth Canto of Purgatory; where it appears that, although on the present occaision they espoused contrary sides, some important favours were nevertheless conferred by that family on our poet at a subsequent perid of his exile in 1307.

Canto XXV

   v.1. The sinner] So Trissino
   Poi facea con le man le fiche al cielo
   Dicendo: Togli, Iddio; che puoi piu farmi?
         L'ital. Lib. c. xii
   v. 12. Thy seed] Thy ancestry.
   v. 15. Not him] Capanaeus. Canto XIV.
   v. 18. On Marenna's marsh.] An extensive tract near the sea-shore in Tuscany.
   v. 24. Cacus.] Virgil, Aen. l. viii. 193.
   v. 31. A hundred blows.] Less than ten blows, out of the hundred Hercules gave him, deprived him of feeling.
   v. 39. Cianfa] He is said to have been of the family of Donati at Florence.
   v. 57. Thus up the shrinking paper.]
   --All my bowels crumble up to dust.
   I am a scribbled form, drawn up with a pen
   Upon a parchment; and against this fire
   Do I shrink up.
         Shakespeare, K. John, a. v. s. 7.
   v. 61. Agnello.] Agnello Brunelleschi
   v. 77. In that part.] The navel.
   v. 81. As if by sleep or fev'rous fit assail'd.]
         O Rome! thy head
   Is drown'd in sleep, and all thy body fev'ry.
         Ben Jonson's Catiline.
   v. 85. Lucan.] Phars. l. ix. 766 and 793.
   v. 87. Ovid.] Metam. l. iv. and v.
   v. 121. His sharpen'd visage.] Compare Milton, P. L. b. x. 511 &c.
   v. 131. Buoso.] He is said to have been of the Donati family.
   v. 138. Sciancato.] Puccio Sciancato, a noted robber, whose familly, Venturi says, he has not been able to discover.
   v. 140. Gaville.] Francesco Guercio Cavalcante was killed at Gaville, near Florence; and in revenge of his death several inhabitants of that district were put to death.

CANTO XXVI

v. 7. But if our minds.]
  Namque sub Auroram, jam dormitante lucerna,
  Somnia quo cerni tempore vera solent.
      Ovid, Epist. xix

The same poetical superstition is alluded to in the Purgatory, Cant. IX. and XXVII.

v. 9. Shall feel what Prato.] The poet prognosticates the calamities which were soon to befal his native city, and which he says, even her nearest neighbor, Prato, would wish her. The calamities more particularly pointed at, are said to be the fall of a wooden bridge over the Arno, in May, 1304, where a large multitude were assembled to witness a representation of hell nnd the infernal torments, in consequence of which accident many lives were lost; and a conflagration that in the following month destroyed more than seventeen hundred houses, many ofthem sumptuous buildings. See G. Villani, Hist. l. viii. c. 70 and 71.

v. 22. More than I am wont.] "When I reflect on the punishment allotted to those who do not give sincere and upright advice to others I am more anxious than ever not to abuse to so bad a purpose those talents, whatever they may be, which Nature, or rather Providence, has conferred on me." It is probable that this declaration was the result of real feeling Textd have given great weight to any opinion or party he had espoused, and to whom indigence and exile might have offerred strong temptations to deviate from that line of conduct which a strict sense of duty prescribed.

v. 35. as he, whose wrongs.] Kings, b. ii. c. ii.

v. 54. ascending from that funeral pile.] The flame is said to have divided on the funeral pile which consumed tile bodies of Eteocles and Polynices, as if conscious of the enmity that actuated them while living.

  Ecce iterum fratris, &c.
      Statius, Theb. l. xii.
  Ostendens confectas flamma, &c.
      Lucan, Pharsal. l. 1. 145.

v. 60. The ambush of the horse.] "The ambush of the wooden horse, that caused Aeneas to quit the city of Troy and seek his fortune in Italy, where his descendants founded the Roman empire."

v. 91. Caieta.] Virgil, Aeneid. l. vii. 1.

v. 93. Nor fondness for my son] Imitated hp Tasso, G. L. c. viii.
  Ne timor di fatica o di periglio,
  Ne vaghezza del regno, ne pietade
  Del vecchio genitor, si degno affetto
  Intiepedir nel generoso petto.

This imagined voyage of Ulysses into the Atlantic is alluded to by Pulci.
  E sopratutto commendava Ulisse,
  Che per veder nell' altro mondo gisse.
      Morg. Magg. c. xxv

And by Tasso, G. L. c. xv. 25.

v. 106. The strait pass.] The straits of Gibraltar.

The Divine Comedy

    v. 122. Made our oars wings.] So Chiabrera, Cant. Eroiche. xiii
    Faro de'remi un volo.
And Tasso Ibid. 26.
    v. 128. A mountain dim.] The mountain of Purgatorg

CANTO XXVII.

    v. 6. The Sicilian Bull.] The engine of torture invented by Perillus, for the tyrant Phalaris.
    v. 26. Of the mountains there.] Montefeltro.
    v. 38. Polenta's eagle.] Guido Novello da Polenta, who bore an eagle for his coat of arms. The name of Polenta was derived from a castle so called in the neighbourhood of Brittonoro. Cervia is a small maritime city, about fifteen miles to the south of Ravenna. Guido was the son of Ostasio da Polenta, and made himself master of Ravenna, in 1265. In 1322 he was deprived of his sovereignty, and died at Bologna in the year following. This last and most munificent patron of Dante is himself enumerated, by the historian of Italian literature, among the poets of his time. Tiraboschi, Storia della Lett. Ital. t. v. l. iii. c. ii. 13. The passnge in the text might have removed the uncertainty wwhich Tiraboschi expressed, respecting the duration of Guido's absence from Ravenna, when he was driven from that city in 1295, by the arms of Pietro, archbishop of Monreale. It must evidently have been very short, since his government is here represented (in 1300) as not having suffered any material disturbance for many years.
    v. 41. The land.] The territory of Forli, the inhabitants of which, in 1282, mere enabled, hy the strategem of Guido da Montefeltro, who then governed it, to defeat with great slaughter the French army by which it had been besieged. See G. Villani, l. vii. c. 81. The poet informs Guido, its former ruler, that it is now in the possession of Sinibaldo Ordolaffi, or Ardelaffi, whom he designates by his coat of arms, a lion vert.
    v. 43. The old mastiff of Verucchio and the young.] Malatesta and Malatestino his son, lords of Rimini, called, from their ferocity, the mastiffs of Verruchio, which was the name of their castle.
    v. 44. Montagna.] Montagna de'Parcitati, a noble knight, and leader of the Ghibelline party at Rimini, murdered by Malatestino.
    v. 46. Lamone's city and Santerno's.] Lamone is the river at Faenza, and Santerno at Imola.
    v. 47. The lion of the snowy lair.] Machinardo Pagano, whose arms were a lion azure on a field argent; mentioned again in the Purgatory, Canto XIV. 122. See G. Villani passim, where he is called Machinardo da Susinana.
    v. 50. Whose flank is wash'd of SSavio's wave.] Cesena, situated at the foot of a mountain, and washed by the river Savio, that often descends with a swoln and rapid stream from the Appenine.
    v. 64. A man of arms.] Guido da Montefeltro.
    v. 68. The high priest.] Boniface VIII.
    v. 72. The nature of the lion than the fox.]
    Non furon leonine ma di volpe.
So Pulci, Morg. Magg. c. xix.
    E furon le sua opre e le sue colpe
    Non creder leonine ma di volpe.

v. 81. The chief of the new Pharisee.] Boniface VIII. whose enmity to the family of Colonna prompted him to destroy their houses near the Lateran. Wishing to obtain possession of their other seat, Penestrino, he consulted with Guido da Montefeltro how he might accomplish his purpose, offering him at the same time absolution for his past sins, as well as for that which he was then tempting him to commit. Guido's advice was, that kind words and fair promises nonld put his enemies into his power; and they accordingly soon aftermards fell into the snare laid for them, A.D. 1298. See G. Villani, l. viii. c. 23.

v. 84. Nor against Acre one Had fought.]
He alludes to the renegade Christians, by whom the Saracens, in Apri., 1291, were assisted to recover St.John d'Acre, the last possession of the Christians in the Iloly Land. The regret expressed by the Florentine annalist G. Villani, for the loss of this valuable fortress, is well worthy of observation, l. vii. c. 144.

v. 89. As in Soracte Constantine besought.] So in Dante's treatise De Monarchia: "Dicunt quidam adhue, quod Constantinus Imperator, mundatus a lepra intercessione Syvestri, tunc summni pontificis imperii sedem, scilicet Romam, donavit ecclesiae, cum multis allis imperii dignitatibus." Lib.iii.

v. 101. My predecessor.] Celestine V. See Notes to Canto III.

CANTO XXVIII.

v.8. In that long war.] The war of Hannibal in Italy. "When Mago brought news of his victories to Carthage, in order to make his successes more easily credited, he commanded the golden rings to be poured out in the senate house, which made so large a heap, that, as some relate, they filled three modii and a half. A more probable account represents them not to have exceeded one modius." Livy, Hist.

v. 12. Guiscard's Norman steel.] Robert Guiscard, who conquered the kingdom of Naples, and died in 1110. G. Villani, l. iv. c. 18. He is introduced in the Paradise, Canto XVIII.

v. 13. And those the rest.] The army of Manfredi, which, through the treachery of the Apulian troops, wns overcome by Charles of Anjou in 1205, and fell in such numbers that the bones of the slain were still gathered near Ceperano. G. Villani, l. vii. c. 9. See the Purgatory, Canto III.

v. 10. O Tagliocozzo.] He alludes to tile victory which Charles gained over Conradino, by the sage advice of the Sieur de Valeri, in 1208. G. Villani, l. vii. c. 27.

v. 32. Ali.] The disciple of Mohammed.

v. 53. Dolcino.] "In 1305, a friar, called Dolcino, who belonged to no regular order, contrived to raise in Novarra, in Lombardy, a large company of the meaner sort of people, declaring himself to be a true apostle of Christ, and promulgating a community of property and of wives, with many other such heretical doctrines. He blamed the pope, cardinals, and other prelates of the holy church, for not observing their duty, nor leading the angelic life, and affirmed that he ought to be pope. He was followed by more than three thousand men and women, who lived promiscuously on the mountains together, like beasts, and, when they wanted provisions, supplied themselves by depredation and rapine. This lasted for two years till, many being struck with compunction at the dissolute life they led, his sect was much diminished; and through failure of food, and the severity of the snows, he was taken by the people of Novarra, and burnt, with Margarita his companion and many other men and women whom his errors had seduced." G. Villanni, l. viii. c. 84.

Landino observes, that he was possessed of singular eloquence, and that both he and Margarita endored their fate with a firmness worthy of a better cause. For a further account of him, see Muratori Rer. Ital. Script. t. ix. p. 427.

v. 69. Medicina.] A place in the territory of Bologna. Piero fomented dissensions among the inhabitants of that city, and among the leaders of the neighbouring states.

v. 70. The pleasant land.] Lombardy.

v. 72. The twain.] Guido dal Cassero and Angiolello da Cagnano, two of the worthiest and most distinguished citizens of Fano, were invited by Malatestino da Rimini to an entertainment on pretence that he had some important business to transact with them: and, according to instructions given by him, they mere drowned in their passage near Catolica, between Rimini and Fano.

v. 85. Focara's wind.] Focara is a mountain, from which a wind blows that is peculiarly dangerous to the navigators of that coast.

v. 94. The doubt in Caesar's mind.] Curio, whose speech (according to Lucan) determined Julius Caesar to proceed when he had arrived at Rimini (the ancient Ariminum), and doubted whether he should prosecute the civil war.

    Tolle moras: semper nocuit differre paratis
        Pharsal, l. i. 281.

v. 102. Mosca.] Buondelmonte was engaged to marry a lady of the Amidei family, but broke his promise and united himself to one of the Donati. This was so much resented by the former, that a meeting of themselves and their kinsmen was held, to consider of the best means of revenging the insult. Mosca degli Uberti persuaded them to resolve on the assassination of Buondelmonte, exclaiming to them "the thing once done, there is an end." The counsel and its effects were the source of many terrible calamities to the state of Florence. "This murder," says G. Villani, l. v. c. 38, "was the cause and beginning of the accursed Guelph and Ghibelline parties in Florence." It happened in 1215. See the Paradise, Canto XVI. 139.

v. 111. The boon companion.]
    What stronger breastplate than a heart untainted?
Shakespeare, 2 Hen. VI. a. iii. s. 2.

v. 160. Bertrand.] Bertrand de Born, Vicomte de Hautefort, near Perigueux in Guienne, who incited John to rebel against his father, Henry II. of England. Bertrand holds a distinguished place among the Provencal poets. He is quoted in Dante, "De Vulg. Eloq." l. ii. c. 2. For the translation of some extracts from his poems, see Millot, Hist. Litteraire des Troubadors t. i. p. 210; but the historical parts of that work are, I believe, not to be relied on.

CANTO XXIX.

v. 26. Geri of Bello.] A kinsman of the Poet's, who was murdered by one of the Sacchetti family. His being placed here, may be considered as a proof that Dante was more impartial in the allotment of his punishments than has generally been supposed.

v. 44. As were the torment.] It is very probable that these lines gave Milton the idea of his celebrated description:

> Immediately a place
> Before their eyes appear'd, sad, noisome, dark,
> A lasar-house it seem'd, wherein were laid
> Numbers of all diseas'd, all maladies, &c.
>   P. L. b. xi. 477.

v. 45. Valdichiana.] The valley through which passes the river Chiana, bounded by Arezzo, Cortona, Montepulciano, and Chiusi. In the heat of autumn it was formerly rendered unwholesome by the stagnation of the water, but has since been drained by the Emperor Leopold II. The Chiana is mentioned as a remarkably sluggish stream, in the Paradise, Canto XIII. 21.

v. 47. Maremma's pestilent fen.] See Note to Canto XXV. v. 18.

v. 58. In Aegina.] He alludes to the fable of the ants changed into Myrmidons. Ovid, Met. 1. vii.

v. 104. Arezzo was my dwelling.] Grifolino of Arezzo, who promised Albero, son of the Bishop of Sienna, that he would teach him the art of flying; and because be did not keep his promise, Albero prevailed on his father to have him burnt for a
necromancer.

v. 117. Was ever race
   Light as Sienna's?]
The same imputation is again cast on the Siennese, Purg. Canto XIII. 141.

v. 121. Stricca.] This is said ironically. Stricca, Niccolo Salimbeni, Caccia of Asciano, and Abbagliato, or Meo de Folcacchieri, belonged to a company of prodigal and luxurious young men in Sienna, called the "brigata godereccia." Niccolo was the inventor of a new manner of using cloves in cookery, not very well understood by the commentators, and which was termed the "costuma ricca."

v. 125. In that garden.] Sienna.

v. 134. Cappocchio's ghost.] Capocchio of Sienna, who is said to have been a fellow-student of Dante's in natural philosophy.

CANTO XXX.

v. 4. Athamas.] From Ovid, Metam. 1. iv.
   Protinos Aelides, &c.

v. 16. Hecuba. See Euripedes, Hecuba; and Ovid, Metnm. l. xiii.

v. 33. Schicchi.] Gianni Schicci, who was of the family of Cavalcanti, possessed such a faculty of moulding his features to the resemblance of others, that he was employed by Simon Donati to personate Buoso Donati, then recently deceased, and to make a will, leaving Simon his heir; for which service he was renumerated with a mare of extraordinary value, here called "the lady of the herd."

v. 39. Myrrha.] See Ovid, Metam. l. x.

v. 60. Adamo's woe.] Adamo of Breschia, at the instigation of Cuido Alessandro, and their brother Aghinulfo, lords of Romena, coonterfeited the coin of Florence; for which crime he was burnt. Landino says, that in his time

The Divine Comedy

the peasants still pointed out a pile of stones near Romena as the place of his execution.

    v. 64. Casentino.] Romena is a part of Casentino.

    v. 77. Branda's limpid spring.] A fountain in Sienna.

    v. 88. The florens with three carats of alloy.] The floren was a coin that ought to have had tmenty-four carats of pure gold. Villani relates, that it was first used at Florence in 1253, an aera of great prosperity in the annals of the republic; before which time their most valuable coinage was of silver. Hist. l. vi. c. 54.

    v. 98. The false accuser.] Potiphar's wife.

CANTO XXXI.

    v. 1. The very tongue.]
      Vulnus in Herculeo quae quondam fecerat hoste
      Vulneris auxilium Pellas hasta fuit.
          Ovid, Rem. Amor. 47.

The same allusion was made by Bernard de Ventadour, a Provencal poet in the middle of the twelfth century: and Millot observes, that it was a singular instance of erudition in a Troubadour. But it is not impossible, as Warton remarks, (Hist. of Engl. Poetry, vol. ii. sec. x. p 215.) but that he might have been indebted for it to some of the early romances.

    In Chaucer's Squier's Tale, a sword of similar quality is introduced:
      And other folk have wondred on the sweard,
      That could so piercen through every thing;
      And fell in speech of Telephus the king,
      And of Achillcs for his queint spere,
      For he couth with it both heale and dere.

So Shakspeare, Henry VI. p. ii. a. 5. s. 1.
      Whose smile and frown like to Achilles' spear
      Is able with the change to kill and cure.

    v. 14. Orlando.l
      When Charlemain with all his peerage fell
          At Fontarabia
          Milton, P. L. b. i. 586.

See Warton's Hist. of Eng. Poetrg, v. i. sect. iii. p. 132. "This is the horn which Orlando won from the giant Jatmund, and which as Turpin and the Islandic bards report, was endued with magical power, and might be heard at the distance of twenty miles." Charlemain and Orlando are introduced in the Paradise, Canto XVIII.

    v. 36. Montereggnon.] A castle near Sienna.

    v. 105. The fortunate vale.] The country near Carthage. See Liv. Hist. l. xxx. and Lucan, Phars. l. iv. 590. Dante has kept the latter of these writers in his eye throughout all this passage.

    v. 123. Alcides.] The combat between Hercules Antaeus is adduced by the Poet in his treatise "De Monarchia," l. ii. as a proof of the judgment of God displayed in the duel, according to the singular superstition of those times.

    v. 128. The tower of Carisenda.] The leaning tower at Bologna

CANTO XXXII.

v. 8. A tongue not us'd
To infant babbling.]
  Ne da lingua, che chiami mamma, o babbo.
Dante in his treatise " De Vulg. Eloq." speaking of words not admissble in the loftier, or as he calls it, tragic style of poetry, says- "In quorum numero nec puerilia propter suam simplicitatem ut Mamma et Babbo," l. ii. c. vii.

v. 29. Tabernich or Pietrapana.] The one a mountain in Sclavonia, the other in that tract of country called the Garfagnana, not far from Lucca.

v. 33. To where modest shame appears.] "As high as to the face."

v. 35. Moving their teeth in shrill note like the stork.]
  Mettendo i denti in nota di cicogna.
So Boccaccio, G. viii. n. 7. "Lo scolar cattivello quasi cicogna
divenuto si forte batteva i denti."

v. 53. Who are these two.] Alessandro and Napoleone, sons of Alberto Alberti, who murdered each other. They were proprietors of the valley of Falterona, where the Bisenzio has its source, a river that falls into the Arno about six miles from Florence.

v. 59. Not him,] Mordrec, son of King Arthur.

v. 60. Foccaccia.] Focaccia of Cancellieri, (the Pistoian family) whose atrocious act of revenge against his uncle is said to have given rise to the parties of the Bianchi and Neri, in the year 1300. See G. Villani, Hist. l, viii. c. 37. and Macchiavelli, Hist. l. ii. The account of the latter writer differs much from that given by Landino in his Commentary.

v. 63. Mascheroni.] Sassol Mascheroni, a Florentiue, who also murdered his uncle.

v. 66. Camiccione.] Camiccione de' Pazzi of Valdarno, by whom his kinsman Ubertino was treacherously pnt to death.

v. 67. Carlino.] One of the same family. He betrayed the Castel di Piano Travigne, in Valdarno, to the Florentines, after the refugees of the Bianca and Ghibelline party had defended it against a siege for twenty-nine days, in the summer of 1302. See G. Villani, l. viii. c. 52 and Dino Compagni, l. ii.

v. 81. Montaperto.] The defeat of the Guelfi at Montaperto, occasioned by the treachery of Bocca degli Abbati, who, during the engagement, cut off the hand of Giacopo del Vacca de'Pazzi, bearer of the Florentine standard. G. Villani, l. vi. c. 80, and Notes to Canto X. This event happened in 1260.

v. 113. Him of Duera.] Buoso of Cremona, of the family of Duera, who was bribed by Guy de Montfort, to leave a pass between Piedmont and Parma, with the defence of which he had been entrusted by the Ghibellines, open to the army of Charles of Anjou, A.D. 1265, at which the people of Cremona were so enraged, that they extirpated the whole family. G. Villani, l. vii. c. 4.

v. 118. Beccaria.] Abbot of Vallombrosa, who was the Pope's Legate at Florence, where his intrigues in favour of the Ghibellines being discovered, he was beheaded. I do not find the occurrence in Vallini, nor do the commentators say to what pope he was legate. By Landino he is reported to have been from Parma, by Vellutello from Pavia.

v. 118. Soldanieri.] "Gianni Soldanieri," says Villani, Hist. l. vii. c14, "put himself at the head of the people, in the hopes of rising into power, not aware that the result would be mischief to the Ghibelline party, and his own

The Divine Comedy

ruin; an event which seems ever to have befallen him, who has headed the populace in Florence." A.D. 1266.

v. 119. Ganellon.] The betrayer of Charlemain, mentioned by Archbishop Turpin. He is a common instance of treachery with the poets of the middle ages.

> Trop son fol e mal pensant,
> Pis valent que Guenelon.
> > Thibaut, roi de Navarre
> O new Scariot, and new Ganilion,
> O false dissembler, &c.
> > Chaucer, Nonne's Prieste's Tale

And in the Monke's Tale, Peter of Spaine.

v. 119. Tribaldello.] Tribaldello de'Manfredi, who was bribed to betray the city of Faonza, A. D. 1282. G. Villani, l. vii. c. 80

v. 128. Tydeus.] See Statius, Theb. l. viii. ad finem.

CANTO XXXIII.

v. 14. Count Ugolino.] "In the year 1288, in the month of July, Pisa was much divided by competitors for the sovereignty; one party, composed of certain of the Guelphi, being headed by the Judge Nino di Gallura de'Visconti; another, consisting of others of the same faction, by the Count Ugolino de' Gherardeschi; and the third by the Archbishop Ruggieri degli Ubaldini, with the Lanfranchi, Sismondi, Gualandi, and other Ghibelline houses. The Count Ugolino,to effect his purpose, united with the Archbishop and his party, and having betrayed Nino, his sister's son, they contrived that he and his followers should either be driven out of Pisa, or their persons seized. Nino hearing this, and not seeing any means of defending himself, retired to Calci, his castle, and formed an alliance with the Florentines and people of Lucca, against the Pisans. The Count, before Nino was gone, in order to cover his treachery, when everything was settled for his expulsion, quitted Pisa, and repaired to a manor of his called Settimo; whence, as soon as he was informed of Nino's departure, he returned to Pisa with great rejoicing and festivity, and was elevated to the supreme power with every demonstration of triumph and honour. But his greatness was not of long continuauce. It pleased the Almighty that a total reverse of fortune should ensue, as a punishment for his acts of treachery and guilt: for he was said to have poisoned the Count Anselmo da Capraia, his sister's son, on account of the envy and fear excited in his mind by the high esteem in which the gracious manners of Anselmo were held by the Pisans. The power of the Guelphi being so much diminished, the Archbishop devised means to betray the Count Uglino and caused him to be suddenly attacked in his palace by the fury of the people, whom he had exasperated, by telling them that Ugolino had betrayed Pisa, and given up their castles to the citizens of Florence and of Lucca. He was immediately compelled to surrender; his bastard son and his grandson fell in the assault; and two of his sons, with their two sons also, were conveyed to prison." G. Villani l. vii. c. 120.

"In the following march, the Pisans, who had imprisoned the Count Uglino, with two of his sons and two of his grandchildren, the offspring of his son the Count Guelfo, in a tower on the Piazza of the Anzania, caused the tower to be locked, the key thrown into the Arno, and all food to be withheld from them. In a few days they died of hunger; but the Count first with loud cries declared his penitence, and yet neither priest nor friar was allowed to shrive him. All the five, when dead, were dragged out of the prison, and meanly interred; and from thence forward the tower was called the tower of famine, and so shall ever be." Ibid. c. 127.

Chancer has briefly told Ugolino's story. See Monke's Tale, Hugeline of Pise.

v. 29. Unto the mountain.] The mountain S. Giuliano, between Pisa and Lucca.

v. 59. Thou gav'st.]
  Tu ne vestisti
 Queste misere carni, e tu le spoglia.
Imitated by Filicaja, Canz. iii.
 Di questa imperial caduca spoglia
 Tu, Signor, me vestisti e tu mi spoglia:
 Ben puoi'l Regno me tor tu che me'l desti.
And by Maffei, in the Merope:
  Tu disciogleste
 Queste misere membra e tu le annodi.

v. 79. In that fair region.]
 Del bel paese la, dove'l si suona.
Italy as explained by Dante himself, in his treatise De Vulg. Eloq. l. i. c. 8. "Qui autem Si dicunt a praedictis finibus. (Januensiem) Oreintalem (Meridionalis Europae partem) tenent; videlicet usque ad promontorium illud Italiae, qua sinus Adriatici maris incipit et Siciliam."

v. 82. Capraia and Gorgona.] Small islands near the mouth of the Arno.

v. 94. There very weeping suffers not to weep,]
 Lo pianto stesso li pianger non lascia.
So Giusto de'Conti, Bella Mano. Son. "Quanto il ciel."
 Che il troppo pianto a me pianger non lassa.

v. 116. The friar Albigero.] Alberigo de'Manfredi, of Faenza, one of the Frati Godenti, Joyons Friars who having quarrelled with some of his brotherhood, under pretence of wishing to be reconciled, invited them to a banquet, at the conclusion of which he called for the fruit, a signal for the assassins to rush in and dispatch those whom he had marked for destruction. Hence, adds Landino, it is said proverbially of one who has been stabbed, that he has had some of the friar Alberigo's fruit. Thus Pulci, Morg. Magg. c. xxv.
 Le frutte amare di frate Alberico.

v. 123. Ptolomea.] This circle is named Ptolomea from Ptolemy, the son of Abubus, by whom Simon and his sons were murdered, at a great banquet he had made for them. See Maccabees, ch xvi.

v. 126. The glazed tear-drops.]
 -sorrow's eye, glazed with blinding tears.
  Shakspeare, Rich. II. a. 2. s. 2.

v. 136. Branca Doria.] The family of Doria was possessed of great influence in Genoa. Branca is said to have murdered his father-in-law, Michel Zanche, introduced in Canto XXII.

v. 162 Romagna's darkest spirit.] The friar Alberigo.

The Divine Comedy
Canto XXXIV.

v. 6. A wind-mill.] The author of the Caliph Vathek, in the notes to that tale, justly observes, that it is more than probable that Don Quixote's mistake of the wind-mills for giants was suggested to Cervantes by this simile.

v. 37. Three faces.] It can scarcely be doubted but that Milton derived his description of Satan in those lines,

>> Each passion dimm'd his face
> Thrice chang'd with pale, ire, envy, and despair.
>> P. L. b. iv. 114.

from this passage, coupled with the remark of Vellutello upon it:
"The first of these sins is anger which he signifies by the red face; the second, represented by that between pale and yellow is envy and not, as others have said, avarice; and the third, denoted by the black, is a melancholy humour that causes a man's thoughts to be dark and evil, and averse from all joy and tranquillity."

v. 44. Sails.]

>> --His sail-broad vans
> He spreads for flight.
>> Milton, P. L. b. ii. 927.

Compare Spenser, F. Q. b. i. c. xi. st. 10; Ben Jonson's Every Man out of his humour, v. 7; and Fletcher's Prophetess, a. 2. s. 3.

v. 46. Like a bat.] The description of an imaginary being, who is called Typhurgo, in the Zodiacus Vitae, has some touches very like this of Dante's Lucifer.

> Ingentem vidi regem ingentique sedentem
> In solio, crines flammanti stemmate cinctum
>> ---utrinque patentes
> Alae humeris magnae, quales vespertilionum
> Membranis contextae amplis--
> Nudus erat longis sed opertus corpora villis.
>> M. Palingenii, Zod. Vit. l. ix.
> A mighty king I might discerne,
>> Plac'd hie on lofty chaire,
> His haire with fyry garland deckt
>> Puft up in fiendish wise.
>   x x x   x x   x
>> Large wings on him did grow
> Framde like the wings of flinder mice, &c.
>> Googe's Translation

v. 61. Brutus.] Landino struggles, but I fear in vain, to extricate Brutus from the unworthy lot which is here assigned him. He maintains, that by Brutus and Cassius are not meant the individuals known by those names, but any who put a lawful monarch to death. Yet if Caesar was such, the conspirators might be regarded as deserving of their doom.

v. 89. Within one hour and half of noon.] The poet uses the Hebrew manner of computing the day, according to which the third hour answers to our twelve o'clock at noon.

v. 120. By what of firm land on this side appears.] The mountain of Purgatory.

v.123. The vaulted tomb.] "La tomba." This word is used to express the whole depth of the infernal region.

PURGATORY

CANTO I

O'er better waves to speed her rapid course
The light bark of my genius lifts the sail,
Well pleas'd to leave so cruel sea behind;
And of that second region will I sing,
In which the human spirit from sinful blot
Is purg'd, and for ascent to Heaven prepares.
    Here, O ye hallow'd Nine! for in your train
I follow, here the deadened strain revive;
Nor let Calliope refuse to sound
A somewhat higher song, of that loud tone,
Which when the wretched birds of chattering note
Had heard, they of forgiveness lost all hope.
    Sweet hue of eastern sapphire, that was spread
O'er the serene aspect of the pure air,
High up as the first circle, to mine eyes
Unwonted joy renew'd, soon as I 'scap'd
Forth from the atmosphere of deadly gloom,
That had mine eyes and bosom fill'd with grief.
The radiant planet, that to love invites,
Made all the orient laugh, and veil'd beneath
The Pisces' light, that in his escort came.
    To the right hand I turn'd, and fix'd my mind
On the' other pole attentive, where I saw
Four stars ne'er seen before save by the ken
Of our first parents. Heaven of their rays
Seem'd joyous. O thou northern site, bereft
Indeed, and widow'd, since of these depriv'd!
    As from this view I had desisted, straight
Turning a little tow'rds the other pole,
There from whence now the wain had disappear'd,
I saw an old man standing by my side
Alone, so worthy of rev'rence in his look,
That ne'er from son to father more was ow'd.
Low down his beard and mix'd with hoary white
Descended, like his locks, which parting fell
Upon his breast in double fold. The beams
Of those four luminaries on his face
So brightly shone, and with such radiance clear
Deck'd it, that I beheld him as the sun.

Dante Alighieri

"Say who are ye, that stemming the blind stream,
Forth from th' eternal prison-house have fled?"
He spoke and moved those venerable plumes.
"Who hath conducted, or with lantern sure
Lights you emerging from the depth of night,
That makes the infernal valley ever black?
Are the firm statutes of the dread abyss
Broken, or in high heaven new laws ordain'd,
That thus, condemn'd, ye to my caves approach?"

    My guide, then laying hold on me, by words
And intimations given with hand and head,
Made my bent knees and eye submissive pay
Due reverence; then thus to him replied.

    "Not of myself I come; a Dame from heaven
Descending, had besought me in my charge
To bring. But since thy will implies, that more
Our true condition I unfold at large,
Mine is not to deny thee thy request.
This mortal ne'er hath seen the farthest gloom.
But erring by his folly had approach'd
So near, that little space was left to turn.
Then, as before I told, I was dispatch'd
To work his rescue, and no way remain'd
Save this which I have ta'en. I have display'd
Before him all the regions of the bad;
And purpose now those spirits to display,
That under thy command are purg'd from sin.
How I have brought him would be long to say.
From high descends the virtue, by whose aid
I to thy sight and hearing him have led.
Now may our coming please thee. In the search
Of liberty he journeys: that how dear
They know, who for her sake have life refus'd.
Thou knowest, to whom death for her was sweet
In Utica, where thou didst leave those weeds,
That in the last great day will shine so bright.
For us the' eternal edicts are unmov'd:
He breathes, and I am free of Minos' power,
Abiding in that circle where the eyes
Of thy chaste Marcia beam, who still in look
Prays thee, O hallow'd spirit! to own her shine.
Then by her love we' implore thee, let us pass
Through thy sev'n regions; for which best thanks
I for thy favour will to her return,
If mention there below thou not disdain."

    "Marcia so pleasing in my sight was found,"
He then to him rejoin'd, "while I was there,
That all she ask'd me I was fain to grant.
Now that beyond the' accursed stream she dwells,
She may no longer move me, by that law,

Which was ordain'd me, when I issued thence.
Not so, if Dame from heaven, as thou sayst,
Moves and directs thee; then no flattery needs.
Enough for me that in her name thou ask.
Go therefore now: and with a slender reed
See that thou duly gird him, and his face
Lave, till all sordid stain thou wipe from thence.
For not with eye, by any cloud obscur'd,
Would it be seemly before him to come,
Who stands the foremost minister in heaven.
This islet all around, there far beneath,
Where the wave beats it, on the oozy bed
Produces store of reeds. No other plant,
Cover'd with leaves, or harden'd in its stalk,
There lives, not bending to the water's sway.
After, this way return not; but the sun
Will show you, that now rises, where to take
The mountain in its easiest ascent."

    He disappear'd; and I myself uprais'd
Speechless, and to my guide retiring close,
Toward him turn'd mine eyes. He thus began;
"My son! observant thou my steps pursue.
We must retreat to rearward, for that way
The champain to its low extreme declines."

    The dawn had chas'd the matin hour of prime,
Which deaf before it, so that from afar
I spy'd the trembling of the ocean stream.

    We travers'd the deserted plain, as one
Who, wander'd from his track, thinks every step
Trodden in vain till he regain the path.

    When we had come, where yet the tender dew
Strove with the sun, and in a place, where fresh
The wind breath'd o'er it, while it slowly dried;
Both hands extended on the watery grass
My master plac'd, in graceful act and kind.
Whence I of his intent before appriz'd,
Stretch'd out to him my cheeks suffus'd with tears.
There to my visage he anew restor'd
That hue, which the dun shades of hell conceal'd.

    Then on the solitary shore arriv'd,
That never sailing on its waters saw
Man, that could after measure back his course,
He girt me in such manner as had pleas'd
Him who instructed, and O, strange to tell!
As he selected every humble plant,
Wherever one was pluck'd, another there
Resembling, straightway in its place arose.

Dante Alighieri

CANTO II

Now had the sun to that horizon reach'd,
That covers, with the most exalted point
Of its meridian circle, Salem's walls,
And night, that opposite to him her orb
Sounds, from the stream of Ganges issued forth,
Holding the scales, that from her hands are dropp'd
When she reigns highest: so that where I was,
Aurora's white and vermeil-tinctur'd cheek
To orange turn'd as she in age increas'd.

    Meanwhile we linger'd by the water's brink,
Like men, who, musing on their road, in thought
Journey, while motionless the body rests.
When lo! as near upon the hour of dawn,
Through the thick vapours Mars with fiery beam
Glares down in west, over the ocean floor;
So seem'd, what once again I hope to view,
A light so swiftly coming through the sea,
No winged course might equal its career.
From which when for a space I had withdrawn
Thine eyes, to make inquiry of my guide,
Again I look'd and saw it grown in size
And brightness: thou on either side appear'd
Something, but what I knew not of bright hue,
And by degrees from underneath it came
Another. My preceptor silent yet
Stood, while the brightness, that we first discern'd,
Open'd the form of wings: then when he knew
The pilot, cried aloud, "Down, down; bend low
Thy knees; behold God's angel: fold thy hands:
Now shalt thou see true Ministers indeed.
Lo how all human means he sets at naught!
So that nor oar he needs, nor other sail
Except his wings, between such distant shores.
Lo how straight up to heaven he holds them rear'd,
Winnowing the air with those eternal plumes,
That not like mortal hairs fall off or change!"

    As more and more toward us came, more bright
Appear'd the bird of God, nor could the eye
Endure his splendor near: I mine bent down.
He drove ashore in a small bark so swift
And light, that in its course no wave it drank.
The heav'nly steersman at the prow was seen,
Visibly written blessed in his looks.
Within a hundred spirits and more there sat.
"In Exitu Israel de Aegypto;"
All with one voice together sang, with what
In the remainder of that hymn is writ.

139

Then soon as with the sign of holy cross
He bless'd them, they at once leap'd out on land,
The swiftly as he came return'd. The crew,
There left, appear'd astounded with the place,
Gazing around as one who sees new sights.

     From every side the sun darted his beams,
And with his arrowy radiance from mid heav'n
Had chas'd the Capricorn, when that strange tribe
Lifting their eyes towards us: If ye know,
Declare what path will Lead us to the mount."

     Them Virgil answer'd. "Ye suppose perchance
Us well acquainted with this place: but here,
We, as yourselves, are strangers. Not long erst
We came, before you but a little space,
By other road so rough and hard, that now
The' ascent will seem to us as play." The spirits,
Who from my breathing had perceiv'd I liv'd,
Grew pale with wonder. As the multitude
Flock round a herald, sent with olive branch,
To hear what news he brings, and in their haste
Tread one another down, e'en so at sight
Of me those happy spirits were fix'd, each one
Forgetful of its errand, to depart,
Where cleans'd from sin, it might be made all fair.

     Then one I saw darting before the rest
With such fond ardour to embrace me, I
To do the like was mov'd. O shadows vain
Except in outward semblance! thrice my hands
I clasp'd behind it, they as oft return'd
Empty into my breast again. Surprise
I needs must think was painted in my looks,
For that the shadow smil'd and backward drew.
To follow it I hasten'd, but with voice
Of sweetness it enjoin'd me to desist.
Then who it was I knew, and pray'd of it,
To talk with me, it would a little pause.
It answered: "Thee as in my mortal frame
I lov'd, so loos'd forth it I love thee still,
And therefore pause; but why walkest thou here?"

     "Not without purpose once more to return,
Thou find'st me, my Casella, where I am
Journeying this way;" I said, "but how of thee
Hath so much time been lost?" He answer'd straight:
"No outrage hath been done to me, if he
Who when and whom he chooses takes, me oft
This passage hath denied, since of just will
His will he makes. These three months past indeed,
He, whose chose to enter, with free leave
Hath taken; whence I wand'ring by the shore
Where Tyber's wave grows salt, of him gain'd kind

Admittance, at that river's mouth, tow'rd which
His wings are pointed, for there always throng
All such as not to Archeron descend."
    Then I: "If new laws have not quite destroy'd
Memory and use of that sweet song of love,
That while all my cares had power to 'swage;
Please thee with it a little to console
My spirit, that incumber'd with its frame,
Travelling so far, of pain is overcome."
    "Love that discourses in my thoughts." He then
Began in such soft accents, that within
The sweetness thrills me yet. My gentle guide
And all who came with him, so well were pleas'd,
That seem'd naught else might in their thoughts have room.
    Fast fix'd in mute attention to his notes
We stood, when lo! that old man venerable
Exclaiming, "How is this, ye tardy spirits?
What negligence detains you loit'ring here?
Run to the mountain to cast off those scales,
That from your eyes the sight of God conceal."
    As a wild flock of pigeons, to their food
Collected, blade or tares, without their pride
Accustom'd, and in still and quiet sort,
If aught alarm them, suddenly desert
Their meal, assail'd by more important care;
So I that new-come troop beheld, the song
Deserting, hasten to the mountain's side,
As one who goes yet where he tends knows not.
Nor with less hurried step did we depart.

CANTO III

Them sudden flight had scatter'd over the plain,
Turn'd tow'rds the mountain, whither reason's voice
Drives us; I to my faithful company
Adhering, left it not. For how of him
Depriv'd, might I have sped, or who beside
Would o'er the mountainous tract have led my steps
He with the bitter pang of self-remorse
Seem'd smitten. O clear conscience and upright
How doth a little fling wound thee sore!
    Soon as his feet desisted (slack'ning pace),
From haste, that mars all decency of act,
My mind, that in itself before was wrapt,
Its thoughts expanded, as with joy restor'd:
And full against the steep ascent I set
My face, where highest to heav'n its top o'erflows.
    The sun, that flar'd behind, with ruddy beam
Before my form was broken; for in me

His rays resistance met. I turn'd aside
With fear of being left, when I beheld
Only before myself the ground obscur'd.
When thus my solace, turning him around,
Bespake me kindly: "Why distrustest thou?
Believ'st not I am with thee, thy sure guide?
It now is evening there, where buried lies
The body, in which I cast a shade, remov'd
To Naples from Brundusium's wall. Nor thou
Marvel, if before me no shadow fall,
More than that in the sky element
One ray obstructs not other. To endure
Torments of heat and cold extreme, like frames
That virtue hath dispos'd, which how it works
Wills not to us should be reveal'd. Insane
Who hopes, our reason may that space explore,
Which holds three persons in one substance knit.
Seek not the wherefore, race of human kind;
Could ye have seen the whole, no need had been
For Mary to bring forth. Moreover ye
Have seen such men desiring fruitlessly;
To whose desires repose would have been giv'n,
That now but serve them for eternal grief.
I speak of Plato, and the Stagyrite,
And others many more." And then he bent
Downwards his forehead, and in troubled mood
Broke off his speech. Meanwhile we had arriv'd
Far as the mountain's foot, and there the rock
Found of so steep ascent, that nimblest steps
To climb it had been vain. The most remote
Most wild untrodden path, in all the tract
'Twixt Lerice and Turbia were to this
A ladder easy' and open of access.

    "Who knows on which hand now the steep declines?"
My master said and paus'd, "so that he may
Ascend, who journeys without aid of wine,?"
And while with looks directed to the ground
The meaning of the pathway he explor'd,
And I gaz'd upward round the stony height,
Of spirits, that toward us mov'd their steps,
Yet moving seem'd not, they so slow approach'd.

    I thus my guide address'd: "Upraise thine eyes,
Lo that way some, of whom thou may'st obtain
Counsel, if of thyself thou find'st it not!"

    Straightway he look'd, and with free speech replied:
"Let us tend thither: they but softly come.
And thou be firm in hope, my son belov'd."

    Now was that people distant far in space
A thousand paces behind ours, as much
As at a throw the nervous arm could fling,

When all drew backward on the messy crags
Of the steep bank, and firmly stood unmov'd
As one who walks in doubt might stand to look.
    "O spirits perfect! O already chosen!"
Virgil to them began, "by that blest peace,
Which, as I deem, is for you all prepar'd,
Instruct us where the mountain low declines,
So that attempt to mount it be not vain.
For who knows most, him loss of time most grieves."
    As sheep, that step from forth their fold, by one,
Or pairs, or three at once; meanwhile the rest
Stand fearfully, bending the eye and nose
To ground, and what the foremost does, that do
The others, gath'ring round her, if she stops,
Simple and quiet, nor the cause discern;
So saw I moving to advance the first,
Who of that fortunate crew were at the head,
Of modest mien and graceful in their gait.
When they before me had beheld the light
From my right side fall broken on the ground,
So that the shadow reach'd the cave, they stopp'd
And somewhat back retir'd: the same did all,
Who follow'd, though unweeting of the cause
    "Unask'd of you, yet freely I confess,
This is a human body which ye see.
That the sun's light is broken on the ground,
Marvel not: but believe, that not without
Virtue deriv'd from Heaven, we to climb
Over this wall aspire." So them bespake
My master; and that virtuous tribe rejoin'd;
" Turn, and before you there the entrance lies,"
Making a signal to us with bent hands.
    Then of them one began. "Whoe'er thou art,
Who journey'st thus this way, thy visage turn,
Think if me elsewhere thou hast ever seen."
    I tow'rds him turn'd, and with fix'd eye beheld.
Comely, and fair, and gentle of aspect,
He seem'd, but on one brow a gash was mark'd.
    When humbly I disclaim'd to have beheld
Him ever: "Now behold!" he said, and show'd
High on his breast a wound: then smiling spake.
    "I am Manfredi, grandson to the Queen
Costanza: whence I pray thee, when return'd,
To my fair daughter go, the parent glad
Of Aragonia and Sicilia's pride;
And of the truth inform her, if of me
Aught else be told. When by two mortal blows
My frame was shatter'd, I betook myself
Weeping to him, who of free will forgives.
My sins were horrible; but so wide arms

Hath goodness infinite, that it receives
All who turn to it. Had this text divine
Been of Cosenza's shepherd better scann'd,
Who then by Clement on my hunt was set,
Yet at the bridge's head my bones had lain,
Near Benevento, by the heavy mole
Protected; but the rain now drenches them,
And the wind drives, out of the kingdom's bounds,
Far as the stream of Verde, where, with lights
Extinguish'd, he remov'd them from their bed.
Yet by their curse we are not so destroy'd,
But that the eternal love may turn, while hope
Retains her verdant blossoms. True it is,
That such one as in contumacy dies
Against the holy church, though he repent,
Must wander thirty-fold for all the time
In his presumption past; if such decree
Be not by prayers of good men shorter made
Look therefore if thou canst advance my bliss;
Revealing to my good Costanza, how
Thou hast beheld me, and beside the terms
Laid on me of that interdict; for here
By means of those below much profit comes."

CANTO IV

When by sensations of delight or pain,
That any of our faculties hath seiz'd,
Entire the soul collects herself, it seems
She is intent upon that power alone,
And thus the error is disprov'd which holds
The soul not singly lighted in the breast.
And therefore when as aught is heard or seen,
That firmly keeps the soul toward it turn'd,
Time passes, and a man perceives it not.
For that, whereby he hearken, is one power,
Another that, which the whole spirit hash;
This is as it were bound, while that is free.
    This found I true by proof, hearing that spirit
And wond'ring; for full fifty steps aloft
The sun had measur'd unobserv'd of me,
When we arriv'd where all with one accord
The spirits shouted, "Here is what ye ask."
    A larger aperture ofttimes is stopp'd
With forked stake of thorn by villager,
When the ripe grape imbrowns, than was the path,
By which my guide, and I behind him close,
Ascended solitary, when that troop
Departing left us. On Sanleo's road

Dante Alighieri

Who journeys, or to Noli low descends,
Or mounts Bismantua's height, must use his feet;
But here a man had need to fly, I mean
With the swift wing and plumes of high desire,
Conducted by his aid, who gave me hope,
And with light furnish'd to direct my way.

    We through the broken rock ascended, close
Pent on each side, while underneath the ground
Ask'd help of hands and feet. When we arriv'd
Near on the highest ridge of the steep bank,
Where the plain level open'd I exclaim'd,
"O master! say which way can we proceed?"

    He answer'd, "Let no step of thine recede.
Behind me gain the mountain, till to us
Some practis'd guide appear." That eminence
Was lofty that no eye might reach its point,
And the side proudly rising, more than line
From the mid quadrant to the centre drawn.
I wearied thus began: "Parent belov'd!
Turn, and behold how I remain alone,
If thou stay not." --" My son!" He straight reply'd,
"Thus far put forth thy strength; "and to a track
Pointed, that, on this side projecting, round
Circles the hill. His words so spurr'd me on,
That I behind him clamb'ring, forc'd myself,
Till my feet press'd the circuit plain beneath.
There both together seated, turn'd we round
To eastward, whence was our ascent: and oft
Many beside have with delight look'd back.

    First on the nether shores I turn'd my eyes,
Then rais'd them to the sun, and wond'ring mark'd
That from the left it smote us. Soon perceiv'd
That Poet sage how at the car of light
Amaz'd I stood, where 'twixt us and the north
Its course it enter'd. Whence he thus to me:
"Were Leda's offspring now in company
Of that broad mirror, that high up and low
Imparts his light beneath, thou might'st behold
The ruddy zodiac nearer to the bears
Wheel, if its ancient course it not forsook.
How that may be if thou would'st think; within
Pond'ring, imagine Sion with this mount
Plac'd on the earth, so that to both be one
Horizon, and two hemispheres apart,
Where lies the path that Phaeton ill knew
To guide his erring chariot: thou wilt see
How of necessity by this on one
He passes, while by that on the' other side,
If with clear view shine intellect attend."

"Of truth, kind teacher!" I exclaim'd, "so clear
Aught saw I never, as I now discern
Where seem'd my ken to fail, that the mid orb
Of the supernal motion (which in terms
Of art is called the Equator, and remains
Ever between the sun and winter) for the cause
Thou hast assign'd, from hence toward the north
Departs, when those who in the Hebrew land
Inhabit, see it tow'rds the warmer part.
But if it please thee, I would gladly know,
How far we have to journey: for the hill
Mounts higher, than this sight of mine can mount."

    He thus to me: "Such is this steep ascent,
That it is ever difficult at first,
But, more a man proceeds, less evil grows.
When pleasant it shall seem to thee, so much
That upward going shall be easy to thee.
As in a vessel to go down the tide,
Then of this path thou wilt have reach'd the end.
There hope to rest thee from thy toil. No more
I answer, and thus far for certain know."
As he his words had spoken, near to us
A voice there sounded: "Yet ye first perchance
May to repose you by constraint be led."
At sound thereof each turn'd, and on the left
A huge stone we beheld, of which nor I
Nor he before was ware. Thither we drew,
find there were some, who in the shady place
Behind the rock were standing, as a man
Thru' idleness might stand. Among them one,
Who seem'd to me much wearied, sat him down,
And with his arms did fold his knees about,
Holding his face between them downward bent.

    "Sweet Sir!" I cry'd, "behold that man, who shows
Himself more idle, than if laziness
Were sister to him." Straight he turn'd to us,
And, o'er the thigh lifting his face, observ'd,
Then in these accents spake: "Up then, proceed
Thou valiant one." Straight who it was I knew;
Nor could the pain I felt (for want of breath
Still somewhat urg'd me) hinder my approach.
And when I came to him, he scarce his head
Uplifted, saying "Well hast thou discern'd,
How from the left the sun his chariot leads."

    His lazy acts and broken words my lips
To laughter somewhat mov'd; when I began:
"Belacqua, now for thee I grieve no more.
But tell, why thou art seated upright there?
Waitest thou escort to conduct thee hence?
Or blame I only shine accustom'd ways?"

Dante Alighieri

Then he: "My brother, of what use to mount,
When to my suffering would not let me pass
The bird of God, who at the portal sits?
Behooves so long that heav'n first bear me round
Without its limits, as in life it bore,
Because I to the end repentant Sighs
Delay'd, if prayer do not aid me first,
That riseth up from heart which lives in grace.
What other kind avails, not heard in heaven?'"
  Before me now the Poet up the mount
Ascending, cried: "Haste thee, for see the sun
Has touch'd the point meridian, and the night
Now covers with her foot Marocco's shore."

CANTO V

Now had I left those spirits, and pursued
The steps of my Conductor, when beheld
Pointing the finger at me one exclaim'd:
"See how it seems as if the light not shone
From the left hand of him beneath, and he,
As living, seems to be led on." Mine eyes
I at that sound reverting, saw them gaze
Through wonder first at me, and then at me
And the light broken underneath, by turns.
"Why are thy thoughts thus riveted?" my guide
Exclaim'd, "that thou hast slack'd thy pace? or how
Imports it thee, what thing is whisper'd here?
Come after me, and to their babblings leave
The crowd. Be as a tower, that, firmly set,
Shakes not its top for any blast that blows!
He, in whose bosom thought on thought shoots out,
Still of his aim is wide, in that the one
Sicklies and wastes to nought the other's strength."
  What other could I answer save "I come?"
I said it, somewhat with that colour ting'd
Which ofttimes pardon meriteth for man.
  Meanwhile traverse along the hill there came,
A little way before us, some who sang
The "Miserere" in responsive Strains.
When they perceiv'd that through my body I
Gave way not for the rays to pass, their song
Straight to a long and hoarse exclaim they chang'd;
And two of them, in guise of messengers,
Ran on to meet us, and inquiring ask'd:
Of your condition we would gladly learn."
  To them my guide. "Ye may return, and bear
Tidings to them who sent you, that his frame
Is real flesh. If, as I deem, to view

147

The Divine Comedy

His shade they paus'd, enough is answer'd them.
Him let them honour, they may prize him well."
    Ne'er saw I fiery vapours with such speed
Cut through the serene air at fall of night,
Nor August's clouds athwart the setting sun,
That upward these did not in shorter space
Return; and, there arriving, with the rest
Wheel back on us, as with loose rein a troop.
    "Many," exclaim'd the bard, "are these, who throng
Around us: to petition thee they come.
Go therefore on, and listen as thou go'st."
    "O spirit! who go'st on to blessedness
With the same limbs, that clad thee at thy birth."
Shouting they came, "a little rest thy step.
Look if thou any one amongst our tribe
Hast e'er beheld, that tidings of him there
Thou mayst report. Ah, wherefore go'st thou on?
Ah wherefore tarriest thou not? We all
By violence died, and to our latest hour
Were sinners, but then warn'd by light from heav'n,
So that, repenting and forgiving, we
Did issue out of life at peace with God,
Who with desire to see him fills our heart."
    Then I: "The visages of all I scan
Yet none of ye remember. But if aught,
That I can do, may please you, gentle spirits!
Speak; and I will perform it, by that peace,
Which on the steps of guide so excellent
Following from world to world intent I seek."
    In answer he began: "None here distrusts
Thy kindness, though not promis'd with an oath;
So as the will fail not for want of power.
Whence I, who sole before the others speak,
Entreat thee, if thou ever see that land,
Which lies between Romagna and the realm
Of Charles, that of thy courtesy thou pray
Those who inhabit Fano, that for me
Their adorations duly be put up,
By which I may purge off my grievous sins.
From thence I came. But the deep passages,
Whence issued out the blood wherein I dwelt,
Upon my bosom in Antenor's land
Were made, where to be more secure I thought.
The author of the deed was Este's prince,
Who, more than right could warrant, with his wrath
Pursued me. Had I towards Mira fled,
When overta'en at Oriaco, still
Might I have breath'd. But to the marsh I sped,
And in the mire and rushes tangled there
Fell, and beheld my life-blood float the plain."

Dante Alighieri

    Then said another: "Ah! so may the wish,
That takes thee o'er the mountain, be fulfill'd,
As thou shalt graciously give aid to mine.
Of Montefeltro I; Buonconte I:
Giovanna nor none else have care for me,
Sorrowing with these I therefore go." I thus:
"From Campaldino's field what force or chance
Drew thee, that ne'er thy sepulture was known?"
    "Oh!" answer'd he, "at Casentino's foot
A stream there courseth, nam'd Archiano, sprung
In Apennine above the Hermit's seat.
E'en where its name is cancel'd, there came I,
Pierc'd in the heart, fleeing away on foot,
And bloodying the plain. Here sight and speech
Fail'd me, and finishing with Mary's name
I fell, and tenantless my flesh remain'd.
I will report the truth; which thou again0
Tell to the living. Me God's angel took,
Whilst he of hell exclaim'd: "O thou from heav'n!
Say wherefore hast thou robb'd me? Thou of him
Th' eternal portion bear'st with thee away
For one poor tear that he deprives me of.
But of the other, other rule I make."
    "Thou knowest how in the atmosphere collects
That vapour dank, returning into water,
Soon as it mounts where cold condenses it.
That evil will, which in his intellect
Still follows evil, came, and rais'd the wind
And smoky mist, by virtue of the power
Given by his nature. Thence the valley, soon
As day was spent, he cover'd o'er with cloud
From Pratomagno to the mountain range,
And stretch'd the sky above, so that the air
Impregnate chang'd to water. Fell the rain,
And to the fosses came all that the land
Contain'd not; and, as mightiest streams are wont,
To the great river with such headlong sweep
Rush'd, that nought stay'd its course. My stiffen'd frame
Laid at his mouth the fell Archiano found,
And dash'd it into Arno, from my breast
Loos'ning the cross, that of myself I made
When overcome with pain. He hurl'd me on,
Along the banks and bottom of his course;
Then in his muddy spoils encircling wrapt."
    "Ah! when thou to the world shalt be return'd,
And rested after thy long road," so spake
Next the third spirit; "then remember me.
I once was Pia. Sienna gave me life,
Maremma took it from me. That he knows,
Who me with jewell'd ring had first espous'd."

The Divine Comedy
CANTO VI

When from their game of dice men separate,
He, who hath lost, remains in sadness fix'd,
Revolving in his mind, what luckless throws
He cast: but meanwhile all the company
Go with the other; one before him runs,
And one behind his mantle twitches, one
Fast by his side bids him remember him.
He stops not; and each one, to whom his hand
Is stretch'd, well knows he bids him stand aside;
And thus he from the press defends himself.
E'en such was I in that close-crowding throng;
And turning so my face around to all,
And promising, I 'scap'd from it with pains.

    Here of Arezzo him I saw, who fell
By Ghino's cruel arm; and him beside,
Who in his chase was swallow'd by the stream.
Here Frederic Novello, with his hand
Stretch'd forth, entreated; and of Pisa he,
Who put the good Marzuco to such proof
Of constancy. Count Orso I beheld;
And from its frame a soul dismiss'd for spite
And envy, as it said, but for no crime:
I speak of Peter de la Brosse; and here,
While she yet lives, that Lady of Brabant
Let her beware; lest for so false a deed
She herd with worse than these. When I was freed
From all those spirits, who pray'd for others' prayers
To hasten on their state of blessedness;
Straight I began: "O thou, my luminary!
It seems expressly in thy text denied,
That heaven's supreme decree can never bend
To supplication; yet with this design
Do these entreat. Can then their hope be vain,
Or is thy saying not to me reveal'd?"

    He thus to me: "Both what I write is plain,
And these deceiv'd not in their hope, if well
Thy mind consider, that the sacred height
Of judgment doth not stoop, because love's flame
In a short moment all fulfils, which he
Who sojourns here, in right should satisfy.
Besides, when I this point concluded thus,
By praying no defect could be supplied;
Because the pray'r had none access to God.
Yet in this deep suspicion rest thou not
Contented unless she assure thee so,
Who betwixt truth and mind infuses light.
I know not if thou take me right; I mean

Dante Alighieri

Beatrice. Her thou shalt behold above,
Upon this mountain's crown, fair seat of joy."
    Then I: "Sir! let us mend our speed; for now
I tire not as before; and lo! the hill
Stretches its shadow far." He answer'd thus:
"Our progress with this day shall be as much
As we may now dispatch; but otherwise
Than thou supposest is the truth. For there
Thou canst not be, ere thou once more behold
Him back returning, who behind the steep
Is now so hidden, that as erst his beam
Thou dost not break. But lo! a spirit there
Stands solitary, and toward us looks:
It will instruct us in the speediest way."
    We soon approach'd it. O thou Lombard spirit!
How didst thou stand, in high abstracted mood,
Scarce moving with slow dignity thine eyes!
It spoke not aught, but let us onward pass,
Eyeing us as a lion on his watch.
I3ut Virgil with entreaty mild advanc'd,
Requesting it to show the best ascent.
It answer to his question none return'd,
But of our country and our kind of life
Demanded. When my courteous guide began,
"Mantua," the solitary shadow quick
Rose towards us from the place in which it stood,
And cry'd, "Mantuan! I am thy countryman
Sordello." Each the other then embrac'd.
    Ah slavish Italy! thou inn of grief,
Vessel without a pilot in loud storm,
Lady no longer of fair provinces,
But brothel-house impure! this gentle spirit,
Ev'n from the Pleasant sound of his dear land
Was prompt to greet a fellow citizen
With such glad cheer; while now thy living ones
In thee abide not without war; and one
Malicious gnaws another, ay of those
Whom the same wall and the same moat contains,
Seek, wretched one! around thy sea-coasts wide;
Then homeward to thy bosom turn, and mark
If any part of the sweet peace enjoy.
What boots it, that thy reins Justinian's hand
Befitted, if thy saddle be unpress'd?
Nought doth he now but aggravate thy shame.
Ah people! thou obedient still shouldst live,
And in the saddle let thy Caesar sit,
If well thou marked'st that which God commands
    Look how that beast to felness hath relaps'd
From having lost correction of the spur,
Since to the bridle thou hast set thine hand,

O German Albert! who abandon'st her,
That is grown savage and unmanageable,
When thou should'st clasp her flanks with forked heels.
Just judgment from the stars fall on thy blood!
And be it strange and manifest to all!
Such as may strike thy successor with dread!
For that thy sire and thou have suffer'd thus,
Through greediness of yonder realms detain'd,
The garden of the empire to run waste.
Come see the Capulets and Montagues,
The Philippeschi and Monaldi! man
Who car'st for nought! those sunk in grief, and these
With dire suspicion rack'd. Come, cruel one!
Come and behold the' oppression of the nobles,
And mark their injuries: and thou mayst see.
What safety Santafiore can supply.
Come and behold thy Rome, who calls on thee,
Desolate widow! day and night with moans:
"My Caesar, why dost thou desert my side?"
Come and behold what love among thy people:
And if no pity touches thee for us,
Come and blush for thine own report. For me,
If it be lawful, O Almighty Power,
Who wast in earth for our sakes crucified!
Are thy just eyes turn'd elsewhere? or is this
A preparation in the wond'rous depth
Of thy sage counsel made, for some good end,
Entirely from our reach of thought cut off?
So are the' Italian cities all o'erthrong'd
With tyrants, and a great Marcellus made
Of every petty factious villager.

    My Florence! thou mayst well remain unmov'd
At this digression, which affects not thee:
Thanks to thy people, who so wisely speed.
Many have justice in their heart, that long
Waiteth for counsel to direct the bow,
Or ere it dart unto its aim: but shine
Have it on their lip's edge. Many refuse
To bear the common burdens: readier thine
Answer uneall'd, and cry, "Behold I stoop!"

    Make thyself glad, for thou hast reason now,
Thou wealthy! thou at peace! thou wisdom-fraught!
Facts best witness if I speak the truth.
Athens and Lacedaemon, who of old
Enacted laws, for civil arts renown'd,
Made little progress in improving life
Tow'rds thee, who usest such nice subtlety,
That to the middle of November scarce
Reaches the thread thou in October weav'st.
How many times, within thy memory,

Customs, and laws, and coins, and offices
Have been by thee renew'd, and people chang'd!
    If thou remember'st well and can'st see clear,
Thou wilt perceive thyself like a sick wretch,
Who finds no rest upon her down, hut oft
Shifting her side, short respite seeks from pain.

CANTO VII

After their courteous greetings joyfully
Sev'n times exchang'd, Sordello backward drew
Exclaiming, "Who are ye?" "Before this mount
By spirits worthy of ascent to God
Was sought, my bones had by Octavius' care
Been buried. I am Virgil, for no sin
Depriv'd of heav'n, except for lack of faith."
    So answer'd him in few my gentle guide.
    As one, who aught before him suddenly
Beholding, whence his wonder riseth, cries
"It is yet is not," wav'ring in belief;
Such he appear'd; then downward bent his eyes,
And drawing near with reverential step,
Caught him, where of mean estate might clasp
His lord. "Glory of Latium!" he exclaim'd,
"In whom our tongue its utmost power display'd!
Boast of my honor'd birth-place! what desert
Of mine, what favour rather undeserv'd,
Shows thee to me? If I to hear that voice
Am worthy, say if from below thou com'st
And from what cloister's pale?"--"Through every orb
Of that sad region," he reply'd, "thus far
Am I arriv'd, by heav'nly influence led
And with such aid I come. There is a place
There underneath, not made by torments sad,
But by dun shades alone; where mourning's voice
Sounds not of anguish sharp, but breathes in sighs.
There I with little innocents abide,
Who by death's fangs were bitten, ere exempt
From human taint. There I with those abide,
Who the three holy virtues put not on,
But understood the rest, and without blame
Follow'd them all. But if thou know'st and canst,
Direct us, how we soonest may arrive,
Where Purgatory its true beginning takes."
    He answer'd thus: "We have no certain place
Assign'd us: upwards I may go or round,
Far as I can, I join thee for thy guide.
But thou beholdest now how day declines:
And upwards to proceed by night, our power

The Divine Comedy

Excels: therefore it may be well to choose
A place of pleasant sojourn. To the right
Some spirits sit apart retir'd. If thou
Consentest, I to these will lead thy steps:
And thou wilt know them, not without delight."

    "How chances this?" was answer'd; "who so wish'd
To ascend by night, would he be thence debarr'd
By other, or through his own weakness fail?"

    The good Sordello then, along the ground
Trailing his finger, spoke: "Only this line
Thou shalt not overpass, soon as the sun
Hath disappear'd; not that aught else impedes
Thy going upwards, save the shades of night.
These with the wont of power perplex the will.
With them thou haply mightst return beneath,
Or to and fro around the mountain's side
Wander, while day is in the horizon shut."

    My master straight, as wond'ring at his speech,
Exclaim'd: "Then lead us quickly, where thou sayst,
That, while we stay, we may enjoy delight."

    A little space we were remov'd from thence,
When I perceiv'd the mountain hollow'd out.
Ev'n as large valleys hollow'd out on earth,

    "That way," the' escorting spirit cried, "we go,
Where in a bosom the high bank recedes:
And thou await renewal of the day."

    Betwixt the steep and plain a crooked path
Led us traverse into the ridge's side,
Where more than half the sloping edge expires.
Refulgent gold, and silver thrice refin'd,
And scarlet grain and ceruse, Indian wood
Of lucid dye serene, fresh emeralds
But newly broken, by the herbs and flowers
Plac'd in that fair recess, in color all
Had been surpass'd, as great surpasses less.
Nor nature only there lavish'd her hues,
But of the sweetness of a thousand smells
A rare and undistinguish'd fragrance made.

    "Salve Regina," on the grass and flowers
Here chanting I beheld those spirits sit
Who not beyond the valley could be seen.

    "Before the west'ring sun sink to his bed,"
Began the Mantuan, who our steps had turn'd,
    "'Mid those desires not that I lead ye on.
For from this eminence ye shall discern
Better the acts and visages of all,
Than in the nether vale among them mix'd.
He, who sits high above the rest, and seems
To have neglected that he should have done,
And to the others' song moves not his lip,

Dante Alighieri

The Emperor Rodolph call, who might have heal'd
The wounds whereof fair Italy hath died,
So that by others she revives but slowly,
He, who with kindly visage comforts him,
Sway'd in that country, where the water springs,
That Moldaw's river to the Elbe, and Elbe
Rolls to the ocean: Ottocar his name:
Who in his swaddling clothes was of more worth
Than Winceslaus his son, a bearded man,
Pamper'd with rank luxuriousness and ease.
And that one with the nose depress, who close
In counsel seems with him of gentle look,
Flying expir'd, with'ring the lily's flower.
Look there how he doth knock against his breast!
The other ye behold, who for his cheek
Makes of one hand a couch, with frequent sighs.
They are the father and the father-in-law
Of Gallia's bane: his vicious life they know
And foul; thence comes the grief that rends them thus.

    "He, so robust of limb, who measure keeps
In song, with him of feature prominent,
With ev'ry virtue bore his girdle brac'd.
And if that stripling who behinds him sits,
King after him had liv'd, his virtue then
From vessel to like vessel had been pour'd;
Which may not of the other heirs be said.
By James and Frederick his realms are held;
Neither the better heritage obtains.
Rarely into the branches of the tree
Doth human worth mount up; and so ordains
He who bestows it, that as his free gift
It may be call'd. To Charles my words apply
No less than to his brother in the song;
Which Pouille and Provence now with grief confess.
So much that plant degenerates from its seed,
As more than Beatrice and Margaret
Costanza still boasts of her valorous spouse.

    "Behold the king of simple life and plain,
Harry of England, sitting there alone:
He through his branches better issue spreads.

    "That one, who on the ground beneath the rest
Sits lowest, yet his gaze directs aloft,
Us William, that brave Marquis, for whose cause
The deed of Alexandria and his war
Makes Conferrat and Canavese weep."

The Divine Comedy
CANTO VIII

Now was the hour that wakens fond desire
In men at sea, and melts their thoughtful heart,
Who in the morn have bid sweet friends farewell,
And pilgrim newly on his road with love
Thrills, if he hear the vesper bell from far,
That seems to mourn for the expiring day:
When I, no longer taking heed to hear
Began, with wonder, from those spirits to mark
One risen from its seat, which with its hand
Audience implor'd. Both palms it join'd and rais'd,
Fixing its steadfast gaze towards the east,
As telling God, "I care for naught beside."

"Te Lucis Ante," so devoutly then
Came from its lip, and in so soft a strain,
That all my sense in ravishment was lost.
And the rest after, softly and devout,
Follow'd through all the hymn, with upward gaze
Directed to the bright supernal wheels.

Here, reader! for the truth makes thine eyes keen:
For of so subtle texture is this veil,
That thou with ease mayst pass it through unmark'd.

I saw that gentle band silently next
Look up, as if in expectation held,
Pale and in lowly guise; and from on high
I saw forth issuing descend beneath
Two angels with two flame-illumin'd swords,
Broken and mutilated at their points.
Green as the tender leaves but newly born,
Their vesture was, the which by wings as green
Beaten, they drew behind them, fann'd in air.
A little over us one took his stand,
The other lighted on the' Opposing hill,
So that the troop were in the midst contain'd.

Well I descried the whiteness on their heads;
But in their visages the dazzled eye
Was lost, as faculty that by too much
Is overpower'd. "From Mary's bosom both
Are come," exclaim'd Sordello, "as a guard
Over the vale, ganst him, who hither tends,
The serpent." Whence, not knowing by which path
He came, I turn'd me round, and closely press'd,
All frozen, to my leader's trusted side.

Sordello paus'd not: "To the valley now
(For it is time) let us descend; and hold
Converse with those great shadows: haply much
Their sight may please ye." Only three steps down
Methinks I measur'd, ere I was beneath,

Dante Alighieri

And noted one who look'd as with desire
To know me. Time was now that air arrow dim;
Yet not so dim, that 'twixt his eyes and mine
It clear'd not up what was conceal'd before.
Mutually tow'rds each other we advanc'd.
Nino, thou courteous judge! what joy I felt,
When I perceiv'd thou wert not with the bad!
    No salutation kind on either part
Was left unsaid. He then inquir'd: "How long
Since thou arrived'st at the mountain's foot,
Over the distant waves?" --"O!" answer'd I,
"Through the sad seats of woe this morn I came,
And still in my first life, thus journeying on,
The other strive to gain." Soon as they heard
My words, he and Sordello backward drew,
As suddenly amaz'd. To Virgil one,
The other to a spirit turn'd, who near
Was seated, crying: "Conrad! up with speed:
Come, see what of his grace high God hath will'd."
Then turning round to me: "By that rare mark
Of honour which thou ow'st to him, who hides
So deeply his first cause, it hath no ford,
When thou shalt he beyond the vast of waves.
Tell my Giovanna, that for me she call
There, where reply to innocence is made.
Her mother, I believe, loves me no more;
Since she has chang'd the white and wimpled folds,
Which she is doom'd once more with grief to wish.
By her it easily may be perceiv'd,
How long in women lasts the flame of love,
If sight and touch do not relume it oft.
For her so fair a burial will not make
The viper which calls Milan to the field,
As had been made by shrill Gallura's bird."
    He spoke, and in his visage took the stamp
Of that right seal, which with due temperature
Glows in the bosom. My insatiate eyes
Meanwhile to heav'n had travel'd, even there
Where the bright stars are slowest, as a wheel
Nearest the axle; when my guide inquir'd:
"What there aloft, my son, has caught thy gaze?"
    I answer'd: "The three torches, with which here
The pole is all on fire. "He then to me:
"The four resplendent stars, thou saw'st this morn
Are there beneath, and these ris'n in their stead."
    While yet he spoke. Sordello to himself
Drew him, and cry'd: "Lo there our enemy!"
And with his hand pointed that way to look.
    Along the side, where barrier none arose
Around the little vale, a serpent lay,

Such haply as gave Eve the bitter food.
Between the grass and flowers, the evil snake
Came on, reverting oft his lifted head;
And, as a beast that smoothes its polish'd coat,
Licking his hack. I saw not, nor can tell,
How those celestial falcons from their seat
Mov'd, but in motion each one well descried,
Hearing the air cut by their verdant plumes.
The serpent fled; and to their stations back
The angels up return'd with equal flight.

     The Spirit (who to Nino, when he call'd,
Had come), from viewing me with fixed ken,
Through all that conflict, loosen'd not his sight.

     "So may the lamp, which leads thee up on high,
Find, in thy destin'd lot, of wax so much,
As may suffice thee to the enamel's height."
It thus began: "If any certain news
Of Valdimagra and the neighbour part
Thou know'st, tell me, who once was mighty there
They call'd me Conrad Malaspina, not
That old one, but from him I sprang. The love
I bore my people is now here refin'd."

     "In your dominions," I answer'd, "ne'er was I.
But through all Europe where do those men dwell,
To whom their glory is not manifest?
The fame, that honours your illustrious house,
Proclaims the nobles and proclaims the land;
So that he knows it who was never there.
I swear to you, so may my upward route
Prosper! your honour'd nation not impairs
The value of her coffer and her sword.
Nature and use give her such privilege,
That while the world is twisted from his course
By a bad head, she only walks aright,
And has the evil way in scorn." He then:
"Now pass thee on: sev'n times the tired sun
Revisits not the couch, which with four feet
The forked Aries covers, ere that kind
Opinion shall be nail'd into thy brain
With stronger nails than other's speech can drive,
If the sure course of judgment be not stay'd."

CANTO IX

Now the fair consort of Tithonus old,
Arisen from her mate's beloved arms,
Look'd palely o'er the eastern cliff: her brow,
Lucent with jewels, glitter'd, set in sign
Of that chill animal, who with his train

Dante Alighieri

Smites fearful nations: and where then we were,
Two steps of her ascent the night had past,
And now the third was closing up its wing,
When I, who had so much of Adam with me,
Sank down upon the grass, o'ercome with sleep,
There where all five were seated. In that hour,
When near the dawn the swallow her sad lay,
Rememb'ring haply ancient grief, renews,
And with our minds more wand'rers from the flesh,
And less by thought restrain'd are, as 't were, full
Of holy divination in their dreams,
Then in a vision did I seem to view
A golden-feather'd eagle in the sky,
With open wings, and hov'ring for descent,
And I was in that place, methought, from whence
Young Ganymede, from his associates 'reft,
Was snatch'd aloft to the high consistory.
"Perhaps," thought I within me, "here alone
He strikes his quarry, and elsewhere disdains
To pounce upon the prey." Therewith, it seem'd,
A little wheeling in his airy tour
Terrible as the lightning rush'd he down,
And snatch'd me upward even to the fire.
There both, I thought, the eagle and myself
Did burn; and so intense th' imagin'd flames,
That needs my sleep was broken off. As erst
Achilles shook himself, and round him roll'd
His waken'd eyeballs wond'ring where he was,
Whenas his mother had from Chiron fled
To Scyros, with him sleeping in her arms;
E'en thus I shook me, soon as from my face
The slumber parted, turning deadly pale,
Like one ice-struck with dread. Solo at my side
My comfort stood: and the bright sun was now
More than two hours aloft: and to the sea
My looks were turn'd. "Fear not," my master cried,
"Assur'd we are at happy point. Thy strength
Shrink not, but rise dilated. Thou art come
To Purgatory now. Lo! there the cliff
That circling bounds it! Lo! the entrance there,
Where it doth seem disparted! Ere the dawn
Usher'd the daylight, when thy wearied soul
Slept in thee, o'er the flowery vale beneath
A lady came, and thus bespake me: "I
Am Lucia. Suffer me to take this man,
Who slumbers. Easier so his way shall speed."
Sordello and the other gentle shapes
Tarrying, she bare thee up: and, as day shone,
This summit reach'd: and I pursued her steps.
Here did she place thee. First her lovely eyes

That open entrance show'd me; then at once
She vanish'd with thy sleep." Like one, whose doubts
Are chas'd by certainty, and terror turn'd
To comfort on discovery of the truth,
Such was the change in me: and as my guide
Beheld me fearless, up along the cliff
He mov'd, and I behind him, towards the height.

    Reader! thou markest how my theme doth rise,
Nor wonder therefore, if more artfully
I prop the structure! Nearer now we drew,
Arriv'd' whence in that part, where first a breach
As of a wall appear'd, I could descry
A portal, and three steps beneath, that led
For inlet there, of different colour each,
And one who watch'd, but spake not yet a word.
As more and more mine eye did stretch its view,
I mark'd him seated on the highest step,
In visage such, as past my power to bear.
Grasp'd in his hand a naked sword, glanc'd back
The rays so toward me, that I oft in vain
My sight directed. "Speak from whence ye stand:"
He cried: "What would ye? Where is your escort?
Take heed your coming upward harm ye not."

    "A heavenly dame, not skilless of these things,"
Replied the' instructor, "told us, even now,
'Pass that way: here the gate is." --"And may she
Befriending prosper your ascent," resum'd
The courteous keeper of the gate: "Come then
Before our steps." We straightway thither came.

    The lowest stair was marble white so smooth
And polish'd, that therein my mirror'd form
Distinct I saw. The next of hue more dark
Than sablest grain, a rough and singed block,
Crack'd lengthwise and across. The third, that lay
Massy above, seem'd porphyry, that flam'd
Red as the life-blood spouting from a vein.
On this God's angel either foot sustain'd,
Upon the threshold seated, which appear'd
A rock of diamond. Up the trinal steps
My leader cheerily drew me. "Ask," said he,
"With humble heart, that he unbar the bolt."

    Piously at his holy feet devolv'd
I cast me, praying him for pity's sake
That he would open to me: but first fell
Thrice on my bosom prostrate. Seven times0
The letter, that denotes the inward stain,
He on my forehead with the blunted point
Of his drawn sword inscrib'd. And "Look," he cried,
"When enter'd, that thou wash these scars away."

Dante Alighieri

     Ashes, or earth ta'en dry out of the ground,
Were of one colour with the robe he wore.
From underneath that vestment forth he drew
Two keys of metal twain: the one was gold,
Its fellow silver. With the pallid first,
And next the burnish'd, he so ply'd the gate,
As to content me well. "Whenever one
Faileth of these, that in the keyhole straight
It turn not, to this alley then expect
Access in vain." Such were the words he spake.
"One is more precious: but the other needs
Skill and sagacity, large share of each,
Ere its good task to disengage the knot
Be worthily perform'd. From Peter these
I hold, of him instructed, that I err
Rather in opening than in keeping fast;
So but the suppliant at my feet implore."
     Then of that hallow'd gate he thrust the door,
Exclaiming, "Enter, but this warning hear:
He forth again departs who looks behind."
     As in the hinges of that sacred ward
The swivels turn'd, sonorous metal strong,
Harsh was the grating; nor so surlily
Roar'd the Tarpeian, when by force bereft
Of good Metellus, thenceforth from his loss
To leanness doom'd. Attentively I turn'd,
List'ning the thunder, that first issued forth;
And "We praise thee, O God," methought I heard
In accents blended with sweet melody.
The strains came o'er mine ear, e'en as the sound
Of choral voices, that in solemn chant
With organ mingle, and, now high and clear,
Come swelling, now float indistinct away.

CANTO X

When we had passed the threshold of the gate
(Which the soul's ill affection doth disuse,
Making the crooked seem the straighter path),
I heard its closing sound. Had mine eyes turn'd,
For that offence what plea might have avail'd?
     We mounted up the riven rock, that wound
On either side alternate, as the wave
Flies and advances. "Here some little art
Behooves us," said my leader, "that our steps
Observe the varying flexure of the path."
     Thus we so slowly sped, that with cleft orb
The moon once more o'erhangs her wat'ry couch,
Ere we that strait have threaded. But when free

The Divine Comedy

We came and open, where the mount above
One solid mass retires, I spent, with toil,
And both, uncertain of the way, we stood,
Upon a plain more lonesome, than the roads
That traverse desert wilds. From whence the brink
Borders upon vacuity, to foot
Of the steep bank, that rises still, the space
Had measur'd thrice the stature of a man:
And, distant as mine eye could wing its flight,
To leftward now and now to right dispatch'd,
That cornice equal in extent appear'd.

   Not yet our feet had on that summit mov'd,
When I discover'd that the bank around,
Whose proud uprising all ascent denied,
Was marble white, and so exactly wrought
With quaintest sculpture, that not there alone
Had Polycletus, but e'en nature's self
Been sham'd. The angel who came down to earth
With tidings of the peace so many years
Wept for in vain, that op'd the heavenly gates
From their long interdict) before us seem'd,
In a sweet act, so sculptur'd to the life,
He look'd no silent image. One had sworn
He had said, "Hail!" for she was imag'd there,
By whom the key did open to God's love,
And in her act as sensibly impress
That word, "Behold the handmaid of the Lord,"
As figure seal'd on wax. "Fix not thy mind
On one place only," said the guide belov'd,
Who had me near him on that part where lies
The heart of man. My sight forthwith I turn'd
And mark'd, behind the virgin mother's form,
Upon that side, where he, that mov'd me, stood,
Another story graven on the rock.

   I passed athwart the bard, and drew me near,
That it might stand more aptly for my view.
There in the self-same marble were engrav'd
The cart and kine, drawing the sacred ark,
That from unbidden office awes mankind.
Before it came much people; and the whole
Parted in seven quires. One sense cried, "Nay,"
Another, "Yes, they sing." Like doubt arose
Betwixt the eye and smell, from the curl'd fume
Of incense breathing up the well-wrought toil.
Preceding the blest vessel, onward came
With light dance leaping, girt in humble guise,
Sweet Israel's harper: in that hap he seem'd
Less and yet more than kingly. Opposite,
At a great palace, from the lattice forth
Look'd Michol, like a lady full of scorn

Dante Alighieri

And sorrow. To behold the tablet next,
Which at the back of Michol whitely shone,
I mov'd me. There was storied on the rock
The' exalted glory of the Roman prince,
Whose mighty worth mov'd Gregory to earn
His mighty conquest, Trajan th' Emperor.
A widow at his bridle stood, attir'd
In tears and mourning. Round about them troop'd
Full throng of knights, and overhead in gold
The eagles floated, struggling with the wind.
The wretch appear'd amid all these to say:
"Grant vengeance, sire! for, woe beshrew this heart
My son is murder'd." He replying seem'd;
    "Wait now till I return." And she, as one
Made hasty by her grief; "O sire, if thou
Dost not return?"--"Where I am, who then is,
May right thee."--" What to thee is other's good,
If thou neglect thy own?"--"Now comfort thee,"
At length he answers. "It beseemeth well
My duty be perform'd, ere I move hence:
So justice wills; and pity bids me stay."
    He, whose ken nothing new surveys, produc'd
That visible speaking, new to us and strange
The like not found on earth. Fondly I gaz'd
Upon those patterns of meek humbleness,
Shapes yet more precious for their artist's sake,
When "Lo," the poet whisper'd, "where this way
(But slack their pace), a multitude advance.
These to the lofty steps shall guide us on."
    Mine eyes, though bent on view of novel sights
Their lov'd allurement, were not slow to turn.
    Reader! I would not that amaz'd thou miss
Of thy good purpose, hearing how just God
Decrees our debts be cancel'd. Ponder not
The form of suff'ring. Think on what succeeds,
Think that at worst beyond the mighty doom
It cannot pass. "Instructor," I began,
"What I see hither tending, bears no trace
Of human semblance, nor of aught beside
That my foil'd sight can guess." He answering thus:
"So courb'd to earth, beneath their heavy teems
Of torment stoop they, that mine eye at first
Struggled as thine. But look intently thither,
An disentangle with thy lab'ring view,
What underneath those stones approacheth: now,
E'en now, mayst thou discern the pangs of each."
    Christians and proud! O poor and wretched ones!
That feeble in the mind's eye, lean your trust
Upon unstaid perverseness! Know ye not
That we are worms, yet made at last to form

The winged insect, imp'd with angel plumes
That to heaven's justice unobstructed soars?
Why buoy ye up aloft your unfleg'd souls?
Abortive then and shapeless ye remain,
Like the untimely embryon of a worm!
     As, to support incumbent floor or roof,
For corbel is a figure sometimes seen,
That crumples up its knees unto its breast,
With the feign'd posture stirring ruth unfeign'd
In the beholder's fancy; so I saw
These fashion'd, when I noted well their guise.
     Each, as his back was laden, came indeed
Or more or less contract; but it appear'd
As he, who show'd most patience in his look,
Wailing exclaim'd: "I can endure no more."

CANTO XI

O thou Almighty Father, who dost make
The heavens thy dwelling, not in bounds confin'd,
But that with love intenser there thou view'st
Thy primal effluence, hallow'd be thy name:
Join each created being to extol
Thy might, for worthy humblest thanks and praise
Is thy blest Spirit. May thy kingdom's peace
Come unto us; for we, unless it come,
With all our striving thither tend in vain.
As of their will the angels unto thee
Tender meet sacrifice, circling thy throne
With loud hosannas, so of theirs be done
By saintly men on earth. Grant us this day
Our daily manna, without which he roams
Through this rough desert retrograde, who most
Toils to advance his steps. As we to each
Pardon the evil done us, pardon thou
Benign, and of our merit take no count.
'Gainst the old adversary prove thou not
Our virtue easily subdu'd; but free
From his incitements and defeat his wiles.
This last petition, dearest Lord! is made
Not for ourselves, since that were needless now,
But for their sakes who after us remain."
     Thus for themselves and us good speed imploring,
Those spirits went beneath a weight like that
We sometimes feel in dreams, all, sore beset,
But with unequal anguish, wearied all,
Round the first circuit, purging as they go,
The world's gross darkness off: In our behalf
If there vows still be offer'd, what can here

Dante Alighieri

For them be vow'd and done by such, whose wills
Have root of goodness in them? Well beseems
That we should help them wash away the stains
They carried hence, that so made pure and light,
They may spring upward to the starry spheres.

   "Ah! so may mercy-temper'd justice rid
Your burdens speedily, that ye have power
To stretch your wing, which e'en to your desire
Shall lift you, as ye show us on which hand
Toward the ladder leads the shortest way.
And if there be more passages than one,
Instruct us of that easiest to ascend;
For this man who comes with me, and bears yet
The charge of fleshly raiment Adam left him,
Despite his better will but slowly mounts."
From whom the answer came unto these words,
Which my guide spake, appear'd not; but 'twas said

   "Along the bank to rightward come with us,
And ye shall find a pass that mocks not toil
Of living man to climb: and were it not
That I am hinder'd by the rock, wherewith
This arrogant neck is tam'd, whence needs I stoop
My visage to the ground, him, who yet lives,
Whose name thou speak'st not him I fain would view.
To mark if e'er I knew him? and to crave
His pity for the fardel that I bear.
I was of Latiun, of a Tuscan horn
A mighty one: Aldobranlesco's name
My sire's, I know not if ye e'er have heard.
My old blood and forefathers' gallant deeds
Made me so haughty, that I clean forgot
The common mother, and to such excess,
Wax'd in my scorn of all men, that I fell,
Fell therefore; by what fate Sienna's sons,
Each child in Campagnatico, can tell.
I am Omberto; not me only pride
Hath injur'd, but my kindred all involv'd
In mischief with her. Here my lot ordains
Under this weight to groan, till I appease
God's angry justice, since I did it not
Amongst the living, here amongst the dead."

   List'ning I bent my visage down: and one
(Not he who spake) twisted beneath the weight
That urg'd him, saw me, knew me straight, and call'd,
Holding his eyes With difficulty fix'd
Intent upon me, stooping as I went
Companion of their way. "O!" I exclaim'd,

   "Art thou not Oderigi, art not thou
Agobbio's glory, glory of that art
Which they of Paris call the limmer's skill?"

"Brother!" said he, "with tints that gayer smile,
Bolognian Franco's pencil lines the leaves.
His all the honour now; mine borrow'd light.
In truth I had not been thus courteous to him,
The whilst I liv'd, through eagerness of zeal
For that pre-eminence my heart was bent on.
Here of such pride the forfeiture is paid.
Nor were I even here; if, able still
To sin, I had not turn'd me unto God.
O powers of man! how vain your glory, nipp'd
E'en in its height of verdure, if an age
Less bright succeed not! Cimabue thought
To lord it over painting's field; and now
The cry is Giotto's, and his name eclips'd.
Thus hath one Guido from the other snatch'd
The letter'd prize: and he perhaps is born,
Who shall drive either from their nest. The noise
Of worldly fame is but a blast of wind,
That blows from divers points, and shifts its name
Shifting the point it blows from. Shalt thou more
Live in the mouths of mankind, if thy flesh
Part shrivel'd from thee, than if thou hadst died,
Before the coral and the pap were left,
Or ere some thousand years have passed? and that
Is, to eternity compar'd, a space,
Briefer than is the twinkling of an eye
To the heaven's slowest orb. He there who treads
So leisurely before me, far and wide
Through Tuscany resounded once; and now
Is in Sienna scarce with whispers nam'd:
There was he sov'reign, when destruction caught
The madd'ning rage of Florence, in that day
Proud as she now is loathsome. Your renown
Is as the herb, whose hue doth come and go,
And his might withers it, by whom it sprang
Crude from the lap of earth." I thus to him:
"True are thy sayings: to my heart they breathe
The kindly spirit of meekness, and allay
What tumours rankle there. But who is he
Of whom thou spak'st but now?" --"This," he replied,
"Is Provenzano. He is here, because
He reach'd, with grasp presumptuous, at the sway
Of all Sienna. Thus he still hath gone,
Thus goeth never-resting, since he died.
Such is th' acquittance render'd back of him,
Who, beyond measure, dar'd on earth." I then:
"If soul that to the verge of life delays
Repentance, linger in that lower space,
Nor hither mount, unless good prayers befriend,
How chanc'd admittance was vouchsaf'd to him?"

Dante Alighieri

"When at his glory's topmost height," said he,
"Respect of dignity all cast aside,
Freely He fix'd him on Sienna's plain,
A suitor to redeem his suff'ring friend,
Who languish'd in the prison-house of Charles,
Nor for his sake refus'd through every vein
To tremble. More I will not say; and dark,
I know, my words are, but thy neighbours soon
Shall help thee to a comment on the text.
This is the work, that from these limits freed him."

CANTO XII

With equal pace as oxen in the yoke,
I with that laden spirit journey'd on
Long as the mild instructor suffer'd me;
But when he bade me quit him, and proceed
(For "here," said he, "behooves with sail and oars
Each man, as best he may, push on his bark"),
Upright, as one dispos'd for speed, I rais'd
My body, still in thought submissive bow'd.

   I now my leader's track not loth pursued;
And each had shown how light we far'd along
When thus he warn'd me: "Bend thine eyesight down:
For thou to ease the way shall find it good
To ruminate the bed beneath thy feet."

   As in memorial of the buried, drawn
Upon earth-level tombs, the sculptur'd form
Of what was once, appears (at sight whereof
Tears often stream forth by remembrance wak'd,
Whose sacred stings the piteous only feel),
So saw I there, but with more curious skill
Of portraiture o'erwrought, whate'er of space
From forth the mountain stretches. On one part
Him I beheld, above all creatures erst
Created noblest, light'ning fall from heaven:
On th' other side with bolt celestial pierc'd
Briareus: cumb'ring earth he lay through dint
Of mortal ice-stroke. The Thymbraean god
With Mars, I saw, and Pallas, round their sire,
Arm'd still, and gazing on the giant's limbs
Strewn o'er th' ethereal field. Nimrod I saw:
At foot of the stupendous work he stood,
As if bewilder'd, looking on the crowd
Leagued in his proud attempt on Sennaar's plain.

   O Niobe! in what a trance of woe
Thee I beheld, upon that highway drawn,
Sev'n sons on either side thee slain! O Saul!
How ghastly didst thou look! on thine own sword

167

The Divine Comedy

Expiring in Gilboa, from that hour
Ne'er visited with rain from heav'n or dew!
    O fond Arachne! thee I also saw
Half spider now in anguish crawling up
Th' unfinish'd web thou weaved'st to thy bane!
    O Rehoboam! here thy shape doth seem
Louring no more defiance! but fear-smote
With none to chase him in his chariot whirl'd.
    Was shown beside upon the solid floor
How dear Alcmaeon forc'd his mother rate
That ornament in evil hour receiv'd:
How in the temple on Sennacherib fell
His sons, and how a corpse they left him there.
Was shown the scath and cruel mangling made
By Tomyris on Cyrus, when she cried:
"Blood thou didst thirst for, take thy fill of blood!"
Was shown how routed in the battle fled
Th' Assyrians, Holofernes slain, and e'en
The relics of the carnage. Troy I mark'd
In ashes and in caverns. Oh! how fall'n,
How abject, Ilion, was thy semblance there!
    What master of the pencil or the style
Had trac'd the shades and lines, that might have made
The subtlest workman wonder? Dead the dead,
The living seem'd alive; with clearer view
His eye beheld not who beheld the truth,
Than mine what I did tread on, while I went
Low bending. Now swell out; and with stiff necks
Pass on, ye sons of Eve! veil not your looks,
Lest they descry the evil of your path!
    I noted not (so busied was my thought)
How much we now had circled of the mount,
And of his course yet more the sun had spent,
When he, who with still wakeful caution went,
Admonish'd: "Raise thou up thy head: for know
Time is not now for slow suspense. Behold
That way an angel hasting towards us! Lo
Where duly the sixth handmaid doth return
From service on the day. Wear thou in look
And gesture seemly grace of reverent awe,
That gladly he may forward us aloft.
Consider that this day ne'er dawns again."
    Time's loss he had so often warn'd me 'gainst,
I could not miss the scope at which he aim'd.
    The goodly shape approach'd us, snowy white
In vesture, and with visage casting streams
Of tremulous lustre like the matin star.
His arms he open'd, then his wings; and spake:
"Onward: the steps, behold! are near; and now
Th' ascent is without difficulty gain'd."

Dante Alighieri

    A scanty few are they, who when they hear
Such tidings, hasten. O ye race of men
Though born to soar, why suffer ye a wind
So slight to baffle ye? He led us on
Where the rock parted; here against my front
Did beat his wings, then promis'd I should fare
In safety on my way. As to ascend
That steep, upon whose brow the chapel stands
(O'er Rubaconte, looking lordly down
On the well-guided city,) up the right
Th' impetuous rise is broken by the steps
Carv'd in that old and simple age, when still
The registry and label rested safe;
Thus is th' acclivity reliev'd, which here
Precipitous from the other circuit falls:
But on each hand the tall cliff presses close.

    As ent'ring there we turn'd, voices, in strain
Ineffable, sang: "Blessed are the poor
In spirit." Ah how far unlike to these
The straits of hell; here songs to usher us,
There shrieks of woe! We climb the holy stairs:
And lighter to myself by far I seem'd
Than on the plain before, whence thus I spake:
"Say, master, of what heavy thing have I
Been lighten'd, that scarce aught the sense of toil
Affects me journeying?" He in few replied:
"When sin's broad characters, that yet remain
Upon thy temples, though well nigh effac'd,
Shall be, as one is, all clean razed out,
Then shall thy feet by heartiness of will
Be so o'ercome, they not alone shall feel
No sense of labour, but delight much more
Shall wait them urg'd along their upward way."

    Then like to one, upon whose head is plac'd
Somewhat he deems not of but from the becks
Of others as they pass him by; his hand
Lends therefore help to' assure him, searches, finds,
And well performs such office as the eye
Wants power to execute: so stretching forth
The fingers of my right hand, did I find
Six only of the letters, which his sword
Who bare the keys had trac'd upon my brow.
The leader, as he mark'd mine action, smil'd.

CANTO XIII

We reach'd the summit of the scale, and stood
Upon the second buttress of that mount
Which healeth him who climbs. A cornice there,

Like to the former, girdles round the hill;
Save that its arch with sweep less ample bends.
    Shadow nor image there is seen; all smooth
The rampart and the path, reflecting nought
But the rock's sullen hue. "If here we wait
For some to question," said the bard, "I fear
Our choice may haply meet too long delay."
    Then fixedly upon the sun his eyes
He fastn'd, made his right the central point
From whence to move, and turn'd the left aside.
"O pleasant light, my confidence and hope,
Conduct us thou," he cried, "on this new way,
Where now I venture, leading to the bourn
We seek. The universal world to thee
Owes warmth and lustre. If no other cause
Forbid, thy beams should ever be our guide."
    Far, as is measur'd for a mile on earth,
In brief space had we journey'd; such prompt will
Impell'd; and towards us flying, now were heard
Spirits invisible, who courteously
Unto love's table bade the welcome guest.
The voice, that first? flew by, call'd forth aloud,
"They have no wine;" so on behind us past,
Those sounds reiterating, nor yet lost
In the faint distance, when another came
Crying, "I am Orestes," and alike
Wing'd its fleet way. "Oh father!" I exclaim'd,
"What tongues are these?" and as I question'd, lo!
A third exclaiming, "Love ye those have wrong'd you."
    "This circuit," said my teacher, "knots the scourge
For envy, and the cords are therefore drawn
By charity's correcting hand. The curb
Is of a harsher sound, as thou shalt hear
(If I deem rightly), ere thou reach the pass,
Where pardon sets them free. But fix thine eyes
Intently through the air, and thou shalt see
A multitude before thee seated, each
Along the shelving grot." Then more than erst
I op'd my eyes, before me view'd, and saw
Shadows with garments dark as was the rock;
And when we pass'd a little forth, I heard
A crying, "Blessed Mary! pray for us,
Michael and Peter! all ye saintly host!"
    I do not think there walks on earth this day
Man so remorseless, that he hath not yearn'd
With pity at the sight that next I saw.
Mine eyes a load of sorrow teemed, when now
I stood so near them, that their semblances
Came clearly to my view. Of sackcloth vile
Their cov'ring seem'd; and on his shoulder one

Dante Alighieri

Did stay another, leaning, and all lean'd
Against the cliff. E'en thus the blind and poor,
Near the confessionals, to crave an alms,
Stand, each his head upon his fellow's sunk,
So most to stir compassion, not by sound
Of words alone, but that, which moves not less,
The sight of mis'ry. And as never beam
Of noonday visiteth the eyeless man,
E'en so was heav'n a niggard unto these
Of his fair light; for, through the orbs of all,
A thread of wire, impiercing, knits them up,
As for the taming of a haggard hawk.

    It were a wrong, methought, to pass and look
On others, yet myself the while unseen.
To my sage counsel therefore did I turn.
He knew the meaning of the mute appeal,
Nor waited for my questioning, but said:
"Speak; and be brief, be subtle in thy words."

    On that part of the cornice, whence no rim
Engarlands its steep fall, did Virgil come;
On the' other side me were the spirits, their cheeks
Bathing devout with penitential tears,
That through the dread impalement forc'd a way.

    I turn'd me to them, and "O shades!" said I,
"Assur'd that to your eyes unveil'd shall shine
The lofty light, sole object of your wish,
So may heaven's grace clear whatsoe'er of foam
Floats turbid on the conscience, that thenceforth
The stream of mind roll limpid from its source,
As ye declare (for so shall ye impart
A boon I dearly prize) if any soul
Of Latium dwell among ye; and perchance
That soul may profit, if I learn so much."

    "My brother, we are each one citizens
Of one true city. Any thou wouldst say,
Who lived a stranger in Italia's land."

    So heard I answering, as appeal'd, a voice
That onward came some space from whence I stood.

    A spirit I noted, in whose look was mark'd
Expectance. Ask ye how? The chin was rais'd
As in one reft of sight. "Spirit," said I,
"Who for thy rise are tutoring (if thou be
That which didst answer to me,) or by place
Or name, disclose thyself, that I may know thee."

    "I was," it answer'd, "of Sienna: here
I cleanse away with these the evil life,
Soliciting with tears that He, who is,
Vouchsafe him to us. Though Sapia nam'd
In sapience I excell'd not, gladder far
Of others' hurt, than of the good befell me.

The Divine Comedy

That thou mayst own I now deceive thee not,
Hear, if my folly were not as I speak it.
When now my years slop'd waning down the arch,
It so bechanc'd, my fellow citizens
Near Colle met their enemies in the field,
And I pray'd God to grant what He had will'd.
There were they vanquish'd, and betook themselves
Unto the bitter passages of flight.
I mark'd the hunt, and waxing out of bounds
In gladness, lifted up my shameless brow,
And like the merlin cheated by a gleam,
Cried, "It is over. Heav'n! I fear thee not."
Upon my verge of life I wish'd for peace
With God; nor repentance had supplied
What I did lack of duty, were it not
The hermit Piero, touch'd with charity,
In his devout orisons thought on me.
But who art thou that question'st of our state,
Who go'st to my belief, with lids unclos'd,
And breathest in thy talk?" --"Mine eyes," said I,
"May yet be here ta'en from me; but not long;
For they have not offended grievously
With envious glances. But the woe beneath
Urges my soul with more exceeding dread.
That nether load already weighs me down."
      She thus: "Who then amongst us here aloft
Hath brought thee, if thou weenest to return?"
      "He," answer'd I, "who standeth mute beside me.
I live: of me ask therefore, chosen spirit,
If thou desire I yonder yet should move
For thee my mortal feet." --"Oh!" she replied,
"This is so strange a thing, it is great sign
That God doth love thee. Therefore with thy prayer
Sometime assist me: and by that I crave,
Which most thou covetest, that if thy feet
E'er tread on Tuscan soil, thou save my fame
Amongst my kindred. Them shalt thou behold
With that vain multitude, who set their hope
On Telamone's haven, there to fail
Confounded, more shall when the fancied stream
They sought of Dian call'd: but they who lead
Their navies, more than ruin'd hopes shall mourn."

CANTO XIV

"Say who is he around our mountain winds,
Or ever death has prun'd his wing for flight,
That opes his eyes and covers them at will?"

Dante Alighieri

"I know not who he is, but know thus much
He comes not singly. Do thou ask of him,
For thou art nearer to him, and take heed
Accost him gently, so that he may speak."
    Thus on the right two Spirits bending each
Toward the other, talk'd of me, then both
Addressing me, their faces backward lean'd,
And thus the one began: "O soul, who yet
Pent in the body, tendest towards the sky!
For charity, we pray thee' comfort us,
Recounting whence thou com'st, and who thou art:
For thou dost make us at the favour shown thee
Marvel, as at a thing that ne'er hath been."
    "There stretches through the midst of Tuscany,
I straight began: "a brooklet, whose well-head
Springs up in Falterona, with his race
Not satisfied, when he some hundred miles
Hath measur'd. From his banks bring, I this frame.
To tell you who I am were words misspent:
For yet my name scarce sounds on rumour's lip."
    "If well I do incorp'rate with my thought
The meaning of thy speech," said he, who first
Addrest me, "thou dost speak of Arno's wave."
    To whom the other: "Why hath he conceal'd
The title of that river, as a man
Doth of some horrible thing?" The spirit, who
Thereof was question'd, did acquit him thus:
"I know not: but 'tis fitting well the name
Should perish of that vale; for from the source
Where teems so plenteously the Alpine steep
Maim'd of Pelorus, (that doth scarcely pass
Beyond that limit,) even to the point
Whereunto ocean is restor'd, what heaven
Drains from th' exhaustless store for all earth's streams,
Throughout the space is virtue worried down,
As 'twere a snake, by all, for mortal foe,
Or through disastrous influence on the place,
Or else distortion of misguided wills,
That custom goads to evil: whence in those,
The dwellers in that miserable vale,
Nature is so transform'd, it seems as they
Had shar'd of Circe's feeding. 'Midst brute swine,
Worthier of acorns than of other food
Created for man's use, he shapeth first
His obscure way; then, sloping onward, finds
Curs, snarlers more in spite than power, from whom
He turns with scorn aside: still journeying down,
By how much more the curst and luckless foss
Swells out to largeness, e'en so much it finds
Dogs turning into wolves. Descending still

Through yet more hollow eddies, next he meets
A race of foxes, so replete with craft,
They do not fear that skill can master it.
Nor will I cease because my words are heard
By other ears than thine. It shall be well
For this man, if he keep in memory
What from no erring Spirit I reveal.
Lo! I behold thy grandson, that becomes
A hunter of those wolves, upon the shore
Of the fierce stream, and cows them all with dread:
Their flesh yet living sets he up to sale,
Then like an aged beast to slaughter dooms.
Many of life he reaves, himself of worth
And goodly estimation. Smear'd with gore
Mark how he issues from the rueful wood,
Leaving such havoc, that in thousand years
It spreads not to prime lustihood again."
     As one, who tidings hears of woe to come,
Changes his looks perturb'd, from whate'er part
The peril grasp him, so beheld I change
That spirit, who had turn'd to listen, struck
With sadness, soon as he had caught the word.
     His visage and the other's speech did raise
Desire in me to know the names of both,
whereof with meek entreaty I inquir'd.
     The shade, who late addrest me, thus resum'd:
"Thy wish imports that I vouchsafe to do
For thy sake what thou wilt not do for mine.
But since God's will is that so largely shine
His grace in thee, I will be liberal too.
Guido of Duca know then that I am.
Envy so parch'd my blood, that had I seen
A fellow man made joyous, thou hadst mark'd
A livid paleness overspread my cheek.
Such harvest reap I of the seed I sow'd.
O man, why place thy heart where there doth need
Exclusion of participants in good?
This is Rinieri's spirit, this the boast
And honour of the house of Calboli,
Where of his worth no heritage remains.
Nor his the only blood, that hath been stript
('twixt Po, the mount, the Reno, and the shore,)
Of all that truth or fancy asks for bliss;
But in those limits such a growth has sprung
Of rank and venom'd roots, as long would mock
Slow culture's toil. Where is good Lizio? where
Manardi, Traversalo, and Carpigna?
O bastard slips of old Romagna's line!
When in Bologna the low artisan,
And in Faenza yon Bernardin sprouts,

Dante Alighieri

A gentle cyon from ignoble stem.
Wonder not, Tuscan, if thou see me weep,
When I recall to mind those once lov'd names,
Guido of Prata, and of Azzo him
That dwelt with you; Tignoso and his troop,
With Traversaro's house and Anastagio s,
(Each race disherited) and beside these,
The ladies and the knights, the toils and ease,
That witch'd us into love and courtesy;
Where now such malice reigns in recreant hearts.
O Brettinoro! wherefore tarriest still,
Since forth of thee thy family hath gone,
And many, hating evil, join'd their steps?
Well doeth he, that bids his lineage cease,
Bagnacavallo; Castracaro ill,
And Conio worse, who care to propagate
A race of Counties from such blood as theirs.
Well shall ye also do, Pagani, then
When from amongst you tries your demon child.
Not so, howe'er, that henceforth there remain
True proof of what ye were. O Hugolin!
Thou sprung of Fantolini's line! thy name
Is safe, since none is look'd for after thee
To cloud its lustre, warping from thy stock.
But, Tuscan, go thy ways; for now I take
Far more delight in weeping than in words.
Such pity for your sakes hath wrung my heart."

    We knew those gentle spirits at parting heard
Our steps. Their silence therefore of our way
Assur'd us. Soon as we had quitted them,
Advancing onward, lo! a voice that seem'd
Like vollied light'ning, when it rives the air,
Met us, and shouted, "Whosoever finds
Will slay me," then fled from us, as the bolt
Lanc'd sudden from a downward-rushing cloud.
When it had giv'n short truce unto our hearing,
Behold the other with a crash as loud
As the quick-following thunder: "Mark in me
Aglauros turn'd to rock." I at the sound
Retreating drew more closely to my guide.

    Now in mute stillness rested all the air:
And thus he spake: "There was the galling bit.
But your old enemy so baits his hook,
He drags you eager to him. Hence nor curb
Avails you, nor reclaiming call. Heav'n calls
And round about you wheeling courts your gaze
With everlasting beauties. Yet your eye
Turns with fond doting still upon the earth.
Therefore He smites you who discerneth all."

The Divine Comedy

CANTO XV

As much as 'twixt the third hour's close and dawn,
Appeareth of heav'n's sphere, that ever whirls
As restless as an infant in his play,
So much appear'd remaining to the sun
Of his slope journey towards the western goal.
    Evening was there, and here the noon of night;
and full upon our forehead smote the beams.
For round the mountain, circling, so our path
Had led us, that toward the sun-set now
Direct we journey'd: when I felt a weight
Of more exceeding splendour, than before,
Press on my front. The cause unknown, amaze
Possess'd me, and both hands against my brow
Lifting, I interpos'd them, as a screen,
That of its gorgeous superflux of light
Clipp'd the diminish'd orb. As when the ray,
Striking On water or the surface clear
Of mirror, leaps unto the opposite part,
Ascending at a glance, e'en as it fell,
(And so much differs from the stone, that falls
Through equal space, as practice skill hath shown;
Thus with refracted light before me seemed
The ground there smitten; whence in sudden haste
My sight recoil'd. "What is this, sire belov'd!
'Gainst which I strive to shield the sight in vain?"
Cried I, "and which towards us moving seems?"
    "Marvel not, if the family of heav'n,"
He answer'd, "yet with dazzling radiance dim
Thy sense it is a messenger who comes,
Inviting man's ascent. Such sights ere long,
Not grievous, shall impart to thee delight,
As thy perception is by nature wrought
Up to their pitch." The blessed angel, soon
As we had reach'd him, hail'd us with glad voice:
"Here enter on a ladder far less steep
Than ye have yet encounter'd." We forthwith
Ascending, heard behind us chanted sweet,
"Blessed the merciful," and "happy thou!
That conquer'st." Lonely each, my guide and I
Pursued our upward way; and as we went,
Some profit from his words I hop'd to win,
And thus of him inquiring, fram'd my speech:
    "What meant Romagna's spirit, when he spake
Of bliss exclusive with no partner shar'd?"
    He straight replied: "No wonder, since he knows,
What sorrow waits on his own worst defect,
If he chide others, that they less may mourn.

Dante Alighieri

Because ye point your wishes at a mark,
Where, by communion of possessors, part
Is lessen'd, envy bloweth up the sighs of men.
No fear of that might touch ye, if the love
Of higher sphere exalted your desire.
For there, by how much more they call it ours,
So much propriety of each in good
Increases more, and heighten'd charity
Wraps that fair cloister in a brighter flame."
    "Now lack I satisfaction more," said I,
"Than if thou hadst been silent at the first,
And doubt more gathers on my lab'ring thought.
How can it chance, that good distributed,
The many, that possess it, makes more rich,
Than if 't were shar'd by few?" He answering thus:
"Thy mind, reverting still to things of earth,
Strikes darkness from true light. The highest good
Unlimited, ineffable, doth so speed
To love, as beam to lucid body darts,
Giving as much of ardour as it finds.
The sempiternal effluence streams abroad
Spreading, wherever charity extends.
So that the more aspirants to that bliss
Are multiplied, more good is there to love,
And more is lov'd; as mirrors, that reflect,
Each unto other, propagated light.
If these my words avail not to allay
Thy thirsting, Beatrice thou shalt see,
Who of this want, and of all else thou hast,
Shall rid thee to the full. Provide but thou
That from thy temples may be soon eras'd,
E'en as the two already, those five scars,
That when they pain thee worst, then kindliest heal,"
    "Thou," I had said, "content'st me," when I saw
The other round was gain'd, and wond'ring eyes
Did keep me mute. There suddenly I seem'd
By an ecstatic vision wrapt away;
And in a temple saw, methought, a crowd
Of many persons; and at th' entrance stood
A dame, whose sweet demeanour did express
A mother's love, who said, "Child! why hast thou
Dealt with us thus? Behold thy sire and I
Sorrowing have sought thee;" and so held her peace,
And straight the vision fled. A female next
Appear'd before me, down whose visage cours'd
Those waters, that grief forces out from one
By deep resentment stung, who seem'd to say:
"If thou, Pisistratus, be lord indeed
Over this city, nam'd with such debate
Of adverse gods, and whence each science sparkles,

Avenge thee of those arms, whose bold embrace
Hath clasp'd our daughter; "and to fuel, meseem'd,
Benign and meek, with visage undisturb'd,
Her sovran spake: "How shall we those requite,
Who wish us evil, if we thus condemn
The man that loves us?" After that I saw
A multitude, in fury burning, slay
With stones a stripling youth, and shout amain
"Destroy, destroy: "and him I saw, who bow'd
Heavy with death unto the ground, yet made
His eyes, unfolded upward, gates to heav'n,
Praying forgiveness of th' Almighty Sire,
Amidst that cruel conflict, on his foes,
With looks, that With compassion to their aim.

    Soon as my spirit, from her airy flight
Returning, sought again the things, whose truth
Depends not on her shaping, I observ'd
How she had rov'd to no unreal scenes

    Meanwhile the leader, who might see I mov'd,
As one, who struggles to shake off his sleep,
Exclaim'd: "What ails thee, that thou canst not hold
Thy footing firm, but more than half a league
Hast travel'd with clos'd eyes and tott'ring gait,
Like to a man by wine or sleep o'ercharg'd?"

    "Beloved father! so thou deign," said I,
"To listen, I will tell thee what appear'd
Before me, when so fail'd my sinking steps."

    He thus: "Not if thy Countenance were mask'd
With hundred vizards, could a thought of thine
How small soe'er, elude me. What thou saw'st
Was shown, that freely thou mightst ope thy heart
To the waters of peace, that flow diffus'd
From their eternal fountain. I not ask'd,
What ails thee? for such cause as he doth, who
Looks only with that eye which sees no more,
When spiritless the body lies; but ask'd,
To give fresh vigour to thy foot. Such goads
The slow and loit'ring need; that they be found
Not wanting, when their hour of watch returns."

    So on we journey'd through the evening sky
Gazing intent, far onward, as our eyes
With level view could stretch against the bright
Vespertine ray: and lo! by slow degrees
Gath'ring, a fog made tow'rds us, dark as night.
There was no room for 'scaping; and that mist
Bereft us, both of sight and the pure air.

Dante Alighieri

CANTO XVI

Hell's dunnest gloom, or night unlustrous, dark,
Of every planes 'reft, and pall'd in clouds,
Did never spread before the sight a veil
In thickness like that fog, nor to the sense
So palpable and gross. Ent'ring its shade,
Mine eye endured not with unclosed lids;
Which marking, near me drew the faithful guide,
Offering me his shoulder for a stay.
    As the blind man behind his leader walks,
Lest he should err, or stumble unawares
On what might harm him, or perhaps destroy,
I journey'd through that bitter air and foul,
Still list'ning to my escort's warning voice,
"Look that from me thou part not." Straight I heard
Voices, and each one seem'd to pray for peace,
And for compassion, to the Lamb of God
That taketh sins away. Their prelude still
Was "Agnus Dei," and through all the choir,
One voice, one measure ran, that perfect seem'd
The concord of their song. "Are these I hear
Spirits, O master?" I exclaim'd; and he:
"Thou aim'st aright: these loose the bonds of wrath."
    "Now who art thou, that through our smoke dost cleave?
And speak'st of us, as thou thyself e'en yet
Dividest time by calends?" So one voice
Bespake me; whence my master said: "Reply;
And ask, if upward hence the passage lead."
    "O being! who dost make thee pure, to stand
Beautiful once more in thy Maker's sight!
Along with me: and thou shalt hear and wonder."
Thus I, whereto the spirit answering spake:
"Long as 't is lawful for me, shall my steps
Follow on thine; and since the cloudy smoke
Forbids the seeing, hearing in its stead
Shall keep us join'd." I then forthwith began
"Yet in my mortal swathing, I ascend
To higher regions, and am hither come
Through the fearful agony of hell.
And, if so largely God hath doled his grace,
That, clean beside all modern precedent,
He wills me to behold his kingly state,
From me conceal not who thou wast, ere death
Had loos'd thee; but instruct me: and instruct
If rightly to the pass I tend; thy words
The way directing as a safe escort."
    "I was of Lombardy, and Marco call'd:
Not inexperienc'd of the world, that worth

179

The Divine Comedy
I still affected, from which all have turn'd
The nerveless bow aside. Thy course tends right
Unto the summit:" and, replying thus,
He added, "I beseech thee pray for me,
When thou shalt come aloft." And I to him:
"Accept my faith for pledge I will perform
What thou requirest. Yet one doubt remains,
That wrings me sorely, if I solve it not,
Singly before it urg'd me, doubled now
By thine opinion, when I couple that
With one elsewhere declar'd, each strength'ning other.
The world indeed is even so forlorn
Of all good as thou speak'st it and so swarms
With every evil. Yet, beseech thee, point
The cause out to me, that myself may see,
And unto others show it: for in heaven
One places it, and one on earth below."

    Then heaving forth a deep and audible sigh,
"Brother!" he thus began, "the world is blind;
And thou in truth com'st from it. Ye, who live,
Do so each cause refer to heav'n above,
E'en as its motion of necessity
Drew with it all that moves. If this were so,
Free choice in you were none; nor justice would
There should be joy for virtue, woe for ill.
Your movements have their primal bent from heaven;
Not all; yet said I all; what then ensues?
Light have ye still to follow evil or good,
And of the will free power, which, if it stand
Firm and unwearied in Heav'n's first assay,
Conquers at last, so it be cherish'd well,
Triumphant over all. To mightier force,
To better nature subject, ye abide
Free, not constrain'd by that, which forms in you
The reasoning mind uninfluenc'd of the stars.
If then the present race of mankind err,
Seek in yourselves the cause, and find it there.
Herein thou shalt confess me no false spy.

    "Forth from his plastic hand, who charm'd beholds
Her image ere she yet exist, the soul
Comes like a babe, that wantons sportively
Weeping and laughing in its wayward moods,
As artless and as ignorant of aught,
Save that her Maker being one who dwells
With gladness ever, willingly she turns
To whate'er yields her joy. Of some slight good
The flavour soon she tastes; and, snar'd by that,
With fondness she pursues it, if no guide
Recall, no rein direct her wand'ring course.
Hence it behov'd, the law should be a curb;

Dante Alighieri

A sovereign hence behov'd, whose piercing view
Might mark at least the fortress and main tower
Of the true city. Laws indeed there are:
But who is he observes them? None; not he,
Who goes before, the shepherd of the flock,
Who chews the cud but doth not cleave the hoof.
Therefore the multitude, who see their guide
Strike at the very good they covet most,
Feed there and look no further. Thus the cause
Is not corrupted nature in yourselves,
But ill-conducting, that hath turn'd the world
To evil. Rome, that turn'd it unto good,
Was wont to boast two suns, whose several beams
Cast light on either way, the world's and God's.
One since hath quench'd the other; and the sword
Is grafted on the crook; and so conjoin'd
Each must perforce decline to worse, unaw'd
By fear of other. If thou doubt me, mark
The blade: each herb is judg'd of by its seed.
That land, through which Adice and the Po
Their waters roll, was once the residence
Of courtesy and velour, ere the day,
That frown'd on Frederick; now secure may pass
Those limits, whosoe'er hath left, for shame,
To talk with good men, or come near their haunts.
Three aged ones are still found there, in whom
The old time chides the new: these deem it long
Ere God restore them to a better world:
The good Gherardo, of Palazzo he
Conrad, and Guido of Castello, nam'd
In Gallic phrase more fitly the plain Lombard.
On this at last conclude. The church of Rome,
Mixing two governments that ill assort,
Hath miss'd her footing, fall'n into the mire,
And there herself and burden much defil'd."

    "O Marco!" I replied, shine arguments
Convince me: and the cause I now discern
Why of the heritage no portion came
To Levi's offspring. But resolve me this
Who that Gherardo is, that as thou sayst
Is left a sample of the perish'd race,
And for rebuke to this untoward age?"

    "Either thy words," said he, "deceive; or else
Are meant to try me; that thou, speaking Tuscan,
Appear'st not to have heard of good Gherado;
The sole addition that, by which I know him;
Unless I borrow'd from his daughter Gaia
Another name to grace him. God be with you.
I bear you company no more. Behold
The dawn with white ray glimm'ring through the mist.

I must away--the angel comes--ere he
Appear." He said, and would not hear me more.

CANTO XVII

Call to remembrance, reader, if thou e'er
Hast, on a mountain top, been ta'en by cloud,
Through which thou saw'st no better, than the mole
Doth through opacous membrane; then, whene'er
The wat'ry vapours dense began to melt
Into thin air, how faintly the sun's sphere
Seem'd wading through them; so thy nimble thought
May image, how at first I re-beheld
The sun, that bedward now his couch o'erhung.
    Thus with my leader's feet still equaling pace
From forth that cloud I came, when now expir'd
The parting beams from off the nether shores.
    O quick and forgetive power! that sometimes dost
So rob us of ourselves, we take no mark
Though round about us thousand trumpets clang!
What moves thee, if the senses stir not? Light
Kindled in heav'n, spontaneous, self-inform'd,
Or likelier gliding down with swift illapse
By will divine. Portray'd before me came
The traces of her dire impiety,
Whose form was chang'd into the bird, that most
Delights itself in song: and here my mind
Was inwardly so wrapt, it gave no place
To aught that ask'd admittance from without.
    Next shower'd into my fantasy a shape
As of one crucified, whose visage spake
Fell rancour, malice deep, wherein he died;
And round him Ahasuerus the great king,
Esther his bride, and Mordecai the just,
Blameless in word and deed. As of itself
That unsubstantial coinage of the brain
Burst, like a bubble, Which the water fails
That fed it; in my vision straight uprose
A damsel weeping loud, and cried, "O queen!
O mother! wherefore has intemperate ire
Driv'n thee to loath thy being? Not to lose
Lavinia, desp'rate thou hast slain thyself.
Now hast thou lost me. I am she, whose tears
Mourn, ere I fall, a mother's timeless end."
    E'en as a sleep breaks off, if suddenly
New radiance strike upon the closed lids,
The broken slumber quivering ere it dies;
Thus from before me sunk that imagery
Vanishing, soon as on my face there struck

Dante Alighieri

The light, outshining far our earthly beam.
As round I turn'd me to survey what place
I had arriv'd at, "Here ye mount," exclaim'd
A voice, that other purpose left me none,
Save will so eager to behold who spake,
I could not choose but gaze. As 'fore the sun,
That weighs our vision down, and veils his form
In light transcendent, thus my virtue fail'd
Unequal. "This is Spirit from above,
Who marshals us our upward way, unsought;
And in his own light shrouds him;. As a man
Doth for himself, so now is done for us.
For whoso waits imploring, yet sees need
Of his prompt aidance, sets himself prepar'd
For blunt denial, ere the suit be made.
Refuse we not to lend a ready foot
At such inviting: haste we to ascend,
Before it darken: for we may not then,
Till morn again return." So spake my guide;
And to one ladder both address'd our steps;
And the first stair approaching, I perceiv'd
Near me as 'twere the waving of a wing,
That fann'd my face and whisper'd: "Blessed they
The peacemakers: they know not evil wrath."

    Now to such height above our heads were rais'd
The last beams, follow'd close by hooded night,
That many a star on all sides through the gloom
Shone out. "Why partest from me, O my strength?"
So with myself I commun'd; for I felt
My o'ertoil'd sinews slacken. We had reach'd
The summit, and were fix'd like to a bark
Arriv'd at land. And waiting a short space,
If aught should meet mine ear in that new round,
Then to my guide I turn'd, and said: "Lov'd sire!
Declare what guilt is on this circle purg'd.
If our feet rest, no need thy speech should pause."

    He thus to me: "The love of good, whate'er
Wanted of just proportion, here fulfils.
Here plies afresh the oar, that loiter'd ill.
But that thou mayst yet clearlier understand,
Give ear unto my words, and thou shalt cull
Some fruit may please thee well, from this delay.

    "Creator, nor created being, ne'er,
My son," he thus began, "was without love,
Or natural, or the free spirit's growth.
Thou hast not that to learn. The natural still
Is without error; but the other swerves,
If on ill object bent, or through excess
Of vigour, or defect. While e'er it seeks
The primal blessings, or with measure due

The Divine Comedy

Th' inferior, no delight, that flows from it,
Partakes of ill. But let it warp to evil,
Or with more ardour than behooves, or less.
Pursue the good, the thing created then
Works 'gainst its Maker. Hence thou must infer
That love is germin of each virtue in ye,
And of each act no less, that merits pain.
Now since it may not be, but love intend
The welfare mainly of the thing it loves,
All from self-hatred are secure; and since
No being can be thought t' exist apart
And independent of the first, a bar
Of equal force restrains from hating that.

    "Grant the distinction just; and it remains
The' evil must be another's, which is lov'd.
Three ways such love is gender'd in your clay.
There is who hopes (his neighbour's worth deprest,)
Preeminence himself, and coverts hence
For his own greatness that another fall.
There is who so much fears the loss of power,
Fame, favour, glory (should his fellow mount
Above him), and so sickens at the thought,
He loves their opposite: and there is he,
Whom wrong or insult seems to gall and shame
That he doth thirst for vengeance, and such needs
Must doat on other's evil. Here beneath
This threefold love is mourn'd. Of th' other sort
Be now instructed, that which follows good
But with disorder'd and irregular course.

    "All indistinctly apprehend a bliss
On which the soul may rest, the hearts of all
Yearn after it, and to that wished bourn
All therefore strive to tend. If ye behold
Or seek it with a love remiss and lax,
This cornice after just repenting lays
Its penal torment on ye. Other good
There is, where man finds not his happiness:
It is not true fruition, not that blest
Essence, of every good the branch and root.
The love too lavishly bestow'd on this,
Along three circles over us, is mourn'd.
Account of that division tripartite
Expect not, fitter for thine own research.

CANTO XVIII

The teacher ended, and his high discourse
Concluding, earnest in my looks inquir'd
If I appear'd content; and I, whom still

Dante Alighieri

Unsated thirst to hear him urg'd, was mute,
Mute outwardly, yet inwardly I said:
"Perchance my too much questioning offends
But he, true father, mark'd the secret wish
By diffidence restrain'd, and speaking, gave
Me boldness thus to speak: "Master, my Sight
Gathers so lively virtue from thy beams,
That all, thy words convey, distinct is seen.
Wherefore I pray thee, father, whom this heart
Holds dearest! thou wouldst deign by proof t' unfold
That love, from which as from their source thou bring'st
All good deeds and their opposite." He then:
"To what I now disclose be thy clear ken
Directed, and thou plainly shalt behold
How much those blind have err'd, who make themselves
The guides of men. The soul, created apt
To love, moves versatile which way soe'er
Aught pleasing prompts her, soon as she is wak'd
By pleasure into act. Of substance true
Your apprehension forms its counterfeit,
And in you the ideal shape presenting
Attracts the soul's regard. If she, thus drawn,
incline toward it, love is that inclining,
And a new nature knit by pleasure in ye.
Then as the fire points up, and mounting seeks
His birth-place and his lasting seat, e'en thus
Enters the captive soul into desire,
Which is a spiritual motion, that ne'er rests
Before enjoyment of the thing it loves.
Enough to show thee, how the truth from those
Is hidden, who aver all love a thing
Praise-worthy in itself: although perhaps
Its substance seem still good. Yet if the wax
Be good, it follows not th' impression must."
"What love is," I return'd, "thy words, O guide!
And my own docile mind, reveal. Yet thence
New doubts have sprung. For from without if love
Be offer'd to us, and the spirit knows
No other footing, tend she right or wrong,
Is no desert of hers." He answering thus:
"What reason here discovers I have power
To show thee: that which lies beyond, expect
From Beatrice, faith not reason's task.
Spirit, substantial form, with matter join'd
Not in confusion mix'd, hath in itself
Specific virtue of that union born,
Which is not felt except it work, nor prov'd
But through effect, as vegetable life
By the green leaf. From whence his intellect
Deduced its primal notices of things,

The Divine Comedy

Man therefore knows not, or his appetites
Their first affections; such in you, as zeal
In bees to gather honey; at the first,
Volition, meriting nor blame nor praise.
But o'er each lower faculty supreme,
That as she list are summon'd to her bar,
Ye have that virtue in you, whose just voice
Uttereth counsel, and whose word should keep
The threshold of assent. Here is the source,
Whence cause of merit in you is deriv'd,
E'en as the affections good or ill she takes,
Or severs, winnow'd as the chaff. Those men
Who reas'ning went to depth profoundest, mark'd
That innate freedom, and were thence induc'd
To leave their moral teaching to the world.
Grant then, that from necessity arise
All love that glows within you; to dismiss
Or harbour it, the pow'r is in yourselves.
Remember, Beatrice, in her style,
Denominates free choice by eminence
The noble virtue, if in talk with thee
She touch upon that theme." The moon, well nigh
To midnight hour belated, made the stars
Appear to wink and fade; and her broad disk
Seem'd like a crag on fire, as up the vault
That course she journey'd, which the sun then warms,
When they of Rome behold him at his set.
Betwixt Sardinia and the Corsic isle.
And now the weight, that hung upon my thought,
Was lighten'd by the aid of that clear spirit,
Who raiseth Andes above Mantua's name.
I therefore, when my questions had obtain'd
Solution plain and ample, stood as one
Musing in dreary slumber; but not long
Slumber'd; for suddenly a multitude,
The steep already turning, from behind,
Rush'd on. With fury and like random rout,
As echoing on their shores at midnight heard
Ismenus and Asopus, for his Thebes
If Bacchus' help were needed; so came these
Tumultuous, curving each his rapid step,
By eagerness impell'd of holy love.

    Soon they o'ertook us; with such swiftness mov'd
The mighty crowd. Two spirits at their head
Cried weeping; "Blessed Mary sought with haste
The hilly region. Caesar to subdue
Ilerda, darted in Marseilles his sting,
And flew to Spain."--"Oh tarry not: away;"
The others shouted; "let not time be lost
Through slackness of affection. Hearty zeal

To serve reanimates celestial grace."
    "O ye, in whom intenser fervency
Haply supplies, where lukewarm erst ye fail'd,
Slow or neglectful, to absolve your part
Of good and virtuous, this man, who yet lives,
(Credit my tale, though strange) desires t' ascend,
So morning rise to light us. Therefore say
Which hand leads nearest to the rifted rock?"
    So spake my guide, to whom a shade return'd:
"Come after us, and thou shalt find the cleft.
We may not linger: such resistless will
Speeds our unwearied course. Vouchsafe us then
Thy pardon, if our duty seem to thee
Discourteous rudeness. In Verona I
Was abbot of San Zeno, when the hand
Of Barbarossa grasp'd Imperial sway,
That name, ne'er utter'd without tears in Milan.
And there is he, hath one foot in his grave,
Who for that monastery ere long shall weep,
Ruing his power misus'd: for that his son,
Of body ill compact, and worse in mind,
And born in evil, he hath set in place
Of its true pastor." Whether more he spake,
Or here was mute, I know not: he had sped
E'en now so far beyond us. Yet thus much
I heard, and in rememb'rance treasur'd it.
    He then, who never fail'd me at my need,
Cried, "Hither turn. Lo! two with sharp remorse
Chiding their sin!" In rear of all the troop
These shouted: "First they died, to whom the sea
Open'd, or ever Jordan saw his heirs:
And they, who with Aeneas to the end
Endur'd not suffering, for their portion chose
Life without glory." Soon as they had fled
Past reach of sight, new thought within me rose
By others follow'd fast, and each unlike
Its fellow: till led on from thought to thought,
And pleasur'd with the fleeting train, mine eye
Was clos'd, and meditation chang'd to dream.

CANTO XIX

It was the hour, when of diurnal heat
No reliques chafe the cold beams of the moon,
O'erpower'd by earth, or planetary sway
Of Saturn; and the geomancer sees
His Greater Fortune up the east ascend,
Where gray dawn checkers first the shadowy cone;
When 'fore me in my dream a woman's shape

The Divine Comedy

There came, with lips that stammer'd, eyes aslant,
Distorted feet, hands maim'd, and colour pale.
    I look'd upon her; and as sunshine cheers
Limbs numb'd by nightly cold, e'en thus my look
Unloos'd her tongue, next in brief space her form
Decrepit rais'd erect, and faded face
With love's own hue illum'd. Recov'ring speech
She forthwith warbling such a strain began,
That I, how loth soe'er, could scarce have held
Attention from the song. "I," thus she sang,
"I am the Siren, she, whom mariners
On the wide sea are wilder'd when they hear:
Such fulness of delight the list'ner feels.
I from his course Ulysses by my lay
Enchanted drew. Whoe'er frequents me once
Parts seldom; so I charm him, and his heart
Contented knows no void." Or ere her mouth
Was clos'd, to shame her at her side appear'd
A dame of semblance holy. With stern voice
She utter'd; "Say, O Virgil, who is this?"
Which hearing, he approach'd, with eyes still bent
Toward that goodly presence: th' other seiz'd her,
And, her robes tearing, open'd her before,
And show'd the belly to me, whence a smell,
Exhaling loathsome, wak'd me. Round I turn'd
Mine eyes, and thus the teacher: "At the least
Three times my voice hath call'd thee. Rise, begone.
Let us the opening find where thou mayst pass."
    I straightway rose. Now day, pour'd down from high,
Fill'd all the circuits of the sacred mount;
And, as we journey'd, on our shoulder smote
The early ray. I follow'd, stooping low
My forehead, as a man, o'ercharg'd with thought,
Who bends him to the likeness of an arch,
That midway spans the flood; when thus I heard,
"Come, enter here," in tone so soft and mild,
As never met the ear on mortal strand.
    With swan-like wings dispread and pointing up,
Who thus had spoken marshal'd us along,
Where each side of the solid masonry
The sloping, walls retir'd; then mov'd his plumes,
And fanning us, affirm'd that those, who mourn,
Are blessed, for that comfort shall be theirs.
    "What aileth thee, that still thou look'st to earth?"
Began my leader; while th' angelic shape
A little over us his station took.
    "New vision," I replied, "hath rais'd in me
8urmisings strange and anxious doubts, whereon
My soul intent allows no other thought
Or room or entrance.--"Hast thou seen," said he,

Dante Alighieri

"That old enchantress, her, whose wiles alone
The spirits o'er us weep for? Hast thou seen
How man may free him of her bonds? Enough.
Let thy heels spurn the earth, and thy rais'd ken
Fix on the lure, which heav'n's eternal King
Whirls in the rolling spheres." As on his feet
The falcon first looks down, then to the sky
Turns, and forth stretches eager for the food,
That woos him thither; so the call I heard,
So onward, far as the dividing rock
Gave way, I journey'd, till the plain was reach'd.

  On the fifth circle when I stood at large,
A race appear'd before me, on the ground
All downward lying prone and weeping sore.
"My soul hath cleaved to the dust," I heard
With sighs so deep, they well nigh choak'd the words.
"O ye elect of God, whose penal woes
Both hope and justice mitigate, direct
Tow'rds the steep rising our uncertain way."

  "If ye approach secure from this our doom,
Prostration--and would urge your course with speed,
See that ye still to rightward keep the brink."

  So them the bard besought; and such the words,
Beyond us some short space, in answer came.

  I noted what remain'd yet hidden from them:
Thence to my liege's eyes mine eyes I bent,
And he, forthwith interpreting their suit,
Beckon'd his glad assent. Free then to act,
As pleas'd me, I drew near, and took my stand
O`er that shade, whose words I late had mark'd.
And, "Spirit!" I said, "in whom repentant tears
Mature that blessed hour, when thou with God
Shalt find acceptance, for a while suspend
For me that mightier care. Say who thou wast,
Why thus ye grovel on your bellies prone,
And if in aught ye wish my service there,
Whence living I am come." He answering spake
"The cause why Heav'n our back toward his cope
Reverses, shalt thou know: but me know first
The successor of Peter, and the name
And title of my lineage from that stream,
That' twixt Chiaveri and Siestri draws
His limpid waters through the lowly glen.
A month and little more by proof I learnt,
With what a weight that robe of sov'reignty
Upon his shoulder rests, who from the mire
Would guard it: that each other fardel seems
But feathers in the balance. Late, alas!
Was my conversion: but when I became
Rome's pastor, I discern'd at once the dream

And cozenage of life, saw that the heart
Rested not there, and yet no prouder height
Lur'd on the climber: wherefore, of that life
No more enamour'd, in my bosom love
Of purer being kindled. For till then
I was a soul in misery, alienate
From God, and covetous of all earthly things;
Now, as thou seest, here punish'd for my doting.
Such cleansing from the taint of avarice
Do spirits converted need. This mount inflicts
No direr penalty. E'en as our eyes
Fasten'd below, nor e'er to loftier clime
Were lifted, thus hath justice level'd us
Here on the earth. As avarice quench'd our love
Of good, without which is no working, thus
Here justice holds us prison'd, hand and foot
Chain'd down and bound, while heaven's just Lord shall please.
So long to tarry motionless outstretch'd."

    My knees I stoop'd, and would have spoke; but he,
Ere my beginning, by his ear perceiv'd
I did him reverence; and "What cause," said he,
"Hath bow'd thee thus!"--" Compunction," I rejoin'd.
"And inward awe of your high dignity."

    "Up," he exclaim'd, "brother! upon thy feet
Arise: err not: thy fellow servant I,
(Thine and all others') of one Sovran Power.
If thou hast ever mark'd those holy sounds
Of gospel truth, 'nor shall be given ill marriage,'
Thou mayst discern the reasons of my speech.
Go thy ways now; and linger here no more.
Thy tarrying is a let unto the tears,
With which I hasten that whereof thou spak'st.
I have on earth a kinswoman; her name
Alagia, worthy in herself, so ill
Example of our house corrupt her not:
And she is all remaineth of me there."

CANTO XX

Ill strives the will, 'gainst will more wise that strives
His pleasure therefore to mine own preferr'd,
I drew the sponge yet thirsty from the wave.

    Onward I mov'd: he also onward mov'd,
Who led me, coasting still, wherever place
Along the rock was vacant, as a man
Walks near the battlements on narrow wall.
For those on th' other part, who drop by drop
Wring out their all-infecting malady,
Too closely press the verge. Accurst be thou!

Dante Alighieri

Inveterate wolf! whose gorge ingluts more prey,
Than every beast beside, yet is not fill'd!
So bottomless thy maw! --Ye spheres of heaven!
To whom there are, as seems, who attribute
All change in mortal state, when is the day
Of his appearing, for whom fate reserves
To chase her hence? --With wary steps and slow
We pass'd; and I attentive to the shades,
Whom piteously I heard lament and wail;
And, 'midst the wailing, one before us heard
Cry out "O blessed Virgin!" as a dame
In the sharp pangs of childbed; and "How poor
Thou wast," it added, "witness that low roof
Where thou didst lay thy sacred burden down.
O good Fabricius! thou didst virtue choose
With poverty, before great wealth with vice."
  The words so pleas'd me, that desire to know
The spirit, from whose lip they seem'd to come,
Did draw me onward. Yet it spake the gift
Of Nicholas, which on the maidens he
Bounteous bestow'd, to save their youthful prime
Unblemish'd. "Spirit! who dost speak of deeds
So worthy, tell me who thou was," I said,
"And why thou dost with single voice renew
Memorial of such praise. That boon vouchsaf'd
Haply shall meet reward; if I return
To finish the Short pilgrimage of life,
Still speeding to its close on restless wing."
  "I," answer'd he, "will tell thee, not for hell,
Which thence I look for; but that in thyself
Grace so exceeding shines, before thy time
Of mortal dissolution. I was root
Of that ill plant, whose shade such poison sheds
O'er all the Christian land, that seldom thence
Good fruit is gather'd. Vengeance soon should come,
Had Ghent and Douay, Lille and Bruges power;
And vengeance I of heav'n's great Judge implore.
Hugh Capet was I high: from me descend
The Philips and the Louis, of whom France
Newly is govern'd; born of one, who ply'd
The slaughterer's trade at Paris. When the race
Of ancient kings had vanish'd (all save one
Wrapt up in sable weeds) within my gripe
I found the reins of empire, and such powers
Of new acquirement, with full store of friends,
That soon the widow'd circlet of the crown
Was girt upon the temples of my son,
He, from whose bones th' anointed race begins.
Till the great dower of Provence had remov'd
The stains, that yet obscur'd our lowly blood,

The Divine Comedy
Its sway indeed was narrow, but howe'er
It wrought no evil: there, with force and lies,
Began its rapine; after, for amends,
Poitou it seiz'd, Navarre and Gascony.
To Italy came Charles, and for amends
Young Conradine an innocent victim slew,
And sent th' angelic teacher back to heav'n,
Still for amends. I see the time at hand,
That forth from France invites another Charles
To make himself and kindred better known.
Unarm'd he issues, saving with that lance,
Which the arch-traitor tilted with; and that
He carries with so home a thrust, as rives
The bowels of poor Florence. No increase
Of territory hence, but sin and shame
Shall be his guerdon, and so much the more
As he more lightly deems of such foul wrong.
I see the other, who a prisoner late
Had steps on shore, exposing to the mart
His daughter, whom he bargains for, as do
The Corsairs for their slaves. O avarice!
What canst thou more, who hast subdued our blood
So wholly to thyself, they feel no care
Of their own flesh? To hide with direr guilt
Past ill and future, lo! the flower-de-luce
Enters Alagna! in his Vicar Christ
Himself a captive, and his mockery
Acted again! Lo! to his holy lip
The vinegar and gall once more applied!
And he 'twixt living robbers doom'd to bleed!
Lo! the new Pilate, of whose cruelty
Such violence cannot fill the measure up,
With no degree to sanction, pushes on
Into the temple his yet eager sails!
    "O sovran Master! when shall I rejoice
To see the vengeance, which thy wrath well-pleas'd
In secret silence broods?--While daylight lasts,
So long what thou didst hear of her, sole spouse
Of the Great Spirit, and on which thou turn'dst
To me for comment, is the general theme
Of all our prayers: but when it darkens, then
A different strain we utter, then record
Pygmalion, whom his gluttonous thirst of gold
Made traitor, robber, parricide: the woes
Of Midas, which his greedy wish ensued,
Mark'd for derision to all future times:
And the fond Achan, how he stole the prey,
That yet he seems by Joshua's ire pursued.
Sapphira with her husband next, we blame;
And praise the forefeet, that with furious ramp

Dante Alighieri

Spurn'd Heliodorus. All the mountain round
Rings with the infamy of Thracia's king,
Who slew his Phrygian charge: and last a shout
Ascends: "Declare, O Crassus! for thou know'st,
The flavour of thy gold." The voice of each
Now high now low, as each his impulse prompts,
Is led through many a pitch, acute or grave.
Therefore, not singly, I erewhile rehears'd
That blessedness we tell of in the day:
But near me none beside his accent rais'd."
    From him we now had parted, and essay'd
With utmost efforts to surmount the way,
When I did feel, as nodding to its fall,
The mountain tremble; whence an icy chill
Seiz'd on me, as on one to death convey'd.
So shook not Delos, when Latona there
Couch'd to bring forth the twin-born eyes of heaven.
    Forthwith from every side a shout arose
So vehement, that suddenly my guide
Drew near, and cried: "Doubt not, while I conduct thee."
"Glory!" all shouted (such the sounds mine ear
Gather'd from those, who near me swell'd the sounds)
"Glory in the highest be to God." We stood
Immovably suspended, like to those,
The shepherds, who first heard in Bethlehem's field
That song: till ceas'd the trembling, and the song
Was ended: then our hallow'd path resum'd,
Eying the prostrate shadows, who renew'd
Their custom'd mourning. Never in my breast
Did ignorance so struggle with desire
Of knowledge, if my memory do not err,
As in that moment; nor through haste dar'd I
To question, nor myself could aught discern,
So on I far'd in thoughtfulness and dread.

CANTO XXI

The natural thirst, ne'er quench'd but from the well,
Whereof the woman of Samaria crav'd,
Excited: haste along the cumber'd path,
After my guide, impell'd; and pity mov'd
My bosom for the 'vengeful deed, though just.
When lo! even as Luke relates, that Christ
Appear'd unto the two upon their way,
New-risen from his vaulted grave; to us
A shade appear'd, and after us approach'd,
Contemplating the crowd beneath its feet.
We were not ware of it; so first it spake,
Saying, "God give you peace, my brethren!" then

The Divine Comedy

Sudden we turn'd: and Virgil such salute,
As fitted that kind greeting, gave, and cried:
"Peace in the blessed council be thy lot
Awarded by that righteous court, which me
To everlasting banishment exiles!"

    "How!" he exclaim'd, nor from his speed meanwhile
Desisting, "If that ye be spirits, whom God
Vouchsafes not room above, who up the height
Has been thus far your guide?" To whom the bard:
"If thou observe the tokens, which this man
Trac'd by the finger of the angel bears,
'Tis plain that in the kingdom of the just
He needs must share. But sithence she, whose wheel
Spins day and night, for him not yet had drawn
That yarn, which, on the fatal distaff pil'd,
Clotho apportions to each wight that breathes,
His soul, that sister is to mine and thine,
Not of herself could mount, for not like ours
Her ken: whence I, from forth the ample gulf
Of hell was ta'en, to lead him, and will lead
Far as my lore avails. But, if thou know,
Instruct us for what cause, the mount erewhile
Thus shook and trembled: wherefore all at once
Seem'd shouting, even from his wave-wash'd foot."

    That questioning so tallied with my wish,
The thirst did feel abatement of its edge
E'en from expectance. He forthwith replied,
"In its devotion nought irregular
This mount can witness, or by punctual rule
Unsanction'd; here from every change exempt.
Other than that, which heaven in itself
Doth of itself receive, no influence
Can reach us. Tempest none, shower, hail or snow,
Hoar frost or dewy moistness, higher falls
Than that brief scale of threefold steps: thick clouds
Nor scudding rack are ever seen: swift glance
Ne'er lightens, nor Thaumantian Iris gleams,
That yonder often shift on each side heav'n.
Vapour adust doth never mount above
The highest of the trinal stairs, whereon
Peter's vicegerent stands. Lower perchance,
With various motion rock'd, trembles the soil:
But here, through wind in earth's deep hollow pent,
I know not how, yet never trembled: then
Trembles, when any spirit feels itself
So purified, that it may rise, or move
For rising, and such loud acclaim ensues.
Purification by the will alone
Is prov'd, that free to change society
Seizes the soul rejoicing in her will.

Dante Alighieri

Desire of bliss is present from the first;
But strong propension hinders, to that wish
By the just ordinance of heav'n oppos'd;
Propension now as eager to fulfil
Th' allotted torment, as erewhile to sin.
And I who in this punishment had lain
Five hundred years and more, but now have felt
Free wish for happier clime. Therefore thou felt'st
The mountain tremble, and the spirits devout
Heard'st, over all his limits, utter praise
To that liege Lord, whom I entreat their joy
To hasten." Thus he spake: and since the draught
Is grateful ever as the thirst is keen,
No words may speak my fullness of content.

    "Now," said the instructor sage, "I see the net
That takes ye here, and how the toils are loos'd,
Why rocks the mountain and why ye rejoice.
Vouchsafe, that from thy lips I next may learn,
Who on the earth thou wast, and wherefore here
So many an age wert prostrate." --"In that time,
When the good Titus, with Heav'n's King to help,
Aveng'd those piteous gashes, whence the blood
By Judas sold did issue, with the name
Most lasting and most honour'd there was I
Abundantly renown'd," the shade reply'd,
"Not yet with faith endued. So passing sweet
My vocal Spirit, from Tolosa, Rome
To herself drew me, where I merited
A myrtle garland to inwreathe my brow.
Statius they name me still. Of Thebes I sang,
And next of great Achilles: but i' th' way
Fell with the second burthen. Of my flame
Those sparkles were the seeds, which I deriv'd
From the bright fountain of celestial fire
That feeds unnumber'd lamps, the song I mean
Which sounds Aeneas' wand'rings: that the breast
I hung at, that the nurse, from whom my veins
Drank inspiration: whose authority
Was ever sacred with me. To have liv'd
Coeval with the Mantuan, I would bide
The revolution of another sun
Beyond my stated years in banishment."

    The Mantuan, when he heard him, turn'd to me,
And holding silence: by his countenance
Enjoin'd me silence but the power which wills,
Bears not supreme control: laughter and tears
Follow so closely on the passion prompts them,
They wait not for the motions of the will
In natures most sincere. I did but smile,
As one who winks; and thereupon the shade

Broke off, and peer'd into mine eyes, where best
Our looks interpret. "So to good event
Mayst thou conduct such great emprize," he cried,
"Say, why across thy visage beam'd, but now,
The lightning of a smile!" On either part
Now am I straiten'd; one conjures me speak,
Th' other to silence binds me: whence a sigh
I utter, and the sigh is heard. "Speak on; "
The teacher cried; "and do not fear to speak,
But tell him what so earnestly he asks."
Whereon I thus: "Perchance, O ancient spirit!
Thou marvel'st at my smiling. There is room
For yet more wonder. He who guides my ken
On high, he is that Mantuan, led by whom
Thou didst presume of men arid gods to sing.
If other cause thou deem'dst for which I smil'd,
Leave it as not the true one; and believe
Those words, thou spak'st of him, indeed the cause."
 Now down he bent t' embrace my teacher's feet;
But he forbade him: "Brother! do it not:
Thou art a shadow, and behold'st a shade."
He rising answer'd thus: "Now hast thou prov'd
The force and ardour of the love I bear thee,
When I forget we are but things of air,
And as a substance treat an empty shade."

CANTO XXII

Now we had left the angel, who had turn'd
To the sixth circle our ascending step,
One gash from off my forehead raz'd: while they,
Whose wishes tend to justice, shouted forth:
"Blessed!" and ended with, "I thirst:" and I,
More nimble than along the other straits,
So journey'd, that, without the sense of toil,
I follow'd upward the swift-footed shades;
When Virgil thus began: "Let its pure flame
From virtue flow, and love can never fail
To warm another's bosom' so the light
Shine manifestly forth. Hence from that hour,
When 'mongst us in the purlieus of the deep,
Came down the spirit of Aquinum's hard,
Who told of thine affection, my good will
Hath been for thee of quality as strong
As ever link'd itself to one not seen.
Therefore these stairs will now seem short to me.
But tell me: and if too secure I loose
The rein with a friend's license, as a friend
Forgive me, and speak now as with a friend:

Dante Alighieri

How chanc'd it covetous desire could find
Place in that bosom, 'midst such ample store
Of wisdom, as thy zeal had treasur'd there?"
    First somewhat mov'd to laughter by his words,
Statius replied: "Each syllable of thine
Is a dear pledge of love. Things oft appear
That minister false matters to our doubts,
When their true causes are remov'd from sight.
Thy question doth assure me, thou believ'st
I was on earth a covetous man, perhaps
Because thou found'st me in that circle plac'd.
Know then I was too wide of avarice:
And e'en for that excess, thousands of moons
Have wax'd and wan'd upon my sufferings.
And were it not that I with heedful care
Noted where thou exclaim'st as if in ire
With human nature, 'Why, thou cursed thirst
Of gold! dost not with juster measure guide
The appetite of mortals?' I had met
The fierce encounter of the voluble rock.
Then was I ware that with too ample wing
The hands may haste to lavishment, and turn'd,
As from my other evil, so from this
In penitence. How many from their grave
Shall with shorn locks arise, who living, aye
And at life's last extreme, of this offence,
Through ignorance, did not repent. And know,
The fault which lies direct from any sin
In level opposition, here With that
Wastes its green rankness on one common heap.
Therefore if I have been with those, who wail
Their avarice, to cleanse me, through reverse
Of their transgression, such hath been my lot."
    To whom the sovran of the pastoral song:
"While thou didst sing that cruel warfare wag'd
By the twin sorrow of Jocasta's womb,
From thy discourse with Clio there, it seems
As faith had not been shine: without the which
Good deeds suffice not. And if so, what sun
Rose on thee, or what candle pierc'd the dark
That thou didst after see to hoist the sail,
And follow, where the fisherman had led?"
    He answering thus: "By thee conducted first,
I enter'd the Parnassian grots, and quaff'd
Of the clear spring; illumin'd first by thee
Open'd mine eyes to God. Thou didst, as one,
Who, journeying through the darkness, hears a light
Behind, that profits not himself, but makes
His followers wise, when thou exclaimedst, 'Lo!
A renovated world! Justice return'd!

The Divine Comedy

Times of primeval innocence restor'd!
And a new race descended from above!'
Poet and Christian both to thee I owed.
That thou mayst mark more clearly what I trace,
My hand shall stretch forth to inform the lines
With livelier colouring. Soon o'er all the world,
By messengers from heav'n, the true belief
Teem'd now prolific, and that word of thine
Accordant, to the new instructors chim'd.
Induc'd by which agreement, I was wont
Resort to them; and soon their sanctity
So won upon me, that, Domitian's rage
Pursuing them, I mix'd my tears with theirs,
And, while on earth I stay'd, still succour'd them;
And their most righteous customs made me scorn
All sects besides. Before I led the Greeks
In tuneful fiction, to the streams of Thebes,
I was baptiz'd; but secretly, through fear,
Remain'd a Christian, and conform'd long time
To Pagan rites. Five centuries and more,
T for that lukewarmness was fain to pace
Round the fourth circle. Thou then, who hast rais'd
The covering, which did hide such blessing from me,
Whilst much of this ascent is yet to climb,
Say, if thou know, where our old Terence bides,
Caecilius, Plautus, Varro: if condemn'd
They dwell, and in what province of the deep."
"These," said my guide, "with Persius and myself,
And others many more, are with that Greek,
Of mortals, the most cherish'd by the Nine,
In the first ward of darkness. There ofttimes
We of that mount hold converse, on whose top
For aye our nurses live. We have the bard
Of Pella, and the Teian, Agatho,
Simonides, and many a Grecian else
Ingarlanded with laurel. Of thy train
Antigone is there, Deiphile,
Argia, and as sorrowful as erst
Ismene, and who show'd Langia's wave:
Deidamia with her sisters there,
And blind Tiresias' daughter, and the bride
Sea-born of Peleus." Either poet now
Was silent, and no longer by th' ascent
Or the steep walls obstructed, round them cast
Inquiring eyes. Four handmaids of the day
Had finish'd now their office, and the fifth
Was at the chariot-beam, directing still
Its balmy point aloof, when thus my guide:
"Methinks, it well behooves us to the brink
Bend the right shoulder' circuiting the mount,

As we have ever us'd." So custom there
Was usher to the road, the which we chose
Less doubtful, as that worthy shade complied.

     They on before me went; I sole pursued,
List'ning their speech, that to my thoughts convey'd
Mysterious lessons of sweet poesy.
But soon they ceas'd; for midway of the road
A tree we found, with goodly fruitage hung,
And pleasant to the smell: and as a fir
Upward from bough to bough less ample spreads,
So downward this less ample spread, that none.
Methinks, aloft may climb. Upon the side,
That clos'd our path, a liquid crystal fell
From the steep rock, and through the sprays above
Stream'd showering. With associate step the bards
Drew near the plant; and from amidst the leaves
A voice was heard: "Ye shall be chary of me;"
And after added: "Mary took more thought
For joy and honour of the nuptial feast,
Than for herself who answers now for you.
The women of old Rome were satisfied
With water for their beverage. Daniel fed
On pulse, and wisdom gain'd. The primal age
Was beautiful as gold; and hunger then
Made acorns tasteful, thirst each rivulet
Run nectar. Honey and locusts were the food,
Whereon the Baptist in the wilderness
Fed, and that eminence of glory reach'd
And greatness, which the' Evangelist records."

CANTO XXIII

On the green leaf mine eyes were fix'd, like his
Who throws away his days in idle chase
Of the diminutive, when thus I heard
The more than father warn me: "Son! our time
Asks thriftier using. Linger not: away."

     Thereat my face and steps at once I turn'd
Toward the sages, by whose converse cheer'd
I journey'd on, and felt no toil: and lo!
A sound of weeping and a song: "My lips,
O Lord!" and these so mingled, it gave birth
To pleasure and to pain. "O Sire, belov'd!
Say what is this I hear?" Thus I inquir'd.

     "Spirits," said he, "who as they go, perchance,
Their debt of duty pay." As on their road
The thoughtful pilgrims, overtaking some
Not known unto them, turn to them, and look,
But stay not; thus, approaching from behind

The Divine Comedy

With speedier motion, eyed us, as they pass'd,
A crowd of spirits, silent and devout.
The eyes of each were dark and hollow: pale
Their visage, and so lean withal, the bones
Stood staring thro' the skin. I do not think
Thus dry and meagre Erisicthon show'd,
When pinc'ed by sharp-set famine to the quick.

    "Lo!" to myself I mus'd, "the race, who lost
Jerusalem, when Mary with dire beak
Prey'd on her child." The sockets seem'd as rings,
From which the gems were drops. Who reads the name
Of man upon his forehead, there the M
Had trac'd most plainly. Who would deem, that scent
Of water and an apple, could have prov'd
Powerful to generate such pining want,
Not knowing how it wrought? While now I stood
Wond'ring what thus could waste them (for the cause
Of their gaunt hollowness and scaly rind
Appear'd not) lo! a spirit turn'd his eyes
In their deep-sunken cell, and fasten'd then
On me, then cried with vehemence aloud:
"What grace is this vouchsaf'd me?" By his looks
I ne'er had recogniz'd him: but the voice
Brought to my knowledge what his cheer conceal'd.
Remembrance of his alter'd lineaments
Was kindled from that spark; and I agniz'd
The visage of Forese. "Ah! respect
This wan and leprous wither'd skin," thus he
Suppliant implor'd, "this macerated flesh.
Speak to me truly of thyself. And who
Are those twain spirits, that escort thee there?
Be it not said thou Scorn'st to talk with me."

    "That face of thine," I answer'd him, "which dead
I once bewail'd, disposes me not less
For weeping, when I see It thus transform'd.
Say then, by Heav'n, what blasts ye thus? The whilst
I wonder, ask not Speech from me: unapt
Is he to speak, whom other will employs.

    He thus: "The water and tee plant we pass'd,
Virtue possesses, by th' eternal will
Infus'd, the which so pines me. Every spirit,
Whose song bewails his gluttony indulg'd
Too grossly, here in hunger and in thirst
Is purified. The odour, which the fruit,
And spray, that showers upon the verdure, breathe,
Inflames us with desire to feed and drink.
Nor once alone encompassing our route
We come to add fresh fuel to the pain:
Pain, said I? solace rather: for that will
To the tree leads us, by which Christ was led

Dante Alighieri

To call Elias, joyful when he paid
Our ransom from his vein." I answering thus:
"Forese! from that day, in which the world
For better life thou changedst, not five years
Have circled. If the power of sinning more
Were first concluded in thee, ere thou knew'st
That kindly grief, which re-espouses us
To God, how hither art thou come so soon?
I thought to find thee lower, there, where time
Is recompense for time." He straight replied:
"To drink up the sweet wormwood of affliction
I have been brought thus early by the tears
Stream'd down my Nella's cheeks. Her prayers devout,
Her sighs have drawn me from the coast, where oft
Expectance lingers, and have set me free
From th' other circles. In the sight of God
So much the dearer is my widow priz'd,
She whom I lov'd so fondly, as she ranks
More singly eminent for virtuous deeds.
The tract most barb'rous of Sardinia's isle,
Hath dames more chaste and modester by far
Than that wherein I left her. O sweet brother!
What wouldst thou have me say? A time to come
Stands full within my view, to which this hour
Shall not be counted of an ancient date,
When from the pulpit shall be loudly warn'd
Th' unblushing dames of Florence, lest they bare
Unkerchief'd bosoms to the common gaze.
What savage women hath the world e'er seen,
What Saracens, for whom there needed scourge
Of spiritual or other discipline,
To force them walk with cov'ring on their limbs!
But did they see, the shameless ones, that Heav'n
Wafts on swift wing toward them, while I speak,
Their mouths were op'd for howling: they shall taste
Of borrow (unless foresight cheat me here)
Or ere the cheek of him be cloth'd with down
Who is now rock'd with lullaby asleep.
Ah! now, my brother, hide thyself no more,
Thou seest how not I alone but all
Gaze, where thou veil'st the intercepted sun."
        Whence I replied: "If thou recall to mind
What we were once together, even yet
Remembrance of those days may grieve thee sore.
That I forsook that life, was due to him
Who there precedes me, some few evenings past,
When she was round, who shines with sister lamp
To his, that glisters yonder," and I show'd
The sun. "Tis he, who through profoundest night
Of the true dead has brought me, with this flesh

201

As true, that follows. From that gloom the aid
Of his sure comfort drew me on to climb,
And climbing wind along this mountain-steep,
Which rectifies in you whate'er the world
Made crooked and deprav'd I have his word,
That he will bear me company as far
As till I come where Beatrice dwells:
But there must leave me. Virgil is that spirit,
Who thus hath promis'd," and I pointed to him;
"The other is that shade, for whom so late
Your realm, as he arose, exulting shook
Through every pendent cliff and rocky bound."

CANTO XXIV

Our journey was not slacken'd by our talk,
Nor yet our talk by journeying. Still we spake,
And urg'd our travel stoutly, like a ship
When the wind sits astern. The shadowy forms,
That seem'd things dead and dead again, drew in
At their deep-delved orbs rare wonder of me,
Perceiving I had life; and I my words
Continued, and thus spake; "He journeys up
Perhaps more tardily then else he would,
For others' sake. But tell me, if thou know'st,
Where is Piccarda? Tell me, if I see
Any of mark, among this multitude,
Who eye me thus."--"My sister (she for whom,
'Twixt beautiful and good I cannot say
Which name was fitter) wears e'en now her crown,
And triumphs in Olympus." Saying this,
He added: "Since spare diet hath so worn
Our semblance out, 't is lawful here to name
Each one . This," and his finger then he rais'd,
"Is Buonaggiuna,--Buonaggiuna, he
Of Lucca: and that face beyond him, pierc'd
Unto a leaner fineness than the rest,
Had keeping of the church: he was of Tours,
And purges by wan abstinence away
Bolsena's eels and cups of muscadel."

    He show'd me many others, one by one,
And all, as they were nam'd, seem'd well content;
For no dark gesture I discern'd in any.
I saw through hunger Ubaldino grind
His teeth on emptiness; and Boniface,
That wav'd the crozier o'er a num'rous flock.
I saw the Marquis, who tad time erewhile
To swill at Forli with less drought, yet so
Was one ne'er sated. I howe'er, like him,

Dante Alighieri

That gazing 'midst a crowd, singles out one,
So singled him of Lucca; for methought
Was none amongst them took such note of me.
Somewhat I heard him whisper of Gentucca:
The sound was indistinct, and murmur'd there,
Where justice, that so strips them, fix'd her sting.
    "Spirit!" said I, "it seems as thou wouldst fain
Speak with me. Let me hear thee. Mutual wish
To converse prompts, which let us both indulge."
    He, answ'ring, straight began: "Woman is born,
Whose brow no wimple shades yet, that shall make
My city please thee, blame it as they may.
Go then with this forewarning. If aught false
My whisper too implied, th' event shall tell
But say, if of a truth I see the man
Of that new lay th' inventor, which begins
With 'Ladies, ye that con the lore of love'."
    To whom I thus: "Count of me but as one
Who am the scribe of love; that, when he breathes,
Take up my pen, and, as he dictates, write."
    "Brother!" said he, "the hind'rance which once held
The notary with Guittone and myself,
Short of that new and sweeter style I hear,
Is now disclos'd. I see how ye your plumes
Stretch, as th' inditer guides them; which, no question,
Ours did not. He that seeks a grace beyond,
Sees not the distance parts one style from other."
And, as contented, here he held his peace.
    Like as the bird, that winter near the Nile,
In squared regiment direct their course,
Then stretch themselves in file for speedier flight;
Thus all the tribe of spirits, as they turn'd
Their visage, faster deaf, nimble alike
Through leanness and desire. And as a man,
Tir'd With the motion of a trotting steed,
Slacks pace, and stays behind his company,
Till his o'erbreathed lungs keep temperate time;
E'en so Forese let that holy crew
Proceed, behind them lingering at my side,
And saying: "When shall I again behold thee?"
    "How long my life may last," said I, "I know not;
This know, how soon soever I return,
My wishes will before me have arriv'd.
Sithence the place, where I am set to live,
Is, day by day, more scoop'd of all its good,
And dismal ruin seems to threaten it."
    "Go now," he cried: "lo! he, whose guilt is most,
Passes before my vision, dragg'd at heels
Of an infuriate beast. Toward the vale,
Where guilt hath no redemption, on it speeds,

The Divine Comedy
Each step increasing swiftness on the last;
Until a blow it strikes, that leaveth him
A corse most vilely shatter'd. No long space
Those wheels have yet to roll" (therewith his eyes
Look'd up to heav'n) "ere thou shalt plainly see
That which my words may not more plainly tell.
I quit thee: time is precious here: I lose
Too much, thus measuring my pace with shine."

    As from a troop of well-rank'd chivalry
One knight, more enterprising than the rest,
Pricks forth at gallop, eager to display
His prowess in the first encounter prov'd
So parted he from us with lengthen'd strides,
And left me on the way with those twain spirits,
Who were such mighty marshals of the world.

    When he beyond us had so fled mine eyes
No nearer reach'd him, than my thought his words,
The branches of another fruit, thick hung,
And blooming fresh, appear'd. E'en as our steps
Turn'd thither, not far off it rose to view.
Beneath it were a multitude, that rais'd
Their hands, and shouted forth I know not What
Unto the boughs; like greedy and fond brats,
That beg, and answer none obtain from him,
Of whom they beg; but more to draw them on,
He at arm's length the object of their wish
Above them holds aloft, and hides it not.

    At length, as undeceiv'd they went their way:
And we approach the tree, who vows and tears
Sue to in vain, the mighty tree. "Pass on,
And come not near. Stands higher up the wood,
Whereof Eve tasted, and from it was ta'en
'this plant." Such sounds from midst the thickets came.
Whence I, with either bard, close to the side
That rose, pass'd forth beyond. "Remember," next
We heard, "those noblest creatures of the clouds,
How they their twofold bosoms overgorg'd
Oppos'd in fight to Theseus: call to mind
The Hebrews, how effeminate they stoop'd
To ease their thirst; whence Gideon's ranks were thinn'd,
As he to Midian march'd adown the hills."

    Thus near one border coasting, still we heard
The sins of gluttony, with woe erewhile
Reguerdon'd. Then along the lonely path,
Once more at large, full thousand paces on
We travel'd, each contemplative and mute.

    "Why pensive journey thus ye three alone?"
Thus suddenly a voice exclaim'd: whereat
I shook, as doth a scar'd and paltry beast;
Then rais'd my head to look from whence it came.

Was ne'er, in furnace, glass, or metal seen
So bright and glowing red, as was the shape
I now beheld. "If ye desire to mount,"
He cried, "here must ye turn. This way he goes,
Who goes in quest of peace." His countenance
Had dazzled me; and to my guides I fac'd
Backward, like one who walks, as sound directs.

    As when, to harbinger the dawn, springs up
On freshen'd wing the air of May, and breathes
Of fragrance, all impregn'd with herb and flowers,
E'en such a wind I felt upon my front
Blow gently, and the moving of a wing
Perceiv'd, that moving shed ambrosial smell;
And then a voice: "Blessed are they, whom grace
Doth so illume, that appetite in them
Exhaleth no inordinate desire,
Still hung'ring as the rule of temperance wills."

CANTO XXV

It was an hour, when he who climbs, had need
To walk uncrippled: for the sun had now
To Taurus the meridian circle left,
And to the Scorpion left the night. As one
That makes no pause, but presses on his road,
Whate'er betide him, if some urgent need
Impel: so enter'd we upon our way,
One before other; for, but singly, none
That steep and narrow scale admits to climb.

    E'en as the young stork lifteth up his wing
Through wish to fly, yet ventures not to quit
The nest, and drops it; so in me desire
Of questioning my guide arose, and fell,
Arriving even to the act, that marks
A man prepar'd for speech. Him all our haste
Restrain'd not, but thus spake the sire belov'd:
Fear not to speed the shaft, that on thy lip
Stands trembling for its flight." Encourag'd thus
I straight began: "How there can leanness come,
Where is no want of nourishment to feed?"

    "If thou," he answer'd, "hadst remember'd thee,
How Meleager with the wasting brand
Wasted alike, by equal fires consm'd,
This would not trouble thee: and hadst thou thought,
How in the mirror your reflected form
With mimic motion vibrates, what now seems
Hard, had appear'd no harder than the pulp
Of summer fruit mature. But that thy will
In certainty may find its full repose,

The Divine Comedy

Lo Statius here! on him I call, and pray
That he would now be healer of thy wound."
    "If in thy presence I unfold to him
The secrets of heaven's vengeance, let me plead
Thine own injunction, to exculpate me."
So Statius answer'd, and forthwith began:
"Attend my words, O son, and in thy mind
Receive them: so shall they be light to clear
The doubt thou offer'st. Blood, concocted well,
Which by the thirsty veins is ne'er imbib'd,
And rests as food superfluous, to be ta'en
From the replenish'd table, in the heart
Derives effectual virtue, that informs
The several human limbs, as being that,
Which passes through the veins itself to make them.
Yet more concocted it descends, where shame
Forbids to mention: and from thence distils
In natural vessel on another's blood.
Then each unite together, one dispos'd
T' endure, to act the other, through meet frame
Of its recipient mould: that being reach'd,
It 'gins to work, coagulating first;
Then vivifies what its own substance caus'd
To bear. With animation now indued,
The active virtue (differing from a plant
No further, than that this is on the way
And at its limit that) continues yet
To operate, that now it moves, and feels,
As sea sponge clinging to the rock: and there
Assumes th' organic powers its seed convey'd.
'This is the period, son! at which the virtue,
That from the generating heart proceeds,
Is pliant and expansive; for each limb
Is in the heart by forgeful nature plann'd.
How babe of animal becomes, remains
For thy consid'ring. At this point, more wise,
Than thou hast err'd, making the soul disjoin'd
From passive intellect, because he saw
No organ for the latter's use assign'd.
    "Open thy bosom to the truth that comes.
Know soon as in the embryo, to the brain,
Articulation is complete, then turns
The primal Mover with a smile of joy
On such great work of nature, and imbreathes
New spirit replete with virtue, that what here
Active it finds, to its own substance draws,
And forms an individual soul, that lives,
And feels, and bends reflective on itself.
And that thou less mayst marvel at the word,
Mark the sun's heat, how that to wine doth change,

Dante Alighieri

Mix'd with the moisture filter'd through the vine.
    "When Lachesis hath spun the thread, the soul
Takes with her both the human and divine,
Memory, intelligence, and will, in act
Far keener than before, the other powers
Inactive all and mute. No pause allow'd,
In wond'rous sort self-moving, to one strand
Of those, where the departed roam, she falls,
Here learns her destin'd path. Soon as the place
Receives her, round the plastic virtue beams,
Distinct as in the living limbs before:
And as the air, when saturate with showers,
The casual beam refracting, decks itself
With many a hue; so here the ambient air
Weareth that form, which influence of the soul
Imprints on it; and like the flame, that where
The fire moves, thither follows, so henceforth
The new form on the spirit follows still:
Hence hath it semblance, and is shadow call'd,
With each sense even to the sight endued:
Hence speech is ours, hence laughter, tears, and sighs
Which thou mayst oft have witness'd on the mount
Th' obedient shadow fails not to present
Whatever varying passion moves within us.
And this the cause of what thou marvel'st at."
    Now the last flexure of our way we reach'd,
And to the right hand turning, other care
Awaits us. Here the rocky precipice
Hurls forth redundant flames, and from the rim
A blast upblown, with forcible rebuff
Driveth them back, sequester'd from its bound.
    Behoov'd us, one by one, along the side,
That border'd on the void, to pass; and I
Fear'd on one hand the fire, on th' other fear'd
Headlong to fall: when thus th' instructor warn'd:
"Strict rein must in this place direct the eyes.
A little swerving and the way is lost."
    Then from the bosom of the burning mass,
"O God of mercy!" heard I sung; and felt
No less desire to turn. And when I saw
Spirits along the flame proceeding, I
Between their footsteps and mine own was fain
To share by turns my view. At the hymn's close
They shouted loud, "I do not know a man;"
Then in low voice again took up the strain,
Which once more ended, "To the wood," they cried,
"Ran Dian, and drave forth Callisto, stung
With Cytherea's poison:" then return'd
Unto their song; then marry a pair extoll'd,
Who liv'd in virtue chastely, and the bands

Of wedded love. Nor from that task, I ween,
Surcease they; whilesoe'er the scorching fire
Enclasps them. Of such skill appliance needs
To medicine the wound, that healeth last.

CANTO XXVI

While singly thus along the rim we walk'd,
Oft the good master warn'd me: "Look thou well.
Avail it that I caution thee." The sun
Now all the western clime irradiate chang'd
From azure tinct to white; and, as I pass'd,
My passing shadow made the umber'd flame
Burn ruddier. At so strange a sight I mark'd
That many a spirit marvel'd on his way.

    This bred occasion first to speak of me,
"He seems," said they, "no insubstantial frame:"
Then to obtain what certainty they might,
Stretch'd towards me, careful not to overpass
The burning pale. "O thou, who followest
The others, haply not more slow than they,
But mov'd by rev'rence, answer me, who burn
In thirst and fire: nor I alone, but these
All for thine answer do more thirst, than doth
Indian or Aethiop for the cooling stream.
Tell us, how is it that thou mak'st thyself
A wall against the sun, as thou not yet
Into th' inextricable toils of death
Hadst enter'd?" Thus spake one, and I had straight
Declar'd me, if attention had not turn'd
To new appearance. Meeting these, there came,
Midway the burning path, a crowd, on whom
Earnestly gazing, from each part I view
The shadows all press forward, sev'rally
Each snatch a hasty kiss, and then away.
E'en so the emmets, 'mid their dusky troops,
Peer closely one at other, to spy out
Their mutual road perchance, and how they thrive.

    That friendly greeting parted, ere dispatch
Of the first onward step, from either tribe
Loud clamour rises: those, who newly come,
Shout Sodom and Gomorrah!" these, "The cow
Pasiphae enter'd, that the beast she woo'd
Might rush unto her luxury." Then as cranes,
That part towards the Riphaean mountains fly,
Part towards the Lybic sands, these to avoid
The ice, and those the sun; so hasteth off
One crowd, advances th' other; and resume
Their first song weeping, and their several shout.

Dante Alighieri

     Again drew near my side the very same,
Who had erewhile besought me, and their looks
Mark'd eagerness to listen. I, who twice
Their will had noted, spake: "O spirits secure,
Whene'er the time may be, of peaceful end!
My limbs, nor crude, nor in mature old age,
Have I left yonder: here they bear me, fed
With blood, and sinew-strung. That I no more
May live in blindness, hence I tend aloft.
There is a dame on high, who wind for us
This grace, by which my mortal through your realm
I bear. But may your utmost wish soon meet
Such full fruition, that the orb of heaven,
Fullest of love, and of most ample space,
Receive you, as ye tell (upon my page
Henceforth to stand recorded) who ye are,
And what this multitude, that at your backs
Have past behind us." As one, mountain-bred,
Rugged and clownish, if some city's walls
He chance to enter, round him stares agape,
Confounded and struck dumb; e'en such appear'd
Each spirit. But when rid of that amaze,
(Not long the inmate of a noble heart)
He, who before had question'd, thus resum'd:
"O blessed, who, for death preparing, tak'st
Experience of our limits, in thy bark!
Their crime, who not with us proceed, was that,
For which, as he did triumph, Caesar heard
The snout of 'queen,' to taunt him. Hence their cry
Of 'Sodom,' as they parted, to rebuke
Themselves, and aid the burning by their shame.
Our sinning was Hermaphrodite: but we,
Because the law of human kind we broke,
Following like beasts our vile concupiscence,
Hence parting from them, to our own disgrace
Record the name of her, by whom the beast
In bestial tire was acted. Now our deeds
Thou know'st, and how we sinn'd. If thou by name
Wouldst haply know us, time permits not now
To tell so much, nor can I. Of myself
Learn what thou wishest. Guinicelli I,
Who having truly sorrow'd ere my last,
Already cleanse me." With such pious joy,
As the two sons upon their mother gaz'd
From sad Lycurgus rescu'd, such my joy
(Save that I more represt it) when I heard
From his own lips the name of him pronounc'd,
Who was a father to me, and to those
My betters, who have ever us'd the sweet
And pleasant rhymes of love. So nought I heard

The Divine Comedy

Nor spake, but long time thoughtfully I went,
Gazing on him; and, only for the fire,
Approach'd not nearer. When my eyes were fed
By looking on him, with such solemn pledge,
As forces credence, I devoted me
Unto his service wholly. In reply
He thus bespake me: "What from thee I hear
Is grav'd so deeply on my mind, the waves
Of Lethe shall not wash it off, nor make
A whit less lively. But as now thy oath
Has seal'd the truth, declare what cause impels
That love, which both thy looks and speech bewray."

    "Those dulcet lays," I answer'd, "which, as long
As of our tongue the beauty does not fade,
Shall make us love the very ink that trac'd them."

    "Brother!" he cried, and pointed at a shade
Before him, "there is one, whose mother speech
Doth owe to him a fairer ornament.
He in love ditties and the tales of prose
Without a rival stands, and lets the fools
Talk on, who think the songster of Limoges
O'ertops him. Rumour and the popular voice
They look to more than truth, and so confirm
Opinion, ere by art or reason taught.
Thus many of the elder time cried up
Guittone, giving him the prize, till truth
By strength of numbers vanquish'd. If thou own
So ample privilege, as to have gain'd
Free entrance to the cloister, whereof Christ
Is Abbot of the college, say to him
One paternoster for me, far as needs
For dwellers in this world, where power to sin
No longer tempts us." Haply to make way
For one, that follow'd next, when that was said,
He vanish'd through the fire, as through the wave
A fish, that glances diving to the deep.

    I, to the spirit he had shown me, drew
A little onward, and besought his name,
For which my heart, I said, kept gracious room.
He frankly thus began: "Thy courtesy
So wins on me, I have nor power nor will
To hide me. I am Arnault; and with songs,
Sorely lamenting for my folly past,
Thorough this ford of fire I wade, and see
The day, I hope for, smiling in my view.
I pray ye by the worth that guides ye up
Unto the summit of the scale, in time
Remember ye my suff'rings." With such words
He disappear'd in the refining flame.

CANTO XXVII

Now was the sun so station'd, as when first
His early radiance quivers on the heights,
Where stream'd his Maker's blood, while Libra hangs
Above Hesperian Ebro, and new fires
Meridian flash on Ganges' yellow tide.

    So day was sinking, when the' angel of God
Appear'd before us. Joy was in his mien.
Forth of the flame he stood upon the brink,
And with a voice, whose lively clearness far
Surpass'd our human, "Blessed are the pure
In heart," he Sang: then near him as we came,
"Go ye not further, holy spirits!" he cried,
"Ere the fire pierce you: enter in; and list
Attentive to the song ye hear from thence."

    I, when I heard his saying, was as one
Laid in the grave. My hands together clasp'd,
And upward stretching, on the fire I look'd,
And busy fancy conjur'd up the forms
Erewhile beheld alive consum'd in flames.

    Th' escorting spirits turn'd with gentle looks
Toward me, and the Mantuan spake: "My son,
Here torment thou mayst feel, but canst not death.
Remember thee, remember thee, if I
Safe e'en on Geryon brought thee: now I come
More near to God, wilt thou not trust me now?
Of this be sure: though in its womb that flame
A thousand years contain'd thee, from thy head
No hair should perish. If thou doubt my truth,
Approach, and with thy hands thy vesture's hem
Stretch forth, and for thyself confirm belief.
Lay now all fear, O lay all fear aside.
Turn hither, and come onward undismay'd."
I still, though conscience urg'd' no step advanc'd.

    When still he saw me fix'd and obstinate,
Somewhat disturb'd he cried: "Mark now, my son,
From Beatrice thou art by this wall
Divided." As at Thisbe's name the eye
Of Pyramus was open'd (when life ebb'd
Fast from his veins), and took one parting glance,
While vermeil dyed the mulberry; thus I turn'd
To my sage guide, relenting, when I heard
The name, that springs forever in my breast.

    He shook his forehead; and, "How long," he said,
"Linger we now?" then smil'd, as one would smile
Upon a child, that eyes the fruit and yields.
Into the fire before me then he walk'd;
And Statius, who erewhile no little space

The Divine Comedy

Had parted us, he pray'd to come behind.
    I would have cast me into molten glass
To cool me, when I enter'd; so intense
Rag'd the conflagrant mass. The sire belov'd,
To comfort me, as he proceeded, still
Of Beatrice talk'd. "Her eyes," saith he,
"E'en now I seem to view." From the other side
A voice, that sang, did guide us, and the voice
Following, with heedful ear, we issued forth,
There where the path led upward. "Come," we heard,
"Come, blessed of my Father." Such the sounds,
That hail'd us from within a light, which shone
So radiant, I could not endure the view.
"The sun," it added, "hastes: and evening comes.
Delay not: ere the western sky is hung
With blackness, strive ye for the pass." Our way
Upright within the rock arose, and fac'd
Such part of heav'n, that from before my steps
The beams were shrouded of the sinking sun.
    Nor many stairs were overpass, when now
By fading of the shadow we perceiv'd
The sun behind us couch'd: and ere one face
Of darkness o'er its measureless expanse
Involv'd th' horizon, and the night her lot
Held individual, each of us had made
A stair his pallet: not that will, but power,
Had fail'd us, by the nature of that mount
Forbidden further travel. As the goats,
That late have skipp'd and wanton'd rapidly
Upon the craggy cliffs, ere they had ta'en
Their supper on the herb, now silent lie
And ruminate beneath the umbrage brown,
While noonday rages; and the goatherd leans
Upon his staff, and leaning watches them:
And as the swain, that lodges out all night
In quiet by his flock, lest beast of prey
Disperse them; even so all three abode,
I as a goat and as the shepherds they,
Close pent on either side by shelving rock.
    A little glimpse of sky was seen above;
Yet by that little I beheld the stars
In magnitude and rustle shining forth
With more than wonted glory. As I lay,
Gazing on them, and in that fit of musing,
Sleep overcame me, sleep, that bringeth oft
Tidings of future hap. About the hour,
As I believe, when Venus from the east
First lighten'd on the mountain, she whose orb
Seems always glowing with the fire of love,
A lady young and beautiful, I dream'd,

Dante Alighieri

Was passing o'er a lea; and, as she came,
Methought I saw her ever and anon
Bending to cull the flowers; and thus she sang:
"Know ye, whoever of my name would ask,
That I am Leah: for my brow to weave
A garland, these fair hands unwearied ply.
To please me at the crystal mirror, here
I deck me. But my sister Rachel, she
Before her glass abides the livelong day,
Her radiant eyes beholding, charm'd no less,
Than I with this delightful task. Her joy
In contemplation, as in labour mine."
    And now as glimm'ring dawn appear'd, that breaks
More welcome to the pilgrim still, as he
Sojourns less distant on his homeward way,
Darkness from all sides fled, and with it fled
My slumber; whence I rose and saw my guide
Already risen. "That delicious fruit,
Which through so many a branch the zealous care
Of mortals roams in quest of, shall this day
Appease thy hunger." Such the words I heard
From Virgil's lip; and never greeting heard
So pleasant as the sounds. Within me straight
Desire so grew upon desire to mount,
Thenceforward at each step I felt the wings
Increasing for my flight. When we had run
O'er all the ladder to its topmost round,
As there we stood, on me the Mantuan fix'd
His eyes, and thus he spake: "Both fires, my son,
The temporal and eternal, thou hast seen,
And art arriv'd, where of itself my ken
No further reaches. I with skill and art
Thus far have drawn thee. Now thy pleasure take
For guide. Thou hast o'ercome the steeper way,
O'ercome the straighter. Lo! the sun, that darts
His beam upon thy forehead! lo! the herb,
The arboreta and flowers, which of itself
This land pours forth profuse! Till those bright eyes
With gladness come, which, weeping, made me haste
To succour thee, thou mayst or seat thee down,
Or wander where thou wilt. Expect no more
Sanction of warning voice or sign from me,
Free of thy own arbitrement to choose,
Discreet, judicious. To distrust thy sense
Were henceforth error. I invest thee then
With crown and mitre, sovereign o'er thyself."

The Divine Comedy
CANTO XXVIII

Through that celestial forest, whose thick shade
With lively greenness the new-springing day
Attemper'd, eager now to roam, and search
Its limits round, forthwith I left the bank,
Along the champain leisurely my way
Pursuing, o'er the ground, that on all sides
Delicious odour breath'd. A pleasant air,
That intermitted never, never veer'd,
Smote on my temples, gently, as a wind
Of softest influence: at which the sprays,
Obedient all, lean'd trembling to that part
Where first the holy mountain casts his shade,
Yet were not so disorder'd, but that still
Upon their top the feather'd quiristers
Applied their wonted art, and with full joy
Welcom'd those hours of prime, and warbled shrill
Amid the leaves, that to their jocund lays
inept tenor; even as from branch to branch,
Along the piney forests on the shore
Of Chiassi, rolls the gath'ring melody,
When Eolus hath from his cavern loos'd
The dripping south. Already had my steps,
Though slow, so far into that ancient wood
Transported me, I could not ken the place
Where I had enter'd, when behold! my path
Was bounded by a rill, which to the left
With little rippling waters bent the grass,
That issued from its brink. On earth no wave
How clean soe'er, that would not seem to have
Some mixture in itself, compar'd with this,
Transpicuous, clear; yet darkly on it roll'd,
Darkly beneath perpetual gloom, which ne'er
Admits or sun or moon light there to shine.
   My feet advanc'd not; but my wond'ring eyes
Pass'd onward, o'er the streamlet, to survey
The tender May-bloom, flush'd through many a hue,
In prodigal variety: and there,
As object, rising suddenly to view,
That from our bosom every thought beside
With the rare marvel chases, I beheld
A lady all alone, who, singing, went,
And culling flower from flower, wherewith her way
Was all o'er painted. "Lady beautiful!
Thou, who (if looks, that use to speak the heart,
Are worthy of our trust), with love's own beam
Dost warm thee," thus to her my speech I fram'd:
"Ah! please thee hither towards the streamlet bend

Dante Alighieri

Thy steps so near, that I may list thy song.
Beholding thee and this fair place, methinks,
I call to mind where wander'd and how look'd
Proserpine, in that season, when her child
The mother lost, and she the bloomy spring."

    As when a lady, turning in the dance,
Doth foot it featly, and advances scarce
One step before the other to the ground;
Over the yellow and vermilion flowers
Thus turn'd she at my suit, most maiden-like,
Valing her sober eyes, and came so near,
That I distinctly caught the dulcet sound.
Arriving where the limped waters now
Lav'd the green sward, her eyes she deign'd to raise,
That shot such splendour on me, as I ween
Ne'er glanced from Cytherea's, when her son
Had sped his keenest weapon to her heart.
Upon the opposite bank she stood and smil'd
through her graceful fingers shifted still
The intermingling dyes, which without seed
That lofty land unbosoms. By the stream
Three paces only were we sunder'd: yet
The Hellespont, where Xerxes pass'd it o'er,
(A curb for ever to the pride of man)
Was by Leander not more hateful held
For floating, with inhospitable wave
'Twixt Sestus and Abydos, than by me
That flood, because it gave no passage thence.

    "Strangers ye come, and haply in this place,
That cradled human nature in its birth,
Wond'ring, ye not without suspicion view
My smiles: but that sweet strain of psalmody,
'Thou, Lord! hast made me glad,' will give ye light,
Which may uncloud your minds. And thou, who stand'st
The foremost, and didst make thy suit to me,
Say if aught else thou wish to hear: for I
Came prompt to answer every doubt of thine."

    She spake; and I replied: "l know not how
To reconcile this wave and rustling sound
Of forest leaves, with what I late have heard
Of opposite report." She answering thus:
"I will unfold the cause, whence that proceeds,
Which makes thee wonder; and so purge the cloud
That hath enwraps thee. The First Good, whose joy
Is only in himself, created man
For happiness, and gave this goodly place,
His pledge and earnest of eternal peace.
Favour'd thus highly, through his own defect
He fell, and here made short sojourn; he fell,
And, for the bitterness of sorrow, chang'd

Laughter unblam'd and ever-new delight.
That vapours none, exhal'd from earth beneath,
Or from the waters (which, wherever heat
Attracts them, follow), might ascend thus far
To vex man's peaceful state, this mountain rose
So high toward the heav'n, nor fears the rage
Of elements contending, from that part
Exempted, where the gate his limit bars.
Because the circumambient air throughout
With its first impulse circles still, unless
Aught interpose to cheek or thwart its course;
Upon the summit, which on every side
To visitation of th' impassive air
Is open, doth that motion strike, and makes
Beneath its sway th' umbrageous wood resound:
And in the shaken plant such power resides,
That it impregnates with its efficacy
The voyaging breeze, upon whose subtle plume
That wafted flies abroad; and th' other land
Receiving (as 't is worthy in itself,
Or in the clime, that warms it), doth conceive,
And from its womb produces many a tree
Of various virtue. This when thou hast heard,
The marvel ceases, if in yonder earth
Some plant without apparent seed be found
To fix its fibrous stem. And further learn,
That with prolific foison of all seeds,
This holy plain is fill'd, and in itself
Bears fruit that ne'er was pluck'd on other soil.
 "The water, thou behold'st, springs not from vein,
As stream, that intermittently repairs
And spends his pulse of life, but issues forth
From fountain, solid, undecaying, sure;
And by the will omnific, full supply
Feeds whatsoe'er On either side it pours;
On this devolv'd with power to take away
Remembrance of offence, on that to bring
Remembrance back of every good deed done.
From whence its name of Lethe on this part;
On th' other Eunoe: both of which must first
Be tasted ere it work; the last exceeding
All flavours else. Albeit thy thirst may now
Be well contented, if I here break off,
No more revealing: yet a corollary
I freely give beside: nor deem my words
Less grateful to thee, if they somewhat pass
The stretch of promise. They, whose verse of yore
The golden age recorded and its bliss,
On the Parnassian mountain, of this place
Perhaps had dream'd. Here was man guiltless, here

Perpetual spring and every fruit, and this
The far-fam'd nectar." Turning to the bards,
When she had ceas'd, I noted in their looks
A smile at her conclusion; then my face
Again directed to the lovely dame.

CANTO XXIX

Singing, as if enamour'd, she resum'd
And clos'd the song, with "Blessed they whose sins
Are cover'd." Like the wood-nymphs then, that tripp'd
Singly across the sylvan shadows, one
Eager to view and one to 'scape the sun,
So mov'd she on, against the current, up
The verdant rivage. I, her mincing step
Observing, with as tardy step pursued.
    Between us not an hundred paces trod,
The bank, on each side bending equally,
Gave me to face the orient. Nor our way
Far onward brought us, when to me at once
She turn'd, and cried: "My brother! look and hearken."
And lo! a sudden lustre ran across
Through the great forest on all parts, so bright
I doubted whether lightning were abroad;
But that expiring ever in the spleen,
That doth unfold it, and this during still
And waxing still in splendor, made me question
What it might be: and a sweet melody
Ran through the luminous air. Then did I chide
With warrantable zeal the hardihood
Of our first parent, for that there were earth
Stood in obedience to the heav'ns, she only,
Woman, the creature of an hour, endur'd not
Restraint of any veil: which had she borne
Devoutly, joys, ineffable as these,
Had from the first, and long time since, been mine.
    While through that wilderness of primy sweets
That never fade, suspense I walk'd, and yet
Expectant of beatitude more high,
Before us, like a blazing fire, the air
Under the green boughs glow'd; and, for a song,
Distinct the sound of melody was heard.
    O ye thrice holy virgins! for your sakes
If e'er I suffer'd hunger, cold and watching,
Occasion calls on me to crave your bounty.
Now through my breast let Helicon his stream
Pour copious; and Urania with her choir
Arise to aid me: while the verse unfolds
Things that do almost mock the grasp of thought.

	Onward a space, what seem'd seven trees of gold,
The intervening distance to mine eye
Falsely presented; but when I was come
So near them, that no lineament was lost
Of those, with which a doubtful object, seen
Remotely, plays on the misdeeming sense,
Then did the faculty, that ministers
Discourse to reason, these for tapers of gold
Distinguish, and it th' singing trace the sound
"Hosanna." Above, their beauteous garniture
Flam'd with more ample lustre, than the moon
Through cloudless sky at midnight in her full.
	I turn'd me full of wonder to my guide;
And he did answer with a countenance
Charg'd with no less amazement: whence my view
Reverted to those lofty things, which came
So slowly moving towards us, that the bride
Would have outstript them on her bridal day.
	The lady called aloud: "Why thus yet burns
Affection in thee for these living lights,
And dost not look on that which follows them?"
	I straightway mark'd a tribe behind them walk,
As if attendant on their leaders, cloth'd
With raiment of such whiteness, as on earth
Was never. On my left, the wat'ry gleam
Borrow'd, and gave me back, when there I look'd,
As in a mirror, my left side portray'd.
	When I had chosen on the river's edge
Such station, that the distance of the stream
Alone did separate me; there I stay'd
My steps for clearer prospect, and beheld
The flames go onward, leaving, as they went,
The air behind them painted as with trail
Of liveliest pencils! so distinct were mark'd
All those sev'n listed colours, whence the sun
Maketh his bow, and Cynthia her zone.
These streaming gonfalons did flow beyond
My vision; and ten paces, as I guess,
Parted the outermost. Beneath a sky
So beautiful, came foul and-twenty elders,
By two and two, with flower-de-luces crown'd.
All sang one song: "Blessed be thou among
The daughters of Adam! and thy loveliness
Blessed for ever!" After that the flowers,
And the fresh herblets, on the opposite brink,
Were free from that elected race; as light
In heav'n doth second light, came after them
Four animals, each crown'd with verdurous leaf.
With six wings each was plum'd, the plumage full
Of eyes, and th' eyes of Argus would be such,

Dante Alighieri

Were they endued with life. Reader, more rhymes
Will not waste in shadowing forth their form:
For other need no straitens, that in this
I may not give my bounty room. But read
Ezekiel; for he paints them, from the north
How he beheld them come by Chebar's flood,
In whirlwind, cloud and fire; and even such
As thou shalt find them character'd by him,
Here were they; save as to the pennons; there,
From him departing, John accords with me.

    The space, surrounded by the four, enclos'd
A car triumphal: on two wheels it came
Drawn at a Gryphon's neck; and he above
Stretch'd either wing uplifted, 'tween the midst
And the three listed hues, on each side three;
So that the wings did cleave or injure none;
And out of sight they rose. The members, far
As he was bird, were golden; white the rest
With vermeil intervein'd. So beautiful
A car in Rome ne'er grac'd Augustus pomp,
Or Africanus': e'en the sun's itself
Were poor to this, that chariot of the sun
Erroneous, which in blazing ruin fell
At Tellus' pray'r devout, by the just doom
Mysterious of all-seeing Jove. Three nymphs
,k the right wheel, came circling in smooth dance;
The one so ruddy, that her form had scarce
Been known within a furnace of clear flame:
The next did look, as if the flesh and bones
Were emerald: snow new-fallen seem'd the third.
Now seem'd the white to lead, the ruddy now;
And from her song who led, the others took
Their treasure, swift or slow. At th' other wheel,
A band quaternion, each in purple clad,
Advanc'd with festal step, as of them one
The rest conducted, one, upon whose front
Three eyes were seen. In rear of all this group,
Two old men I beheld, dissimilar
In raiment, but in port and gesture like,
Solid and mainly grave; of whom the one
Did show himself some favour'd counsellor
Of the great Coan, him, whom nature made
To serve the costliest creature of her tribe.
His fellow mark'd an opposite intent,
Bearing a sword, whose glitterance and keen edge,
E'en as I view'd it with the flood between,
Appall'd me. Next four others I beheld,
Of humble seeming: and, behind them all,
One single old man, sleeping, as he came,
With a shrewd visage. And these seven, each

Like the first troop were habited, hut wore
No braid of lilies on their temples wreath'd.
Rather with roses and each vermeil flower,
A sight, but little distant, might have sworn,
That they were all on fire above their brow.
   Whenas the car was o'er against me, straight.
Was heard a thund'ring, at whose voice it seem'd
The chosen multitude were stay'd; for there,
With the first ensigns, made they solemn halt.

CANTO XXX

Soon as the polar light, which never knows
Setting nor rising, nor the shadowy veil
Of other cloud than sin, fair ornament
Of the first heav'n, to duty each one there
Safely convoying, as that lower doth
The steersman to his port, stood firmly fix'd;
Forthwith the saintly tribe, who in the van
Between the Gryphon and its radiance came,
Did turn them to the car, as to their rest:
And one, as if commission'd from above,
In holy chant thrice shorted forth aloud:
"Come, spouse, from Libanus!" and all the rest
Took up the song--At the last audit so
The blest shall rise, from forth his cavern each
Uplifting lightly his new-vested flesh,
As, on the sacred litter, at the voice
Authoritative of that elder, sprang
A hundred ministers and messengers
Of life eternal. "Blessed thou! who com'st!"
And, "O," they cried, "from full hands scatter ye
Unwith'ring lilies;" and, so saying, cast
Flowers over head and round them on all sides.
   I have beheld, ere now, at break of day,
The eastern clime all roseate, and the sky
Oppos'd, one deep and beautiful serene,
And the sun's face so shaded, and with mists
Attemper'd at lids rising, that the eye
Long while endur'd the sight: thus in a cloud
Of flowers, that from those hands angelic rose,
And down, within and outside of the car,
Fell showering, in white veil with olive wreath'd,
A virgin in my view appear'd, beneath
Green mantle, rob'd in hue of living flame:
And o'er my Spirit, that in former days
Within her presence had abode so long,
No shudd'ring terror crept. Mine eyes no more
Had knowledge of her; yet there mov'd from her

Dante Alighieri

A hidden virtue, at whose touch awak'd,
The power of ancient love was strong within me.
    No sooner on my vision streaming, smote
The heav'nly influence, which years past, and e'en
In childhood, thrill'd me, than towards Virgil I
Turn'd me to leftward, panting, like a babe,
That flees for refuge to his mother's breast,
If aught have terrified or work'd him woe:
And would have cried: "There is no dram of blood,
That doth not quiver in me. The old flame
Throws out clear tokens of reviving fire:"
But Virgil had bereav'd us of himself,
Virgil, my best-lov'd father; Virgil, he
To whom I gave me up for safety: nor,
All, our prime mother lost, avail'd to save
My undew'd cheeks from blur of soiling tears.
    "Dante, weep not, that Virgil leaves thee: nay,
Weep thou not yet: behooves thee feel the edge
Of other sword, and thou shalt weep for that."
    As to the prow or stern, some admiral
Paces the deck, inspiriting his crew,
When 'mid the sail-yards all hands ply aloof;
Thus on the left side of the car I saw,
(Turning me at the sound of mine own name,
Which here I am compell'd to register)
The virgin station'd, who before appeared
Veil'd in that festive shower angelical.
    Towards me, across the stream, she bent her eyes;
Though from her brow the veil descending, bound
With foliage of Minerva, suffer'd not
That I beheld her clearly; then with act
Full royal, still insulting o'er her thrall,
Added, as one, who speaking keepeth back
The bitterest saying, to conclude the speech:
"Observe me well. I am, in sooth, I am
Beatrice. What! and hast thou deign'd at last
Approach the mountain? knewest not, O man!
Thy happiness is whole?" Down fell mine eyes
On the clear fount, but there, myself espying,
Recoil'd, and sought the greensward: such a weight
Of shame was on my forehead. With a mien
Of that stern majesty, which doth surround
mother's presence to her awe-struck child,
She look'd; a flavour of such bitterness
Was mingled in her pity. There her words
Brake off, and suddenly the angels sang:
"In thee, O gracious Lord, my hope hath been:"
But went no farther than, "Thou Lord, hast set
My feet in ample room." As snow, that lies
Amidst the living rafters on the back

The Divine Comedy

Of Italy congeal'd when drifted high
And closely pil'd by rough Sclavonian blasts,
Breathe but the land whereon no shadow falls,
And straightway melting it distils away,
Like a fire-wasted taper: thus was I,
Without a sigh or tear, or ever these
Did sing, that with the chiming of heav'n's sphere,
Still in their warbling chime: but when the strain
Of dulcet symphony, express'd for me
Their soft compassion, more than could the words
"Virgin, why so consum'st him?" then the ice,
Congeal'd about my bosom, turn'd itself
To spirit and water, and with anguish forth
Gush'd through the lips and eyelids from the heart.

    Upon the chariot's right edge still she stood,
Immovable, and thus address'd her words
To those bright semblances with pity touch'd:
"Ye in th' eternal day your vigils keep,
So that nor night nor slumber, with close stealth,
Conveys from you a single step in all
The goings on of life: thence with more heed
I shape mine answer, for his ear intended,
Who there stands weeping, that the sorrow now
May equal the transgression. Not alone
Through operation of the mighty orbs,
That mark each seed to some predestin'd aim,
As with aspect or fortunate or ill
The constellations meet, but through benign
Largess of heav'nly graces, which rain down
From such a height, as mocks our vision, this man
Was in the freshness of his being, such,
So gifted virtually, that in him
All better habits wond'rously had thriv'd.
The more of kindly strength is in the soil,
So much doth evil seed and lack of culture
Mar it the more, and make it run to wildness.
These looks sometime upheld him; for I show'd
My youthful eyes, and led him by their light
In upright walking. Soon as I had reach'd
The threshold of my second age, and chang'd
My mortal for immortal, then he left me,
And gave himself to others. When from flesh
To spirit I had risen, and increase
Of beauty and of virtue circled me,
I was less dear to him, and valued less.
His steps were turn'd into deceitful ways,
Following false images of good, that make
No promise perfect. Nor avail'd me aught
To sue for inspirations, with the which,
I, both in dreams of night, and otherwise,

Did call him back; of them so little reck'd him,
Such depth he fell, that all device was short
Of his preserving, save that he should view
The children of perdition. To this end
I visited the purlieus of the dead:
And one, who hath conducted him thus high,
Receiv'd my supplications urg'd with weeping.
It were a breaking of God's high decree,
If Lethe should be past, and such food tasted
Without the cost of some repentant tear."

CANTO XXXI

"O Thou!" her words she thus without delay
Resuming, turn'd their point on me, to whom
They but with lateral edge seem'd harsh before,
'Say thou, who stand'st beyond the holy stream,
If this be true. A charge so grievous needs
Thine own avowal." On my faculty
Such strange amazement hung, the voice expir'd
Imperfect, ere its organs gave it birth.
　　A little space refraining, then she spake:
"What dost thou muse on? Answer me. The wave
On thy remembrances of evil yet
Hath done no injury." A mingled sense
Of fear and of confusion, from my lips
Did such a "Yea " produce, as needed help
Of vision to interpret. As when breaks
In act to be discharg'd, a cross-bow bent
Beyond its pitch, both nerve and bow o'erstretch'd,
The flagging weapon feebly hits the mark;
Thus, tears and sighs forth gushing, did I burst
Beneath the heavy load, and thus my voice
Was slacken'd on its way. She straight began:
"When my desire invited thee to love
The good, which sets a bound to our aspirings,
What bar of thwarting foss or linked chain
Did meet thee, that thou so should'st quit the hope
Of further progress, or what bait of ease
Or promise of allurement led thee on
Elsewhere, that thou elsewhere should'st rather wait?"
　　A bitter sigh I drew, then scarce found voice
To answer, hardly to these sounds my lips
Gave utterance, wailing: "Thy fair looks withdrawn,
Things present, with deceitful pleasures, turn'd
My steps aside." She answering spake: "Hadst thou
Been silent, or denied what thou avow'st,
Thou hadst not hid thy sin the more: such eye
Observes it. But whene'er the sinner's cheek

The Divine Comedy

Breaks forth into the precious-streaming tears
Of self-accusing, in our court the wheel
Of justice doth run counter to the edge.
Howe'er that thou may'st profit by thy shame
For errors past, and that henceforth more strength
May arm thee, when thou hear'st the Siren-voice,
Lay thou aside the motive to this grief,
And lend attentive ear, while I unfold
How opposite a way my buried flesh
Should have impell'd thee. Never didst thou spy
In art or nature aught so passing sweet,
As were the limbs, that in their beauteous frame
Enclos'd me, and are scatter'd now in dust.
If sweetest thing thus fail'd thee with my death,
What, afterward, of mortal should thy wish
Have tempted? When thou first hadst felt the dart
Of perishable things, in my departing
For better realms, thy wing thou should'st have prun'd
To follow me, and never stoop'd again
To 'bide a second blow for a slight girl,
Or other gaud as transient and as vain.
The new and inexperienc'd bird awaits,
Twice it may be, or thrice, the fowler's aim;
But in the sight of one, whose plumes are full,
In vain the net is spread, the arrow wing'd."

    I stood, as children silent and asham'd
Stand, list'ning, with their eyes upon the earth,
Acknowledging their fault and self-condemn'd.
And she resum'd: "If, but to hear thus pains thee,
Raise thou thy beard, and lo! what sight shall do!"

    With less reluctance yields a sturdy holm,
Rent from its fibers by a blast, that blows
From off the pole, or from Iarbas' land,
Than I at her behest my visage rais'd:
And thus the face denoting by the beard,
I mark'd the secret sting her words convey'd.

    No sooner lifted I mine aspect up,
Than downward sunk that vision I beheld
Of goodly creatures vanish; and mine eyes
Yet unassur'd and wavering, bent their light
On Beatrice. Towards the animal,
Who joins two natures in one form, she turn'd,
And, even under shadow of her veil,
And parted by the verdant rill, that flow'd
Between, in loveliness appear'd as much
Her former self surpassing, as on earth
All others she surpass'd. Remorseful goads
Shot sudden through me. Each thing else, the more
Its love had late beguil'd me, now the more
I Was loathsome. On my heart so keenly smote

Dante Alighieri

The bitter consciousness, that on the ground
O'erpower'd I fell: and what my state was then,
She knows who was the cause. When now my strength
Flow'd back, returning outward from the heart,
The lady, whom alone I first had seen,
I found above me. "Loose me not," she cried:
"Loose not thy hold;" and lo! had dragg'd me high
As to my neck into the stream, while she,
Still as she drew me after, swept along,
Swift as a shuttle, bounding o'er the wave.
    The blessed shore approaching then was heard
So sweetly, "Tu asperges me," that I
May not remember, much less tell the sound.
The beauteous dame, her arms expanding, clasp'd
My temples, and immerg'd me, where 't was fit
The wave should drench me: and thence raising up,
Within the fourfold dance of lovely nymphs
Presented me so lav'd, and with their arm
They each did cover me. "Here are we nymphs,
And in the heav'n are stars. Or ever earth
Was visited of Beatrice, we
Appointed for her handmaids, tended on her.
We to her eyes will lead thee; but the light
Of gladness that is in them, well to scan,
Those yonder three, of deeper ken than ours,
Thy sight shall quicken." Thus began their song;
And then they led me to the Gryphon's breast,
While, turn'd toward us, Beatrice stood.
"Spare not thy vision. We have stationed thee
Before the emeralds, whence love erewhile
Hath drawn his weapons on thee. "As they spake,
A thousand fervent wishes riveted
Mine eyes upon her beaming eyes, that stood
Still fix'd toward the Gryphon motionless.
As the sun strikes a mirror, even thus
Within those orbs the twofold being, shone,
For ever varying, in one figure now
Reflected, now in other. Reader! muse
How wond'rous in my sight it seem'd to mark
A thing, albeit steadfast in itself,
Yet in its imag'd semblance mutable.
    Full of amaze, and joyous, while my soul
Fed on the viand, whereof still desire
Grows with satiety, the other three
With gesture, that declar'd a loftier line,
Advanc'd: to their own carol on they came
Dancing in festive ring angelical.
    "Turn, Beatrice!" was their song: "O turn
Thy saintly sight on this thy faithful one,
Who to behold thee many a wearisome pace

The Divine Comedy

Hath measur'd. Gracious at our pray'r vouchsafe
Unveil to him thy cheeks: that he may mark
Thy second beauty, now conceal'd." O splendour!
O sacred light eternal! who is he
So pale with musing in Pierian shades,
Or with that fount so lavishly imbued,
Whose spirit should not fail him in th' essay
To represent thee such as thou didst seem,
When under cope of the still-chiming heaven
Thou gav'st to open air thy charms reveal'd.

CANTO XXXII

Mine eyes with such an eager coveting,
Were bent to rid them of their ten years' thirst,
No other sense was waking: and e'en they
Were fenc'd on either side from heed of aught;
So tangled in its custom'd toils that smile
Of saintly brightness drew me to itself,
When forcibly toward the left my sight
The sacred virgins turn'd; for from their lips
I heard the warning sounds: "Too fix'd a gaze!"
    Awhile my vision labor'd; as when late
Upon the' o'erstrained eyes the sun hath smote:
But soon to lesser object, as the view
Was now recover'd (lesser in respect
To that excess of sensible, whence late
I had perforce been sunder'd) on their right
I mark'd that glorious army wheel, and turn,
Against the sun and sev'nfold lights, their front.
As when, their bucklers for protection rais'd,
A well-rang'd troop, with portly banners curl'd,
Wheel circling, ere the whole can change their ground:
E'en thus the goodly regiment of heav'n
Proceeding, all did pass us, ere the car
Had slop'd his beam. Attendant at the wheels
The damsels turn'd; and on the Gryphon mov'd
The sacred burden, with a pace so smooth,
No feather on him trembled. The fair dame
Who through the wave had drawn me, companied
By Statius and myself, pursued the wheel,
Whose orbit, rolling, mark'd a lesser arch.
    Through the high wood, now void (the more her blame,
Who by the serpent was beguil'd) I past
With step in cadence to the harmony
Angelic. Onward had we mov'd, as far
Perchance as arrow at three several flights
Full wing'd had sped, when from her station down
Descended Beatrice. With one voice

Dante Alighieri

All murmur'd "Adam," circling next a plant
Despoil'd of flowers and leaf on every bough.
Its tresses, spreading more as more they rose,
Were such, as 'midst their forest wilds for height
The Indians might have gaz'd at. "Blessed thou!
Gryphon, whose beak hath never pluck'd that tree
Pleasant to taste: for hence the appetite
Was warp'd to evil." Round the stately trunk
Thus shouted forth the rest, to whom return'd
The animal twice-gender'd: "Yea: for so
The generation of the just are sav'd."
And turning to the chariot-pole, to foot
He drew it of the widow'd branch, and bound
There left unto the stock whereon it grew.

 As when large floods of radiance from above
Stream, with that radiance mingled, which ascends
Next after setting of the scaly sign,
Our plants then burgeon, and each wears anew
His wonted colours, ere the sun have yok'd
Beneath another star his flamy steeds;
Thus putting forth a hue, more faint than rose,
And deeper than the violet, was renew'd
The plant, erewhile in all its branches bare.

 Unearthly was the hymn, which then arose.
I understood it not, nor to the end
Endur'd the harmony. Had I the skill
To pencil forth, how clos'd th' unpitying eyes
Slumb'ring, when Syrinx warbled, (eyes that paid
So dearly for their watching,) then like painter,
That with a model paints, I might design
The manner of my falling into sleep.
But feign who will the slumber cunningly;
I pass it by to when I wak'd, and tell
How suddenly a flash of splendour rent
The curtain of my sleep, and one cries out:
"Arise, what dost thou?" As the chosen three,
On Tabor's mount, admitted to behold
The blossoming of that fair tree, whose fruit
Is coveted of angels, and doth make
Perpetual feast in heaven, to themselves
Returning at the word, whence deeper sleeps
Were broken, that they their tribe diminish'd saw,
Both Moses and Elias gone, and chang'd
The stole their master wore: thus to myself
Returning, over me beheld I stand
The piteous one, who cross the stream had brought
My steps. "And where," all doubting, I exclaim'd,
"Is Beatrice?"--"See her," she replied,
"Beneath the fresh leaf seated on its root.
Behold th' associate choir that circles her.

The Divine Comedy
The others, with a melody more sweet
And more profound, journeying to higher realms,
Upon the Gryphon tend." If there her words
Were clos'd, I know not; but mine eyes had now
Ta'en view of her, by whom all other thoughts
Were barr'd admittance. On the very ground
Alone she sat, as she had there been left
A guard upon the wain, which I beheld
Bound to the twyform beast. The seven nymphs
Did make themselves a cloister round about her,
And in their hands upheld those lights secure
From blast septentrion and the gusty south.

   "A little while thou shalt be forester here:
And citizen shalt be forever with me,
Of that true Rome, wherein Christ dwells a Roman
To profit the misguided world, keep now
Thine eyes upon the car; and what thou seest,
Take heed thou write, returning to that place."

   Thus Beatrice: at whose feet inclin'd
Devout, at her behest, my thought and eyes,
I, as she bade, directed. Never fire,
With so swift motion, forth a stormy cloud
Leap'd downward from the welkin's farthest bound,
As I beheld the bird of Jove descending
Pounce on the tree, and, as he rush'd, the rind,
Disparting crush beneath him, buds much more
And leaflets. On the car with all his might
He struck, whence, staggering like a ship, it reel'd,
At random driv'n, to starboard now, o'ercome,
And now to larboard, by the vaulting waves.

   Next springing up into the chariot's womb
A fox I saw, with hunger seeming pin'd
Of all good food. But, for his ugly sins
The saintly maid rebuking him, away
Scamp'ring he turn'd, fast as his hide-bound corpse
Would bear him. Next, from whence before he came,
I saw the eagle dart into the hull
O' th' car, and leave it with his feathers lin'd;
And then a voice, like that which issues forth
From heart with sorrow riv'd, did issue forth
From heav'n, and, "O poor bark of mine!" it cried,
"How badly art thou freighted!" Then, it seem'd,
That the earth open'd between either wheel,
And I beheld a dragon issue thence,
That through the chariot fix'd his forked train;
And like a wasp that draggeth back the sting,
So drawing forth his baleful train, he dragg'd
Part of the bottom forth, and went his way
Exulting. What remain'd, as lively turf
With green herb, so did clothe itself with plumes,

Which haply had with purpose chaste and kind
Been offer'd; and therewith were cloth'd the wheels,
Both one and other, and the beam, so quickly
A sigh were not breath'd sooner. Thus transform'd,
The holy structure, through its several parts,
Did put forth heads, three on the beam, and one
On every side; the first like oxen horn'd,
But with a single horn upon their front
The four. Like monster sight hath never seen.
O'er it methought there sat, secure as rock
On mountain's lofty top, a shameless whore,
Whose ken rov'd loosely round her. At her side,
As 't were that none might bear her off, I saw
A giant stand; and ever, and anon
They mingled kisses. But, her lustful eyes
Chancing on me to wander, that fell minion
Scourg'd her from head to foot all o'er; then full
Of jealousy, and fierce with rage, unloos'd
The monster, and dragg'd on, so far across
The forest, that from me its shades alone
Shielded the harlot and the new-form'd brute.

CANTO XXXIII

"The heathen, Lord! are come!" responsive thus,
The trinal now, and now the virgin band
Quaternion, their sweet psalmody began,
Weeping; and Beatrice listen'd, sad
And sighing, to the song', in such a mood,
That Mary, as she stood beside the cross,
Was scarce more chang'd. But when they gave her place
To speak, then, risen upright on her feet,
She, with a colour glowing bright as fire,
Did answer: "Yet a little while, and ye
Shall see me not; and, my beloved sisters,
Again a little while, and ye shall see me."
     Before her then she marshall'd all the seven,
And, beck'ning only motion'd me, the dame,
And that remaining sage, to follow her.
     So on she pass'd; and had not set, I ween,
Her tenth step to the ground, when with mine eyes
Her eyes encounter'd; and, with visage mild,
"So mend thy pace," she cried, "that if my words
Address thee, thou mayst still be aptly plac'd
To hear them." Soon as duly to her side
I now had hasten'd: "Brother!" she began,
"Why mak'st thou no attempt at questioning,
As thus we walk together?" Like to those
Who, speaking with too reverent an awe

The Divine Comedy

Before their betters, draw not forth the voice
Alive unto their lips, befell me shell
That I in sounds imperfect thus began:
"Lady! what I have need of, that thou know'st,
And what will suit my need." She answering thus:
"Of fearfulness and shame, I will, that thou
Henceforth do rid thee: that thou speak no more,
As one who dreams. Thus far be taught of me:
The vessel, which thou saw'st the serpent break,
Was and is not: let him, who hath the blame,
Hope not to scare God's vengeance with a sop.
Without an heir for ever shall not be
That eagle, he, who left the chariot plum'd,
Which monster made it first and next a prey.
Plainly I view, and therefore speak, the stars
E'en now approaching, whose conjunction, free
From all impediment and bar, brings on
A season, in the which, one sent from God,
(Five hundred, five, and ten, do mark him out)
That foul one, and th' accomplice of her guilt,
The giant, both shall slay. And if perchance
My saying, dark as Themis or as Sphinx,
Fail to persuade thee, (since like them it foils
The intellect with blindness) yet ere long
Events shall be the Naiads, that will solve
This knotty riddle, and no damage light
On flock or field. Take heed; and as these words
By me are utter'd, teach them even so
To those who live that life, which is a race
To death: and when thou writ'st them, keep in mind
Not to conceal how thou hast seen the plant,
That twice hath now been spoil'd. This whoso robs,
This whoso plucks, with blasphemy of deed
Sins against God, who for his use alone
Creating hallow'd it. For taste of this,
In pain and in desire, five thousand years
And upward, the first soul did yearn for him,
Who punish'd in himself the fatal gust.

  "Thy reason slumbers, if it deem this height
And summit thus inverted of the plant,
Without due cause: and were not vainer thoughts,
As Elsa's numbing waters, to thy soul,
And their fond pleasures had not dyed it dark
As Pyramus the mulberry, thou hadst seen,
In such momentous circumstance alone,
God's equal justice morally implied
In the forbidden tree. But since I mark thee
In understanding harden'd into stone,
And, to that hardness, spotted too and stain'd,
So that thine eye is dazzled at my word,

Dante Alighieri

I will, that, if not written, yet at least
Painted thou take it in thee, for the cause,
That one brings home his staff inwreath'd with palm.
    "I thus: "As wax by seal, that changeth not
Its impress, now is stamp'd my brain by thee.
But wherefore soars thy wish'd-for speech so high
Beyond my sight, that loses it the more,
The more it strains to reach it?" --"To the end
That thou mayst know," she answer'd straight, "the school,
That thou hast follow'd; and how far behind,
When following my discourse, its learning halts:
And mayst behold your art, from the divine
As distant, as the disagreement is
'Twixt earth and heaven's most high and rapturous orb."
    "I not remember," I replied, "that e'er
I was estrang'd from thee, nor for such fault
Doth conscience chide me." Smiling she return'd:
"If thou canst, not remember, call to mind
How lately thou hast drunk of Lethe's wave;
And, sure as smoke doth indicate a flame,
In that forgetfulness itself conclude
Blame from thy alienated will incurr'd.
From henceforth verily my words shall be
As naked as will suit them to appear
In thy unpractis'd view." More sparkling now,
And with retarded course the sun possess'd
The circle of mid-day, that varies still
As th' aspect varies of each several clime,
When, as one, sent in vaward of a troop
For escort, pauses, if perchance he spy
Vestige of somewhat strange and rare: so paus'd
The sev'nfold band, arriving at the verge
Of a dun umbrage hoar, such as is seen,
Beneath green leaves and gloomy branches, oft
To overbrow a bleak and alpine cliff.
And, where they stood, before them, as it seem'd,
Tigris and Euphrates both beheld,
Forth from one fountain issue; and, like friends,
Linger at parting. "O enlight'ning beam!
O glory of our kind! beseech thee say
What water this, which from one source deriv'd
Itself removes to distance from itself?"
    To such entreaty answer thus was made:
"Entreat Matilda, that she teach thee this."
    And here, as one, who clears himself of blame
Imputed, the fair dame return'd: "Of me
He this and more hath learnt; and I am safe
That Lethe's water hath not hid it from him."
    And Beatrice: "Some more pressing care
That oft the memory 'reeves, perchance hath made

The Divine Comedy

His mind's eye dark. But lo! where Eunoe cows!
Lead thither; and, as thou art wont, revive
His fainting virtue." As a courteous spirit,
That proffers no excuses, but as soon
As he hath token of another's will,
Makes it his own; when she had ta'en me, thus
The lovely maiden mov'd her on, and call'd
To Statius with an air most lady-like:
"Come thou with him." Were further space allow'd,
Then, Reader, might I sing, though but in part,
That beverage, with whose sweetness I had ne'er
Been sated. But, since all the leaves are full,
Appointed for this second strain, mine art
With warning bridle checks me. I return'd
From the most holy wave, regenerate,
If 'en as new plants renew'd with foliage new,
Pure and made apt for mounting to the stars.

NOTES TO PURGATORY

CANTO I

Verse 1. O'er better waves.] Berni, Orl. Inn. L 2. c. i. Per correr maggior acqua alza le vele, O debil navicella del mio ingegno.
v. 11. Birds of chattering note.] For the fable of the daughters of Pierus, who challenged the muses to sing, and were by them changed into magpies, see Ovid, Met. 1. v. fab. 5.
v. 19. Planet.] Venus.
v. 20. Made all the orient laugh.] Hence Chaucer, Knight's Tale: And all the orisont laugheth of the sight.
It is sometimes read "orient."
v. 24. Four stars.] Symbolical of the four cardinal virtues, Prudence Justice, Fortitude, and Temperance. See Canto XXXI v. 105.
v. 30. The wain.] Charles's wain, or Bootes.
v. 31. An old man.] Cato.
v. 92. Venerable plumes.] The same metaphor has occurred in Hell Canto XX. v. 41:
--the plumes,
That mark'd the better sex.
It is used by Ford in the Lady's Trial, a. 4. s. 2.
Now the down
Of softness is exchang'd for plumes of age.
v. 58. The farthest gloom.] L'ultima sera. Ariosto, Oroando Furioso c. xxxiv st. 59: Che non hen visto ancor l'ultima sera.
And Filicaja, c. ix. Al Sonno.
L'ultima sera.
v. 79. Marcia.]
Da fredera prisci
Illibata tori: da tantum nomen inane
Connubil: liceat tumulo scripsisse, Catonis
Martia
Lucan, Phars. 1. ii. 344.
v. 110. I spy'd the trembling of the ocean stream.] Connubil il tremolar della marina.
Trissino, in the Sofonisba.]
E resta in tremolar l'onda marina
And Fortiguerra, Rleelardetto, c. ix. st. 17.
--visto il tremolar della marine.
v. 135. another.] From Virg, Aen. 1. vi. 143. Primo avulso non deficit alter

The Divine Comedy
CANTO II

v. 1. Now had the sun.] Dante was now antipodal to Jerusalem, so that while the sun was setting with respect to that place which he supposes to be the middle of the inhabited earth, to him it was rising.

v. 6. The scales.] The constellation Libra.

v. 35. Winnowing the air.]
Trattando l'acre con l'eterne penne.
80 Filicaja, canz. viii. st. 11.
Ma trattar l'acre coll' eterne plume

v. 45. In exitu.] "When Israel came out of Egypt." Ps. cxiv.

v. 75. Thrice my hands.]
Ter conatus ibi eollo dare brachia eircum,
Ter frustra eomprensa manus effugit imago,
Par levibus ventis voluerique simillima sommo.
Virg. Aen. ii. 794.
Compare Homer, Od. xl. 205.

v. 88. My Casella.] A Florentine, celebrated for his skill in music, "in whose company," says Landine, "Dante often recreated his spirits wearied by severe studies." See Dr. Burney's History of Music, vol. ii. c. iv. p. 322. Milton has a fine allusion to this meeting in his sonnet to Henry Lawes.

v. 90. Hath so much time been lost.] Casella had been dead some years but was only just arrived.

v. 91. He.] The eonducting angel.

v. 94. These three months past.] Since the time of the Jubilee, during which all spirits not condemned to eternal punishment, were supposed to pass over to Purgatory as soon as they pleased.

v. 96. The shore.] Ostia.

v. 170. "Love that discourses in my thoughts."]
"Amor che nella mente mi ragiona."
The first verse of a eanzone or song in the Convito of Dante, which he again cites in his Treatise de Vulg. Eloq. 1. ii. c. vi.

CANTO III

v. 9. How doth a little failing wound thee sore.] (Ch'era al cor picciol fallo amaro morso. Tasso, G. L. c. x. st. 59.

v. 11. Haste, that mars all decency of act. Aristotle in his Physiog iii. reekons it among the "the signs of an impudent man," that he is "quick in his motions." Compare Sophoeles, Electra, 878.

v. 26. To Naples.]
Virgil died at Brundusium, from whence his body is said to have been removed to Naples.

v. 38. Desiring fruitlessly.] See H. Canto IV, 39.

v. 49. 'Twixt Lerice and Turbia.] At that time the two extremities of the Genoese republic, the former on the east, the latter on the west. A very ingenious writer has had occasion, for a different purpose, to mention one of these places as remarkably secluded by its mountainous situation "On an eminence among the mountains, between the two little cities, Nice and Manoca, is the village of Torbia, a name formed from the Greek [GREEK HERE] Mitford on the Harmony of Language, sect. x. p. 351. 2d edit.

v. 78. As sheep.] The imitative nature of these animals supplies our Poet with another comparison in his Convito Opere, t. i. p 34. Ediz. Ven. 1793.

v. 110. Manfredi. King of Naples and Sicily, and the natural son of Frederick II. He was lively end agreeable in his manners, and delighted in poetry, music, and dancing. But he was luxurious and ambitious. Void of religion, and in his philosophy an Epicurean. See G. Villani l. vi. c. xlvii. and Mr. Matthias's Tiraboschi, v. I. p. 38. He fell in the battle with Charles of Anjou in 1265, alluded to in Canto XXVIII, of Hell, v. 13, "Dying, excommunicated, King Charles did allow of his being buried in sacred ground, but he was interred near the bridge of Benevento, and on his grave there was cast a stone by every one of the army whence there was formed a great mound of stones. But some ave said, that afterwards, by command of the Pope. the Bishop of Cosenza took up his body and sent it out of the kingdom, because it was the land of the church, and that it was buried by the river Verde, on the borders of the kingdom and of Carapagna. this, however, we do not affirm." G. Villani, Hist. l. vii. c. 9.

v. 111. Costanza.] See Paradise Canto III. v. 121.

v. 112. My fair daughter.] Costanza, the daughter of Manfredi, and wife of Peter III. King of Arragon, by whom she was mother to Frederick, King of Sicily and James, King of Arragon With the latter of these she was at Rome 1296. See G. Villani, 1. viii. c. 18. and notes to Canto VII.

v. 122. Clement.] Pope Clement IV.

v. 127. The stream of Verde.] A river near Ascoli, that falls into he Toronto. The "xtinguished lights " formed part of the ceremony t the interment of one excommunicated.

v. 130. Hope.]
Mentre che la speranza ha fior del verde.
Tasso, G. L. c. xix. st. 53.
--infin che verde e fior di speme.

CANTO IV

v. 1. When.] It must be owned the beginning of this Canto is somewhat obscure. Bellutello refers, for an elucidation of it, to the reasoning of Statius in the twenty-fifth canto. Perhaps some illustration may be derived from the following, passage in South's Sermons, in which I have ventured to supply the words between crotchets that seemed to be wanting to complete the sense. Now whether these three, judgement memory, and invention, are three distinct things, both in being distinguished from one another, and likewise from the substance of the soul itself, considered without any such faculties, (or whether the soul be one individual substance) but only receiving these several denominations rom the several respects arising from the several actions exerted immediately by itself upon several objects, or several qualities of the same object, I say whether of these it is, is not easy to decide, and it is well that it is not necessary Aquinas, and most with him, affirm the former, and Scotus with his followers the latter." Vol. iv. Serm. 1.

v. 23. Sanleo.] A fortress on the summit of Montefeltro.

v. 24. Noli.] In the Genoese territory, between Finale and Savona.

v. 25. Bismantua.] A steep mountain in the territory of Reggio.

v. 55. From the left.] Vellutello observes an imitation of Lucan in this passage:

Ignotum vobis, Arabes, venistis in orbem,
Umbras mirati nemornm non ire sinistras.
Phars. s. 1. iii. 248

v. 69 Thou wilt see.] "If you consider that this mountain of Purgatory and that of Sion are antipodal to each other, you will perceive that the sun must rise on opposite sides of the respective eminences."

v. 119. Belacqua.] Concerning this man, the commentators afford no information.

CANTO V

v. 14. Be as a tower.] Sta ome torre ferma
Berni, Orl. Inn. 1. 1. c. xvi. st. 48:
In quei due piedi sta fermo il gigante
Com' una torre in mezzo d'un castello.
And Milton, P. L. b. i. 591.
Stood like a tower.

v. 36. Ne'er saw I fiery vapours.] Imitated by Tasso, G. L, c. xix t. 62:
Tal suol fendendo liquido sereno
Stella cader della gran madre in seno.
And by Milton, P. L. b. iv. 558:
Swift as a shooting star
In autumn thwarts the night, when vapours fir'd
Impress the air.

v. 67. That land.] The Marca d'Ancona, between Romagna and Apulia, the kingdom of Charles of Anjou.

v. 76. From thence I came.] Giacopo del Cassero, a citizen of Fano who having spoken ill of Azzo da Este, Marquis of Ferrara, was by his orders put to death. Giacopo, was overtaken by the assassins at Oriaco a place near the Brenta, from whence, if he had fled towards Mira, higher up on that river, instead of making for the marsh on the sea shore, he might have escaped.

v. 75. Antenor's land.] The city of Padua, said to be founded by Antenor.

v. 87. Of Montefeltro I.] Buonconte (son of Guido da Montefeltro, whom we have had in the twenty-seventh Canto of Hell) fell in the battle of Campaldino (1289), fighting on the side of the Aretini.

v. 88. Giovanna.] Either the wife, or kinswoman, of Buonconte.

v. 91. The hermit's seat.] The hermitage of Camaldoli.

v. 95. Where its name is cancel'd.] That is, between Bibbiena and Poppi, where the Archiano falls into the Arno.

v. 115. From Pratomagno to the mountain range.] From Pratomagno now called Prato Vecchio (which divides the Valdarno from Casentino) as far as to the Apennine.

v. 131. Pia.] She is said to have been a Siennese lady, of the family of Tolommei, secretly made away with by her husband, Nello della Pietra, of the same city, in Maremma, where he had some possessions.

CANTO VI

v. 14. Of Arezzo him.] Benincasa of Arezzo, eminent for his skill in jurisprudence, who, having condemned to death Turrino da Turrita brother of Ghino di Tacco, for his robberies in Maremma, was murdered by Ghino, in an apartment of his own house, in the presence of many witnesses. Ghino was not only suffered to escape in safety, but (as the commentators inform us) obtained so high a reputation by the liberality with which he was accustomed to dispense the fruits of his plunder, and treated those who fell into his hands with so much courtesy, that he was afterwards invited to Rome, and knighted by Boniface VIII. A story is told of him by Boccaccio, G. x. N. 2.

v. 15. Him beside.] Ciacco de' Tariatti of Arezzo. He is said to have been carried by his horse into the Arno, and there drowned, while he was in pursuit of certain of his enemies.

v. 17. Frederic Novello.] Son of the Conte Guido da Battifolle, and slain by one of the family of Bostoli.

v. 18. Of Pisa he.] Farinata de' Scornigiani of Pisa. His father Marzuco, who had entered the order of the Frati Minori, so entirely overcame the feelings of resentment, that he even kissed the hands of the slayer of his son, and, as he was following the funeral, exhorted his kinsmen to reconciliation.

v. 20. Count Orso.] Son of Napoleone da Cerbaia, slain by Alberto da Mangona, his uncle.

v. 23. Peter de la Brosse.] Secretary of Philip III of France. The courtiers, envying the high place which he held in the king's favour, prevailed on Mary of Brabant to charge him falsely with an attempt upon her person for which supposed crime he suffered death. So say the Italian commentators. Henault represents the matter very differently: "Pierre de la Brosse, formerly barber to St. Louis, afterwards the favorite of Philip, fearing the too great attachment of the king for his wife Mary, accuses this princess of having poisoned Louis, eldest son of Philip, by his first marriage. This calumny is discovered by a nun of Nivelle in Flanders. La Brosse is hung." Abrege Chron. t. 275, &c.

v. 30. In thy text.] He refers to Virgil, Aen. 1, vi. 376. Desine fata deum flecti sperare precando, 37. The sacred height Of judgment. Shakespeare, Measure for Measure, a. ii. s. 2. If he, which is the top of judgment

v. 66. Eyeing us as a lion on his watch.]
A guisa di Leon quando si posa.
A line taken by Tasso, G. L. c. x. st. 56.

v. 76. Sordello.] The history of Sordello's life is wrapt in the obscurity of romance. That he distinguished himself by his skill in Provencal poetry is certain. It is probable that he was born towards the end of the twelfth, and died about the middle of the succeeding century. Tiraboschi has taken much pains to sift all the notices he could collect relating to him. Honourable mention of his name is made by our Poet in the Treatise de Vulg. Eloq. 1. i. c. 15.

v. 76. Thou inn of grief.]
Thou most beauteous inn
Why should hard-favour'd grief be lodg'd in thee?
Shakespeare, Richard II a. 5. s. 1.

v. 89. Justinian's hand.] "What avails it that Justinian delivered thee from the Goths, and reformed thy laws, if thou art no longer under the control of his successors in the empire?"

v. 94. That which God commands.] He alludes to the precept- "Render unto Caesar the things which are Caesar's."

v. 98. O German Albert!] The Emperor Albert I. succeeded Adolphus in 1298, and was murdered in 1308. See Par Canto XIX 114 v. 103. Thy successor.] The successor of Albert was Henry of Luxembourg, by whose interposition in the affairs of Italy our Poet hoped to have been reinstated in his native city.

v. 101. Thy sire.] The Emperor Rodolph, too intent on increasing his power in Germany to give much of his thoughts to Italy, "the garden of the empire."

v. 107. Capulets and Montagues.] Our ears are so familiarized to the names of these rival families in the language of Shakespeare, that I have used them instead of the "Montecchi" and "Cappelletti."

v. 108. Philippeschi and Monaldi.] Two other rival families in Orvieto.

v. 113. What safety, Santafiore can supply.] A place between Pisa and Sienna. What he alludes to is so doubtful, that it is not certain whether we should not read "come si cura"--" How Santafiore is governed." Perhaps the event related in the note to v. 58, Canto XI. may be pointed at.

v. 127. Marcellus.]
Un Marcel diventa
Ogni villan che parteggiando viene.
Repeated by Alamanni in his Coltivazione, 1. i.

v. 51. I sick wretch.] Imitated by the Cardinal de Polignac in his Anti-Lucretius, 1. i. 1052.

Ceu lectum peragrat membris languentibus aeger
In latus alterne faevum dextrumque recumbens
Nec javat: inde oculos tollit resupinus in altum:
Nusquam inventa quies; semper quaesita: quod illi
Primum in deliciis fuerat, mox torquet et angit:
Nec morburm sanat, nec fallit taedia morbi.

CANTO VII

v. 14. Where one of mean estate might clasp his lord.] Ariosto Orl. F. c. xxiv. st. 19
E l'abbracciaro, ove il maggior s'abbraccia
Col capo nudo e col ginocchio chino.

v. 31. The three holy virtues.] Faith, Hope and Charity.

v. 32. The red.] Prudence, Justice, Fortitude, and Temperance.

v. 72. Fresh emeralds.]
Under foot the violet,
Crocus, and hyacinth with rich inlay
Broider'd the ground, more colour'd than with stone
Of costliest emblem.
Milton, P. L. b. iv. 793
Compare Ariosto, Orl. F. c. xxxiv. st. 49.

v. 79. Salve Regina.] The beginning of a prayer to the Virgin. It is sufficient here to observe, that in similar instances I shall either preserve the original Latin words or translate them, as it may seem best to suit the purpose of the verse.

v. 91. The Emperor Rodolph.] See the last Canto, v. 104. He died in 1291.

v. 95. That country.] Bohemia.

v. 97. Ottocar.] King of Bohemia, was killed in the battle of Marchfield, fought with Rodolph, August 26, 1278. Winceslaus II. His son, who succeeded him in the kingdom of Bohemia. died in 1305. He is again taxed with luxury in the Paradise Canto XIX. 123.

v. 101. That one with the nose deprest.] Philip III of France, who died in 1285, at Perpignan, in his retreat from Arragon.

v. 102. Him of gentle look.] Henry of Naverre, father of Jane married to Philip IV of France, whom Dante calls "mal di Francia" -" Gallia's bane."

v. 110. He so robust of limb.] Peter III called the Great, King of Arragon, who died in 1285, leaving four sons, Alonzo, James, Frederick and Peter. The two former succeeded him in the kingdom of Arragon, and Frederick in that of Sicily. See G. Villani, 1. vii. c. 102. and Mariana, I. xiv. c. 9. He is enumerated among the Provencal poets by Millot, Hist. Litt. Des Troubadours, t. iii. p. 150.

v. 111. Him of feature prominent.] "Dal maschio naso"-with the masculine nose." Charles I. King of Naples, Count of Anjou, and brother of St. Lonis. He died in 1284. The annalist of Florence remarks, that "there had been no sovereign of the house of France, since the time of Charlemagne, by whom Charles was surpassed either in military renown, and prowess, or in the loftiness of his understanding." G. Villani, 1. vii. c. 94. We shall, however, find many of his actions severely reprobated in the twentieth Canto.

v. 113. That stripling.] Either (as the old commentators suppose) Alonzo III King of Arragon, the eldest son of Peter III who died in 1291, at the age of 27, or, according to Venturi, Peter the youngest son. The former was a young prince of virtue sufficient to have justified the eulogium and the hopes of Dante.

See Mariana, 1. xiv. c. 14.

v. 119. Rarely.]
Full well can the wise poet of Florence
That hight Dante, speaken in this sentence
Lo! in such manner rime is Dantes tale.
Full selde upriseth by his branches smale
Prowesse of man for God of his goodnesse
Woll that we claim of him our gentlenesse:
For of our elders may we nothing claime
But temporal thing, that men may hurt and maime.
Chaucer, Wife of Bathe's Tale.

Compare Homer, Od. b. ii. v. 276; Pindar, Nem. xi. 48 and Euripides, Electra, 369.

v. 122. To Charles.] "Al Nasuto." -"Charles II King of Naples, is no less inferior to his father Charles I. than James and Frederick to theirs, Peter III."

v. 127. Costanza.] Widow of Peter III She has been already mentioned in the third Canto, v. 112. By Beatrice and Margaret are probably meant two of the daughters of Raymond Berenger, Count of Provence; the former married to St. Louis of France, the latter to his brother Charles of Anjou.

See Paradise, Canto VI. 135. Dante therefore considers Peter as the most illustrious of the three monarchs.

v. 129. Harry of England.] Henry III.

The Divine Comedy

v. 130. Better issue.] Edward 1. of whose glory our Poet was perhaps a witness, in his visit to England.

v. 133. William, that brave Marquis.] William, Marquis of Monferrat, was treacherously seized by his own subjects, at Alessandria, in Lombardy, A.D. 1290, and ended his life in prison. See G. Villani, 1. vii. c. 135. A war ensued between the people of Alessandria and those of Monferrat and the Canavese.

CANTO VIII

v. 6. That seems to mourn for the expiring day.] The curfew tolls the knell of parting day. Gray's Elegy.

v. 13. Te Lucis Ante.] The beginning of one of the evening hymns.

v. 36. As faculty.]
My earthly by his heav'nly overpower'd
* * * *
As with an object, that excels the sense,
Dazzled and spent.
Milton, P. L. b. viii. 457.

v. 53. Nino, thou courteous judge.] Nino di Gallura de' Visconti nephew to Count Ugolino de' Gherardeschi, and betrayed by him. See Notes to Hell Canto XXXIII.

v. 65. Conrad.] Currado Malaspina.

v. 71 My Giovanna.] The daughter of Nino, and wife of Riccardo da Cammino of Trevigi.

v. 73. Her mother.] Beatrice, marchioness of Este wife of Nino, and after his death married to Galeazzo de' Visconti of Milan.

v. 74. The white and wimpled folds.] The weeds of widowhood.

v. 80. The viper.] The arms of Galeazzo and the ensign of the Milanese.

v. 81. Shrill Gallura's bird.] The cock was the ensign of Gallura, Nino's province in Sardinia. Hell, Canto XXII. 80. and Notes.

v. 115. Valdimagra.] See Hell, Canto XXIV. 144. and Notes.

v. 133. Sev'n times the tired sun.] "The sun shall not enter into the constellation of Aries seven times more, before thou shalt have still better cause for the good opinion thou expresses" of Valdimagra, in the kind reception thou shalt there meet with." Dante was hospitably received by the Marchese Marcello Malaspina, during his banishment. A.D. 1307.

CANTO IX

v. 1. Now the fair consort of Tithonus old.]
La concubina di Titone antico.
So Tassoni, Secchia Rapita, c. viii. st. 15.
La puttanella del canuto amante.

v. 5. Of that chill animal.] The scorpion.

v. 14. Our minds.] Compare Hell, Canto XXVI. 7.

v. 18. A golden-feathered eagle.] Chaucer, in the house of Fame at the conclusion of the first book and beginning of the second, represents himself carried up by the "grim pawes" of a golden eagle. Much of his description is closely imitated from Dante.

v. 50. Lucia.] The enlightening, grace of heaven Hell, Canto II. 97.

v. 85. The lowest stair.] By the white step is meant the distinctness with which the conscience of the penitent reflects his offences, by the burnt and cracked one, his contrition on, their account; and by that of porphyry, the fervour with which he resolves on the future pursuit of piety and virtue. Hence, no doubt, Milton describing "the gate of heaven," P. L. b. iii. 516.

Each stair mysteriously was meant.

v. 100. Seven times.] Seven P's, to denote the seven sins (Peccata) of which he was to be cleansed in his passage through purgatory.

v. 115. One is more precious.] The golden key denotes the divine authority by which the priest absolves the sinners the silver expresses the learning and judgment requisite for the due discharge of that office.

v. 127. Harsh was the grating.]
On a sudden open fly
With impetuous recoil and jarring, sound
Th' infernal doors, and on their hinges grate
Harsh thunder
Milton, P. L. b. ii 882

v. 128. The Turpeian.]
Protinus, abducto patuerunt temple Metello.
Tunc rupes Tarpeia sonat: magnoque reclusas
Testatur stridore fores: tune conditus imo
Eruitur tempo multis intactus ab annnis
Romani census populi, &c.
Lucan. Ph. 1. iii. 157.

CANTO X

v. 6. That Wound.] Venturi justly observes, that the Padre d'Aquino has misrepresented the sense of this passage in his translation.

--dabat ascensum tendentibus ultra
Scissa tremensque silex, tenuique erratica motu.

The verb "muover'" is used in the same signification in the Inferno, Canto XVIII. 21.

Cosi da imo della roccia scogli
Moven.
--from the rock's low base
Thus flinty paths advanc'd.
In neither place is actual motion intended to be expressed.

v. 52. That from unbidden. office awes mankind.] Seo 2 Sam. G.

v 58. Preceding.] Ibid. 14, &c.

v. 68. Gregory.] St. Gregory's prayers are said to have delivered Trajan from hell. See Paradise, Canto XX. 40.

v. 69. Trajan the Emperor. For this story, Landino refers to two writers, whom he calls "Heunando," of France, by whom he means Elinand, a monk and chronicler, in the reign of Philip Augustus, and "Polycrato," of England, by whom is meant John of Salisbury, author of the Polycraticus de Curialium Nugis, in the twelfth century. The passage in the text I find to be nearly a translation from that work, 1. v. c. 8. The original appears to be in Dio Cassius, where it is told of the Emperor Hadrian, lib. I xix. [GREEK HERE]

When a woman appeared to him with a suit, as he was on a journey, at first he answered her, 'I have no leisure,' but she crying out to him, 'then reign no longer' he turned about, and heard her cause."

v. 119. As to support.] Chillingworth, ch.vi. 54. speaks of "those crouching anticks, which seem in great buildings to labour under the weight they bear." And Lord Shaftesbury has a similar illustration in his Essay on Wit and Humour, p. 4. s. 3.

CANTO XI

v. 1. 0 thou Mighty Father.] The first four lines are borrowed by Pulci, Morg. Magg. c. vi.

Dante, in his 'Credo,' has again versified the Lord's prayer.

v. 58. I was of Latinum.] Omberto, the son of Guglielino Aldobrandeseo, Count of Santafiore, in the territory of Sienna His arrogance provoked his countrymen to such a pitch of fury against him, that he was murdered by them at Campagnatico.

v. 79. Oderigi.] The illuminator, or miniature painter, a friend of Giotto and Dante

v. 83. Bolognian Franco.] Franco of Bologna, who is said to have been a pupil of Oderigi's.

v. 93. Cimabue.] Giovanni Cimabue, the restorer of painting, was born at Florence, of a noble family, in 1240, and died in 1300. The passage in the text is an illusion to his epitaph:

Credidit ut Cimabos picturae castra tenere,
Sic tenuit vivens: nunc tenet astra poli.

v. 95. The cry is Giotto's.] In Giotto we have a proof at how early a period the fine arts were encouraged in Italy. His talents were discovered by Cimabue, while he was tending sheep for his father in the neighbourhood of Florence, and he was afterwards patronized by Pope Benedict XI and Robert King of Naples, and enjoyed the society and friendship of Dante, whose likeness he has transmitted to posterity. He died in 1336, at the age of 60.

v. 96. One Guido from the other.] Guido Cavalcanti, the friend of our Poet, (see Hell, Canto X. 59.) had eclipsed the literary fame of Guido Guinicelli, of a noble family in Bologna, whom we shall meet with in the twenty-sixth Canto and of whom frequent mention is made by our Poet in his Treatise de Vulg. Eloq. Guinicelli died in 1276. Many of Cavalcanti's writings, hitherto in MS. are now publishing at Florence" Esprit des Journaux, Jan. 1813.

v. 97. He perhaps is born.] Some imagine, with much probability, that Dante here augurs the greatness of his own poetical reputation. Others have fancied that he prophesies the glory of Petrarch. But Petrarch was not yet born.

v. 136. suitor.] Provenzano salvani humbled himself so far for the sake of one of his friends, who was detained in captivity by Charles I of Sicily, as personally to supplicate the people of Sienna to contribute the sum required by the king for his ransom:

and this act of self-abasement atoned for his general ambition and pride.

v. 140. Thy neighbours soon.] "Thou wilt know in the time of thy banishment, which is near at hand, what it is to solicit favours of others and 'tremble through every vein,' lest they should be refused thee."

CANTO XII

v. 26. The Thymbraen god.] Apollo
Si modo, quem perhibes, pater est Thymbraeus Apollo. Virg. Georg. iv. 323.

v. 37. Mars.]
With such a grace,
The giants that attempted to scale heaven
When they lay dead on the Phlegren plain
Mars did appear to Jove.
Beaumont and Fletcher, The Prophetess, a. 2. s. 3.

v. 42. O Rehoboam.] 1 Kings, c. xii. 18.

v. 46. Alcmaeon.] Virg. Aen. l. vi. 445, and Homer, Od. xi. 325.

v. 48. Sennacherib.] 2 Kings, c. xix. 37.

v. 58. What master of the pencil or the style.]
--inimitable on earth
By model, or by shading pencil drawn.
Milton, P. L. b. iii. 509.

v. 94. The chapel stands.] The church of San Miniato in Florence situated on a height that overlooks the Arno, where it is crossed by the bridge Rubaconte, so called from Messer Rubaconte da Mandelia, of Milan chief magistrate of Florence, by whom the bridge was founded in 1237. See G. Villani, 1. vi. c. 27.

v. 96. The well-guided city] This is said ironically of Florence.

v. 99. The registry.] In allusion to certain instances of fraud committed with respect to the public accounts and measures See Paradise Canto XVI. 103.

CANTO XIII

v. 26. They have no wine.] John, ii. 3. These words of the Virgin are referred to as an instance of charity.

v. 29. Orestes] Alluding to his friendship with Pylades

v. 32. Love ye those have wrong'd you.] Matt. c. v. 44.

v. 33. The scourge.] "The chastisement of envy consists in hearing examples of the opposite virtue, charity. As a curb and restraint on this vice, you will presently hear very different sounds, those of threatening and punishment."

v. 87. Citizens Of one true city.]
"For here we have no continuing city, but we seek to come." Heb. C. xiii. 14.

v. 101. Sapia.] A lady of Sienna, who, living in exile at Colle, was so overjoyed at a defeat which her countrymen sustained near that place that she declared nothing more was wanting to make her die contented.

v. 114. The merlin.] The story of the merlin is that having been induced by a gleam of fine weather in the winter to escape from his master, he was soon oppressed by the rigour of the season.

v. 119. The hermit Piero.] Piero Pettinagno, a holy hermit of Florence.

v. 141. That vain multitude.] The Siennese. See Hell, Canto XXIX. 117. "Their acquisition of Telamone, a seaport on the confines of the Maremma, has led them to conceive hopes of becoming a naval power: but this scheme will prove as chimerical as their former plan for the discovery of a subterraneous stream under their city." Why they gave the appellation of Diana to the imagined stream, Venturi says he leaves it to the antiquaries of Sienna to conjecture.

CANTO XIV

v. 34. Maim'd of Pelorus.] Virg. Aen. 1. iii. 414.
--a hill
Torn from Pelorus
Milton P. L. b. i. 232

v. 45. 'Midst brute swine.] The people of Casentino.

v. 49. Curs.] The Arno leaves Arezzo about four miles to the left.

v. 53. Wolves.] The Florentines.

v. 55. Foxes.] The Pisans

v. 61. Thy grandson.] Fulcieri de' Calboli, grandson of Rinieri de' Calboli, who is here spoken to. The atrocities predicted came to pass in 1302. See G. Villani, 1. viii c. 59

v. 95. 'Twixt Po, the mount, the Reno, and the shore.] The boundaries of Romagna.

v. 99. Lizio.] Lizio da Valbona, introduced into Boccaccio's Decameron, G. v. N, 4.

v. 100. Manardi, Traversaro, and Carpigna.1 Arrigo Manardi of Faenza, or as some say, of Brettinoro, Pier Traversaro, lord of Ravenna, and Guido di Carpigna of Montefeltro.

v. 102. In Bologna the low artisan.] One who had been a mechanic named Lambertaccio, arrived at almost supreme power in Bologna.

v. 103. Yon Bernardin.] Bernardin di Fosco, a man of low origin but great talents, who governed at Faenza.

v. 107. Prata.] A place between Faenza and Ravenna

v. 107. Of Azzo him.] Ugolino of the Ubaldini family in Tuscany He is recounted among the poets by Crescimbeni and Tiraboschi.

v. 108. Tignoso.] Federigo Tignoso of Rimini.

v. 109. Traversaro's house and Anastagio's.] Two noble families of Ravenna. She to whom Dryden has given the name of Honoria, in the fable so admirably paraphrased from Boccaccio, was of the former: her lover and the specter were of the Anastagi family.

v. 111. The ladies, &c.] These two lines express the true spirit of chivalry. "Agi" is understood by the commentators whom I have consulted,to mean "the ease procured for others by the exertions of knight-errantry." But surely it signifies the alternation of ease with labour.

v. 114. O Brettinoro.] A beautifully situated castle in Romagna, the hospitable residence of Guido del Duca, who is here speaking.

v. 118. Baynacavallo.] A castle between Imola and Ravenna

v. 118. Castracaro ill
And Conio worse.] Both in Romagna.

v. 121. Pagani.] The Pagani were lords of Faenza and Imola. One of them Machinardo, was named the Demon, from his treachery. See Hell, Canto XXVII. 47, and Note.

v. 124. Hugolin.] Ugolino Ubaldini, a noble and virtuous person in Faenza, who, on account of his age probably, was not likely to leave any offspring behind him. He is enumerated among the poets by Crescimbeni, and Tiraboschi. Mr. Matthias's edit. vol. i. 143

v. 136. Whosoever finds Will slay me.] The words of Cain, Gen. e. iv. 14.

v. 142. Aglauros.] Ovid, Met. I, ii. fate. 12.

v. 145. There was the galling bit.] Referring to what had been before said, Canto XIII. 35.

CANTO XV

v. 1. As much.] It wanted three hours of sunset.

v. 16. As when the ray.] Compare Virg. Aen. 1.viii. 22, and Apol. Rhod. 1. iii. 755.

v. 19. Ascending at a glance.] Lucretius, 1. iv. 215.

v. 20. Differs from the stone.] The motion of light being quicker than that of a stone through an equal space.

v. 38. Blessed the merciful. Matt. c. v. 7.

v. 43. Romagna's spirit.] Guido del Duea, of Brettinoro whom we have seen in the preceding Canto.

v. 87. A dame.] Luke, c. ii. 18

v. 101. How shall we those requite.] The answer of Pisistratus the tyrant to his wife, when she urged him to inflict the punishment of death on a young man, who, inflamed with love for his daughter, had snatched from her a kiss in public. The story is told by Valerius Maximus, 1.v. 1.

v. 105. A stripling youth.] The protomartyr Stephen.

CANTO XVI

v. 94. As thou.] "If thou wert still living."

v. 46. I was of Lombardy, and Marco call'd.] A Venetian gentleman. "Lombardo" both was his surname and denoted the country to which he belonged. G. Villani, 1. vii. c. 120, terms him "a wise and worthy courtier."

v. 58. Elsewhere.] He refers to what Guido del Duca had said in the thirteenth Canto, concerning the degeneracy of his countrymen.

v. 70. If this were so.] Mr. Crowe in his Lewesdon Hill has expressed similar sentiments with much energy.

Of this be sure,
Where freedom is not, there no virtue is, &c.

Compare Origen in Genesim, Patrum Graecorum, vol. xi. p. 14. Wirer burgi, 1783. 8vo.

v. 79. To mightier force.] "Though ye are subject to a higher power than that of the heavenly constellations, e`en to the power of the great Creator himself, yet ye are still left in the possession of liberty."

v. 88. Like a babe that wantons sportively.] This reminds one of the Emperor Hadrian's verses to his departing soul:

Animula vagula blandula, &c

v. 99. The fortress.] Justice, the most necessary virtue in the chief magistrate, as the commentators explain it.

v. 103. Who.] He compares the Pope, on account of the union of the temporal with the spiritual power in his person, to an unclean beast in the levitical law. "The camel, because he cheweth the cud, but divideth not the hoof, he is unclean unto you." Levit. c. xi. 4.

v. 110. Two sons.] The Emperor and the Bishop of Rome.

v. 117. That land.] Lombardy.

v. 119. Ere the day.] Before the Emperor Frederick II was defeated before Parma, in 1248. G. Villani, 1. vi. c. 35.

v. 126. The good Gherardo.] Gherardo di Camino of Trevigi. He is honourably mentioned in our Poet's "Convito." Opere di Dante, t. i. p. 173 Venez. 8vo. 1793. And Tiraboschi supposes him to have been the same Gherardo with whom the Provencal poets were used to meet with hospitable reception. See Mr. Matthias's edition, t. i. p. 137,

v. 127. Conrad.] Currado da Palazzo, a gentleman of Brescia.

v. 127. Guido of Castello.] Of Reggio. All the Italians were called Lombards by the French.

v. 144. His daughter Gaia.] A lady equally admired for her modesty, the beauty of her person, and the excellency of her talents. Gaia, says Tiraboschi, may perhaps lay claim to the praise of having been the first among the Italian ladies, by whom the vernacular poetry was cultivated. Ibid. p. 137.

CANTO XVII

v. 21. The bird, that most Delights itself in song.] I cannot think with Vellutello, that the swallow is here meant. Dante probably alludes to the story of Philomela, as it is found in Homer's Odyssey, b. xix. 518 rather than as later poets have told it. "She intended to slay the son of her husband's brother Amphion, incited to it, by the envy of his wife, who had six children, while herself had only two, but through mistake slew her own son Itylus, and for her punishment was transformed by Jupiter into a nightingale."

Cowper's note on the passage.

In speaking of the nightingale, let me observe, that while some have considered its song as a melancholy, and others as a cheerful one, Chiabrera appears to have come nearest the truth, when he says, in the Alcippo, a. l. s. 1,

Non mal si stanca d' iterar le note
O gioconde o dogliose,
Al sentir dilettose.
Unwearied still reiterates her lays,
Jocund or sad, delightful to the ear.

v. 26. One crucified.] Haman. See the book of Esther, c. vii.

v. 34. A damsel.] Lavinia, mourning for her mother Amata, who, impelled by grief and indignation for the supposed death of Turnus, destroyed herself. Aen. 1. xii. 595.

v. 43. The broken slumber quivering ere it dies.] Venturi suggests that this bold and unusual metaphor may have been formed on that in Virgil.

Tempus erat quo prima quies mortalibus aegris
Incipit, et dono divun gratissima serpit.
Aen. 1. ii. 268.

v. 68. The peace-makers.] Matt. c. v. 9.

v. 81. The love.] "A defect in our love towards God, or lukewarmness in piety, is here removed."

v. 94. The primal blessings.] Spiritual good.

v. 95. Th' inferior.] Temporal good.

v. 102. Now.] "It is impossible for any being, either to hate itself, or to hate the First Cause of all, by which it exists. We can therefore only rejoice in the evil which befalls others."

v. 111. There is.] The proud.

v. 114. There is.] The envious.

v. 117. There is he.] The resentful.

v. 135. Along Three circles.] According to the allegorical commentators, as Venturi has observed, Reason is represented under the person of Virgil, and Sense under that of Dante. The former leaves to the latter to discover for itself the three carnal sins, avarice, gluttony and libidinousness; having already declared the nature of the spiritual sins, pride, envy, anger, and indifference, or lukewarmness in piety, which the Italians call accidia, from the Greek word. [GREEK HERE]

CANTO XVIII

v. 1. The teacher ended.] Compare Plato, Protagoras, v. iii. p. 123. Bip. edit. [GREEK HERE] Apoll. Rhod. 1. i. 513, and Milton, P. L. b. viii. 1.

The angel ended, &c.

v. 23. Your apprehension.] It is literally, "Your apprehensive faculty derives intention from a thing really existing, and displays the intention within you, so that it makes the soul turn to it." The commentators labour in explaining this; and whatever sense they have elicited may, I think, be resolved into the words of the translation in the text.

v. 47. Spirit.] The human soul, which differs from that of brutes, inasmuch as, though united with the body, it has a separate existence of its own.

v. 65. Three men.] The great moral philosophers among the heathens.

v. 78. A crag.] I have preferred the reading of Landino, scheggion, "crag," conceiving it to be more poetical than secchion, "bucket," which is the common reading. The same cause, the vapours, which the commentators say might give the appearance of increased magnitude to the moon, might also make her seem broken at her rise.

v. 78. Up the vault.] The moon passed with a motion opposite to that of the heavens, through the constellation of the scorpion, in which the sun is, when to those who are in Rome he appears to set between the isles of Corsica and Sardinia.

v. 84. Andes.] Andes, now Pietola, made more famous than Mantua near which it is situated, by having been the birthplace of Virgil.

v. 92. Ismenus and Asopus.] Rivers near Thebes

v. 98. Mary.] Luke, c i. 39, 40

v. 99. Caesar.] See Lucan, Phars. l. iii. and iv, and Caesar de Bello Civiii, l. i. Caesar left Brutus to complete the siege of Marseilles, and hastened on to the attack of Afranius and Petreius, the generals of Pompey, at Ilerda (Lerida) in Spain.

v. 118. abbot.] Alberto, abbot of San Zeno in Verona, when Frederick I was emperor, by whom Milan was besieged and reduced to ashes.

The Divine Comedy

v. 121. There is he.] Alberto della Scala, lord of Verona, who had made his natural son abbot of San Zeno.

v. 133. First they died.] The Israelites, who, on account of their disobedience, died before reaching the promised land.

v. 135. And they.] Virg Aen. 1. v.

CANTO XIX

v. 1. The hour.] Near the dawn.

v. 4. The geomancer.] The geomancers, says Landino, when they divined, drew a figure consisting of sixteen marks, named from so many stars which constitute the end of Aquarius and the beginning of Pisces. One of these they called "the greater fortune."

v. 7. A woman's shape.] Worldly happiness. This allegory reminds us of the "Choice of Hercules."

v. 14. Love's own hue.]
A smile that glow'd
Celestial rosy red, love's proper hue.
Milton, P. L. b. viii. 619
--facies pulcherrima tune est
Quum porphyriaco variatur candida rubro
Quid color hic roseus sibi vult? designat amorem:
Quippe amor est igni similis; flammasque rubentes
Ignus habere solet.
Palingenii Zodiacus Vitae, 1. xii.

v. 26. A dame.] Philosophy.

v. 49. Who mourn.] Matt. c. v. 4.

v. 72. My soul.] Psalm cxix. 5

v. 97. The successor of Peter Ottobuono, of the family of Fieschi Counts of Lavagna, died thirty-nine days after he became Pope, with the title of Adrian V, in 1276.

v. 98. That stream.] The river Lavagna, in the Genoese territory.

v. 135. nor shall be giv'n in marriage.] Matt. c. xxii. 30. "Since in this state we neither marry nor are given in marriage, I am no longer the spouse of the church, and therefore no longer retain my former dignity.

v. 140. A kinswoman.] Alagia is said to have been the wife of the Marchese Marcello Malaspina, one of the poet's protectors during his exile. See Canto VIII. 133.

CANTO XX

v. 3. I drew the sponge.] "I did not persevere in my inquiries from the spirit though still anxious to learn more."

v. 11. Wolf.] Avarice.

v. 16. Of his appearing.] He is thought to allude to Can Grande della Scala. See Hell, Canto I. 98.

v. 25. Fabricius.] Compare Petrarch, Tr. della Fama, c. 1.
Un Curio ed un Fabricio, &c.

v. 30. Nicholas.] The story of Nicholas is, that an angel having revealed to him that the father of a family was so impoverished as to resolve on exposing the chastity of his three daughters to sale, he threw in at the window of their house three bags of money, containing a sufficient portion for each of them.

v. 42. Root.] Hugh Capet, ancestor of Philip IV.

v. 46. Had Ghent and Douay, Lille and Bruges power.] These cities had lately been seized by Philip IV. The spirit is made to imitate the approaching defeat of the French army by the Flemings, in the battle of Courtrai, which happened in 1302.

v. 51. The slaughter's trade.] This reflection on the birth of his ancestor induced Francis I to forbid the reading of Dante in his dominions Hugh Capet, who came to the throne of France in 987, was however the grandson of Robert, who was the brother of Eudes, King of France in 888.

v. 52. All save one.] The posterity of Charlemagne, the second race of French monarchs, had failed, with the exception of Charles of Lorraine who is said, on account of the melancholy temper of his mind, to have always clothed himself in black. Venturi suggest that Dante may have confounded him with Childeric III the last of the Merosvingian, or first, race, who was deposed and made a monk in 751.

v. 57. My son.] Hugh Capet caused his son Robert to be crowned at Orleans.

v. 59. The Great dower of Provence.] Louis IX, and his brother Charles of Anjou, married two of the four daughters of Raymond Berenger Count of Provence. See Par. Canto VI. 135.

v. 63. For amends.] This is ironical

v. 64. Poitou it seiz'd, Navarre and Gascony.] I venture to read-
Potti e Navarra prese e Guascogna,
instead of
Ponti e Normandia prese e Guascogna
Seiz'd Ponthieu, Normandy and Gascogny.

Landino has "Potti," and he is probably right for Poitou was annexed to the French crown by Philip IV. See Henault, Abrege Chron. A.D. 1283, &c. Normandy had been united to it long before by Philip Augustus, a circumstance of which it is difficult to imagine that Dante should have been ignorant, but Philip IV, says Henault, ibid., took the title of King of Navarre: and the subjugation of Navarre is also alluded to in the Paradise, Canto XIX. 140. In 1293, Philip IV summoned Edward I. to do him homage for the duchy of Gascogny, which he had conceived the design of seizing. See G. Villani, l. viii. c. 4.

v. 66. Young Conradine.] Charles of Anjou put Conradine to death in 1268; and became King of Naples. See Hell, Canto XXVIII, 16, and Note.

v. 67. Th' angelic teacher.] Thomas Aquinas. He was reported to have been poisoned by a physician, who wished to ingratiate himself with Charles of Anjou. G. Villani, I. ix. c. 218. We shall find him in the Paradise, Canto X.

v. 69. Another Charles.] Charles of Valois, brother of Philip IV, was sent by Pope Boniface VIII to settle the disturbed state of Florence. In consequence of the measures he adopted for that purpose, our poet and his friend, were condemned to exile and death.

v. 71. -with that lance Which the arch-traitor tilted with.]
con la lancia
Con la qual giostro Guida.

If I remember right, in one of the old romances, Judas is represented tilting with our Saviour.

v. 78. The other.] Charles, King of Naples, the eldest son of Charles of Anjou, having, contrary to the directions of his father, engaged with Ruggier de Lauria, the admiral of Peter of Arragon, was made prisoner and carried into Sicily, June, 1284. He afterwards, in consideration of a large sum of money, married his daughter to Azzo VI11, Marquis of Ferrara.

v. 85. The flower-de-luce.] Boniface VIII was seized at Alagna in Campagna, by order of Philip IV., in the year 1303, and soon after died of grief. G. Villani, 1. viii. c. 63.

v. 94. Into the temple.] It is uncertain whether our Poet alludes still to the event mentioned in the preceding Note, or to the destruction of the order of the Templars in 1310, but the latter appears more probable.

v. 103. Pygmalion.] Virg. Aen. 1. i. 348.

v. 107. Achan.] Joshua, c. vii.

v. 111. Heliodorus.] 2 Maccabees, c. iii. 25. "For there appeared unto them a horse, with a terrible rider upon him, and adorned with a very fair covering, and he ran fiercely and smote at Heliodorus with his forefeet."

v. 112. Thracia's king.] Polymnestor, the murderer of Polydorus. Hell, Canto XXX, 19.

v. 114. Crassus.] Marcus Crassus, who fell miserably in the Parthian war. See Appian, Parthica.

CANTO XXI

v. 26. She.] Lachesis, one of the three fates.

v. 43. --that, which heaven in itself Doth of itself receive.] Venturi, I think rightly interprets this to be light.

v. 49. Thaumantian.] Figlia di Taumante [GREEK HERE]

Compare Plato, Theaet. v. ii. p. 76. Bip. edit., Virg; Aen. ix. 5, and Spenser, Faery Queen, b. v. c. 3. st. 25.

v. 85. The name.] The name of Poet.

v. 89. From Tolosa.] Dante, as many others have done, confounds Statius the poet, who was a Neapolitan, with a rhetorician of the same name, who was of Tolosa, or Thoulouse. Thus Chaucer, Temple of Fame, b. iii. The Tholason, that height Stace.

v. 94. Fell.] Statius lived to write only a small part of the Achilleid.

CANTO XXII

v. 5. Blessed.] Matt. v. 6.

v. 14. Aquinum's bard.] Juvenal had celebrated his contemporary Statius, Sat. vii. 82; though some critics imagine that there is a secret derision couched under his praise.

v. 28. Why.] Quid non mortalia pecaora cogis
Anri sacra fames?
Virg. Aen. 1. iii. 57

Venturi supposes that Dante might have mistaken the meaning of the word sacra, and construed it "holy," instead of "cursed." But I see no necessity for having recourse to so improbable a conjecture.

v. 41. The fierce encounter.] See Hell, Canto VII. 26.
v. 46. With shorn locks.] Ibid. 58.
v. 57. The twin sorrow of Jocasta's womb.] Eteocles and Polynices
v. 71. A renovated world.] Virg. Ecl. iv. 5
v. 100. That Greek.] Homer
v. 107. Of thy train.] Of those celebrated in thy Poem."
v. 112. Tiresias' daughter.] Dante appears to have forgotten that he had placed Manto, the daughter of Tiresias, among the sorcerers. See Hell Canto XX. Vellutello endeavours, rather awkwardly, to reconcile the inconsistency, by observing, that although she was placed there as a sinner, yet, as one of famous memory, she had also a place among the worthies in Limbo.

Lombardi excuses our author better, by observing that Tiresias had a daughter named Daphne. See Diodorus Siculus, 1. iv. 66.

v. 139. Mary took more thought.] "The blessed virgin, who answers for yon now in heaven, when she said to Jesus, at the marriage in Cana of Galilee, 'they have no wine,' regarded not the gratification of her own taste, but the honour of the nuptial banquet."

v. 142 The women of old Rome.] See Valerius Maximus, 1. ii. c. i.

CANTO XXIII

v. 9. My lips.] Psalm ii. 15.
v. 20. The eyes.] Compare Ovid, Metam. 1. viii. 801
v. 26. When Mary.] Josephus, De Bello Jud. 1. vii. c. xxi. p. 954 Ed Genev. fol. 1611. The shocking story is well told
v. 27. Rings.]
In this habit
Met I my father with his bleeding rings
Their precious stones new lost.
Shakespeare, Lear, a. 5. s. 3
v. 28. Who reads the name.] "He, who pretends to distinguish the letters which form OMO in the features of the human face, "might easily have traced out the M on their emaciated countenances." The temples, nose, and forehead are supposed to represent this letter; and the eyes the two O's placed within each side of it.

v. 44. Forese.] One of the brothers of Piccarda, she who is again spoken of in the next Canto, and introduced in the Paradise, Canto III.

V. 72. If the power.] "If thou didst delay thy repentance to the last, when thou hadst lost the power of sinning, how happens it thou art arrived here so early?"

v. 76. Lower.] In the Ante-Purgatory. See Canto II.
v. 80. My Nella.] The wife of Forese.
v. 87. The tract most barb'rous of Sardinia's isle.] The Barbagia is part of Sardinia, to which that name was given, on account of the uncivilized state of its inhabitants, who are said to have gone nearly naked.

v. 91. The' unblushing domes of Florence.] Landino's note exhibits a curious instance of the changeableness of his countrywomen. He even goes beyond the acrimony of the original. "In those days," says the commentator, "no less than in ours, the Florentine ladies exposed the neck and bosom, a dress, no doubt, more suitable to a harlot than a matron. But, as they changed soon after, insomuch that they wore collars up to the chin, covering the whole of the neck and throat, so have I hopes they will change again; not indeed so much from motives of decency, as through that fickleness, which pervades every action of their lives."

v. 97. Saracens.] "This word, during the middle ages, was indiscriminately applied to Pagans and Mahometans; in short, to all nations (except the Jew's) who did not profess Christianity." Mr. Ellis's specimens of Early English Metrical Romances, vol. i. page 196, a note. Lond. 8vo. 1805.

CANTO XXIV

v. 20. Buonaggiunta.] Buonaggiunta Urbiciani, of Lucca. "There is a canzone by this poet, printed in the collection made by the Giunti, (p. 209,).land a sonnet to Guido Guinicelli in that made by Corbinelli, (p 169,) from which we collect that he lived not about 1230, as Quadrio supposes, (t. ii. p. 159,) but towards the end of the thirteenth century. Concerning, other poems by Buonaggiunta, that are preserved in MS. in some libraries, Crescimbeni may be consulted." Tiraboschi, Mr. Matthias's ed. v. i. p. 115.

v. 23. He was of Tours.] Simon of Tours became Pope, with the title of Martin IV in 1281 and died in 1285.

v. 29. Ubaldino.] Ubaldino degli Ubaldini, of Pila, in the Florentine territory.

v. 30. Boniface.] Archbishop of Ravenna. By Venturi he is called Bonifazio de Fieschi, a Genoese, by Vellutello, the son of the above, mentioned Ubaldini and by Laudino Francioso, a Frenchman.

v. 32. The Marquis.] The Marchese de' Rigogliosi, of Forli.

v. 38. gentucca.] Of this lady it is thought that our Poet became enamoured during his exile.

v. 45. Whose brow no wimple shades yet.] "Who has not yet assumed the dress of a woman."

v. 46. Blame it as they may.] See Hell, Canto XXI. 39.

v. 51. Ladies, ye that con the lore of love.]Donne ch' avete intelletto d'amore.The first verse of a canzone in our author's Vita Nuova.

v. 56. The Notary.] Jucopo da Lentino, called the Notary, a poet of these times. He was probably an Apulian: for Dante, (De Vulg. Eloq. I. i. c 12.) quoting a verse which belongs to a canzone of his published by the Giunti, without mentioning the writer's name, terms him one of "the illustrious Apulians," praefulgentes Apuli. See Tiraboschi, Mr. Matthias's edit. vol. i. p. 137. Crescimbeni (1. i. Della Volg. Poes p. 72. 4to. ed. 1698) gives an extract from one of his poems, printed in Allacci's Collection, to show that the whimsical compositions called "Ariette " are not of modern invention.

v. 56. Guittone.] Fra Guittone, of Arezzo, holds a distinguished place in Italian literature, as besides his poems printed in the collection of the Giunti, he has left a collection of letters, forty in number, which afford the earliest specimen of that kind of writing in the language. They were published at Rome in 1743, with learned illustrations by Giovanni Bottari. He was also the first who gave to the sonnet its regular and legitimate form, a species of composition in which not only his own countrymen, but many of the best poets in all the cultivated languages of modern Europe, have since so much delighted.

Guittone, a native of Arezzo, was the son of Viva di Michele. He was of the order of the "Frati Godenti," of which an account may be seen in the Notes to Hell, Canto XXIII. In the year 1293, he founded a monastery of the order of Camaldoli, in Florence, and died in the following year. Tiraboschi, Ibid. p. 119. Dante, in the Treatise de Vulg. Eloq. 1. i. c. 13, and 1. ii. c. 6., blames him for preferring the plebeian to the mor courtly style; and Petrarch twice places him in the company of our Poet. Triumph of Love, cap. iv. and Son. Par. See "Sennuccio mio"

v. 63. The birds.] Hell, Canto V. 46, Euripides, Helena, 1495, and Statius; Theb. 1. V. 12.

v. 81. He.] Corso Donati was suspected of aiming at the sovereignty of Florence. To escape the fury of his fellow citizens, he fled away on horseback, but failing, was overtaken and slain, A.D. 1308. The contemporary annalist, after relating at length the circumstances of his fate, adds, "that he was one of the wisest and most valorous knights the best speaker, the most expert statesman, the most renowned and enterprising, man of his age in Italy, a comely knight and of graceful carriage, but very worldly, and in his time had formed many conspiracies in Florence and entered into many scandalous practices, for the sake of attaining state and lordship." G. Villani, 1. viii. c. 96. The character of Corso is forcibly drawn by another of his contemporaries Dino Compagni. 1. iii., Muratori, Rer. Ital. Script. t. ix. p. 523.

v. 129. Creatures of the clouds.] The Centaurs. Ovid. Met. 1. fab. 4 v. 123. The Hebrews.] Judges, c. vii.

CANTO XXV

v. 58. As sea-sponge.] The fetus is in this stage is zoophyte.

v. 66. -More wise Than thou, has erred.]
Averroes is said to be here meant. Venturi refers to his commentary on Aristotle, De Anim 1. iii. c. 5. for the opinion that there is only one universal intellect or mind pervading every individual of the human race. Much of the knowledge displayed by our Poet in the present Canto appears to have been derived from the medical work o+ Averroes, called the Colliget. Lib. ii. f. 10. Ven. 1400. fol.

v. 79. Mark the sun's heat.] Redi and Tiraboschi (Mr. Matthias's ed. v. ii. p. 36.) have considered this an anticipation of a profound discovery of Galileo's in natural philosophy, but it is in reality taken from a passage in Cicero "de Senectute," where, speaking of the grape, he says, " quae, et succo terrae et calore solis augescens, primo est peracerba gustatu, deinde maturata dulcescit."

v. 123. I do, not know a man.] Luke, c. i. 34.
v. 126. Callisto.] See Ovid, Met. 1. ii. fab. 5.

CANTO XXVI

v. 70. Caesar.] For the opprobrium east on Caesar's effeminacy, see Suetonius, Julius Caesar, c. 49.

v. 83. Guinicelli.] See Note to Canto XI. 96.

v. 87. lycurgus.] Statius, Theb. 1. iv. and v. Hypsipile had left her infant charge, the son of Lycurgus, on a bank, where it was destroyed by a serpent, when she went to show the Argive army the river of Langia: and, on her escaping the effects of Lycurgus's resentment, the joy her own children felt at the sight of her was such as our Poet felt on beholding his predecessor Guinicelli.

    The incidents are beautifully described in Statius, and seem to have made an impression on Dante, for he again (Canto XXII. 110.) characterizes Hypsipile, as her- Who show'd Langia's wave.

    v. 111. He.] The united testimony of Dante, and of Petrarch, in his Triumph of Love, e. iv. places Arnault Daniel at the head of the Provencal poets. That he was born of poor but noble parents, at the castle of Ribeyrae in Perigord, and that he was at the English court, is the amount of Millot's information concerning him (t. ii. p. 479).

    The account there given of his writings is not much more satisfactory, and the criticism on them must go for little better than nothing.

    It is to be regretted that we have not an opportunity of judging for ourselves of his "love ditties and his tales of prose "

    Versi d'amore e prose di romanzi.

    Our Poet frequently cities him in the work De Vulgari Eloquentia. According to Crescimbeni, (Della Volg. Poes. 1. 1. p. 7. ed. 1698.) He died in 1189.

    v. 113. The songster of Limoges.] Giraud de Borneil, of Sideuil, a castle in Limoges. He was a troubadour, much admired and caressed in his day, and appears to have been in favour with the monarchs of Castile, Leon, Navarre, and Arragon He is quoted by Dante, De Vulg. Eloq., and many of his poems are still remaining in MS. According to Nostradamus he died in 1278. Millot, Hist. Litt. des Troub. t. ii. p. 1 and 23. But I suspect that there is some error in this date, and that he did not live to see so late a period.

    v. 118. Guittone.] See Cano XXIV. 56.

    v. 123. Far as needs.] See Canto XI. 23.

    v. 132. Thy courtesy.] Arnault is here made to speak in his own tongue, the Provencal. According to Dante, (De Vulg. Eloq. 1. 1. c. 8.) the Provencal was one language with the Spanish. What he says on this subject is so curious, that the reader will perhaps not be displeased it I give an abstract of it.

    He first makes three great divisions of the European languages. "One of these extends from the mouths of the Danube, or the lake of Maeotis, to the western limits of England, and is bounded by the limits of the French and Italians, and by the ocean. One idiom obtained over the whole of this space: but was afterwards subdivided into, the Sclavonian, Hungarian, Teutonic, Saxon, English, and the vernacular tongues of several other people, one sign remaining to all, that they use the affirmative io, (our English ay.) The whole of Europe, beginning from the Hungarian limits and stretching towards the east, has a second idiom which reaches still further than the end of Europe into Asia. This is the Greek. In all that remains of Europe, there is a third idiom subdivided into three dialects, which may be severally distinguished by the use of the affirmatives, oc, oil, and si; the first spoken by the Spaniards, the next by the French, and the third by the Latins (or Italians). The first occupy the western part of southern Europe, beginning from the limits of the Genoese. The third occupy the eastern part from the said limits, as far, that is, as the promontory of Italy, where the Adriatic sea begins, and to Sicily. The second are in a manner northern with respect to these for they have the Germans to the east and north, on the west they are bounded by the English sea, and the mountains of Arragon, and on the south by the people of Provence and the declivity of the Apennine." Ibid. c. x. "Each of these three," he observes, "has its own claims to distinction The excellency of the French language consists in its being best adapted, on account of its facility and agreeableness, to prose narration, (quicquid redactum, sive inventum est ad vulgare prosaicum suum est); and he instances the books compiled on the gests of the Trojans and Romans and the delightful adventures of King Arthur, with many other histories and works of instruction. The Spanish (or Provencal) may boast of its having produced such as first cultivated in this as in a more perfect and sweet language, the vernacular poetry: among whom are Pierre d'Auvergne, and others more ancient. The privileges of the Latin, or Italian are two: first that it may reckon for its own those writers who have adopted a more sweet and subtle style of poetry, in the number of whom are Cino, da Pistoia and his friend, and the next, that its writers seem to adhere to, certain general rules of grammar, and in so doing give it, in the opinion of the intelligent, a very weighty pretension to preference."

CANTO XXVII

v. 1. The sun.] At Jerusalem it was dawn, in Spain midnight, and in India noonday, while it was sunset in Purgatory

v. 10. Blessed.] Matt. c. v. 8.

v. 57. Come.] Matt. c. xxv. 34.

v. 102. I am Leah.] By Leah is understood the active life, as Rachel figures the contemplative. The divinity is the mirror in which the latter looks. Michel Angelo has made these allegorical personages the subject of two statues on the monument of Julius II. in the church of S. Pietro in Vincolo. See Mr. Duppa's Life of Michel Angelo, Sculpture viii. And x. and p 247.

v. 135. Those bright eyes.] The eyes of Beatrice.

CANTO XXVIII

v. 11. To that part.] The west.

v. 14. The feather'd quiristers] Imitated by Boccaccio, Fiammetta, 1. iv. "Odi i queruli uccelli," &c. --"Hear the querulous birds plaining with sweet songs, and the boughs trembling, and, moved by a gentle wind, as it were keeping tenor to their notes."

v. 7. A pleasant air.] Compare Ariosto, O. F. c. xxxiv. st. 50.

v. Chiassi.] This is the wood where the scene of Boccaccio's sublimest story is laid. See Dec. g. 5. n. 8. and Dryden's Theodore and Honoria Our Poet perhaps wandered in it daring his abode with Guido Novello da Polenta.

v. 41. A lady.] Most of the commentators suppose, that by this lady, who in the last Canto is called Matilda, is to be understood the Countess Matilda, who endowed the holy see with the estates called the Patrimony of St. Peter, and died in 1115. See G. Villani, 1. iv. e. 20 But it seems more probable that she should be intended for an allegorical personage.

v. 80. Thou, Lord hast made me glad.] Psalm xcii. 4

v. 146. On the Parnassian mountain.]
In bicipiti somniasse Parnasso.

Persius Prol.

CANTO XXIX

v. 76. Listed colours.]
Di sette liste tutte in quel colori, &c.
--a bow
Conspicuous with three listed colours gay.
Milton, P. L. b. xi. 865.

v. 79. Ten paces.] For an explanation of the allegorical meaning of this mysterious procession, Venturi refers those "who would see in the dark" to the commentaries of Landino, Vellutello, and others: and adds that it is evident the Poet has accommodated to his own fancy many sacred images in the Apocalypse. In Vasari's Life of Giotto, we learn that Dante recommended that book to his friend, as affording fit subjects for his pencil.

v. 89. Four.] The four evangelists.

v. 96. Ezekiel.] Chap. 1. 4.

v. 101. John.] Rev. c. iv. 8.

v. 104. Gryphon.] Under the Gryphon, an imaginary creature, the forepart of which is an eagle, and the hinder a lion, is shadowed forth the union of the divine and human nature in Jesus Christ. The car is the church.

v. 115. Tellus' prayer.] Ovid, Met. 1. ii. v. 279.

v. 116. 'Three nymphs.] The three evangelical virtues: the first Charity, the next Hope, and the third Faith. Faith may be produced by charity, or charity by faith, but the inducements to hope must arise either from one or other of these.

v. 125. A band quaternion.] The four moral or cardinal virtues, of whom Prudence directs the others.

v. 129. Two old men.] Saint Luke, characterized as the writer of the Arts of the Apostles and Saint Paul.

v. 133. Of the great Coan.] Hippocrates, "whom nature made for the benefit of her favourite creature, man."

v. 138. Four others.] "The commentators," says Venturi; "suppose these four to be the four evangelists, but I should rather take them to be four principal doctors of the church." Yet both Landino and Vellutello expressly call them the authors of the epistles, James, Peter, John and Jude.

v. 140. One single old man.] As some say, St. John, under his character of the author of the Apocalypse. But in the poem attributed to Giacopo, the son of our Poet, which in some MSS, accompanies the original of this work, and is descriptive of its plan, this old man is said to be Moses.

E'l vecchio, ch' era dietro a tutti loro
Fu Moyse.
And the old man, who was behind them all,
Was Moses.
See No. 3459 of the Harl. MSS. in the British Museum.

CANTO XXX

v. 1. The polar light.] The seven candlesticks.
v. 12. Come.] Song of Solomon, c. iv. 8.
v. 19. Blessed.] Matt. c. xxi. 9.
v. 20. From full hands.] Virg. Aen 1. vi. 884.
v. 97. The old flame.]
Agnosco veteris vestigia flammae
Virg. Aen. I. I. 23.
Conosco i segni dell' antico fuoco.
Giusto de' Conti, La Bella Mano.
v. 61. Nor.] "Not all the beauties of the terrestrial Paradise; in which I was, were sufficient to allay my grief."
v. 85. But.] They sang the thirty-first Psalm, to the end of the eighth verse.
v. 87. The living rafters.] The leafless woods on the Apennine.
v. 90. The land whereon no shadow falls.] "When the wind blows, from off Africa, where, at the time of the equinox, bodies being under the equator cast little or no shadow; or, in other words, when the wind is south."
v. 98. The ice.] Milton has transferred this conceit, though scarcely worth the pains of removing, into one of his Italian poems, son.

CANTO XXXI

v. 3. With lateral edge.] The words of Beatrice, when not addressed directly to himself, but speaking to the angel of hell, Dante had thought sufficiently harsh.
v. 39. Counter to the edge.] "The weapons of divine justice are blunted by the confession and sorrow of the offender."
v. 58. Bird.] Prov. c. i. 17
v. 69. From Iarbas' land.] The south.
v. 71. The beard.] "I perceived, that when she desired me to raise my beard, instead of telling me to lift up my head, a severe reflection was implied on my want of that wisdom which should accompany the age of manhood."
v. 98. Tu asperges me.] A prayer repeated by the priest at sprinkling the holy water.
v. 106. And in the heaven are stars.] See Canto I. 24.
v. 116. The emeralds.] The eyes of Beatrice.

CANTO XXXII

v. 2. Their ten years' thirst.] Beatrice had been dead ten years.
v. 9. Two fix'd a gaze.] The allegorical interpretation of Vellutello whether it be considered as justly terrible from the text or not, conveys so useful a lesson, that it deserves our notice. "The understanding is sometimes so intently engaged in contemplating the light of divine truth in the scriptures, that it becomes dazzled, and is made less capable of attaining such knowledge, than if it had sought after it with greater moderation"
v. 39. Its tresses.] Daniel, c. iv. 10, &c.
v. 41. The Indians.]

Quos oceano proprior gerit India lucos.
Virg. Georg. 1. ii. 122,
Such as at this day to Indians known.
Milton, P. L. b. ix. 1102.

v. 51. When large floods of radiance.] When the sun enters into Aries, the constellation next to that of the Fish.

v. 63. Th' unpitying eyes.] See Ovid, Met. 1. i. 689.

v. 74. The blossoming of that fair tree.] Our Saviour's transfiguration.

v. 97. Those lights.] The tapers of gold.

v. 101. That true Rome.] Heaven.

v. 110. The bird of Jove.] This, which is imitated from Ezekiel, c. xvii. 3, 4. appears to be typical of the persecutions which the church sustained from the Roman Emperors.

v. 118. A fox.] By the fox perhaps is represented the treachery of the heretics.

v. 124. With his feathers lin'd.]. An allusion to the donations made by the Roman Emperors to the church.

v. 130. A dragon.] Probably Mahomet.

v. 136. With plumes.] The donations before mentioned.

v. 142. Heads.] By the seven heads, it is supposed with sufficient probability, are meant the seven capital sins, by the three with two horns, pride, anger, and avarice, injurious both to man himself and to his neighbor: by the four with one horn, gluttony, lukewarmness, concupiscence, and envy, hurtful, at least in their primary effects, chiefly to him who is guilty of them.

v. 146. O'er it.] The harlot is thought to represent the state of the church under Boniface VIII and the giant to figure Philip IV of France.

v. 155. Dragg'd on.] The removal of the Pope's residence from Rome to Avignon is pointed at.

CANTO XXXIII

v. 1. The Heathen.] Psalm lxxix. 1.

v. 36. Hope not to scare God's vengeance with a sop.] "Let not him who hath occasioned the destruction of the church, that vessel which the serpent brake, hope to appease the anger of the Deity by any outward acts of religious, or rather superstitious, ceremony, such as was that, in our poet's time, performed by a murderer at Florence, who imagined himself secure from vengeance, if he ate a sop of bread in wine, upon the grave of the person murdered, within the space of nine days."

v. 38. That eagle.] He prognosticates that the Emperor of Germany will not always continue to submit to the usurpations of the Pope, and foretells the coming of Henry VII Duke of Luxembourg signified by the numerical figures DVX; or, as Lombardi supposes, of Can Grande della Scala, appointed the leader of the Ghibelline forces. It is unnecessary to point out the imitation of the Apocalypse in the manner of this prophecy.

v. 50. The Naiads.] Dante, it is observed, has been led into a mistake by a corruption in the text of Ovid's Metam. I. vii. 75, where he found-
    Carmina Naiades non intellecta priorum;
instead of Carmina Laiades, &c. as it has been since corrected. Lombardi refers to Pansanias, where "the Nymphs" are spoken of as expounders of oracles for a

vindication of the poet's accuracy. Should the reader blame me for not departing from the error of the original (if error it be), he may substitute

Events shall be the Oedipus will solve, &c.

v. 67. Elsa's numbing waters.] The Elsa, a little stream, which flows into the Arno about twenty miles below Florence, is said to possess a petrifying quality.

v. 78. That one brings home his staff inwreath'd with palm.] "For the same cause that the pilgrim, returning from Palestine, brings home his staff, or bourdon, bound with palm," that is, to show where he has been.

Che si reca 'l bordon di palma cinto.

"In regard to the word bourdon, why it has been applied to a pilgrim's staff, it is not easy to guess. I believe, however that this name has been given to such sort of staves, because pilgrims usually travel and perform their pilgrimages on foot, their staves serving them instead of horses or mules, then called bourdons and burdones, by writers in the middle ages." Mr. Johnes's Translation of Joinville's Memoirs. Dissertation xv, by M. du Cange p. 152. 4to. edit. The word is thrice used by Chaucer in the Romaunt of the Rose.

PARADISE

CANTO I

His glory, by whose might all things are mov'd,
Pierces the universe, and in one part
Sheds more resplendence, elsewhere less. In heav'n,
That largeliest of his light partakes, was I,
Witness of things, which to relate again
Surpasseth power of him who comes from thence;
For that, so near approaching its desire
Our intellect is to such depth absorb'd,
That memory cannot follow. Nathless all,
That in my thoughts I of that sacred realm
Could store, shall now be matter of my song.
     Benign Apollo! this last labour aid,
And make me such a vessel of thy worth,
As thy own laurel claims of me belov'd.
Thus far hath one of steep Parnassus' brows
Suffic'd me; henceforth there is need of both
For my remaining enterprise Do thou
Enter into my bosom, and there breathe
So, as when Marsyas by thy hand was dragg'd
Forth from his limbs unsheath'd. O power divine!
If thou to me of shine impart so much,
That of that happy realm the shadow'd form
Trac'd in my thoughts I may set forth to view,
Thou shalt behold me of thy favour'd tree
Come to the foot, and crown myself with leaves;
For to that honour thou, and my high theme
Will fit me. If but seldom, mighty Sire!
To grace his triumph gathers thence a wreath
Caesar or bard (more shame for human wills
Deprav'd) joy to the Delphic god must spring
From the Pierian foliage, when one breast
Is with such thirst inspir'd. From a small spark
Great flame hath risen: after me perchance
Others with better voice may pray, and gain
From the Cirrhaean city answer kind.
     Through diver passages, the world's bright lamp
Rises to mortals, but through that which joins
Four circles with the threefold cross, in best
Course, and in happiest constellation set

Dante Alighieri

He comes, and to the worldly wax best gives
Its temper and impression. Morning there,
Here eve was by almost such passage made;
And whiteness had o'erspread that hemisphere,
Blackness the other part; when to the left
I saw Beatrice turn'd, and on the sun
Gazing, as never eagle fix'd his ken.
As from the first a second beam is wont
To issue, and reflected upwards rise,
E'en as a pilgrim bent on his return,
So of her act, that through the eyesight pass'd
Into my fancy, mine was form'd; and straight,
Beyond our mortal wont, I fix'd mine eyes
Upon the sun. Much is allowed us there,
That here exceeds our pow'r; thanks to the place
Made for the dwelling of the human kind

    I suffer'd it not long, and yet so long
That I beheld it bick'ring sparks around,
As iron that comes boiling from the fire.
And suddenly upon the day appear'd
A day new-ris'n, as he, who hath the power,
Had with another sun bedeck'd the sky.

    Her eyes fast fix'd on the eternal wheels,
Beatrice stood unmov'd; and I with ken
Fix'd upon her, from upward gaze remov'd
At her aspect, such inwardly became
As Glaucus, when he tasted of the herb,
That made him peer among the ocean gods;
Words may not tell of that transhuman change:
And therefore let the example serve, though weak,
For those whom grace hath better proof in store

    If I were only what thou didst create,
Then newly, Love! by whom the heav'n is rul'd,
Thou know'st, who by thy light didst bear me up.
Whenas the wheel which thou dost ever guide,
Desired Spirit! with its harmony
Temper'd of thee and measur'd, charm'd mine ear,
Then seem'd to me so much of heav'n to blaze
With the sun's flame, that rain or flood ne'er made
A lake so broad. The newness of the sound,
And that great light, inflam'd me with desire,
Keener than e'er was felt, to know their cause.

    Whence she who saw me, clearly as myself,
To calm my troubled mind, before I ask'd,
Open'd her lips, and gracious thus began:
"With false imagination thou thyself
Mak'st dull, so that thou seest not the thing,
Which thou hadst seen, had that been shaken off.
Thou art not on the earth as thou believ'st;
For light'ning scap'd from its own proper place

Ne'er ran, as thou hast hither now return'd."
    Although divested of my first-rais'd doubt,
By those brief words, accompanied with smiles,
Yet in new doubt was I entangled more,
And said: "Already satisfied, I rest
From admiration deep, but now admire
How I above those lighter bodies rise."
    Whence, after utt'rance of a piteous sigh,
She tow'rds me bent her eyes, with such a look,
As on her frenzied child a mother casts;
Then thus began: "Among themselves all things
Have order; and from hence the form, which makes
The universe resemble God. In this
The higher creatures see the printed steps
Of that eternal worth, which is the end
Whither the line is drawn. All natures lean,
In this their order, diversely, some more,
Some less approaching to their primal source.
Thus they to different havens are mov'd on
Through the vast sea of being, and each one
With instinct giv'n, that bears it in its course;
This to the lunar sphere directs the fire,
This prompts the hearts of mortal animals,
This the brute earth together knits, and binds.
Nor only creatures, void of intellect,
Are aim'd at by this bow; hut even those,
That have intelligence and love, are pierc'd.
That Providence, who so well orders all,
With her own light makes ever calm the heaven,
In which the substance, that hath greatest speed,
Is turn'd: and thither now, as to our seat
Predestin'd, we are carried by the force
Of that strong cord, that never looses dart,
But at fair aim and glad. Yet is it true,
That as ofttimes but ill accords the form
To the design of art, through sluggishness
Of unreplying matter, so this course
Is sometimes quitted by the creature, who
Hath power, directed thus, to bend elsewhere;
As from a cloud the fire is seen to fall,
From its original impulse warp'd, to earth,
By vicious fondness. Thou no more admire
Thy soaring, (if I rightly deem,) than lapse
Of torrent downwards from a mountain's height.
There would in thee for wonder be more cause,
If, free of hind'rance, thou hadst fix'd thyself
Below, like fire unmoving on the earth."
    So said, she turn'd toward the heav'n her face.

Dante Alighieri

CANTO II

All ye, who in small bark have following sail'd,
Eager to listen, on the advent'rous track
Of my proud keel, that singing cuts its way,
Backward return with speed, and your own shores
Revisit, nor put out to open sea,
Where losing me, perchance ye may remain
Bewilder'd in deep maze. The way I pass
Ne'er yet was run: Minerva breathes the gale,
Apollo guides me, and another Nine
To my rapt sight the arctic beams reveal.
Ye other few, who have outstretch'd the neck.
Timely for food of angels, on which here
They live, yet never know satiety,
Through the deep brine ye fearless may put out
Your vessel, marking, well the furrow broad
Before you in the wave, that on both sides
Equal returns. Those, glorious, who pass'd o'er
To Colchos, wonder'd not as ye will do,
When they saw Jason following the plough.
    The increate perpetual thirst, that draws
Toward the realm of God's own form, bore us
Swift almost as the heaven ye behold.
    Beatrice upward gaz'd, and I on her,
And in such space as on the notch a dart
Is plac'd, then loosen'd flies, I saw myself
Arriv'd, where wond'rous thing engag'd my sight.
Whence she, to whom no work of mine was hid,
Turning to me, with aspect glad as fair,
Bespake me: "Gratefully direct thy mind
To God, through whom to this first star we come."
    Me seem'd as if a cloud had cover'd us,
Translucent, solid, firm, and polish'd bright,
Like adamant, which the sun's beam had smit
Within itself the ever-during pearl
Receiv'd us, as the wave a ray of light
Receives, and rests unbroken. If I then
Was of corporeal frame, and it transcend
Our weaker thought, how one dimension thus
Another could endure, which needs must be
If body enter body, how much more
Must the desire inflame us to behold
That essence, which discovers by what means
God and our nature join'd! There will be seen
That which we hold through faith, not shown by proof,
But in itself intelligibly plain,
E'en as the truth that man at first believes.

The Divine Comedy

     I answered: "Lady! I with thoughts devout,
Such as I best can frame, give thanks to Him,
Who hath remov'd me from the mortal world.
But tell, I pray thee, whence the gloomy spots
Upon this body, which below on earth
Give rise to talk of Cain in fabling quaint?"
     She somewhat smil'd, then spake: "If mortals err
In their opinion, when the key of sense
Unlocks not, surely wonder's weapon keen
Ought not to pierce thee; since thou find'st, the wings
Of reason to pursue the senses' flight
Are short. But what thy own thought is, declare."
     Then I: "What various here above appears,
Is caus'd, I deem, by bodies dense or rare."
     She then resum'd: "Thou certainly wilt see
In falsehood thy belief o'erwhelm'd, if well
Thou listen to the arguments, which I
Shall bring to face it. The eighth sphere displays
Numberless lights, the which in kind and size
May be remark'd of different aspects;
If rare or dense of that were cause alone,
One single virtue then would be in all,
Alike distributed, or more, or less.
Different virtues needs must be the fruits
Of formal principles, and these, save one,
Will by thy reasoning be destroy'd. Beside,
If rarity were of that dusk the cause,
Which thou inquirest, either in some part
That planet must throughout be void, nor fed
With its own matter; or, as bodies share
Their fat and leanness, in like manner this
Must in its volume change the leaves. The first,
If it were true, had through the sun's eclipse
Been manifested, by transparency
Of light, as through aught rare beside effus'd.
But this is not. Therefore remains to see
The other cause: and if the other fall,
Erroneous so must prove what seem'd to thee.
If not from side to side this rarity
Pass through, there needs must be a limit, whence
Its contrary no further lets it pass.
And hence the beam, that from without proceeds,
Must be pour'd back, as colour comes, through glass
Reflected, which behind it lead conceals.
Now wilt thou say, that there of murkier hue
Than in the other part the ray is shown,
By being thence refracted farther back.
From this perplexity will free thee soon
Experience, if thereof thou trial make,
The fountain whence your arts derive their streame.

Dante Alighieri

Three mirrors shalt thou take, and two remove
From thee alike, and more remote the third.
Betwixt the former pair, shall meet thine eyes;
Then turn'd toward them, cause behind thy back
A light to stand, that on the three shall shine,
And thus reflected come to thee from all.
Though that beheld most distant do not stretch
A space so ample, yet in brightness thou
Will own it equaling the rest. But now,
As under snow the ground, if the warm ray
Smites it, remains dismantled of the hue
And cold, that cover'd it before, so thee,
Dismantled in thy mind, I will inform
With light so lively, that the tremulous beam
Shall quiver where it falls. Within the heaven,
Where peace divine inhabits, circles round
A body, in whose virtue dies the being
Of all that it contains. The following heaven,
That hath so many lights, this being divides,
Through different essences, from it distinct,
And yet contain'd within it. The other orbs
Their separate distinctions variously
Dispose, for their own seed and produce apt.
Thus do these organs of the world proceed,
As thou beholdest now, from step to step,
Their influences from above deriving,
And thence transmitting downwards. Mark me well,
How through this passage to the truth I ford,
The truth thou lov'st, that thou henceforth alone,
May'st know to keep the shallows, safe, untold.

"The virtue and motion of the sacred orbs,
As mallet by the workman's hand, must needs
By blessed movers be inspir'd. This heaven,
Made beauteous by so many luminaries,
From the deep spirit, that moves its circling sphere,
Its image takes an impress as a seal:
And as the soul, that dwells within your dust,
Through members different, yet together form'd,
In different pow'rs resolves itself; e'en so
The intellectual efficacy unfolds
Its goodness multiplied throughout the stars;
On its own unity revolving still.
Different virtue compact different
Makes with the precious body it enlivens,
With which it knits, as life in you is knit.
From its original nature full of joy,
The virtue mingled through the body shines,
As joy through pupil of the living eye.
From hence proceeds, that which from light to light
Seems different, and not from dense or rare.

The Divine Comedy
This is the formal cause, that generates
Proportion'd to its power, the dusk or clear."

CANTO III

That sun, which erst with love my bosom warm'd
Had of fair truth unveil'd the sweet aspect,
By proof of right, and of the false reproof;
And I, to own myself convinc'd and free
Of doubt, as much as needed, rais'd my head
Erect for speech. But soon a sight appear'd,
Which, so intent to mark it, held me fix'd,
That of confession I no longer thought.

    As through translucent and smooth glass, or wave
Clear and unmov'd, and flowing not so deep
As that its bed is dark, the shape returns
So faint of our impictur'd lineaments,
That on white forehead set a pearl as strong
Comes to the eye: such saw I many a face,
All stretch'd to speak, from whence I straight conceiv'd
Delusion opposite to that, which rais'd
Between the man and fountain, amorous flame.

    Sudden, as I perceiv'd them, deeming these
Reflected semblances to see of whom
They were, I turn'd mine eyes, and nothing saw;
Then turn'd them back, directed on the light
Of my sweet guide, who smiling shot forth beams
From her celestial eyes. "Wonder not thou,"
She cry'd, "at this my smiling, when I see
Thy childish judgment; since not yet on truth
It rests the foot, but, as it still is wont,
Makes thee fall back in unsound vacancy.
True substances are these, which thou behold'st,
Hither through failure of their vow exil'd.
But speak thou with them; listen, and believe,
That the true light, which fills them with desire,
Permits not from its beams their feet to stray."

    Straight to the shadow which for converse seem'd
Most earnest, I addressed me, and began,
As one by over-eagerness perplex'd:
"O spirit, born for joy! who in the rays
Of life eternal, of that sweetness know'st
The flavour, which, not tasted, passes far
All apprehension, me it well would please,
If thou wouldst tell me of thy name, and this
Your station here." Whence she, with kindness prompt,
And eyes glist'ning with smiles: "Our charity,
To any wish by justice introduc'd,
Bars not the door, no more than she above,

Dante Alighieri

Who would have all her court be like herself.
I was a virgin sister in the earth;
And if thy mind observe me well, this form,
With such addition grac'd of loveliness,
Will not conceal me long, but thou wilt know
Piccarda, in the tardiest sphere thus plac'd,
Here 'mid these other blessed also blest.
Our hearts, whose high affections burn alone
With pleasure, from the Holy Spirit conceiv'd,
Admitted to his order dwell in joy.
And this condition, which appears so low,
Is for this cause assign'd us, that our vows
Were in some part neglected and made void."

    Whence I to her replied: "Something divine
Beams in your countenance, wond'rous fair,
From former knowledge quite transmuting you.
Therefore to recollect was I so slow.
But what thou sayst hath to my memory
Given now such aid, that to retrace your forms
Is easier. Yet inform me, ye, who here
Are happy, long ye for a higher place
More to behold, and more in love to dwell?"

    She with those other spirits gently smil'd,
Then answer'd with such gladness, that she seem'd
With love's first flame to glow: "Brother! our will
Is in composure settled by the power
Of charity, who makes us will alone
What we possess, and nought beyond desire;
If we should wish to be exalted more,
Then must our wishes jar with the high will
Of him, who sets us here, which in these orbs
Thou wilt confess not possible, if here
To be in charity must needs befall,
And if her nature well thou contemplate.
Rather it is inherent in this state
Of blessedness, to keep ourselves within
The divine will, by which our wills with his
Are one. So that as we from step to step
Are plac'd throughout this kingdom, pleases all,
E'en as our King, who in us plants his will;
And in his will is our tranquillity;
It is the mighty ocean, whither tends
Whatever it creates and nature makes."

    Then saw I clearly how each spot in heav'n
Is Paradise, though with like gracious dew
The supreme virtue show'r not over all.

    But as it chances, if one sort of food
Hath satiated, and of another still
The appetite remains, that this is ask'd,
And thanks for that return'd; e'en so did I

In word and motion, bent from her to learn
What web it was, through which she had not drawn
The shuttle to its point. She thus began:
"Exalted worth and perfectness of life
The Lady higher up enshrine in heaven,
By whose pure laws upon your nether earth
The robe and veil they wear, to that intent,
That e'en till death they may keep watch or sleep
With their great bridegroom, who accepts each vow,
Which to his gracious pleasure love conforms.
from the world, to follow her, when young
Escap'd; and, in her vesture mantling me,
Made promise of the way her sect enjoins.
Thereafter men, for ill than good more apt,
Forth snatch'd me from the pleasant cloister's pale.
God knows how after that my life was fram'd.
This other splendid shape, which thou beholdst
At my right side, burning with all the light
Of this our orb, what of myself I tell
May to herself apply. From her, like me
A sister, with like violence were torn
The saintly folds, that shaded her fair brows.
E'en when she to the world again was brought
In spite of her own will and better wont,
Yet not for that the bosom's inward veil
Did she renounce. This is the luminary
Of mighty Constance, who from that loud blast,
Which blew the second over Suabia's realm,
That power produc'd, which was the third and last."
    She ceas'd from further talk, and then began
"Ave Maria" singing, and with that song
Vanish'd, as heavy substance through deep wave.
    Mine eye, that far as it was capable,
Pursued her, when in dimness she was lost,
Turn'd to the mark where greater want impell'd,
And bent on Beatrice all its gaze.
But she as light'ning beam'd upon my looks:
So that the sight sustain'd it not at first.
Whence I to question her became less prompt.

CANTO IV

Between two kinds of food, both equally
Remote and tempting, first a man might die
Of hunger, ere he one could freely choose.
E'en so would stand a lamb between the maw
Of two fierce wolves, in dread of both alike:
E'en so between two deer a dog would stand,
Wherefore, if I was silent, fault nor praise

Dante Alighieri

I to myself impute, by equal doubts
Held in suspense, since of necessity
It happen'd. Silent was I, yet desire
Was painted in my looks; and thus I spake
My wish more earnestly than language could.
     As Daniel, when the haughty king he freed
From ire, that spurr'd him on to deeds unjust
And violent; so look'd Beatrice then.
     "Well I discern," she thus her words address'd,
"How contrary desires each way constrain thee,
So that thy anxious thought is in itself
Bound up and stifled, nor breathes freely forth.
Thou arguest; if the good intent remain;
What reason that another's violence
Should stint the measure of my fair desert?
     "Cause too thou findst for doubt, in that it seems,
That spirits to the stars, as Plato deem'd,
Return. These are the questions which thy will
Urge equally; and therefore I the first
Of that will treat which hath the more of gall.
Of seraphim he who is most ensky'd,
Moses and Samuel, and either John,
Choose which thou wilt, nor even Mary's self,
Have not in any other heav'n their seats,
Than have those spirits which so late thou saw'st;
Nor more or fewer years exist; but all
Make the first circle beauteous, diversely
Partaking of sweet life, as more or less
Afflation of eternal bliss pervades them.
Here were they shown thee, not that fate assigns
This for their sphere, but for a sign to thee
Of that celestial furthest from the height.
Thus needs, that ye may apprehend, we speak:
Since from things sensible alone ye learn
That, which digested rightly after turns
To intellectual. For no other cause
The scripture, condescending graciously
To your perception, hands and feet to God
Attributes, nor so means: and holy church
Doth represent with human countenance
Gabriel, and Michael, and him who made
Tobias whole. Unlike what here thou seest,
The judgment of Timaeus, who affirms
Each soul restor'd to its particular star,
Believing it to have been taken thence,
When nature gave it to inform her mold:
Since to appearance his intention is
E'en what his words declare: or else to shun
Derision, haply thus he hath disguis'd
His true opinion. If his meaning be,

That to the influencing of these orbs revert
The honour and the blame in human acts,
Perchance he doth not wholly miss the truth.
This principle, not understood aright,
Erewhile perverted well nigh all the world;
So that it fell to fabled names of Jove,
And Mercury, and Mars. That other doubt,
Which moves thee, is less harmful; for it brings
No peril of removing thee from me.

    "That, to the eye of man, our justice seems
Unjust, is argument for faith, and not
For heretic declension. To the end
This truth may stand more clearly in your view,
I will content thee even to thy wish

    "If violence be, when that which suffers, nought
Consents to that which forceth, not for this
These spirits stood exculpate. For the will,
That will not, still survives unquench'd, and doth
As nature doth in fire, tho' violence
Wrest it a thousand times; for, if it yield
Or more or less, so far it follows force.
And thus did these, whom they had power to seek
The hallow'd place again. In them, had will
Been perfect, such as once upon the bars
Held Laurence firm, or wrought in Scaevola
To his own hand remorseless, to the path,
Whence they were drawn, their steps had hasten'd back,
When liberty return'd: but in too few
Resolve so steadfast dwells. And by these words
If duly weigh'd, that argument is void,
Which oft might have perplex'd thee still. But now
Another question thwarts thee, which to solve
Might try thy patience without better aid.
I have, no doubt, instill'd into thy mind,
That blessed spirit may not lie; since near
The source of primal truth it dwells for aye:
And thou might'st after of Piccarda learn
That Constance held affection to the veil;
So that she seems to contradict me here.
Not seldom, brother, it hath chanc'd for men
To do what they had gladly left undone,
Yet to shun peril they have done amiss:
E'en as Alcmaeon, at his father's suit
Slew his own mother, so made pitiless
Not to lose pity. On this point bethink thee,
That force and will are blended in such wise
As not to make the' offence excusable.
Absolute will agrees not to the wrong,
That inasmuch as there is fear of woe
From non-compliance, it agrees. Of will

Thus absolute Piccarda spake, and I
Of th' other; so that both have truly said."
    Such was the flow of that pure rill, that well'd
From forth the fountain of all truth; and such
The rest, that to my wond'ring thoughts I found.
    "O thou of primal love the prime delight!
Goddess! "I straight reply'd, "whose lively words
Still shed new heat and vigour through my soul!
Affection fails me to requite thy grace
With equal sum of gratitude: be his
To recompense, who sees and can reward thee.
Well I discern, that by that truth alone
Enlighten'd, beyond which no truth may roam,
Our mind can satisfy her thirst to know:
Therein she resteth, e'en as in his lair
The wild beast, soon as she hath reach'd that bound,
And she hath power to reach it; else desire
Were given to no end. And thence doth doubt
Spring, like a shoot, around the stock of truth;
And it is nature which from height to height
On to the summit prompts us. This invites,
This doth assure me, lady, rev'rently
To ask thee of other truth, that yet
Is dark to me. I fain would know, if man
By other works well done may so supply
The failure of his vows, that in your scale
They lack not weight." I spake; and on me straight
Beatrice look'd with eyes that shot forth sparks
Of love celestial in such copious stream,
That, virtue sinking in me overpower'd,
I turn'd, and downward bent confus'd my sight.

CANTO V

"If beyond earthly wont, the flame of love
Illume me, so that I o'ercome thy power
Of vision, marvel not: but learn the cause
In that perfection of the sight, which soon
As apprehending, hasteneth on to reach
The good it apprehends. I well discern,
How in thine intellect already shines
The light eternal, which to view alone
Ne'er fails to kindle love; and if aught else
Your love seduces, 't is but that it shows
Some ill-mark'd vestige of that primal beam.
    "This would'st thou know, if failure of the vow
By other service may be so supplied,
As from self-question to assure the soul."

The Divine Comedy

     Thus she her words, not heedless of my wish,
Began; and thus, as one who breaks not off
Discourse, continued in her saintly strain.
"Supreme of gifts, which God creating gave
Of his free bounty, sign most evident
Of goodness, and in his account most priz'd,
Was liberty of will, the boon wherewith
All intellectual creatures, and them sole
He hath endow'd. Hence now thou mayst infer
Of what high worth the vow, which so is fram'd
That when man offers, God well-pleas'd accepts;
For in the compact between God and him,
This treasure, such as I describe it to thee,
He makes the victim, and of his own act.
What compensation therefore may he find?
If that, whereof thou hast oblation made,
By using well thou think'st to consecrate,
Thou would'st of theft do charitable deed.
Thus I resolve thee of the greater point.
     "But forasmuch as holy church, herein
Dispensing, seems to contradict the truth
I have discover'd to thee, yet behooves
Thou rest a little longer at the board,
Ere the crude aliment, which thou hast taken,
Digested fitly to nutrition turn.
Open thy mind to what I now unfold,
And give it inward keeping. Knowledge comes
Of learning well retain'd, unfruitful else.
     "This sacrifice in essence of two things
Consisteth; one is that, whereof 't is made,
The covenant the other. For the last,
It ne'er is cancell'd if not kept: and hence
I spake erewhile so strictly of its force.
For this it was enjoin'd the Israelites,
Though leave were giv'n them, as thou know'st, to change
The offering, still to offer. Th' other part,
The matter and the substance of the vow,
May well be such, to that without offence
It may for other substance be exchang'd.
But at his own discretion none may shift
The burden on his shoulders, unreleas'd
By either key, the yellow and the white.
Nor deem of any change, as less than vain,
If the last bond be not within the new
Included, as the quatre in the six.
No satisfaction therefore can be paid
For what so precious in the balance weighs,
That all in counterpoise must kick the beam.
Take then no vow at random: ta'en, with faith
Preserve it; yet not bent, as Jephthah once,

Dante Alighieri

Blindly to execute a rash resolve,
Whom better it had suited to exclaim,
'1 have done ill,' than to redeem his pledge
By doing worse or, not unlike to him
In folly, that great leader of the Greeks:
Whence, on the alter, Iphigenia mourn'd
Her virgin beauty, and hath since made mourn
Both wise and simple, even all, who hear
Of so fell sacrifice. Be ye more staid,
O Christians, not, like feather, by each wind
Removable: nor think to cleanse ourselves
In every water. Either testament,
The old and new, is yours: and for your guide
The shepherd of the church let this suffice
To save you. When by evil lust entic'd,
Remember ye be men, not senseless beasts;
Nor let the Jew, who dwelleth in your streets,
Hold you in mock'ry. Be not, as the lamb,
That, fickle wanton, leaves its mother's milk,
To dally with itself in idle play."
    Such were the words that Beatrice spake:
These ended, to that region, where the world
Is liveliest, full of fond desire she turn'd.
    Though mainly prompt new question to propose,
Her silence and chang'd look did keep me dumb.
And as the arrow, ere the cord is still,
Leapeth unto its mark; so on we sped
Into the second realm. There I beheld
The dame, so joyous enter, that the orb
Grew brighter at her smiles; and, if the star
Were mov'd to gladness, what then was my cheer,
Whom nature hath made apt for every change!
    As in a quiet and clear lake the fish,
If aught approach them from without, do draw
Towards it, deeming it their food; so drew
Full more than thousand splendours towards us,
And in each one was heard: "Lo! one arriv'd
To multiply our loves!" and as each came
The shadow, streaming forth effulgence new,
Witness'd augmented joy. Here, reader! think,
If thou didst miss the sequel of my tale,
To know the rest how sorely thou wouldst crave;
And thou shalt see what vehement desire
Possess'd me, as soon as these had met my view,
To know their state. "O born in happy hour!
Thou to whom grace vouchsafes, or ere thy close
Of fleshly warfare, to behold the thrones
Of that eternal triumph, know to us
The light communicated, which through heaven
Expatiates without bound. Therefore, if aught

Thou of our beams wouldst borrow for thine aid,
Spare not; and of our radiance take thy fill."
　　　Thus of those piteous spirits one bespake me;
And Beatrice next: "Say on; and trust
As unto gods!" --"How in the light supreme
Thou harbour'st, and from thence the virtue bring'st,
That, sparkling in thine eyes, denotes thy joy,
l mark; but, who thou art, am still to seek;
Or wherefore, worthy spirit! for thy lot
This sphere assign'd, that oft from mortal ken
Is veil'd by others' beams." I said, and turn'd
Toward the lustre, that with greeting, kind
Erewhile had hail'd me. Forthwith brighter far
Than erst, it wax'd: and, as himself the sun
Hides through excess of light, when his warm gaze
Hath on the mantle of thick vapours prey'd;
Within its proper ray the saintly shape
Was, through increase of gladness, thus conceal'd;
And, shrouded so in splendour answer'd me,
E'en as the tenour of my song declares.

CANTO VI

"After that Constantine the eagle turn'd
Against the motions of the heav'n, that roll'd
Consenting with its course, when he of yore,
Lavinia's spouse, was leader of the flight,
A hundred years twice told and more, his seat
At Europe's extreme point, the bird of Jove
Held, near the mountains, whence he issued first.
There, under shadow of his sacred plumes
Swaying the world, till through successive hands
To mine he came devolv'd. Caesar I was,
And am Justinian; destin'd by the will
Of that prime love, whose influence I feel,
From vain excess to clear th' encumber'd laws.
Or ere that work engag'd me, I did hold
Christ's nature merely human, with such faith
Contented. But the blessed Agapete,
Who was chief shepherd, he with warning voice
To the true faith recall'd me. I believ'd
His words: and what he taught, now plainly see,
As thou in every contradiction seest
The true and false oppos'd. Soon as my feet
Were to the church reclaim'd, to my great task,
By inspiration of God's grace impell'd,
I gave me wholly, and consign'd mine arms
To Belisarius, with whom heaven's right hand
Was link'd in such conjointment, 't was a sign

Dante Alighieri

That I should rest. To thy first question thus
I shape mine answer, which were ended here,
But that its tendency doth prompt perforce
To some addition; that thou well, mayst mark
What reason on each side they have to plead,
By whom that holiest banner is withstood,
Both who pretend its power and who oppose.

   "Beginning from that hour, when Pallas died
To give it rule, behold the valorous deeds
Have made it worthy reverence. Not unknown
To thee, how for three hundred years and more
It dwelt in Alba, up to those fell lists
Where for its sake were met the rival three;
Nor aught unknown to thee, which it achiev'd
Down to the Sabines' wrong to Lucrece' woe,
With its sev'n kings conqu'ring the nation round;
Nor all it wrought, by Roman worthies home
'Gainst Brennus and th' Epirot prince, and hosts
Of single chiefs, or states in league combin'd
Of social warfare; hence Torquatus stern,
And Quintius nam'd of his neglected locks,
The Decii, and the Fabii hence acquir'd
Their fame, which I with duteous zeal embalm.
By it the pride of Arab hordes was quell'd,
When they led on by Hannibal o'erpass'd
The Alpine rocks, whence glide thy currents, Po!
Beneath its guidance, in their prime of days
Scipio and Pompey triumph'd; and that hill,
Under whose summit thou didst see the light,
Rued its stern bearing. After, near the hour,
When heav'n was minded that o'er all the world
His own deep calm should brood, to Caesar's hand
Did Rome consign it; and what then it wrought
From Var unto the Rhine, saw Isere's flood,
Saw Loire and Seine, and every vale, that fills
The torrent Rhone. What after that it wrought,
When from Ravenna it came forth, and leap'd
The Rubicon, was of so bold a flight,
That tongue nor pen may follow it. Tow'rds Spain
It wheel'd its bands, then tow'rd Dyrrachium smote,
And on Pharsalia with so fierce a plunge,
E'en the warm Nile was conscious to the pang;
Its native shores Antandros, and the streams
Of Simois revisited, and there
Where Hector lies; then ill for Ptolemy
His pennons shook again; lightning thence fell
On Juba; and the next upon your west,
At sound of the Pompeian trump, return'd.

   "What following and in its next bearer's gripe
It wrought, is now by Cassius and Brutus

The Divine Comedy
Bark'd off in hell, and by Perugia's sons
And Modena's was mourn'd. Hence weepeth still
Sad Cleopatra, who, pursued by it,
Took from the adder black and sudden death.
With him it ran e'en to the Red Sea coast;
With him compos'd the world to such a peace,
That of his temple Janus barr'd the door.

    "But all the mighty standard yet had wrought,
And was appointed to perform thereafter,
Throughout the mortal kingdom which it sway'd,
Falls in appearance dwindled and obscur'd,
If one with steady eye and perfect thought
On the third Caesar look; for to his hands,
The living Justice, in whose breath I move,
Committed glory, e'en into his hands,
To execute the vengeance of its wrath.

    "Hear now and wonder at what next I tell.
After with Titus it was sent to wreak
Vengeance for vengeance of the ancient sin,
And, when the Lombard tooth, with fangs impure,
Did gore the bosom of the holy church,
Under its wings victorious, Charlemagne
Sped to her rescue. Judge then for thyself
Of those, whom I erewhile accus'd to thee,
What they are, and how grievous their offending,
Who are the cause of all your ills. The one
Against the universal ensign rears
The yellow lilies, and with partial aim
That to himself the other arrogates:
So that 't is hard to see which more offends.
Be yours, ye Ghibellines, to veil your arts
Beneath another standard: ill is this
Follow'd of him, who severs it and justice:
And let not with his Guelphs the new-crown'd Charles
Assail it, but those talons hold in dread,
Which from a lion of more lofty port
Have rent the easing. Many a time ere now
The sons have for the sire's transgression wail'd;
Nor let him trust the fond belief, that heav'n
Will truck its armour for his lilied shield.

    "This little star is furnish'd with good spirits,
Whose mortal lives were busied to that end,
That honour and renown might wait on them:
And, when desires thus err in their intention,
True love must needs ascend with slacker beam.
But it is part of our delight, to measure
Our wages with the merit; and admire
The close proportion. Hence doth heav'nly justice
Temper so evenly affection in us,
It ne'er can warp to any wrongfulness.

Of diverse voices is sweet music made:
So in our life the different degrees
Render sweet harmony among these wheels.
   "Within the pearl, that now encloseth us,
Shines Romeo's light, whose goodly deed and fair
Met ill acceptance. But the Provencals,
That were his foes, have little cause for mirth.
Ill shapes that man his course, who makes his wrong
Of other's worth. Four daughters were there born
To Raymond Berenger, and every one
Became a queen; and this for him did Romeo,
Though of mean state and from a foreign land.
Yet envious tongues incited him to ask
A reckoning of that just one, who return'd
Twelve fold to him for ten. Aged and poor
He parted thence: and if the world did know
The heart he had, begging his life by morsels,
'T would deem the praise, it yields him, scantly dealt."

CANTO VII

"Hosanna Sanctus Deus Sabaoth
Superillustrans claritate tua
Felices ignes horum malahoth!"
Thus chanting saw I turn that substance bright
With fourfold lustre to its orb again,
Revolving; and the rest unto their dance
With it mov'd also; and like swiftest sparks,
In sudden distance from my sight were veil'd.
   Me doubt possess'd, and "Speak," it whisper'd me,
"Speak, speak unto thy lady, that she quench
Thy thirst with drops of sweetness." Yet blank awe,
Which lords it o'er me, even at the sound
Of Beatrice's name, did bow me down
As one in slumber held. Not long that mood
Beatrice suffer'd: she, with such a smile,
As might have made one blest amid the flames,
Beaming upon me, thus her words began:
"Thou in thy thought art pond'ring (as I deem,
And what I deem is truth how just revenge
Could be with justice punish'd: from which doubt
I soon will free thee; so thou mark my words;
For they of weighty matter shall possess thee.
   "That man, who was unborn, himself condemn'd,
And, in himself, all, who since him have liv'd,
His offspring: whence, below, the human kind
Lay sick in grievous error many an age;
Until it pleas'd the Word of God to come
Amongst them down, to his own person joining

The Divine Comedy
The nature, from its Maker far estrang'd,
By the mere act of his eternal love.
Contemplate here the wonder I unfold.
The nature with its Maker thus conjoin'd,
Created first was blameless, pure and good;
But through itself alone was driven forth
From Paradise, because it had eschew'd
The way of truth and life, to evil turn'd.
Ne'er then was penalty so just as that
Inflicted by the cross, if thou regard
The nature in assumption doom'd: ne'er wrong
So great, in reference to him, who took
Such nature on him, and endur'd the doom.
God therefore and the Jews one sentence pleas'd:
So different effects flow'd from one act,
And heav'n was open'd, though the earth did quake.
Count it not hard henceforth, when thou dost hear
That a just vengeance was by righteous court
Justly reveng'd. But yet I see thy mind
By thought on thought arising sore perplex'd,
And with how vehement desire it asks
Solution of the maze. What I have heard,
Is plain, thou sayst: but wherefore God this way
For our redemption chose, eludes my search.

    "Brother! no eye of man not perfected,
Nor fully ripen'd in the flame of love,
May fathom this decree. It is a mark,
In sooth, much aim'd at, and but little kenn'd:
And I will therefore show thee why such way
Was worthiest. The celestial love, that spume
All envying in its bounty, in itself
With such effulgence blazeth, as sends forth
All beauteous things eternal. What distils
Immediate thence, no end of being knows,
Bearing its seal immutably impress'd.
Whatever thence immediate falls, is free,
Free wholly, uncontrollable by power
Of each thing new: by such conformity
More grateful to its author, whose bright beams,
Though all partake their shining, yet in those
Are liveliest, which resemble him the most.
These tokens of pre-eminence on man
Largely bestow'd, if any of them fail,
He needs must forfeit his nobility,
No longer stainless. Sin alone is that,
Which doth disfranchise him, and make unlike
To the chief good; for that its light in him
Is darken'd. And to dignity thus lost
Is no return; unless, where guilt makes void,
He for ill pleasure pay with equal pain.

Dante Alighieri

Your nature, which entirely in its seed
Trangress'd, from these distinctions fell, no less
Than from its state in Paradise; nor means
Found of recovery (search all methods out
As strickly as thou may) save one of these,
The only fords were left through which to wade,
Either that God had of his courtesy
Releas'd him merely, or else man himself
For his own folly by himself aton'd.

    "Fix now thine eye, intently as thou canst,
On th' everlasting counsel, and explore,
Instructed by my words, the dread abyss.

    "Man in himself had ever lack'd the means
Of satisfaction, for he could not stoop
Obeying, in humility so low,
As high he, disobeying, thought to soar:
And for this reason he had vainly tried
Out of his own sufficiency to pay
The rigid satisfaction. Then behooved
That God should by his own ways lead him back
Unto the life, from whence he fell, restor'd:
By both his ways, I mean, or one alone.
But since the deed is ever priz'd the more,
The more the doer's good intent appears,
Goodness celestial, whose broad signature
Is on the universe, of all its ways
To raise ye up, was fain to leave out none,
Nor aught so vast or so magnificent,
Either for him who gave or who receiv'd
Between the last night and the primal day,
Was or can be. For God more bounty show'd.
Giving himself to make man capable
Of his return to life, than had the terms
Been mere and unconditional release.
And for his justice, every method else
Were all too scant, had not the Son of God
Humbled himself to put on mortal flesh.

    "Now, to fulfil each wish of thine, remains
I somewhat further to thy view unfold.
That thou mayst see as clearly as myself.

    "I see, thou sayst, the air, the fire I see,
The earth and water, and all things of them
Compounded, to corruption turn, and soon
Dissolve. Yet these were also things create,
Because, if what were told me, had been true
They from corruption had been therefore free.

    "The angels, O my brother! and this clime
Wherein thou art, impassible and pure,
I call created, as indeed they are
In their whole being. But the elements,

Which thou hast nam'd, and what of them is made,
Are by created virtue' inform'd: create
Their substance, and create the' informing virtue
In these bright stars, that round them circling move
The soul of every brute and of each plant,
The ray and motion of the sacred lights,
With complex potency attract and turn.
But this our life the' eternal good inspires
Immediate, and enamours of itself;
So that our wishes rest for ever here.
    "And hence thou mayst by inference conclude
Our resurrection certain, if thy mind
Consider how the human flesh was fram'd,
When both our parents at the first were made."

CANTO VIII

The world was in its day of peril dark
Wont to believe the dotage of fond love
From the fair Cyprian deity, who rolls
In her third epicycle, shed on men
By stream of potent radiance: therefore they
Of elder time, in their old error blind,
Not her alone with sacrifice ador'd
And invocation, but like honours paid
To Cupid and Dione, deem'd of them
Her mother, and her son, him whom they feign'd
To sit in Dido's bosom: and from her,
Whom I have sung preluding, borrow'd they
The appellation of that star, which views,
Now obvious and now averse, the sun.
    I was not ware that I was wafted up
Into its orb; but the new loveliness
That grac'd my lady, gave me ample proof
That we had entered there. And as in flame
A sparkle is distinct, or voice in voice
Discern'd, when one its even tenour keeps,
The other comes and goes; so in that light
I other luminaries saw, that cours'd
In circling motion. rapid more or less,
As their eternal phases each impels.
    Never was blast from vapour charged with cold,
Whether invisible to eye or no,
Descended with such speed, it had not seem'd
To linger in dull tardiness, compar'd
To those celestial lights, that tow'rds us came,
Leaving the circuit of their joyous ring,
Conducted by the lofty seraphim.
And after them, who in the van appear'd,

Dante Alighieri

Such an hosanna sounded, as hath left
Desire, ne'er since extinct in me, to hear
Renew'd the strain. Then parting from the rest
One near us drew, and sole began: "We all
Are ready at thy pleasure, well dispos'd
To do thee gentle service. We are they,
To whom thou in the world erewhile didst Sing
'O ye! whose intellectual ministry
Moves the third heaven!' and in one orb we roll,
One motion, one impulse, with those who rule
Princedoms in heaven; yet are of love so full,
That to please thee 't will be as sweet to rest."

    After mine eyes had with meek reverence
Sought the celestial guide, and were by her
Assur'd, they turn'd again unto the light
Who had so largely promis'd, and with voice
That bare the lively pressure of my zeal,
"Tell who ye are," I cried. Forthwith it grew
In size and splendour, through augmented joy;
And thus it answer'd: "A short date below
The world possess'd me. Had the time been more,
Much evil, that will come, had never chanc'd.
My gladness hides thee from me, which doth shine .
Around, and shroud me, as an animal
In its own silk enswath'd. Thou lov'dst me well,
And had'st good cause; for had my sojourning
Been longer on the earth, the love I bare thee
Had put forth more than blossoms. The left bank,
That Rhone, when he hath mix'd with Sorga, laves.
In me its lord expected, and that horn
Of fair Ausonia, with its boroughs old,
Bari, and Croton, and Gaeta pil'd,
From where the Trento disembogues his waves,
With Verde mingled, to the salt sea-flood.
Already on my temples beam'd the crown,
Which gave me sov'reignty over the land
By Danube wash'd, whenas he strays beyond
The limits of his German shores. The realm,
Where, on the gulf by stormy Eurus lash'd,
Betwixt Pelorus and Pachynian heights,
The beautiful Trinacria lies in gloom
(Not through Typhaeus, but the vap'ry cloud
Bituminous upsteam'd), THAT too did look
To have its scepter wielded by a race
Of monarchs, sprung through me from Charles and Rodolph;
had not ill lording which doth spirit up
The people ever, in Palermo rais'd
The shout of 'death,' re-echo'd loud and long.
Had but my brother's foresight kenn'd as much,
He had been warier that the greedy want

The Divine Comedy

Of Catalonia might not work his bale.
And truly need there is, that he forecast,
Or other for him, lest more freight be laid
On his already over-laden bark.
Nature in him, from bounty fall'n to thrift,
Would ask the guard of braver arms, than such
As only care to have their coffers fill'd."

    "My liege, it doth enhance the joy thy words
Infuse into me, mighty as it is,
To think my gladness manifest to thee,
As to myself, who own it, when thou lookst
Into the source and limit of all good,
There, where thou markest that which thou dost speak,
Thence priz'd of me the more. Glad thou hast made me.
Now make intelligent, clearing the doubt
Thy speech hath raised in me; for much I muse,
How bitter can spring up, when sweet is sown."

    I thus inquiring; he forthwith replied:
"If I have power to show one truth, soon that
Shall face thee, which thy questioning declares
Behind thee now conceal'd. The Good, that guides
And blessed makes this realm, which thou dost mount,
Ordains its providence to be the virtue
In these great bodies: nor th' all perfect Mind
Upholds their nature merely, but in them
Their energy to save: for nought, that lies
Within the range of that unerring bow,
But is as level with the destin'd aim,
As ever mark to arrow's point oppos'd.
Were it not thus, these heavens, thou dost visit,
Would their effect so work, it would not be
Art, but destruction; and this may not chance,
If th' intellectual powers, that move these stars,
Fail not, or who, first faulty made them fail.
Wilt thou this truth more clearly evidenc'd?"

    To whom I thus: "It is enough: no fear,
I see, lest nature in her part should tire."

    He straight rejoin'd: "Say, were it worse for man,
If he liv'd not in fellowship on earth?"

    "Yea," answer'd I; "nor here a reason needs."

    "And may that be, if different estates
Grow not of different duties in your life?
Consult your teacher, and he tells you 'no.'"

    Thus did he come, deducing to this point,
And then concluded: "For this cause behooves,
The roots, from whence your operations come,
Must differ. Therefore one is Solon born;
Another, Xerxes; and Melchisidec
A third; and he a fourth, whose airy voyage
Cost him his son. In her circuitous course,

Nature, that is the seal to mortal wax,
Doth well her art, but no distinctions owns
'Twixt one or other household. Hence befalls
That Esau is so wide of Jacob: hence
Quirinus of so base a father springs,
He dates from Mars his lineage. Were it not
That providence celestial overrul'd,
Nature, in generation, must the path
Trac'd by the generator, still pursue
Unswervingly. Thus place I in thy sight
That, which was late behind thee. But, in sign
Of more affection for thee, 't is my will
Thou wear this corollary. Nature ever
Finding discordant fortune, like all seed
Out of its proper climate, thrives but ill.
And were the world below content to mark
And work on the foundation nature lays,
It would not lack supply of excellence.
But ye perversely to religion strain
Him, who was born to gird on him the sword,
And of the fluent phrasemen make your king;
Therefore your steps have wander'd from the paths."

CANTO IX

After solution of my doubt, thy Charles,
O fair Clemenza, of the treachery spake
That must befall his seed: but, "Tell it not,"
Said he, "and let the destin'd years come round."
Nor may I tell thee more, save that the meed
Of sorrow well-deserv'd shall quit your wrongs.
     And now the visage of that saintly light
Was to the sun, that fills it, turn'd again,
As to the good, whose plenitude of bliss
Sufficeth all. O ye misguided souls!
Infatuate, who from such a good estrange
Your hearts, and bend your gaze on vanity,
Alas for you!--And lo! toward me, next,
Another of those splendent forms approach'd,
That, by its outward bright'ning, testified
The will it had to pleasure me. The eyes
Of Beatrice, resting, as before,
Firmly upon me, manifested forth
Approval of my wish. "And O," I cried,
Blest spirit! quickly be my will perform'd;
And prove thou to me, that my inmost thoughts
I can reflect on thee." Thereat the light,
That yet was new to me, from the recess,
Where it before was singing, thus began,

As one who joys in kindness: "In that part
Of the deprav'd Italian land, which lies
Between Rialto, and the fountain-springs
Of Brenta and of Piava, there doth rise,
But to no lofty eminence, a hill,
From whence erewhile a firebrand did descend,
That sorely sheet the region. From one root
I and it sprang; my name on earth Cunizza:
And here I glitter, for that by its light
This star o'ercame me. Yet I naught repine,
Nor grudge myself the cause of this my lot,
Which haply vulgar hearts can scarce conceive.

    "This jewel, that is next me in our heaven,
Lustrous and costly, great renown hath left,
And not to perish, ere these hundred years
Five times absolve their round. Consider thou,
If to excel be worthy man's endeavour,
When such life may attend the first. Yet they
Care not for this, the crowd that now are girt
By Adice and Tagliamento, still
Impenitent, tho' scourg'd. The hour is near,
When for their stubbornness at Padua's marsh
The water shall be chang'd, that laves Vicena
And where Cagnano meets with Sile, one
Lords it, and bears his head aloft, for whom
The web is now a-warping. Feltro too
Shall sorrow for its godless shepherd's fault,
Of so deep stain, that never, for the like,
Was Malta's bar unclos'd. Too large should be
The skillet, that would hold Ferrara's blood,
And wearied he, who ounce by ounce would weight it,
The which this priest, in show of party-zeal,
Courteous will give; nor will the gift ill suit
The country's custom. We descry above,
Mirrors, ye call them thrones, from which to us
Reflected shine the judgments of our God:
Whence these our sayings we avouch for good."

    She ended, and appear'd on other thoughts
Intent, re-ent'ring on the wheel she late
Had left. That other joyance meanwhile wax'd
A thing to marvel at, in splendour glowing,
Like choicest ruby stricken by the sun,
For, in that upper clime, effulgence comes
Of gladness, as here laughter: and below,
As the mind saddens, murkier grows the shade.

    "God seeth all: and in him is thy sight,"
Said I, "blest Spirit! Therefore will of his
Cannot to thee be dark. Why then delays
Thy voice to satisfy my wish untold,
That voice which joins the inexpressive song,

Dante Alighieri

Pastime of heav'n, the which those ardours sing,
That cowl them with six shadowing wings outspread?
I would not wait thy asking, wert thou known
To me, as thoroughly I to thee am known."
     He forthwith answ'ring, thus his words began:
"The valley' of waters, widest next to that
Which doth the earth engarland, shapes its course,
Between discordant shores, against the sun
Inward so far, it makes meridian there,
Where was before th' horizon. Of that vale
Dwelt I upon the shore, 'twixt Ebro's stream
And Macra's, that divides with passage brief
Genoan bounds from Tuscan. East and west
Are nearly one to Begga and my land,
Whose haven erst was with its own blood warm.
Who knew my name were wont to call me Folco:
And I did bear impression of this heav'n,
That now bears mine: for not with fiercer flame
Glow'd Belus' daughter, injuring alike
Sichaeus and Creusa, than did I,
Long as it suited the unripen'd down
That fledg'd my cheek: nor she of Rhodope,
That was beguiled of Demophoon;
Nor Jove's son, when the charms of Iole
Were shrin'd within his heart. And yet there hides
No sorrowful repentance here, but mirth,
Not for the fault (that doth not come to mind),
But for the virtue, whose o'erruling sway
And providence have wrought thus quaintly. Here
The skill is look'd into, that fashioneth
With such effectual working, and the good
Discern'd, accruing to this upper world
From that below. But fully to content
Thy wishes, all that in this sphere have birth,
Demands my further parle. Inquire thou wouldst,
Who of this light is denizen, that here
Beside me sparkles, as the sun-beam doth
On the clear wave. Know then, the soul of Rahab
Is in that gladsome harbour, to our tribe
United, and the foremost rank assign'd.
He to that heav'n, at which the shadow ends
Of your sublunar world, was taken up,
First, in Christ's triumph, of all souls redeem'd:
For well behoov'd, that, in some part of heav'n,
She should remain a trophy, to declare
The mighty contest won with either palm;
For that she favour'd first the high exploit
Of Joshua on the holy land, whereof
The Pope recks little now. Thy city, plant
Of him, that on his Maker turn'd the back,

And of whose envying so much woe hath sprung,
Engenders and expands the cursed flower,
That hath made wander both the sheep and lambs,
Turning the shepherd to a wolf. For this,
The gospel and great teachers laid aside,
The decretals, as their stuft margins show,
Are the sole study. Pope and Cardinals,
Intent on these, ne'er journey but in thought
To Nazareth, where Gabriel op'd his wings.
Yet it may chance, erelong, the Vatican,
And other most selected parts of Rome,
That were the grave of Peter's soldiery,
Shall be deliver'd from the adult'rous bond."

CANTO X

Looking into his first-born with the love,
Which breathes from both eternal, the first Might
Ineffable, whence eye or mind
Can roam, hath in such order all dispos'd,
As none may see and fail to' enjoy. Raise, then,
O reader! to the lofty wheels, with me,
Thy ken directed to the point, whereat
One motion strikes on th' other. There begin
Thy wonder of the mighty Architect,
Who loves his work so inwardly, his eye
Doth ever watch it. See, how thence oblique
Brancheth the circle, where the planets roll
To pour their wished influence on the world;
Whose path not bending thus, in heav'n above
Much virtue would be lost, and here on earth,
All power well nigh extinct: or, from direct
Were its departure distant more or less,
I' th' universal order, great defect
Must, both in heav'n and here beneath, ensue.
    Now rest thee, reader! on thy bench, and muse
Anticipative of the feast to come;
So shall delight make thee not feel thy toil.
Lo! I have set before thee, for thyself
Feed now: the matter I indite, henceforth
Demands entire my thought. Join'd with the part,
Which late we told of, the great minister
Of nature, that upon the world imprints
The virtue of the heaven, and doles out
Time for us with his beam, went circling on
Along the spires, where each hour sooner comes;
And I was with him, weetless of ascent,
As one, who till arriv'd, weets not his coming.

Dante Alighieri

    For Beatrice, she who passeth on
So suddenly from good to better, time
Counts not the act, oh then how great must needs
Have been her brightness! What she was i' th' sun
(Where I had enter'd), not through change of hue,
But light transparent--did I summon up
Genius, art, practice--I might not so speak,
It should be e'er imagin'd: yet believ'd
It may be, and the sight be justly crav'd.
And if our fantasy fail of such height,
What marvel, since no eye above the sun
Hath ever travel'd? Such are they dwell here,
Fourth family of the Omnipotent Sire,
Who of his spirit and of his offspring shows;
And holds them still enraptur'd with the view.
And thus to me Beatrice: "Thank, oh thank,
The Sun of angels, him, who by his grace
To this perceptible hath lifted thee."
    Never was heart in such devotion bound,
And with complacency so absolute
Dispos'd to render up itself to God,
As mine was at those words: and so entire
The love for Him, that held me, it eclips'd
Beatrice in oblivion. Naught displeas'd
Was she, but smil'd thereat so joyously,
That of her laughing eyes the radiance brake
And scatter'd my collected mind abroad.
    Then saw I a bright band, in liveliness
Surpassing, who themselves did make the crown,
And us their centre: yet more sweet in voice,
Than in their visage beaming. Cinctur'd thus,
Sometime Latona's daughter we behold,
When the impregnate air retains the thread,
That weaves her zone. In the celestial court,
Whence I return, are many jewels found,
So dear and beautiful, they cannot brook
Transporting from that realm: and of these lights
Such was the song. Who doth not prune his wing
To soar up thither, let him look from thence
For tidings from the dumb. When, singing thus,
Those burning suns that circled round us thrice,
As nearest stars around the fixed pole,
Then seem'd they like to ladies, from the dance
Not ceasing, but suspense, in silent pause,
List'ning, till they have caught the strain anew:
Suspended so they stood: and, from within,
Thus heard I one, who spake: "Since with its beam
The grace, whence true love lighteth first his flame,
That after doth increase by loving, shines
So multiplied in thee, it leads thee up

The Divine Comedy

Along this ladder, down whose hallow'd steps
None e'er descend, and mount them not again,
Who from his phial should refuse thee wine
To slake thy thirst, no less constrained were,
Than water flowing not unto the sea.
Thou fain wouldst hear, what plants are these, that bloom
In the bright garland, which, admiring, girds
This fair dame round, who strengthens thee for heav'n.
I then was of the lambs, that Dominic
Leads, for his saintly flock, along the way,
Where well they thrive, not sworn with vanity.
He, nearest on my right hand, brother was,
And master to me: Albert of Cologne
Is this: and of Aquinum, Thomas I.
If thou of all the rest wouldst be assur'd,
Let thine eye, waiting on the words I speak,
In circuit journey round the blessed wreath.
That next resplendence issues from the smile
Of Gratian, who to either forum lent
Such help, as favour wins in Paradise.
The other, nearest, who adorns our quire,
Was Peter, he that with the widow gave
To holy church his treasure. The fifth light,
Goodliest of all, is by such love inspired,
That all your world craves tidings of its doom:
Within, there is the lofty light, endow'd
With sapience so profound, if truth be truth,
That with a ken of such wide amplitude
No second hath arisen. Next behold
That taper's radiance, to whose view was shown,
Clearliest, the nature and the ministry
Angelical, while yet in flesh it dwelt.
In the other little light serenely smiles
That pleader for the Christian temples, he
Who did provide Augustin of his lore.
Now, if thy mind's eye pass from light to light,
Upon my praises following, of the eighth
Thy thirst is next. The saintly soul, that shows
The world's deceitfulness, to all who hear him,
Is, with the sight of all the good, that is,
Blest there. The limbs, whence it was driven, lie
Down in Cieldauro, and from martyrdom
And exile came it here. Lo! further on,
Where flames the arduous Spirit of Isidore,
Of Bede, and Richard, more than man, erewhile,
In deep discernment. Lastly this, from whom
Thy look on me reverteth, was the beam
Of one, whose spirit, on high musings bent,
Rebuk'd the ling'ring tardiness of death.
It is the eternal light of Sigebert,

Who 'scap'd not envy, when of truth he argued,
Reading in the straw-litter'd street." Forthwith,
As clock, that calleth up the spouse of God
To win her bridegroom's love at matin's hour,
Each part of other fitly drawn and urg'd,
Sends out a tinkling sound, of note so sweet,
Affection springs in well-disposed breast;
Thus saw I move the glorious wheel, thus heard
Voice answ'ring voice, so musical and soft,
It can be known but where day endless shines.

CANTO XI

O fond anxiety of mortal men!
How vain and inconclusive arguments
Are those, which make thee beat thy wings below
For statues one, and one for aphorisms
Was hunting; this the priesthood follow'd, that
By force or sophistry aspir'd to rule;
To rob another, and another sought
By civil business wealth; one moiling lay
Tangled in net of sensual delight,
And one to witless indolence resign'd;
What time from all these empty things escap'd,
With Beatrice, I thus gloriously
Was rais'd aloft, and made the guest of heav'n.
   They of the circle to that point, each one,
Where erst it was, had turn'd; and steady glow'd,
As candle in his socket. Then within
The lustre, that erewhile bespake me, smiling
With merer gladness, heard I thus begin:
   "E'en as his beam illumes me, so I look
Into the eternal light, and clearly mark
Thy thoughts, from whence they rise. Thou art in doubt,
And wouldst, that I should bolt my words afresh
In such plain open phrase, as may be smooth
To thy perception, where I told thee late
That 'well they thrive;' and that 'no second such
Hath risen,' which no small distinction needs.
   "The providence, that governeth the world,
In depth of counsel by created ken
Unfathomable, to the end that she,
Who with loud cries was 'spous'd in precious blood,
Might keep her footing towards her well-belov'd,
Safe in herself and constant unto him,
Hath two ordain'd, who should on either hand
In chief escort her: one seraphic all
In fervency; for wisdom upon earth,
The other splendour of cherubic light.

The Divine Comedy

I but of one will tell: he tells of both,
Who one commendeth. which of them so'er
Be taken: for their deeds were to one end.
     "Between Tupino, and the wave, that falls
From blest Ubaldo's chosen hill, there hangs
Rich slope of mountain high, whence heat and cold
Are wafted through Perugia's eastern gate:
And Norcera with Gualdo, in its rear
Mourn for their heavy yoke. Upon that side,
Where it doth break its steepness most, arose
A sun upon the world, as duly this
From Ganges doth: therefore let none, who speak
Of that place, say Ascesi; for its name
Were lamely so deliver'd; but the East,
To call things rightly, be it henceforth styl'd.
He was not yet much distant from his rising,
When his good influence 'gan to bless the earth.
A dame to whom none openeth pleasure's gate
More than to death, was, 'gainst his father's will,
His stripling choice: and he did make her his,
Before the Spiritual court, by nuptial bonds,
And in his father's sight: from day to day,
Then lov'd her more devoutly. She, bereav'd
Of her first husband, slighted and obscure,
Thousand and hundred years and more, remain'd
Without a single suitor, till he came.
Nor aught avail'd, that, with Amyclas, she
Was found unmov'd at rumour of his voice,
Who shook the world: nor aught her constant boldness
Whereby with Christ she mounted on the cross,
When Mary stay'd beneath. But not to deal
Thus closely with thee longer, take at large
The rovers' titles--Poverty and Francis.
Their concord and glad looks, wonder and love,
And sweet regard gave birth to holy thoughts,
So much, that venerable Bernard first
Did bare his feet, and, in pursuit of peace
So heavenly, ran, yet deem'd his footing slow.
O hidden riches! O prolific good!
Egidius bares him next, and next Sylvester,
And follow both the bridegroom; so the bride
Can please them. Thenceforth goes he on his way,
The father and the master, with his spouse,
And with that family, whom now the cord
Girt humbly: nor did abjectness of heart
Weigh down his eyelids, for that he was son
Of Pietro Bernardone, and by men
In wond'rous sort despis'd. But royally
His hard intention he to Innocent
Set forth, and from him first receiv'd the seal

Dante Alighieri

On his religion. Then, when numerous flock'd
The tribe of lowly ones, that trac'd HIS steps,
Whose marvellous life deservedly were sung
In heights empyreal, through Honorius' hand
A second crown, to deck their Guardian's virtues,
Was by the eternal Spirit inwreath'd: and when
He had, through thirst of martyrdom, stood up
In the proud Soldan's presence, and there preach'd
Christ and his followers; but found the race
Unripen'd for conversion: back once more
He hasted (not to intermit his toil),
And reap'd Ausonian lands. On the hard rock,
'Twixt Arno and the Tyber, he from Christ
Took the last Signet, which his limbs two years
Did carry. Then the season come, that he,
Who to such good had destin'd him, was pleas'd
T' advance him to the meed, which he had earn'd
By his self-humbling, to his brotherhood,
As their just heritage, he gave in charge
His dearest lady, and enjoin'd their love
And faith to her: and, from her bosom, will'd
His goodly spirit should move forth, returning
To its appointed kingdom, nor would have
His body laid upon another bier.

 "Think now of one, who were a fit colleague,
To keep the bark of Peter in deep sea
Helm'd to right point; and such our Patriarch was.
Therefore who follow him, as he enjoins,
Thou mayst be certain, take good lading in.
But hunger of new viands tempts his flock,
So that they needs into strange pastures wide
Must spread them: and the more remote from him
The stragglers wander, so much mole they come
Home to the sheep-fold, destitute of milk.
There are of them, in truth, who fear their harm,
And to the shepherd cleave; but these so few,
A little stuff may furnish out their cloaks.

 "Now, if my words be clear, if thou have ta'en
Good heed, if that, which I have told, recall
To mind, thy wish may be in part fulfill'd:
For thou wilt see the point from whence they split,
Nor miss of the reproof, which that implies,
'That well they thrive not sworn with vanity.'"

CANTO XII

Soon as its final word the blessed flame
Had rais'd for utterance, straight the holy mill
Began to wheel, nor yet had once revolv'd,

The Divine Comedy

Or ere another, circling, compass'd it,
Motion to motion, song to song, conjoining,
Song, that as much our muses doth excel,
Our Sirens with their tuneful pipes, as ray
Of primal splendour doth its faint reflex.

    As when, if Juno bid her handmaid forth,
Two arches parallel, and trick'd alike,
Span the thin cloud, the outer taking birth
From that within (in manner of that voice
Whom love did melt away, as sun the mist),
And they who gaze, presageful call to mind
The compact, made with Noah, of the world
No more to be o'erflow'd; about us thus
Of sempiternal roses, bending, wreath'd
Those garlands twain, and to the innermost
E'en thus th' external answered. When the footing,
And other great festivity, of song,
And radiance, light with light accordant, each
Jocund and blythe, had at their pleasure still'd
(E'en as the eyes by quick volition mov'd,
Are shut and rais'd together), from the heart
Of one amongst the new lights mov'd a voice,
That made me seem like needle to the star,
In turning to its whereabout, and thus
Began: "The love, that makes me beautiful,
Prompts me to tell of th' other guide, for whom
Such good of mine is spoken. Where one is,
The other worthily should also be;
That as their warfare was alike, alike
Should be their glory. Slow, and full of doubt,
And with thin ranks, after its banner mov'd
The army of Christ (which it so clearly cost
To reappoint), when its imperial Head,
Who reigneth ever, for the drooping host
Did make provision, thorough grace alone,
And not through its deserving. As thou heard'st,
Two champions to the succour of his spouse
He sent, who by their deeds and words might join
Again his scatter'd people. In that clime,
Where springs the pleasant west-wind to unfold
The fresh leaves, with which Europe sees herself
New-garmented; nor from those billows far,
Beyond whose chiding, after weary course,
The sun doth sometimes hide him, safe abides
The happy Callaroga, under guard
Of the great shield, wherein the lion lies
Subjected and supreme. And there was born
The loving million of the Christian faith,
The hollow'd wrestler, gentle to his own,
And to his enemies terrible. So replete

Dante Alighieri

His soul with lively virtue, that when first
Created, even in the mother's womb,
It prophesied. When, at the sacred font,
The spousals were complete 'twixt faith and him,
Where pledge of mutual safety was exchang'd,
The dame, who was his surety, in her sleep
Beheld the wondrous fruit, that was from him
And from his heirs to issue. And that such
He might be construed, as indeed he was,
She was inspir'd to name him of his owner,
Whose he was wholly, and so call'd him Dominic.
And I speak of him, as the labourer,
Whom Christ in his own garden chose to be
His help-mate. Messenger he seem'd, and friend
Fast-knit to Christ; and the first love he show'd,
Was after the first counsel that Christ gave.
Many a time his nurse, at entering found
That he had ris'n in silence, and was prostrate,
As who should say, "My errand was for this."
O happy father! Felix rightly nam'd!
O favour'd mother! rightly nam'd Joanna!
If that do mean, as men interpret it.
Not for the world's sake, for which now they pore
Upon Ostiense and Taddeo's page,
But for the real manna, soon he grew
Mighty in learning, and did set himself
To go about the vineyard, that soon turns
To wan and wither'd, if not tended well:
And from the see (whose bounty to the just
And needy is gone by, not through its fault,
But his who fills it basely), he besought,
No dispensation for commuted wrong,
Nor the first vacant fortune, nor the tenth),
That to God's paupers rightly appertain,
But, 'gainst an erring and degenerate world,
Licence to fight, in favour of that seed,
From which the twice twelve cions gird thee round.
Then, with sage doctrine and good will to help,
Forth on his great apostleship he far'd,
Like torrent bursting from a lofty vein;
And, dashing 'gainst the stocks of heresy,
Smote fiercest, where resistance was most stout.
Thence many rivulets have since been turn'd,
Over the garden Catholic to lead
Their living waters, and have fed its plants.
     "If such one wheel of that two-yoked car,
Wherein the holy church defended her,
And rode triumphant through the civil broil.
Thou canst not doubt its fellow's excellence,
Which Thomas, ere my coming, hath declar'd

So courteously unto thee. But the track,
Which its smooth fellies made, is now deserted:
That mouldy mother is where late were lees.
His family, that wont to trace his path,
Turn backward, and invert their steps; erelong
To rue the gathering in of their ill crop,
When the rejected tares in vain shall ask
Admittance to the barn. I question not
But he, who search'd our volume, leaf by leaf,
Might still find page with this inscription on't,
'I am as I was wont.' Yet such were not
From Acquasparta nor Casale, whence
Of those, who come to meddle with the text,
One stretches and another cramps its rule.
Bonaventura's life in me behold,
From Bagnororegio, one, who in discharge
Of my great offices still laid aside
All sinister aim. Illuminato here,
And Agostino join me: two they were,
Among the first of those barefooted meek ones,
Who sought God's friendship in the cord: with them
Hugues of Saint Victor, Pietro Mangiadore,
And he of Spain in his twelve volumes shining,
Nathan the prophet, Metropolitan
Chrysostom, and Anselmo, and, who deign'd
To put his hand to the first art, Donatus.
Raban is here: and at my side there shines
Calabria's abbot, Joachim , endow'd
With soul prophetic. The bright courtesy
Of friar Thomas, and his goodly lore,
Have mov'd me to the blazon of a peer
So worthy, and with me have mov'd this throng."

CANTO XIII

Let him, who would conceive what now I saw,
Imagine (and retain the image firm,
As mountain rock, the whilst he hears me speak),
Of stars fifteen, from midst the ethereal host
Selected, that, with lively ray serene,
O'ercome the massiest air: thereto imagine
The wain, that, in the bosom of our sky,
Spins ever on its axle night and day,
With the bright summit of that horn which swells
Due from the pole, round which the first wheel rolls,
T' have rang'd themselves in fashion of two signs
In heav'n, such as Ariadne made,
When death's chill seized her; and that one of them
Did compass in the other's beam; and both

Dante Alighieri

In such sort whirl around, that each should tend
With opposite motion and, conceiving thus,
Of that true constellation, and the dance
Twofold, that circled me, he shall attain
As 't were the shadow; for things there as much
Surpass our usage, as the swiftest heav'n
Is swifter than the Chiana. There was sung
No Bacchus, and no Io Paean, but
Three Persons in the Godhead, and in one
Substance that nature and the human join'd.

    The song fulfill'd its measure; and to us
Those saintly lights attended, happier made
At each new minist'ring. Then silence brake,
Amid th' accordant sons of Deity,
That luminary, in which the wondrous life
Of the meek man of God was told to me;
And thus it spake: "One ear o' th' harvest thresh'd,
And its grain safely stor'd, sweet charity
Invites me with the other to like toil.

    "Thou know'st, that in the bosom, whence the rib
Was ta'en to fashion that fair cheek, whose taste
All the world pays for, and in that, which pierc'd
By the keen lance, both after and before
Such satisfaction offer'd, as outweighs
Each evil in the scale, whate'er of light
To human nature is allow'd, must all
Have by his virtue been infus'd, who form'd
Both one and other: and thou thence admir'st
In that I told thee, of beatitudes
A second, there is none, to his enclos'd
In the fifth radiance. Open now thine eyes
To what I answer thee; and thou shalt see
Thy deeming and my saying meet in truth,
As centre in the round. That which dies not,
And that which can die, are but each the beam
Of that idea, which our Soverign Sire
Engendereth loving; for that lively light,
Which passeth from his brightness; not disjoin'd
From him, nor from his love triune with them,
Doth, through his bounty, congregate itself,
Mirror'd, as 't were in new existences,
Itself unalterable and ever one.

    "Descending hence unto the lowest powers,
Its energy so sinks, at last it makes
But brief contingencies: for so I name
Things generated, which the heav'nly orbs
Moving, with seed or without seed, produce.
Their wax, and that which molds it, differ much:
And thence with lustre, more or less, it shows
Th' ideal stamp impress: so that one tree

The Divine Comedy

According to his kind, hath better fruit,
And worse: and, at your birth, ye, mortal men,
Are in your talents various. Were the wax
Molded with nice exactness, and the heav'n
In its disposing influence supreme,
The lustre of the seal should be complete:
But nature renders it imperfect ever,
Resembling thus the artist in her work,
Whose faultering hand is faithless to his skill.
Howe'er, if love itself dispose, and mark
The primal virtue, kindling with bright view,
There all perfection is vouchsafed; and such
The clay was made, accomplish'd with each gift,
That life can teem with; such the burden fill'd
The virgin's bosom: so that I commend
Thy judgment, that the human nature ne'er
Was or can be, such as in them it was.

    "Did I advance no further than this point,
'How then had he no peer?' thou might'st reply.
But, that what now appears not, may appear
Right plainly, ponder, who he was, and what
(When he was bidden 'Ask'), the motive sway'd
To his requesting. I have spoken thus,
That thou mayst see, he was a king, who ask'd
For wisdom, to the end he might be king
Sufficient: not the number to search out
Of the celestial movers; or to know,
If necessary with contingent e'er
Have made necessity; or whether that
Be granted, that first motion is; or if
Of the mid circle can, by art, be made
Triangle with each corner, blunt or sharp.

    "Whence, noting that, which I have said, and this,
Thou kingly prudence and that ken mayst learn,
At which the dart of my intention aims.
And, marking clearly, that I told thee, 'Risen,'
Thou shalt discern it only hath respect
To kings, of whom are many, and the good
Are rare. With this distinction take my words;
And they may well consist with that which thou
Of the first human father dost believe,
And of our well-beloved. And let this
Henceforth be led unto thy feet, to make
Thee slow in motion, as a weary man,
Both to the 'yea' and to the 'nay' thou seest not.
For he among the fools is down full low,
Whose affirmation, or denial, is
Without distinction, in each case alike
Since it befalls, that in most instances
Current opinion leads to false: and then

Affection bends the judgment to her ply.
    "Much more than vainly doth he loose from shore,
Since he returns not such as he set forth,
Who fishes for the truth and wanteth skill.
And open proofs of this unto the world
Have been afforded in Parmenides,
Melissus, Bryso, and the crowd beside,
Who journey'd on, and knew not whither: so did
Sabellius, Arius, and the other fools,
Who, like to scymitars, reflected back
The scripture-image, by distortion marr'd.
    "Let not the people be too swift to judge,
As one who reckons on the blades in field,
Or ere the crop be ripe. For I have seen
The thorn frown rudely all the winter long
And after bear the rose upon its top;
And bark, that all the way across the sea
Ran straight and speedy, perish at the last,
E'en in the haven's mouth seeing one steal,
Another brine, his offering to the priest,
Let not Dame Birtha and Sir Martin thence
Into heav'n's counsels deem that they can pry:
For one of these may rise, the other fall."

CANTO XIV

From centre to the circle, and so back
From circle to the centre, water moves
In the round chalice, even as the blow
Impels it, inwardly, or from without.
Such was the image glanc'd into my mind,
As the great spirit of Aquinum ceas'd;
And Beatrice after him her words
Resum'd alternate: "Need there is (tho' yet
He tells it to you not in words, nor e'en
In thought) that he should fathom to its depth
Another mystery. Tell him, if the light,
Wherewith your substance blooms, shall stay with you
Eternally, as now: and, if it doth,
How, when ye shall regain your visible forms,
The sight may without harm endure the change,
That also tell." As those, who in a ring
Tread the light measure, in their fitful mirth
Raise loud the voice, and spring with gladder bound;
Thus, at the hearing of that pious suit,
The saintly circles in their tourneying
And wond'rous note attested new delight.
    Whoso laments, that we must doff this garb
Of frail mortality, thenceforth to live

The Divine Comedy

Immortally above, he hath not seen
The sweet refreshing, of that heav'nly shower.
    Him, who lives ever, and for ever reigns
In mystic union of the Three in One,
Unbounded, bounding all, each spirit thrice
Sang, with such melody, as but to hear
For highest merit were an ample meed.
And from the lesser orb the goodliest light,
With gentle voice and mild, such as perhaps
The angel's once to Mary, thus replied:
"Long as the joy of Paradise shall last,
Our love shall shine around that raiment, bright,
As fervent; fervent, as in vision blest;
And that as far in blessedness exceeding,
As it hath grave beyond its virtue great.
Our shape, regarmented with glorious weeds
Of saintly flesh, must, being thus entire,
Show yet more gracious. Therefore shall increase,
Whate'er of light, gratuitous, imparts
The Supreme Good; light, ministering aid,
The better disclose his glory: whence
The vision needs increasing, much increase
The fervour, which it kindles; and that too
The ray, that comes from it. But as the greed
Which gives out flame, yet it its whiteness shines
More lively than that, and so preserves
Its proper semblance; thus this circling sphere
Of splendour, shall to view less radiant seem,
Than shall our fleshly robe, which yonder earth
Now covers. Nor will such excess of light
O'erpower us, in corporeal organs made
Firm, and susceptible of all delight."
    So ready and so cordial an "Amen,"
Followed from either choir, as plainly spoke
Desire of their dead bodies; yet perchance
Not for themselves, but for their kindred dear,
Mothers and sires, and those whom best they lov'd,
Ere they were made imperishable flame.
    And lo! forthwith there rose up round about
A lustre over that already there,
Of equal clearness, like the brightening up
Of the horizon. As at an evening hour
Of twilight, new appearances through heav'n
Peer with faint glimmer, doubtfully descried;
So there new substances, methought began
To rise in view; and round the other twain
Enwheeling, sweep their ampler circuit wide.
    O gentle glitter of eternal beam!
With what a such whiteness did it flow,
O'erpowering vision in me! But so fair,

Dante Alighieri

So passing lovely, Beatrice show'd,
Mind cannot follow it, nor words express
Her infinite sweetness. Thence mine eyes regain'd
Power to look up, and I beheld myself,
Sole with my lady, to more lofty bliss
Translated: for the star, with warmer smile
Impurpled, well denoted our ascent.
    With all the heart, and with that tongue which speaks
The same in all, an holocaust I made
To God, befitting the new grace vouchsaf'd.
And from my bosom had not yet upsteam'd
The fuming of that incense, when I knew
The rite accepted. With such mighty sheen
And mantling crimson, in two listed rays
The splendours shot before me, that I cried,
"God of Sabaoth! that does prank them thus!"
    As leads the galaxy from pole to pole,
Distinguish'd into greater lights and less,
Its pathway, which the wisest fail to spell;
So thickly studded, in the depth of Mars,
Those rays describ'd the venerable sign,
That quadrants in the round conjoining frame.
Here memory mocks the toil of genius. Christ
Beam'd on that cross; and pattern fails me now.
But whoso takes his cross, and follows Christ
Will pardon me for that I leave untold,
When in the flecker'd dawning he shall spy
The glitterance of Christ. From horn to horn,
And 'tween the summit and the base did move
Lights, scintillating, as they met and pass'd.
Thus oft are seen, with ever-changeful glance,
Straight or athwart, now rapid and now slow,
The atomies of bodies, long or short,
To move along the sunbeam, whose slant line
Checkers the shadow, interpos'd by art
Against the noontide heat. And as the chime
Of minstrel music, dulcimer, and harp
With many strings, a pleasant dining makes
To him, who heareth not distinct the note;
So from the lights, which there appear'd to me,
Gather'd along the cross a melody,
That, indistinctly heard, with ravishment
Possess'd me. Yet I mark'd it was a hymn
Of lofty praises; for there came to me
"Arise and conquer," as to one who hears
And comprehends not. Me such ecstasy
O'ercame, that never till that hour was thing
That held me in so sweet imprisonment.
    Perhaps my saying over bold appears,
Accounting less the pleasure of those eyes,

The Divine Comedy
Whereon to look fulfilleth all desire.
But he, who is aware those living seals
Of every beauty work with quicker force,
The higher they are ris'n; and that there
I had not turn'd me to them; he may well
Excuse me that, whereof in my excuse
I do accuse me, and may own my truth;
That holy pleasure here not yet reveal'd,
Which grows in transport as we mount aloof.

CANTO XV

True love, that ever shows itself as clear
In kindness, as loose appetite in wrong,
Silenced that lyre harmonious, and still'd
The sacred chords, that are by heav'n's right hand
Unwound and tighten'd, flow to righteous prayers
Should they not hearken, who, to give me will
For praying, in accordance thus were mute?
He hath in sooth good cause for endless grief,
Who, for the love of thing that lasteth not,
Despoils himself forever of that love.

    As oft along the still and pure serene,
At nightfall, glides a sudden trail of fire,
Attracting with involuntary heed
The eye to follow it, erewhile at rest,
And seems some star that shifted place in heav'n,
Only that, whence it kindles, none is lost,
And it is soon extinct; thus from the horn,
That on the dexter of the cross extends,
Down to its foot, one luminary ran
From mid the cluster shone there; yet no gem
Dropp'd from its foil; and through the beamy list
Like flame in alabaster, glow'd its course.

    So forward stretch'd him (if of credence aught
Our greater muse may claim) the pious ghost
Of old Anchises, in th' Elysian bower,
When he perceiv'd his son. "O thou, my blood!
O most exceeding grace divine! to whom,
As now to thee, hath twice the heav'nly gate
Been e'er unclos'd?" so spake the light; whence I
Turn'd me toward him; then unto my dame
My sight directed, and on either side
Amazement waited me; for in her eyes
Was lighted such a smile, I thought that mine
Had div'd unto the bottom of my grace
And of my bliss in Paradise. Forthwith
To hearing and to sight grateful alike,
The spirit to his proem added things

Dante Alighieri

I understood not, so profound he spake;
Yet not of choice but through necessity
Mysterious; for his high conception scar'd
Beyond the mark of mortals. When the flight
Of holy transport had so spent its rage,
That nearer to the level of our thought
The speech descended, the first sounds I heard
Were, "Best he thou, Triunal Deity!
That hast such favour in my seed vouchsaf'd!"
Then follow'd: "No unpleasant thirst, tho' long,
Which took me reading in the sacred book,
Whose leaves or white or dusky never change,
Thou hast allay'd, my son, within this light,
From whence my voice thou hear'st; more thanks to her.
Who for such lofty mounting has with plumes
Begirt thee. Thou dost deem thy thoughts to me
From him transmitted, who is first of all,
E'en as all numbers ray from unity;
And therefore dost not ask me who I am,
Or why to thee more joyous I appear,
Than any other in this gladsome throng.
The truth is as thou deem'st; for in this hue
Both less and greater in that mirror look,
In which thy thoughts, or ere thou think'st, are shown.
But, that the love, which keeps me wakeful ever,
Urging with sacred thirst of sweet desire,
May be contended fully, let thy voice,
Fearless, and frank and jocund, utter forth
Thy will distinctly, utter forth the wish,
Whereto my ready answer stands decreed."
    I turn'd me to Beatrice; and she heard
Ere I had spoken, smiling, an assent,
That to my will gave wings; and I began
"To each among your tribe, what time ye kenn'd
The nature, in whom naught unequal dwells,
Wisdom and love were in one measure dealt;
For that they are so equal in the sun,
From whence ye drew your radiance and your heat,
As makes all likeness scant. But will and means,
In mortals, for the cause ye well discern,
With unlike wings are fledge. A mortal I
Experience inequality like this,
And therefore give no thanks, but in the heart,
For thy paternal greeting. This howe'er
I pray thee, living topaz! that ingemm'st
This precious jewel, let me hear thy name."
    "I am thy root, O leaf! whom to expect
Even, hath pleas'd me: "thus the prompt reply
Prefacing, next it added; "he, of whom
Thy kindred appellation comes, and who,

The Divine Comedy

These hundred years and more, on its first ledge
Hath circuited the mountain, was my son
And thy great grandsire. Well befits, his long
Endurance should he shorten'd by thy deeds.

    "Florence, within her ancient limit-mark,
Which calls her still to matin prayers and noon,
Was chaste and sober, and abode in peace.
She had no armlets and no head-tires then,
No purfled dames, no zone, that caught the eye
More than the person did. Time was not yet,
When at his daughter's birth the sire grew pale.
For fear the age and dowry should exceed
On each side just proportion. House was none
Void of its family; nor yet had come
Hardanapalus, to exhibit feats
Of chamber prowess. Montemalo yet
O'er our suburban turret rose; as much
To be surpass in fall, as in its rising.
I saw Bellincione Berti walk abroad
In leathern girdle and a clasp of bone;
And, with no artful colouring on her cheeks,
His lady leave the glass. The sons I saw
Of Nerli and of Vecchio well content
With unrob'd jerkin; and their good dames handling
The spindle and the flax; O happy they!
Each sure of burial in her native land,
And none left desolate a-bed for France!
One wak'd to tend the cradle, hushing it
With sounds that lull'd the parent's infancy:
Another, with her maidens, drawing off
The tresses from the distaff, lectur'd them
Old tales of Troy and Fesole and Rome.
A Salterello and Cianghella we
Had held as strange a marvel, as ye would
A Cincinnatus or Cornelia now.

    "In such compos'd and seemly fellowship,
Such faithful and such fair equality,
In so sweet household, Mary at my birth
Bestow'd me, call'd on with loud cries; and there
In your old baptistery, I was made
Christian at once and Cacciaguida; as were
My brethren, Eliseo and Moronto.

    "From Valdipado came to me my spouse,
And hence thy surname grew. I follow'd then
The Emperor Conrad; and his knighthood he
Did gird on me; in such good part he took
My valiant service. After him I went
To testify against that evil law,
Whose people, by the shepherd's fault, possess
Your right, usurping. There, by that foul crew

Dante Alighieri

Was I releas'd from the deceitful world,
Whose base affection many a spirit soils,
And from the martyrdom came to this peace."

CANTO XVI

O slight respect of man's nobility!
I never shall account it marvelous,
That our infirm affection here below
Thou mov'st to boasting, when I could not choose,
E'en in that region of unwarp'd desire,
In heav'n itself, but make my vaunt in thee!
Yet cloak thou art soon shorten'd, for that time,
Unless thou be eked out from day to day,
Goes round thee with his shears. Resuming then
With greeting such, as Rome, was first to bear,
But since hath disaccustom'd I began;
And Beatrice, that a little space
Was sever'd, smil'd reminding me of her,
Whose cough embolden'd (as the story holds)
To first offence the doubting Guenever.
    "You are my sire," said I, "you give me heart
Freely to speak my thought: above myself
You raise me. Through so many streams with joy
My soul is fill'd, that gladness wells from it;
So that it bears the mighty tide, and bursts not
Say then, my honour'd stem! what ancestors
Where those you sprang from, and what years were mark'd
In your first childhood? Tell me of the fold,
That hath Saint John for guardian, what was then
Its state, and who in it were highest seated?"
    As embers, at the breathing of the wind,
Their flame enliven, so that light I saw
Shine at my blandishments; and, as it grew
More fair to look on, so with voice more sweet,
Yet not in this our modern phrase, forthwith
It answer'd: "From the day, when it was said
' Hail Virgin!' to the throes, by which my mother,
Who now is sainted, lighten'd her of me
Whom she was heavy with, this fire had come,
Five hundred fifty times and thrice, its beams
To reilumine underneath the foot
Of its own lion. They, of whom I sprang,
And I, had there our birth-place, where the last
Partition of our city first is reach'd
By him, that runs her annual game. Thus much
Suffice of my forefathers: who they were,
And whence they hither came, more honourable
It is to pass in silence than to tell.

The Divine Comedy

All those, who in that time were there from Mars
Until the Baptist, fit to carry arms,
Were but the fifth of them this day alive.
But then the citizen's blood, that now is mix'd
From Campi and Certaldo and Fighine,
Ran purely through the last mechanic's veins.
O how much better were it, that these people
Were neighbours to you, and that at Galluzzo
And at Trespiano, ye should have your bound'ry,
Than to have them within, and bear the stench
Of Aguglione's hind, and Signa's, him,
That hath his eye already keen for bart'ring!
Had not the people, which of all the world
Degenerates most, been stepdame unto Caesar,
But, as a mother, gracious to her son;
Such one, as hath become a Florentine,
And trades and traffics, had been turn'd adrift
To Simifonte, where his grandsire ply'd
The beggar's craft. The Conti were possess'd
Of Montemurlo still: the Cerchi still
Were in Acone's parish; nor had haply
From Valdigrieve past the Buondelmonte.
The city's malady hath ever source
In the confusion of its persons, as
The body's, in variety of food:
And the blind bull falls with a steeper plunge,
Than the blind lamb; and oftentimes one sword
Doth more and better execution,
Than five. Mark Luni, Urbisaglia mark,
How they are gone, and after them how go
Chiusi and Sinigaglia; and 't will seem
No longer new or strange to thee to hear,
That families fail, when cities have their end.
All things, that appertain t' ye, like yourselves,
Are mortal: but mortality in some
Ye mark not, they endure so long, and you
Pass by so suddenly. And as the moon
Doth, by the rolling of her heav'nly sphere,
Hide and reveal the strand unceasingly;
So fortune deals with Florence. Hence admire not
At what of them I tell thee, whose renown
Time covers, the first Florentines. I saw
The Ughi, Catilini and Filippi,
The Alberichi, Greci and Ormanni,
Now in their wane, illustrious citizens:
And great as ancient, of Sannella him,
With him of Arca saw, and Soldanieri
And Ardinghi, and Bostichi. At the poop,
That now is laden with new felony,
So cumb'rous it may speedily sink the bark,

Dante Alighieri

The Ravignani sat, of whom is sprung
The County Guido, and whoso hath since
His title from the fam'd Bellincione ta'en.
Fair governance was yet an art well priz'd
By him of Pressa: Galigaio show'd
The gilded hilt and pommel, in his house.
The column, cloth'd with verrey, still was seen
Unshaken: the Sacchetti still were great,
Giouchi, Sifanti, Galli and Barucci,
With them who blush to hear the bushel nam'd.
Of the Calfucci still the branchy trunk
Was in its strength: and to the curule chairs
Sizii and Arigucci yet were drawn.
How mighty them I saw, whom since their pride
Hath undone! and in all her goodly deeds
Florence was by the bullets of bright gold
O'erflourish'd. Such the sires of those, who now,
As surely as your church is vacant, flock
Into her consistory, and at leisure
There stall them and grow fat. The o'erweening brood,
That plays the dragon after him that flees,
But unto such, as turn and show the tooth,
Ay or the purse, is gentle as a lamb,
Was on its rise, but yet so slight esteem'd,
That Ubertino of Donati grudg'd
His father-in-law should yoke him to its tribe.
Already Caponsacco had descended
Into the mart from Fesole: and Giuda
And Infangato were good citizens.
A thing incredible I tell, tho' true:
The gateway, named from those of Pera, led
Into the narrow circuit of your walls.
Each one, who bears the sightly quarterings
Of the great Baron (he whose name and worth
The festival of Thomas still revives)
His knighthood and his privilege retain'd;
Albeit one, who borders them with gold,
This day is mingled with the common herd.
In Borgo yet the Gualterotti dwelt,
And Importuni: well for its repose
Had it still lack'd of newer neighbourhood.
The house, from whence your tears have had their spring,
Through the just anger that hath murder'd ye
And put a period to your gladsome days,
Was honour'd, it, and those consorted with it.
O Buondelmonte! what ill counseling
Prevail'd on thee to break the plighted bond
Many, who now are weeping, would rejoice,
Had God to Ema giv'n thee, the first time
Thou near our city cam'st. But so was doom'd:

The Divine Comedy
On that maim'd stone set up to guard the bridge,
At thy last peace, the victim, Florence! fell.
With these and others like to them, I saw
Florence in such assur'd tranquility,
She had no cause at which to grieve: with these
Saw her so glorious and so just, that ne'er
The lily from the lance had hung reverse,
Or through division been with vermeil dyed."

CANTO XVII

Such as the youth, who came to Clymene
To certify himself of that reproach,
Which had been fasten'd on him, (he whose end
Still makes the fathers chary to their sons,
E'en such was I; nor unobserv'd was such
Of Beatrice, and that saintly lamp,
Who had erewhile for me his station mov'd;
When thus by lady: "Give thy wish free vent,
That it may issue, bearing true report
Of the mind's impress; not that aught thy words
May to our knowledge add, but to the end,
That thou mayst use thyself to own thy thirst
And men may mingle for thee when they hear."
    "O plant! from whence I spring! rever'd and lov'd!
Who soar'st so high a pitch, thou seest as clear,
As earthly thought determines two obtuse
In one triangle not contain'd, so clear
Dost see contingencies, ere in themselves
Existent, looking at the point whereto
All times are present, I, the whilst I scal'd
With Virgil the soul purifying mount,
And visited the nether world of woe,
Touching my future destiny have heard
Words grievous, though I feel me on all sides
Well squar'd to fortune's blows. Therefore my will
Were satisfied to know the lot awaits me,
The arrow, seen beforehand, slacks its flight."
    So said I to the brightness, which erewhile
To me had spoken, and my will declar'd,
As Beatrice will'd, explicitly.
Nor with oracular response obscure,
Such, as or ere the Lamb of God was slain,
Beguil'd the credulous nations; but, in terms
Precise and unambiguous lore, replied
The spirit of paternal love, enshrin'd,
Yet in his smile apparent; and thus spake:
"Contingency, unfolded not to view
Upon the tablet of your mortal mold,

Dante Alighieri

Is all depictur'd in the' eternal sight;
But hence deriveth not necessity,
More then the tall ship, hurried down the flood,
Doth from the vision, that reflects the scene.
From thence, as to the ear sweet harmony
From organ comes, so comes before mine eye
The time prepar'd for thee. Such as driv'n out
From Athens, by his cruel stepdame's wiles,
Hippolytus departed, such must thou
Depart from Florence. This they wish, and this
Contrive, and will ere long effectuate, there,
Where gainful merchandize is made of Christ,
Throughout the livelong day. The common cry,
Will, as 't is ever wont, affix the blame
Unto the party injur'd: but the truth
Shall, in the vengeance it dispenseth, find
A faithful witness. Thou shall leave each thing
Belov'd most dearly: this is the first shaft
Shot from the bow of exile. Thou shalt prove
How salt the savour is of other's bread,
How hard the passage to descend and climb
By other's stairs, But that shall gall thee most
Will he the worthless and vile company,
With whom thou must be thrown into these straits.
For all ungrateful, impious all and mad,
Shall turn 'gainst thee: but in a little while
Theirs and not thine shall be the crimson'd brow
Their course shall so evince their brutishness
T' have ta'en thy stand apart shall well become thee.
   "First refuge thou must find, first place of rest,
In the great Lombard's courtesy, who bears
Upon the ladder perch'd the sacred bird.
He shall behold thee with such kind regard,
That 'twixt ye two, the contrary to that
Which falls 'twixt other men, the granting shall
Forerun the asking. With him shalt thou see
That mortal, who was at his birth impress
So strongly from this star, that of his deeds
The nations shall take note. His unripe age
Yet holds him from observance; for these wheels
Only nine years have compass him about.
But, ere the Gascon practice on great Harry,
Sparkles of virtue shall shoot forth in him,
In equal scorn of labours and of gold.
His bounty shall be spread abroad so widely,
As not to let the tongues e'en of his foes
Be idle in its praise. Look thou to him
And his beneficence: for he shall cause
Reversal of their lot to many people,
Rich men and beggars interchanging fortunes.

The Divine Comedy

And thou shalt bear this written in thy soul
Of him, but tell it not; "and things he told
Incredible to those who witness them;
Then added: "So interpret thou, my son,
What hath been told thee.--Lo! the ambushment
That a few circling seasons hide for thee!
Yet envy not thy neighbours: time extends
Thy span beyond their treason's chastisement."

    Soon, as the saintly spirit, by his silence,
Had shown the web, which I had streteh'd for him
Upon the warp, was woven, I began,
As one, who in perplexity desires
Counsel of other, wise, benign and friendly:
"My father! well I mark how time spurs on
Toward me, ready to inflict the blow,
Which falls most heavily on him, who most
Abandoned himself. Therefore 't is good
I should forecast, that driven from the place
Most dear to me, I may not lose myself
All others by my song. Down through the world
Of infinite mourning, and along the mount
From whose fair height my lady's eyes did lift me,
And after through this heav'n from light to light,
Have I learnt that, which if I tell again,
It may with many woefully disrelish;
And, if I am a timid friend to truth,
I fear my life may perish among those,
To whom these days shall be of ancient date."

    The brightness, where enclos'd the treasure smil'd,
Which I had found there, first shone glisteningly,
Like to a golden mirror in the sun;
Next answer'd: "Conscience, dimm'd or by its own
Or other's shame, will feel thy saying sharp.
Thou, notwithstanding, all deceit remov'd,
See the whole vision be made manifest.
And let them wince who have their withers wrung.
What though, when tasted first, thy voice shall prove
Unwelcome, on digestion it will turn
To vital nourishment. The cry thou raisest,
Shall, as the wind doth, smite the proudest summits;
Which is of honour no light argument,
For this there only have been shown to thee,
Throughout these orbs, the mountain, and the deep,
Spirits, whom fame hath note of. For the mind
Of him, who hears, is loth to acquiesce
And fix its faith, unless the instance brought
Be palpable, and proof apparent urge."

Dante Alighieri

CANTO XVIII

Now in his word, sole, ruminating, joy'd
That blessed spirit; and I fed on mine,
Tempting the sweet with bitter: she meanwhile,
Who led me unto God, admonish'd: "Muse
On other thoughts: bethink thee, that near Him
I dwell, who recompenseth every wrong."
　　At the sweet sounds of comfort straight I turn'd;
And, in the saintly eyes what love was seen,
I leave in silence here: nor through distrust
Of my words only, but that to such bliss
The mind remounts not without aid. Thus much
Yet may I speak; that, as I gaz'd on her,
Affection found no room for other wish.
While the everlasting pleasure, that did full
On Beatrice shine, with second view
From her fair countenance my gladden'd soul
Contented; vanquishing me with a beam
Of her soft smile, she spake: "Turn thee, and list.
These eyes are not thy only Paradise."
　　As here we sometimes in the looks may see
Th' affection mark'd, when that its sway hath ta'en
The spirit wholly; thus the hallow'd light,
To whom I turn'd, flashing, bewray'd its will
To talk yet further with me, and began:
"On this fifth lodgment of the tree, whose life
Is from its top, whose fruit is ever fair
And leaf unwith'ring, blessed spirits abide,
That were below, ere they arriv'd in heav'n,
So mighty in renown, as every muse
Might grace her triumph with them. On the horns
Look therefore of the cross: he, whom I name,
Shall there enact, as doth 1n summer cloud
Its nimble fire." Along the cross I saw,
At the repeated name of Joshua,
A splendour gliding; nor, the word was said,
Ere it was done: then, at the naming saw
Of the great Maccabee, another move
With whirling speed; and gladness was the scourge
Unto that top. The next for Charlemagne
And for the peer Orlando, two my gaze
Pursued, intently, as the eye pursues
A falcon flying. Last, along the cross,
William, and Renard, and Duke Godfrey drew
My ken, and Robert Guiscard. And the soul,
Who spake with me among the other lights
Did move away, and mix; and with the choir
Of heav'nly songsters prov'd his tuneful skill.

The Divine Comedy

     To Beatrice on my right I bent,
Looking for intimation or by word
Or act, what next behoov'd; and did descry
Such mere effulgence in her eyes, such joy,
It past all former wont. And, as by sense
Of new delight, the man, who perseveres
In good deeds doth perceive from day to day
His virtue growing; I e'en thus perceiv'd
Of my ascent, together with the heav'n
The circuit widen'd, noting the increase
Of beauty in that wonder. Like the change
In a brief moment on some maiden's cheek,
Which from its fairness doth discharge the weight
Of pudency, that stain'd it; such in her,
And to mine eyes so sudden was the change,
Through silvery whiteness of that temperate star,
Whose sixth orb now enfolded us. I saw,
Within that Jovial cresset, the clear sparks
Of love, that reign'd there, fashion to my view
Our language. And as birds, from river banks
Arisen, now in round, now lengthen'd troop,
Array them in their flight, greeting, as seems,
Their new-found pastures; so, within the lights,
The saintly creatures flying, sang, and made
Now D. now I. now L. figur'd I' th' air.
First, singing, to their notes they mov'd, then one
Becoming of these signs, a little while
Did rest them, and were mute. O nymph divine
Of Pegasean race! whose souls, which thou
Inspir'st, mak'st glorious and long-liv'd, as they
Cities and realms by thee! thou with thyself
Inform me; that I may set forth the shapes,
As fancy doth present them. Be thy power
Display'd in this brief song. The characters,
Vocal and consonant, were five-fold seven.
In order each, as they appear'd, I mark'd.
Diligite Justitiam, the first,
Both verb and noun all blazon'd; and the extreme
Qui judicatis terram. In the M.
Of the fifth word they held their station,
Making the star seem silver streak'd with gold.
And on the summit of the M. I saw
Descending other lights, that rested there,
Singing, methinks, their bliss and primal good.
Then, as at shaking of a lighted brand,
Sparkles innumerable on all sides
Rise scatter'd, source of augury to th' unwise;
Thus more than thousand twinkling lustres hence
Seem'd reascending, and a higher pitch
Some mounting, and some less; e'en as the sun,

Dante Alighieri

Which kindleth them, decreed. And when each one
Had settled in his place, the head and neck
Then saw I of an eagle, lively
Grav'd in that streaky fire. Who painteth there,
Hath none to guide him; of himself he guides;
And every line and texture of the nest
Doth own from him the virtue, fashions it.
The other bright beatitude, that seem'd
Erewhile, with lilied crowning, well content
To over-canopy the M. mov'd forth,
Following gently the impress of the bird.
    Sweet star! what glorious and thick-studded gems
Declar'd to me our justice on the earth
To be the effluence of that heav'n, which thou,
Thyself a costly jewel, dost inlay!
Therefore I pray the Sovran Mind, from whom
Thy motion and thy virtue are begun,
That he would look from whence the fog doth rise,
To vitiate thy beam: so that once more
He may put forth his hand 'gainst such, as drive
Their traffic in that sanctuary, whose walls
With miracles and martyrdoms were built.
    Ye host of heaven! whose glory I survey l
O beg ye grace for those, that are on earth
All after ill example gone astray.
War once had for its instrument the sword:
But now 't is made, taking the bread away
Which the good Father locks from none. --And thou,
That writes but to cancel, think, that they,
Who for the vineyard, which thou wastest, died,
Peter and Paul live yet, and mark thy doings.
Thou hast good cause to cry, "My heart so cleaves
To him, that liv'd in solitude remote,
And from the wilds was dragg'd to martyrdom,
I wist not of the fisherman nor Paul."

CANTO XIX

Before my sight appear'd, with open wings,
The beauteous image, in fruition sweet
Gladdening the thronged spirits. Each did seem
A little ruby, whereon so intense
The sun-beam glow'd that to mine eyes it came
In clear refraction. And that, which next
Befalls me to portray, voice hath not utter'd,
Nor hath ink written, nor in fantasy
Was e'er conceiv'd. For I beheld and heard
The beak discourse; and, what intention form'd
Of many, singly as of one express,

The Divine Comedy

Beginning: "For that I was just and piteous,
I am exalted to this height of glory,
The which no wish exceeds: and there on earth
Have I my memory left, e'en by the bad
Commended, while they leave its course untrod."
    Thus is one heat from many embers felt,
As in that image many were the loves,
And one the voice, that issued from them all.
Whence I address them: "O perennial flowers
Of gladness everlasting! that exhale
In single breath your odours manifold!
Breathe now; and let the hunger be appeas'd,
That with great craving long hath held my soul,
Finding no food on earth. This well I know,
That if there be in heav'n a realm, that shows
In faithful mirror the celestial Justice,
Yours without veil reflects it. Ye discern
The heed, wherewith I do prepare myself
To hearken; ye the doubt that urges me
With such inveterate craving." Straight I saw,
Like to a falcon issuing from the hood,
That rears his head, and claps him with his wings,
His beauty and his eagerness bewraying.
So saw I move that stately sign, with praise
Of grace divine inwoven and high song
Of inexpressive joy. "He," it began,
"Who turn'd his compass on the world's extreme,
And in that space so variously hath wrought,
Both openly, and in secret, in such wise
Could not through all the universe display
Impression of his glory, that the Word
Of his omniscience should not still remain
In infinite excess. In proof whereof,
He first through pride supplanted, who was sum
Of each created being, waited not
For light celestial, and abortive fell.
Whence needs each lesser nature is but scant
Receptacle unto that Good, which knows
No limit, measur'd by itself alone.
Therefore your sight, of th' omnipresent Mind
A single beam, its origin must own
Surpassing far its utmost potency.
The ken, your world is gifted with, descends
In th' everlasting Justice as low down,
As eye doth in the sea; which though it mark
The bottom from the shore, in the wide main
Discerns it not; and ne'ertheless it is,
But hidden through its deepness. Light is none,
Save that which cometh from the pure serene
Of ne'er disturbed ether: for the rest,

Dante Alighieri

'Tis darkness all, or shadow of the flesh,
Or else its poison. Here confess reveal'd
That covert, which hath hidden from thy search
The living justice, of the which thou mad'st
Such frequent question; for thou saidst--'A man
Is born on Indus' banks, and none is there
Who speaks of Christ, nor who doth read nor write,
And all his inclinations and his acts,
As far as human reason sees, are good,
And he offendeth not in word or deed.
But unbaptiz'd he dies, and void of faith.
Where is the justice that condemns him? where
His blame, if he believeth not?'--What then,
And who art thou, that on the stool wouldst sit
To judge at distance of a thousand miles
With the short-sighted vision of a span?
To him, who subtilizes thus with me,
There would assuredly be room for doubt
Even to wonder, did not the safe word
Of scripture hold supreme authority.

    "O animals of clay! O spirits gross I
The primal will, that in itself is good,
Hath from itself, the chief Good, ne'er been mov'd.
Justice consists in consonance with it,
Derivable by no created good,
Whose very cause depends upon its beam."

    As on her nest the stork, that turns about
Unto her young, whom lately she hath fed,
While they with upward eyes do look on her;
So lifted I my gaze; and bending so
The ever-blessed image wav'd its wings,
Lab'ring with such deep counsel. Wheeling round
It warbled, and did say: "As are my notes
To thee, who understand'st them not, such is
Th' eternal judgment unto mortal ken."

    Then still abiding in that ensign rang'd,
Wherewith the Romans over-awed the world,
Those burning splendours of the Holy Spirit
Took up the strain; and thus it spake again:
"None ever hath ascended to this realm,
Who hath not a believer been in Christ,
Either before or after the blest limbs
Were nail'd upon the wood. But lo! of those
Who call 'Christ, Christ,' there shall be many found,
 In judgment, further off from him by far,
Than such, to whom his name was never known.
Christians like these the Ethiop shall condemn:
When that the two assemblages shall part;
One rich eternally, the other poor.

"What may the Persians say unto your kings,
When they shall see that volume, in the which
All their dispraise is written, spread to view?
There amidst Albert's works shall that be read,
Which will give speedy motion to the pen,
When Prague shall mourn her desolated realm.
There shall be read the woe, that he doth work
With his adulterate money on the Seine,
Who by the tusk will perish: there be read
The thirsting pride, that maketh fool alike
The English and Scot, impatient of their bound.
There shall be seen the Spaniard's luxury,
The delicate living there of the Bohemian,
Who still to worth has been a willing stranger.
The halter of Jerusalem shall see
A unit for his virtue, for his vices
No less a mark than million. He, who guards
The isle of fire by old Anchises honour'd
Shall find his avarice there and cowardice;
And better to denote his littleness,
The writing must be letters maim'd, that speak
Much in a narrow space. All there shall know
His uncle and his brother's filthy doings,
Who so renown'd a nation and two crowns
Have bastardized. And they, of Portugal
And Norway, there shall be expos'd with him
Of Ratza, who hath counterfeited ill
The coin of Venice. O blest Hungary!
If thou no longer patiently abid'st
Thy ill-entreating! and, O blest Navarre!
If with thy mountainous girdle thou wouldst arm thee
In earnest of that day, e'en now are heard
Wailings and groans in Famagosta's streets
And Nicosia's, grudging at their beast,
Who keepeth even footing with the rest."

CANTO XX

When, disappearing, from our hemisphere,
The world's enlightener vanishes, and day
On all sides wasteth, suddenly the sky,
Erewhile irradiate only with his beam,
Is yet again unfolded, putting forth
Innumerable lights wherein one shines.
Of such vicissitude in heaven I thought,
As the great sign, that marshaleth the world
And the world's leaders, in the blessed beak
Was silent; for that all those living lights,
Waxing in splendour, burst forth into songs,

Dante Alighieri

Such as from memory glide and fall away.
    Sweet love! that dost apparel thee in smiles,
How lustrous was thy semblance in those sparkles,
Which merely are from holy thoughts inspir'd!
    After the precious and bright beaming stones,
That did ingem the sixth light, ceas'd the chiming
Of their angelic bells; methought I heard
The murmuring of a river, that doth fall
From rock to rock transpicuous, making known
The richness of his spring-head: and as sound
Of cistern, at the fret-board, or of pipe,
Is, at the wind-hole, modulate and tun'd;
Thus up the neck, as it were hollow, rose
That murmuring of the eagle, and forthwith
Voice there assum'd, and thence along the beak
Issued in form of words, such as my heart
Did look for, on whose tables I inscrib'd them.
    "The part in me, that sees, and bears the sun,,
In mortal eagles," it began, "must now
Be noted steadfastly: for of the fires,
That figure me, those, glittering in mine eye,
Are chief of all the greatest. This, that shines
Midmost for pupil, was the same, who sang
The Holy Spirit's song, and bare about
The ark from town to town; now doth he know
The merit of his soul-impassion'd strains
By their well-fitted guerdon. Of the five,
That make the circle of the vision, he
Who to the beak is nearest, comforted
The widow for her son: now doth he know
How dear he costeth not to follow Christ,
Both from experience of this pleasant life,
And of its opposite. He next, who follows
In the circumference, for the over arch,
By true repenting slack'd the pace of death:
Now knoweth he, that the degrees of heav'n
Alter not, when through pious prayer below
Today's is made tomorrow's destiny.
The other following, with the laws and me,
To yield the shepherd room, pass'd o'er to Greece,
From good intent producing evil fruit:
Now knoweth he, how all the ill, deriv'd
From his well doing, doth not helm him aught,
Though it have brought destruction on the world.
That, which thou seest in the under bow,
Was William, whom that land bewails, which weeps
For Charles and Frederick living: now he knows
How well is lov'd in heav'n the righteous king,
Which he betokens by his radiant seeming.
Who in the erring world beneath would deem,

That Trojan Ripheus in this round was set
Fifth of the saintly splendours? now he knows
Enough of that, which the world cannot see,
The grace divine, albeit e'en his sight
Reach not its utmost depth." Like to the lark,
That warbling in the air expatiates long,
Then, trilling out his last sweet melody,
Drops satiate with the sweetness; such appear'd
That image stampt by the' everlasting pleasure,
Which fashions like itself all lovely things.

    I, though my doubting were as manifest,
As is through glass the hue that mantles it,
In silence waited not: for to my lips
"What things are these?" involuntary rush'd,
And forc'd a passage out: whereat I mark'd
A sudden lightening and new revelry.
The eye was kindled: and the blessed sign
No more to keep me wond'ring and suspense,
Replied: "I see that thou believ'st these things,
Because I tell them, but discern'st not how;
So that thy knowledge waits not on thy faith:
As one who knows the name of thing by rote,
But is a stranger to its properties,
Till other's tongue reveal them. Fervent love
And lively hope with violence assail
The kingdom of the heavens, and overcome
The will of the Most high; not in such sort
As man prevails o'er man; but conquers it,
Because 't is willing to be conquer'd, still,
Though conquer'd, by its mercy conquering.

    "Those, in the eye who live the first and fifth,
Cause thee to marvel, in that thou behold'st
The region of the angels deck'd with them.
They quitted not their bodies, as thou deem'st,
Gentiles but Christians, in firm rooted faith,
This of the feet in future to be pierc'd,
That of feet nail'd already to the cross.
One from the barrier of the dark abyss,
Where never any with good will returns,
Came back unto his bones. Of lively hope
Such was the meed; of lively hope, that wing'd
The prayers sent up to God for his release,
And put power into them to bend his will.
The glorious Spirit, of whom I speak to thee,
A little while returning to the flesh,
Believ'd in him, who had the means to help,
And, in believing, nourish'd such a flame
Of holy love, that at the second death
He was made sharer in our gamesome mirth.
The other, through the riches of that grace,

Dante Alighieri

Which from so deep a fountain doth distil,
As never eye created saw its rising,
Plac'd all his love below on just and right:
Wherefore of grace God op'd in him the eye
To the redemption of mankind to come;
Wherein believing, he endur'd no more
The filth of paganism, and for their ways
Rebuk'd the stubborn nations. The three nymphs,
Whom at the right wheel thou beheldst advancing,
Were sponsors for him more than thousand years
Before baptizing. O how far remov'd,
Predestination! is thy root from such
As see not the First cause entire: and ye,
O mortal men! be wary how ye judge:
For we, who see our Maker, know not yet
The number of the chosen: and esteem
Such scantiness of knowledge our delight:
For all our good is in that primal good
Concentrate, and God's will and ours are one."
    So, by that form divine, was giv'n to me
Sweet medicine to clear and strengthen sight,
And, as one handling skillfully the harp,
Attendant on some skilful songster's voice
Bids the chords vibrate, and therein the song
Acquires more pleasure; so, the whilst it spake,
It doth remember me, that I beheld
The pair of blessed luminaries move.
Like the accordant twinkling of two eyes,
Their beamy circlets, dancing to the sounds.

CANTO XXI

Again mine eyes were fix'd on Beatrice,
And with mine eyes my soul, that in her looks
Found all contentment. Yet no smile she wore
And, "Did I smile," quoth she, "thou wouldst be straight
Like Semele when into ashes turn'd:
For, mounting these eternal palace-stairs,
My beauty, which the loftier it climbs,
As thou hast noted, still doth kindle more,
So shines, that, were no temp'ring interpos'd,
Thy mortal puissance would from its rays
Shrink, as the leaf doth from the thunderbolt.
Into the seventh splendour are we wafted,
That underneath the burning lion's breast
Beams, in this hour, commingled with his might,
Thy mind be with thine eyes: and in them mirror'd
The shape, which in this mirror shall be shown."
Whoso can deem, how fondly I had fed

The Divine Comedy

My sight upon her blissful countenance,
May know, when to new thoughts I chang'd, what joy
To do the bidding of my heav'nly guide:
In equal balance poising either weight.
    Within the crystal, which records the name,
(As its remoter circle girds the world)
Of that lov'd monarch, in whose happy reign
No ill had power to harm, I saw rear'd up,
In colour like to sun-illumin'd gold.
A ladder, which my ken pursued in vain,
So lofty was the summit; down whose steps
I saw the splendours in such multitude
Descending, ev'ry light in heav'n, methought,
Was shed thence. As the rooks, at dawn of day
Bestirring them to dry their feathers chill,
Some speed their way a-field, and homeward some,
Returning, cross their flight, while some abide
And wheel around their airy lodge; so seem'd
That glitterance, wafted on alternate wing,
As upon certain stair it met, and clash'd
Its shining. And one ling'ring near us, wax'd
So bright, that in my thought: said: "The love,
Which this betokens me, admits no doubt."
    Unwillingly from question I refrain,
To her, by whom my silence and my speech
Are order'd, looking for a sign: whence she,
Who in the sight of Him, that seeth all,
Saw wherefore I was silent, prompted me
T' indulge the fervent wish; and I began:
"I am not worthy, of my own desert,
That thou shouldst answer me; but for her sake,
Who hath vouchsaf'd my asking, spirit blest!
That in thy joy art shrouded! say the cause,
Which bringeth thee so near: and wherefore, say,
Doth the sweet symphony of Paradise
Keep silence here, pervading with such sounds
Of rapt devotion ev'ry lower sphere?"
"Mortal art thou in hearing as in sight;"
Was the reply: "and what forbade the smile
Of Beatrice interrupts our song.
Only to yield thee gladness of my voice,
And of the light that vests me, I thus far
Descend these hallow'd steps: not that more love
Invites me; for lo! there aloft, as much
Or more of love is witness'd in those flames:
But such my lot by charity assign'd,
That makes us ready servants, as thou seest,
To execute the counsel of the Highest.
"That in this court," said I, "O sacred lamp!
Love no compulsion needs, but follows free

Dante Alighieri

Th' eternal Providence, I well discern:
This harder find to deem, why of thy peers
Thou only to this office wert foredoom'd."
I had not ended, when, like rapid mill,
Upon its centre whirl'd the light; and then
The love, that did inhabit there, replied:
"Splendour eternal, piercing through these folds,
Its virtue to my vision knits, and thus
Supported, lifts me so above myself,
That on the sov'ran essence, which it wells from,
I have the power to gaze: and hence the joy,
Wherewith I sparkle, equaling with my blaze
The keenness of my sight. But not the soul,
That is in heav'n most lustrous, nor the seraph
That hath his eyes most fix'd on God, shall solve
What thou hast ask'd: for in th' abyss it lies
Of th' everlasting statute sunk so low,
That no created ken may fathom it.
And, to the mortal world when thou return'st,
Be this reported; that none henceforth dare
Direct his footsteps to so dread a bourn.
The mind, that here is radiant, on the earth
Is wrapt in mist. Look then if she may do,
Below, what passeth her ability,
When she is ta'en to heav'n." By words like these
Admonish'd, I the question urg'd no more;
And of the spirit humbly sued alone
T' instruct me of its state. "'Twixt either shore
Of Italy, nor distant from thy land,
A stony ridge ariseth, in such sort,
The thunder doth not lift his voice so high,
They call it Catria: at whose foot a cell
Is sacred to the lonely Eremite,
For worship set apart and holy rites."
A third time thus it spake; then added: "There
So firmly to God's service I adher'd,
That with no costlier viands than the juice
Of olives, easily I pass'd the heats
Of summer and the winter frosts, content
In heav'n-ward musings. Rich were the returns
And fertile, which that cloister once was us'd
To render to these heavens: now 't is fall'n
Into a waste so empty, that ere long
Detection must lay bare its vanity
Pietro Damiano there was I y-clept:
Pietro the sinner, when before I dwelt
Beside the Adriatic, in the house
Of our blest Lady. Near upon my close
Of mortal life, through much importuning
I was constrain'd to wear the hat that still

From bad to worse it shifted.--Cephas came;
He came, who was the Holy Spirit's vessel,
Barefoot and lean, eating their bread, as chanc'd,
At the first table. Modern Shepherd's need
Those who on either hand may prop and lead them,
So burly are they grown: and from behind
Others to hoist them. Down the palfrey's sides
Spread their broad mantles, so as both the beasts
Are cover'd with one skin. O patience! thou
That lookst on this and doth endure so long."
I at those accents saw the splendours down
From step to step alight, and wheel, and wax,
Each circuiting, more beautiful. Round this
They came, and stay'd them; uttered them a shout
So loud, it hath no likeness here: nor I
Wist what it spake, so deaf'ning was the thunder.

CANTO XXII

Astounded, to the guardian of my steps
I turn'd me, like the chill, who always runs
Thither for succour, where he trusteth most,
And she was like the mother, who her son
Beholding pale and breathless, with her voice
Soothes him, and he is cheer'd; for thus she spake,
Soothing me: "Know'st not thou, thou art in heav'n?
And know'st not thou, whatever is in heav'n,
Is holy, and that nothing there is done
But is done zealously and well? Deem now,
What change in thee the song, and what my smile
had wrought, since thus the shout had pow'r to move thee.
In which couldst thou have understood their prayers,
The vengeance were already known to thee,
Which thou must witness ere thy mortal hour,
The sword of heav'n is not in haste to smite,
Nor yet doth linger, save unto his seeming,
Who in desire or fear doth look for it.
But elsewhere now I bid thee turn thy view;
So shalt thou many a famous spirit behold."
Mine eyes directing, as she will'd, I saw
A hundred little spheres, that fairer grew
By interchange of splendour. I remain'd,
As one, who fearful of o'er-much presuming,
Abates in him the keenness of desire,
Nor dares to question, when amid those pearls,
One largest and most lustrous onward drew,
That it might yield contentment to my wish;
And from within it these the sounds I heard.

Dante Alighieri

"If thou, like me, beheldst the charity
That burns amongst us, what thy mind conceives,
Were utter'd. But that, ere the lofty bound
Thou reach, expectance may not weary thee,
I will make answer even to the thought,
Which thou hast such respect of. In old days,
That mountain, at whose side Cassino rests,
Was on its height frequented by a race
Deceived and ill dispos'd: and I it was,
Who thither carried first the name of Him,
Who brought the soul-subliming truth to man.
And such a speeding grace shone over me,
That from their impious worship I reclaim'd
The dwellers round about, who with the world
Were in delusion lost. These other flames,
The spirits of men contemplative, were all
Enliven'd by that warmth, whose kindly force
Gives birth to flowers and fruits of holiness.
Here is Macarius; Romoaldo here:
And here my brethren, who their steps refrain'd
Within the cloisters, and held firm their heart."
    I answ'ring, thus; "Thy gentle words and kind,
And this the cheerful semblance, I behold
Not unobservant, beaming in ye all,
Have rais'd assurance in me, wakening it
Full-blossom'd in my bosom, as a rose
Before the sun, when the consummate flower
Has spread to utmost amplitude. Of thee
Therefore entreat I, father! to declare
If I may gain such favour, as to gaze
Upon thine image, by no covering veil'd."
    "Brother!" he thus rejoin'd, "in the last sphere
Expect completion of thy lofty aim,
For there on each desire completion waits,
And there on mine: where every aim is found
Perfect, entire, and for fulfillment ripe.
There all things are as they have ever been:
For space is none to bound, nor pole divides,
Our ladder reaches even to that clime,
And so at giddy distance mocks thy view.
Thither the Patriarch Jacob saw it stretch
Its topmost round, when it appear'd to him
With angels laden. But to mount it now
None lifts his foot from earth: and hence my rule
Is left a profitless stain upon the leaves;
The walls, for abbey rear'd, turned into dens,
The cowls to sacks choak'd up with musty meal.
Foul usury doth not more lift itself
Against God's pleasure, than that fruit which makes
The hearts of monks so wanton: for whate'er

Is in the church's keeping, all pertains.
To such, as sue for heav'n's sweet sake, and not
To those who in respect of kindred claim,
Or on more vile allowance. Mortal flesh
Is grown so dainty, good beginnings last not
From the oak's birth, unto the acorn's setting.
His convent Peter founded without gold
Or silver; I with pray'rs and fasting mine;
And Francis his in meek humility.
And if thou note the point, whence each proceeds,
Then look what it hath err'd to, thou shalt find
The white grown murky. Jordan was turn'd back;
And a less wonder, then the refluent sea,
May at God's pleasure work amendment here."
    So saying, to his assembly back he drew:
And they together cluster'd into one,
Then all roll'd upward like an eddying wind.
    The sweet dame beckon'd me to follow them:
And, by that influence only, so prevail'd
Over my nature, that no natural motion,
Ascending or descending here below,
Had, as I mounted, with my pennon vied.
    So, reader, as my hope is to return
Unto the holy triumph, for the which
I ofttimes wail my sins, and smite my breast,
Thou hadst been longer drawing out and thrusting
Thy finger in the fire, than I was, ere
The sign, that followeth Taurus, I beheld,
And enter'd its precinct. O glorious stars!
O light impregnate with exceeding virtue!
To whom whate'er of genius lifteth me
Above the vulgar, grateful I refer;
With ye the parent of all mortal life
Arose and set, when I did first inhale
The Tuscan air; and afterward, when grace
Vouchsaf'd me entrance to the lofty wheel
That in its orb impels ye, fate decreed
My passage at your clime. To you my soul
Devoutly sighs, for virtue even now
To meet the hard emprize that draws me on.
    "Thou art so near the sum of blessedness,"
Said Beatrice, "that behooves thy ken
Be vigilant and clear. And, to this end,
Or even thou advance thee further, hence
Look downward, and contemplate, what a world
Already stretched under our feet there lies:
So as thy heart may, in its blithest mood,
Present itself to the triumphal throng,
Which through the' etherial concave comes rejoicing."

Dante Alighieri

  I straight obey'd; and with mine eye return'd
Through all the seven spheres, and saw this globe
So pitiful of semblance, that perforce
It moved my smiles: and him in truth I hold
For wisest, who esteems it least: whose thoughts
Elsewhere are fix'd, him worthiest call and best.
I saw the daughter of Latona shine
Without the shadow, whereof late I deem'd
That dense and rare were cause. Here I sustain'd
The visage, Hyperion! of thy sun;
And mark'd, how near him with their circle, round
Move Maia and Dione; here discern'd
Jove's tempering 'twixt his sire and son; and hence
Their changes and their various aspects
Distinctly scann'd. Nor might I not descry
Of all the seven, how bulky each, how swift;
Nor of their several distances not learn.
This petty area (o'er the which we stride
So fiercely), as along the eternal twins
I wound my way, appear'd before me all,
Forth from the havens stretch'd unto the hills.
Then to the beauteous eyes mine eyes return'd.

CANTO XXIII

E'en as the bird, who midst the leafy bower
Has, in her nest, sat darkling through the night,
With her sweet brood, impatient to descry
Their wished looks, and to bring home their food,
In the fond quest unconscious of her toil:
She, of the time prevenient, on the spray,
That overhangs their couch, with wakeful gaze
Expects the sun; nor ever, till the dawn,
Removeth from the east her eager ken;
So stood the dame erect, and bent her glance
Wistfully on that region, where the sun
Abateth most his speed; that, seeing her
Suspense and wand'ring, I became as one,
In whom desire is waken'd, and the hope
Of somewhat new to come fills with delight.
  Short space ensued; I was not held, I say,
Long in expectance, when I saw the heav'n
Wax more and more resplendent; and, "Behold,"
Cried Beatrice, "the triumphal hosts
Of Christ, and all the harvest reap'd at length
Of thy ascending up these spheres." Meseem'd,
That, while she spake her image all did burn,
And in her eyes such fullness was of joy,
And I am fain to pass unconstrued by.

The Divine Comedy

    As in the calm full moon, when Trivia smiles,
In peerless beauty, 'mid th' eternal nympus,
That paint through all its gulfs the blue profound
In bright pre-eminence so saw I there,
O'er million lamps a sun, from whom all drew
Their radiance as from ours the starry train:
And through the living light so lustrous glow'd
The substance, that my ken endur'd it not.
    O Beatrice! sweet and precious guide!
Who cheer'd me with her comfortable words!
"Against the virtue, that o'erpow'reth thee,
Avails not to resist. Here is the might,
And here the wisdom, which did open lay
The path, that had been yearned for so long,
Betwixt the heav'n and earth." Like to the fire,
That, in a cloud imprison'd doth break out
Expansive, so that from its womb enlarg'd,
It falleth against nature to the ground;
Thus in that heav'nly banqueting my soul
Outgrew herself; and, in the transport lost.
Holds now remembrance none of what she was.
    "Ope thou thine eyes, and mark me: thou hast seen
Things, that empower thee to sustain my smile."
    I was as one, when a forgotten dream
Doth come across him, and he strives in vain
To shape it in his fantasy again,
Whenas that gracious boon was proffer'd me,
Which never may be cancel'd from the book,
Wherein the past is written. Now were all
Those tongues to sound, that have on sweetest milk
Of Polyhymnia and her sisters fed
And fatten'd, not with all their help to boot,
Unto the thousandth parcel of the truth,
My song might shadow forth that saintly smile,
flow merely in her saintly looks it wrought.
And with such figuring of Paradise
The sacred strain must leap, like one, that meets
A sudden interruption to his road.
But he, who thinks how ponderous the theme,
And that 't is lain upon a mortal shoulder,
May pardon, if it tremble with the burden.
The track, our ventrous keel must furrow, brooks
No unribb'd pinnace, no self-sparing pilot.
    "Why doth my face," said Beatrice, "thus
Enamour thee, as that thou dost not turn
Unto the beautiful garden, blossoming
Beneath the rays of Christ? Here is the rose,
Wherein the word divine was made incarnate;
And here the lilies, by whose odour known
The way of life was follow'd." Prompt I heard

Dante Alighieri

Her bidding, and encounter once again
The strife of aching vision. As erewhile,
Through glance of sunlight, stream'd through broken cloud,
Mine eyes a flower-besprinkled mead have seen,
Though veil'd themselves in shade; so saw I there
Legions of splendours, on whom burning rays
Shed lightnings from above, yet saw I not
The fountain whence they flow'd. O gracious virtue!
Thou, whose broad stamp is on them, higher up
Thou didst exalt thy glory to give room
To my o'erlabour'd sight: when at the name
Of that fair flower, whom duly I invoke
Both morn and eve, my soul, with all her might
Collected, on the goodliest ardour fix'd.
And, as the bright dimensions of the star
In heav'n excelling, as once here on earth
Were, in my eyeballs lively portray'd,
Lo! from within the sky a cresset fell,
Circling in fashion of a diadem,
And girt the star, and hov'ring round it wheel'd.
    Whatever melody sounds sweetest here,
And draws the spirit most unto itself,
Might seem a rent cloud when it grates the thunder,
Compar'd unto the sounding of that lyre,
Wherewith the goodliest sapphire, that inlays
The floor of heav'n, was crown'd. " Angelic Love
I am, who thus with hov'ring flight enwheel
The lofty rapture from that womb inspir'd,
Where our desire did dwell: and round thee so,
Lady of Heav'n! will hover; long as thou
Thy Son shalt follow, and diviner joy
Shall from thy presence gild the highest sphere."
    Such close was to the circling melody:
And, as it ended, all the other lights
Took up the strain, and echoed Mary's name.
    The robe, that with its regal folds enwraps
The world, and with the nearer breath of God
Doth burn and quiver, held so far retir'd
Its inner hem and skirting over us,
That yet no glimmer of its majesty
Had stream'd unto me: therefore were mine eyes
Unequal to pursue the crowned flame,
That rose and sought its natal seed of fire;
And like to babe, that stretches forth its arms
For very eagerness towards the breast,
After the milk is taken; so outstretch'd
Their wavy summits all the fervent band,
Through zealous love to Mary: then in view
There halted, and "Regina Coeli " sang
So sweetly, the delight hath left me never.

O what o'erflowing plenty is up-pil'd
In those rich-laden coffers, which below
Sow'd the good seed, whose harvest now they keep.
    Here are the treasures tasted, that with tears
Were in the Babylonian exile won,
When gold had fail'd them. Here in synod high
Of ancient council with the new conven'd,
Under the Son of Mary and of God,
Victorious he his mighty triumph holds,
To whom the keys of glory were assign'd.

CANTO XXIV

"O ye! in chosen fellowship advanc'd
To the great supper of the blessed Lamb,
Whereon who feeds hath every wish fulfill'd!
If to this man through God's grace be vouchsaf'd
Foretaste of that, which from your table falls,
Or ever death his fated term prescribe;
Be ye not heedless of his urgent will;
But may some influence of your sacred dews
Sprinkle him. Of the fount ye alway drink,
Whence flows what most he craves." Beatrice spake,
And the rejoicing spirits, like to spheres
On firm-set poles revolving, trail'd a blaze
Of comet splendour; and as wheels, that wind
Their circles in the horologe, so work
The stated rounds, that to th' observant eye
The first seems still, and, as it flew, the last;
E'en thus their carols weaving variously,
They by the measure pac'd, or swift, or slow,
Made me to rate the riches of their joy.
    From that, which I did note in beauty most
Excelling, saw I issue forth a flame
So bright, as none was left more goodly there.
Round Beatrice thrice it wheel'd about,
With so divine a song, that fancy's ear
Records it not; and the pen passeth on
And leaves a blank: for that our mortal speech,
Nor e'en the inward shaping of the brain,
Hath colours fine enough to trace such folds.
    "O saintly sister mine! thy prayer devout
Is with so vehement affection urg'd,
Thou dost unbind me from that beauteous sphere."
    Such were the accents towards my lady breath'd
From that blest ardour, soon as it was stay'd:
To whom she thus: "O everlasting light
Of him, within whose mighty grasp our Lord
Did leave the keys, which of this wondrous bliss

Dante Alighieri

He bare below! tent this man, as thou wilt,
With lighter probe or deep, touching the faith,
By the which thou didst on the billows walk.
If he in love, in hope, and in belief,
Be steadfast, is not hid from thee: for thou
Hast there thy ken, where all things are beheld
In liveliest portraiture. But since true faith
Has peopled this fair realm with citizens,
Meet is, that to exalt its glory more,
Thou in his audience shouldst thereof discourse."
     Like to the bachelor, who arms himself,
And speaks not, till the master have propos'd
The question, to approve, and not to end it;
So I, in silence, arm'd me, while she spake,
Summoning up each argument to aid;
As was behooveful for such questioner,
And such profession: "As good Christian ought,
Declare thee, What is faith?" Whereat I rais'd
My forehead to the light, whence this had breath'd,
Then turn'd to Beatrice, and in her looks
Approval met, that from their inmost fount
I should unlock the waters. "May the grace,
That giveth me the captain of the church
For confessor," said I, "vouchsafe to me
Apt utterance for my thoughts!" then added: "Sire!
E'en as set down by the unerring style
Of thy dear brother, who with thee conspir'd
To bring Rome in unto the way of life,
Faith of things hop'd is substance, and the proof
Of things not seen; and herein doth consist
Methinks its essence,"--" Rightly hast thou deem'd,"
Was answer'd: "if thou well discern, why first
He hath defin'd it, substance, and then proof."
     "The deep things," I replied, "which here I scan
Distinctly, are below from mortal eye
So hidden, they have in belief alone
Their being, on which credence hope sublime
Is built; and therefore substance it intends.
And inasmuch as we must needs infer
From such belief our reasoning, all respect
To other view excluded, hence of proof
Th' intention is deriv'd." Forthwith I heard:
"If thus, whate'er by learning men attain,
Were understood, the sophist would want room
To exercise his wit." So breath'd the flame
Of love: then added: "Current is the coin
Thou utter'st, both in weight and in alloy.
But tell me, if thou hast it in thy purse."
     "Even so glittering and so round," said I,
"I not a whit misdoubt of its assay."

The Divine Comedy

      Next issued from the deep imbosom'd splendour:
"Say, whence the costly jewel, on the which
Is founded every virtue, came to thee."
"The flood," I answer'd, "from the Spirit of God
Rain'd down upon the ancient bond and new,--
Here is the reas'ning, that convinceth me
So feelingly, each argument beside
Seems blunt and forceless in comparison."
Then heard I: "Wherefore holdest thou that each,
The elder proposition and the new,
Which so persuade thee, are the voice of heav'n?"
      "The works, that follow'd, evidence their truth;"
I answer'd: "Nature did not make for these
The iron hot, or on her anvil mould them."
"Who voucheth to thee of the works themselves,
Was the reply, "that they in very deed
Are that they purport? None hath sworn so to thee."
      "That all the world," said I, "should have bee turn'd
To Christian, and no miracle been wrought,
Would in itself be such a miracle,
The rest were not an hundredth part so great.
E'en thou wentst forth in poverty and hunger
To set the goodly plant, that from the vine,
It once was, now is grown unsightly bramble."
That ended, through the high celestial court
Resounded all the spheres. "Praise we one God!"
In song of most unearthly melody.
And when that Worthy thus, from branch to branch,
Examining, had led me, that we now
Approach'd the topmost bough, he straight resum'd;
"The grace, that holds sweet dalliance with thy soul,
So far discreetly hath thy lips unclos'd
That, whatsoe'er has past them, I commend.
Behooves thee to express, what thou believ'st,
The next, and whereon thy belief hath grown."
      "O saintly sire and spirit!" I began,
"Who seest that, which thou didst so believe,
As to outstrip feet younger than thine own,
Toward the sepulchre? thy will is here,
That I the tenour of my creed unfold;
And thou the cause of it hast likewise ask'd.
And I reply: I in one God believe,
One sole eternal Godhead, of whose love
All heav'n is mov'd, himself unmov'd the while.
Nor demonstration physical alone,
Or more intelligential and abstruse,
Persuades me to this faith; but from that truth
It cometh to me rather, which is shed
Through Moses, the rapt Prophets, and the Psalms.
The Gospel, and that ye yourselves did write,

Dante Alighieri

When ye were gifted of the Holy Ghost.
In three eternal Persons I believe,
Essence threefold and one, mysterious league
Of union absolute, which, many a time,
The word of gospel lore upon my mind
Imprints: and from this germ, this firstling spark,
The lively flame dilates, and like heav'n's star
Doth glitter in me." As the master hears,
Well pleas'd, and then enfoldeth in his arms
The servant, who hath joyful tidings brought,
And having told the errand keeps his peace;
Thus benediction uttering with song
Soon as my peace I held, compass'd me thrice
The apostolic radiance, whose behest
Had op'd lips; so well their answer pleas'd.

CANTO XXV

If e'er the sacred poem that hath made
Both heav'n and earth copartners in its toil,
And with lean abstinence, through many a year,
Faded my brow, be destin'd to prevail
Over the cruelty, which bars me forth
Of the fair sheep-fold, where a sleeping lamb
The wolves set on and fain had worried me,
With other voice and fleece of other grain
I shall forthwith return, and, standing up
At my baptismal font, shall claim the wreath
Due to the poet's temples: for I there
First enter'd on the faith which maketh souls
Acceptable to God: and, for its sake,
Peter had then circled my forehead thus.

    Next from the squadron, whence had issued forth
The first fruit of Christ's vicars on the earth,
Toward us mov'd a light, at view whereof
My Lady, full of gladness, spake to me:
"Lo! lo! behold the peer of mickle might,
That makes Falicia throng'd with visitants!"

    As when the ring-dove by his mate alights,
In circles each about the other wheels,
And murmuring cooes his fondness; thus saw I
One, of the other great and glorious prince,
With kindly greeting hail'd, extolling both
Their heavenly banqueting; but when an end
Was to their gratulation, silent, each,
Before me sat they down, so burning bright,
I could not look upon them. Smiling then,
Beatrice spake: "O life in glory shrin'd!"
Who didst the largess of our kingly court

The Divine Comedy

Set down with faithful pen! let now thy voice
Of hope the praises in this height resound.
For thou, who figur'st them in shapes, as clear,
As Jesus stood before thee, well can'st speak them."
    "Lift up thy head, and be thou strong in trust:
For that, which hither from the mortal world
Arriveth, must be ripen'd in our beam."
    Such cheering accents from the second flame
Assur'd me; and mine eyes I lifted up
Unto the mountains that had bow'd them late
With over-heavy burden. "Sith our Liege
Wills of his grace that thou, or ere thy death,
In the most secret council, with his lords
Shouldst be confronted, so that having view'd
The glories of our court, thou mayst therewith
Thyself, and all who hear, invigorate
With hope, that leads to blissful end; declare,
What is that hope, how it doth flourish in thee,
And whence thou hadst it?" Thus proceeding still,
The second light: and she, whose gentle love
My soaring pennons in that lofty flight
Escorted, thus preventing me, rejoin'd:
Among her sons, not one more full of hope,
Hath the church militant: so 't is of him
Recorded in the sun, whose liberal orb
Enlighteneth all our tribe: and ere his term
Of warfare, hence permitted he is come,
From Egypt to Jerusalem, to see.
The other points, both which thou hast inquir'd,
Not for more knowledge, but that he may tell
How dear thou holdst the virtue, these to him
Leave I; for he may answer thee with ease,
And without boasting, so God give him grace."
Like to the scholar, practis'd in his task,
Who, willing to give proof of diligence,
Seconds his teacher gladly, "Hope," said I,
"Is of the joy to come a sure expectance,
Th' effect of grace divine and merit preceding.
This light from many a star visits my heart,
But flow'd to me the first from him, who sang
The songs of the Supreme, himself supreme
Among his tuneful brethren. 'Let all hope
In thee,' so speak his anthem, 'who have known
Thy name;' and with my faith who know not that?
From thee, the next, distilling from his spring,
In thine epistle, fell on me the drops
So plenteously, that I on others shower
The influence of their dew." Whileas I spake,
A lamping, as of quick and vollied lightning,
Within the bosom of that mighty sheen,

Dante Alighieri

Play'd tremulous; then forth these accents breath'd:
"Love for the virtue which attended me
E'en to the palm, and issuing from the field,
Glows vigorous yet within me, and inspires
To ask of thee, whom also it delights;
What promise thou from hope in chief dost win."
  "Both scriptures, new and ancient," I reply'd;
"Propose the mark (which even now I view)
For souls belov'd of God. Isaias saith,
  That, in their own land, each one must be clad
In twofold vesture; and their proper lands this delicious life.
In terms more full,
And clearer far, thy brother hath set forth
This revelation to us, where he tells
Of the white raiment destin'd to the saints."
And, as the words were ending, from above,
"They hope in thee," first heard we cried: whereto
Answer'd the carols all. Amidst them next,
A light of so clear amplitude emerg'd,
That winter's month were but a single day,
Were such a crystal in the Cancer's sign.
  Like as a virgin riseth up, and goes,
And enters on the mazes of the dance,
Though gay, yet innocent of worse intent,
Than to do fitting honour to the bride;
So I beheld the new effulgence come
Unto the other two, who in a ring
Wheel'd, as became their rapture. In the dance
And in the song it mingled. And the dame
Held on them fix'd her looks: e'en as the spouse
Silent and moveless. "This is he, who lay
Upon the bosom of our pelican:
This he, into whose keeping from the cross
The mighty charge was given." Thus she spake,
Yet therefore naught the more remov'd her Sight
From marking them, or ere her words began,
Or when they clos'd. As he, who looks intent,
And strives with searching ken, how he may see
The sun in his eclipse, and, through desire
Of seeing, loseth power of sight: so I
Peer'd on that last resplendence, while I heard:
"Why dazzlest thou thine eyes in seeking that,
Which here abides not? Earth my body is,
In earth: and shall be, with the rest, so long,
As till our number equal the decree
Of the Most High. The two that have ascended,
In this our blessed cloister, shine alone
With the two garments. So report below."
  As when, for ease of labour, or to shun
Suspected peril at a whistle's breath,

The Divine Comedy

The oars, erewhile dash'd frequent in the wave,
All rest; the flamy circle at that voice
So rested, and the mingling sound was still,
Which from the trinal band soft-breathing rose.
I turn'd, but ah! how trembled in my thought,
When, looking at my side again to see
Beatrice, I descried her not, although
Not distant, on the happy coast she stood.

CANTO XXVI

With dazzled eyes, whilst wond'ring I remain'd,
Forth of the beamy flame which dazzled me,
Issued a breath, that in attention mute
Detain'd me; and these words it spake: "'T were well,
That, long as till thy vision, on my form
O'erspent, regain its virtue, with discourse
Thou compensate the brief delay. Say then,
Beginning, to what point thy soul aspires:
And meanwhile rest assur'd, that sight in thee
Is but o'erpowered a space, not wholly quench'd:
Since thy fair guide and lovely, in her look
Hath potency, the like to that which dwelt
In Ananias' hand." I answering thus:
"Be to mine eyes the remedy or late
Or early, at her pleasure; for they were
The gates, at which she enter'd, and did light
Her never dying fire. My wishes here
Are centered; in this palace is the weal,
That Alpha and Omega, is to all
The lessons love can read me." Yet again
The voice which had dispers'd my fear, when daz'd
With that excess, to converse urg'd, and spake:
"Behooves thee sift more narrowly thy terms,
And say, who level'd at this scope thy bow."

"Philosophy," said I, "hath arguments,
And this place hath authority enough
'T' imprint in me such love: for, of constraint,
Good, inasmuch as we perceive the good,
Kindles our love, and in degree the more,
As it comprises more of goodness in 't.
The essence then, where such advantage is,
That each good, found without it, is naught else
But of his light the beam, must needs attract
The soul of each one, loving, who the truth
Discerns, on which this proof is built. Such truth
Learn I from him, who shows me the first love
Of all intelligential substances
Eternal: from his voice I learn, whose word

Dante Alighieri

Is truth, that of himself to Moses saith,
'I will make all my good before thee pass.'
Lastly from thee I learn, who chief proclaim'st,
E'en at the outset of thy heralding,
In mortal ears the mystery of heav'n."
    "Through human wisdom, and th' authority
Therewith agreeing," heard I answer'd, "keep
The choicest of thy love for God. But say,
If thou yet other cords within thee feel'st
That draw thee towards him; so that thou report
How many are the fangs, with which this love
Is grappled to thy soul." I did not miss,
To what intent the eagle of our Lord
Had pointed his demand; yea noted well
Th' avowal, which he led to; and resum'd:
"All grappling bonds, that knit the heart to God,
Confederate to make fast our clarity.
The being of the world, and mine own being,
The death which he endur'd that I should live,
And that, which all the faithful hope, as I do,
To the foremention'd lively knowledge join'd,
Have from the sea of ill love sav'd my bark,
And on the coast secur'd it of the right.
As for the leaves, that in the garden bloom,
My love for them is great, as is the good
Dealt by th' eternal hand, that tends them all."
    I ended, and therewith a song most sweet
Rang through the spheres; and "Holy, holy, holy,"
Accordant with the rest my lady sang.
And as a sleep is broken and dispers'd
Through sharp encounter of the nimble light,
With the eye's spirit running forth to meet
The ray, from membrane on to the membrane urg'd;
And the upstartled wight loathes that be sees;
So, at his sudden waking, he misdeems
Of all around him, till assurance waits
On better judgment: thus the saintly came
Drove from before mine eyes the motes away,
With the resplendence of her own, that cast
Their brightness downward, thousand miles below.
Whence I my vision, clearer shall before,
Recover'd; and, well nigh astounded, ask'd
Of a fourth light, that now with us I saw.
    And Beatrice: "The first diving soul,
That ever the first virtue fram'd, admires
Within these rays his Maker." Like the leaf,
That bows its lithe top till the blast is blown;
By its own virtue rear'd then stands aloof;
So I, the whilst she said, awe-stricken bow'd.
Then eagerness to speak embolden'd me;

The Divine Comedy

And I began: "O fruit! that wast alone
Mature, when first engender'd! Ancient father!
That doubly seest in every wedded bride
Thy daughter by affinity and blood!
Devoutly as I may, I pray thee hold
Converse with me: my will thou seest; and I,
More speedily to hear thee, tell it not "

    It chanceth oft some animal bewrays,
Through the sleek cov'ring of his furry coat.
The fondness, that stirs in him and conforms
His outside seeming to the cheer within:
And in like guise was Adam's spirit mov'd
To joyous mood, that through the covering shone,
Transparent, when to pleasure me it spake:
"No need thy will be told, which I untold
Better discern, than thou whatever thing
Thou holdst most certain: for that will I see
In Him, who is truth's mirror, and Himself
Parhelion unto all things, and naught else
To him. This wouldst thou hear; how long since God
Plac'd me high garden, from whose hounds
She led me up in this ladder, steep and long;
What space endur'd my season of delight;
Whence truly sprang the wrath that banish'd me;
And what the language, which I spake and fram'd
Not that I tasted of the tree, my son,
Was in itself the cause of that exile,
But only my transgressing of the mark
Assign'd me. There, whence at thy lady's hest
The Mantuan mov'd him, still was I debarr'd
This council, till the sun had made complete,
Four thousand and three hundred rounds and twice,
His annual journey; and, through every light
In his broad pathway, saw I him return,
Thousand save sev'nty times, the whilst I dwelt
Upon the earth. The language I did use
Was worn away, or ever Nimrod's race
Their unaccomplishable work began.
For naught, that man inclines to, ere was lasting,
Left by his reason free, and variable,
As is the sky that sways him. That he speaks,
Is nature's prompting: whether thus or thus,
She leaves to you, as ye do most affect it.
Ere I descended into hell's abyss,
El was the name on earth of the Chief Good,
Whose joy enfolds me: Eli then 't was call'd
And so beseemeth: for, in mortals, use
Is as the leaf upon the bough; that goes,
And other comes instead. Upon the mount
Most high above the waters, all my life,

Both innocent and guilty, did but reach
From the first hour, to that which cometh next
(As the sun changes quarter), to the sixth.

CANTO XXVII

Then "Glory to the Father, to the Son,
And to the Holy Spirit," rang aloud
Throughout all Paradise, that with the song
My spirit reel'd, so passing sweet the strain:
And what I saw was equal ecstasy;
One universal smile it seem'd of all things,
Joy past compare, gladness unutterable,
Imperishable life of peace and love,
Exhaustless riches and unmeasur'd bliss.
  Before mine eyes stood the four torches lit;
And that, which first had come, began to wax
In brightness, and in semblance such became,
As Jove might be, if he and Mars were birds,
And interchang'd their plumes. Silence ensued,
Through the blest quire, by Him, who here appoints
Vicissitude of ministry, enjoin'd;
When thus I heard: "Wonder not, if my hue
Be chang'd; for, while I speak, these shalt thou see
All in like manner change with me. My place
He who usurps on earth (my place, ay, mine,
Which in the presence of the Son of God
Is void), the same hath made my cemetery
A common sewer of puddle and of blood:
The more below his triumph, who from hence
Malignant fell." Such colour, as the sun,
At eve or morning, paints and adverse cloud,
Then saw I sprinkled over all the sky.
And as th' unblemish'd dame, who in herself
Secure of censure, yet at bare report
Of other's failing, shrinks with maiden fear;
So Beatrice in her semblance chang'd:
And such eclipse in heav'n methinks was seen,
When the Most Holy suffer'd. Then the words
Proceeded, with voice, alter'd from itself
So clean, the semblance did not alter more.
"Not to this end was Christ's spouse with my blood,
With that of Linus, and of Cletus fed:
That she might serve for purchase of base gold:
But for the purchase of this happy life
Did Sextus, Pius, and Callixtus bleed,
And Urban, they, whose doom was not without
Much weeping seal'd. No purpose was of our
That on the right hand of our successors

The Divine Comedy

Part of the Christian people should be set,
And part upon their left; nor that the keys,
Which were vouchsaf'd me, should for ensign serve
Unto the banners, that do levy war
On the baptiz'd: nor I, for sigil-mark
Set upon sold and lying privileges;
Which makes me oft to bicker and turn red.
In shepherd's clothing greedy wolves below
Range wide o'er all the pastures. Arm of God!
Why longer sleepst thou? Caorsines and Gascona
Prepare to quaff our blood. O good beginning
To what a vile conclusion must thou stoop!
But the high providence, which did defend
Through Scipio the world's glory unto Rome,
Will not delay its succour: and thou, son,
Who through thy mortal weight shall yet again
Return below, open thy lips, nor hide
What is by me not hidden." As a Hood
Of frozen vapours streams adown the air,
What time the she-goat with her skiey horn
Touches the sun; so saw I there stream wide
The vapours, who with us had linger'd late
And with glad triumph deck th' ethereal cope.
Onward my sight their semblances pursued;
So far pursued, as till the space between
From its reach sever'd them: whereat the guide
Celestial, marking me no more intent
On upward gazing, said, "Look down and see
What circuit thou hast compass'd." From the hour
When I before had cast my view beneath,
All the first region overpast I saw,
Which from the midmost to the bound'ry winds;
That onward thence from Gades I beheld
The unwise passage of Laertes' son,
And hitherward the shore, where thou, Europa!
Mad'st thee a joyful burden: and yet more
Of this dim spot had seen, but that the sun,
A constellation off and more, had ta'en
His progress in the zodiac underneath.

    Then by the spirit, that doth never leave
Its amorous dalliance with my lady's looks,
Back with redoubled ardour were mine eyes
Led unto her: and from her radiant smiles,
Whenas I turn'd me, pleasure so divine
Did lighten on me, that whatever bait
Or art or nature in the human flesh,
Or in its limn'd resemblance, can combine
Through greedy eyes to take the soul withal,
Were to her beauty nothing. Its boon influence
From the fair nest of Leda rapt me forth,

Dante Alighieri

And wafted on into the swiftest heav'n.
    What place for entrance Beatrice chose,
I may not say, so uniform was all,
Liveliest and loftiest. She my secret wish
Divin'd; and with such gladness, that God's love
Seem'd from her visage shining, thus began:
"Here is the goal, whence motion on his race
Starts; motionless the centre, and the rest
All mov'd around. Except the soul divine,
Place in this heav'n is none, the soul divine,
Wherein the love, which ruleth o'er its orb,
Is kindled, and the virtue that it sheds;
One circle, light and love, enclasping it,
As this doth clasp the others; and to Him,
Who draws the bound, its limit only known.
Measur'd itself by none, it doth divide
Motion to all, counted unto them forth,
As by the fifth or half ye count forth ten.
The vase, wherein time's roots are plung'd, thou seest,
Look elsewhere for the leaves. O mortal lust!
That canst not lift thy head above the waves
Which whelm and sink thee down! The will in man
Bears goodly blossoms; but its ruddy promise
Is, by the dripping of perpetual rain,
Made mere abortion: faith and innocence
Are met with but in babes, each taking leave
Ere cheeks with down are sprinkled; he, that fasts,
While yet a stammerer, with his tongue let loose
Gluts every food alike in every moon.
One yet a babbler, loves and listens to
His mother; but no sooner hath free use
Of speech, than he doth wish her in her grave.
So suddenly doth the fair child of him,
Whose welcome is the morn and eve his parting,
To negro blackness change her virgin white.
    "Thou, to abate thy wonder, note that none
Bears rule in earth, and its frail family
Are therefore wand'rers. Yet before the date,
When through the hundredth in his reck'ning drops
Pale January must be shor'd aside
From winter's calendar, these heav'nly spheres
Shall roar so loud, that fortune shall be fain
To turn the poop, where she hath now the prow;
So that the fleet run onward; and true fruit,
Expected long, shall crown at last the bloom!"

The Divine Comedy
CANTO XXVIII

So she who doth imparadise my soul,
Had drawn the veil from off our pleasant life,
And bar'd the truth of poor mortality;
When lo! as one who, in a mirror, spies
The shining of a flambeau at his back,
Lit sudden ere he deem of its approach,
And turneth to resolve him, if the glass
Have told him true, and sees the record faithful
As note is to its metre; even thus,
I well remember, did befall to me,
Looking upon the beauteous eyes, whence love
Had made the leash to take me. As I turn'd;
And that, which, in their circles, none who spies,
Can miss of, in itself apparent, struck
On mine; a point I saw, that darted light
So sharp, no lid, unclosing, may bear up
Against its keenness. The least star we view
From hence, had seem'd a moon, set by its side,
As star by side of star. And so far off,
Perchance, as is the halo from the light
Which paints it, when most dense the vapour spreads,
There wheel'd about the point a circle of fire,
More rapid than the motion, which first girds
The world. Then, circle after circle, round
Enring'd each other; till the seventh reach'd
Circumference so ample, that its bow,
Within the span of Juno's messenger,
Had scarce been held entire. Beyond the sev'nth,
Follow'd yet other two. And every one,
As more in number distant from the first,
Was tardier in motion; and that glow'd
With flame most pure, that to the sparkle' of truth
Was nearest, as partaking most, methinks,
Of its reality. The guide belov'd
Saw me in anxious thought suspense, and spake:
"Heav'n, and all nature, hangs upon that point.
The circle thereto most conjoin'd observe;
And know, that by intenser love its course
Is to this swiftness wing'd. "To whom I thus:
"It were enough; nor should I further seek,
Had I but witness'd order, in the world
Appointed, such as in these wheels is seen.
But in the sensible world such diff'rence is,
That is each round shows more divinity,
As each is wider from the centre. Hence,
If in this wondrous and angelic temple,
That hath for confine only light and love,

Dante Alighieri

My wish may have completion I must know,
Wherefore such disagreement is between
Th' exemplar and its copy: for myself,
Contemplating, I fail to pierce the cause."
    "It is no marvel, if thy fingers foil'd
Do leave the knot untied: so hard 't is grown
For want of tenting." Thus she said: "But take,"
She added, "if thou wish thy cure, my words,
And entertain them subtly. Every orb
Corporeal, doth proportion its extent
Unto the virtue through its parts diffus'd.
The greater blessedness preserves the more.
The greater is the body (if all parts
Share equally) the more is to preserve.
Therefore the circle, whose swift course enwheels
The universal frame answers to that,
Which is supreme in knowledge and in love
Thus by the virtue, not the seeming, breadth
Of substance, measure, thou shalt see the heav'ns,
Each to the' intelligence that ruleth it,
Greater to more, and smaller unto less,
Suited in strict and wondrous harmony."
    As when the sturdy north blows from his cheek
A blast, that scours the sky, forthwith our air,
Clear'd of the rack, that hung on it before,
Glitters; and, With his beauties all unveil'd,
The firmament looks forth serene, and smiles;
Such was my cheer, when Beatrice drove
With clear reply the shadows back, and truth
Was manifested, as a star in heaven.
And when the words were ended, not unlike
To iron in the furnace, every cirque
Ebullient shot forth scintillating fires:
And every sparkle shivering to new blaze,
In number did outmillion the account
Reduplicate upon the chequer'd board.
Then heard I echoing on from choir to choir,
"Hosanna," to the fixed point, that holds,
And shall for ever hold them to their place,
From everlasting, irremovable.
    Musing awhile I stood: and she, who saw
by inward meditations, thus began:
"In the first circles, they, whom thou beheldst,
Are seraphim and cherubim. Thus swift
Follow their hoops, in likeness to the point,
Near as they can, approaching; and they can
The more, the loftier their vision. Those,
That round them fleet, gazing the Godhead next,
Are thrones; in whom the first trine ends. And all
Are blessed, even as their sight descends

The Divine Comedy

Deeper into the truth, wherein rest is
For every mind. Thus happiness hath root
In seeing, not in loving, which of sight
Is aftergrowth. And of the seeing such
The meed, as unto each in due degree
Grace and good-will their measure have assign'd.
The other trine, that with still opening buds
In this eternal springtide blossom fair,
Fearless of bruising from the nightly ram,
Breathe up in warbled melodies threefold
Hosannas blending ever, from the three
Transmitted. hierarchy of gods, for aye
Rejoicing, dominations first, next then
Virtues, and powers the third. The next to whom
Are princedoms and archangels, with glad round
To tread their festal ring; and last the band
Angelical, disporting in their sphere.
All, as they circle in their orders, look
Aloft, and downward with such sway prevail,
That all with mutual impulse tend to God.
These once a mortal view beheld. Desire
In Dionysius so intently wrought,
That he, as I have done rang'd them; and nam'd
Their orders, marshal'd in his thought. From him
Dissentient, one refus'd his sacred read.
But soon as in this heav'n his doubting eyes
Were open'd, Gregory at his error smil'd
Nor marvel, that a denizen of earth
Should scan such secret truth; for he had learnt
Both this and much beside of these our orbs,
From an eye-witness to heav'n's mysteries."

CANTO XXIX

No longer than what time Latona's twins
Cover'd of Libra and the fleecy star,
Together both, girding the' horizon hang,
In even balance from the zenith pois'd,
Till from that verge, each, changing hemisphere,
Part the nice level; e'en so brief a space
Did Beatrice's silence hold. A smile
Bat painted on her cheek; and her fix'd gaze
Bent on the point, at which my vision fail'd:
When thus her words resuming she began:
"I speak, nor what thou wouldst inquire demand;
For I have mark'd it, where all time and place
Are present. Not for increase to himself
Of good, which may not be increas'd, but forth
To manifest his glory by its beams,

Dante Alighieri

Inhabiting his own eternity,
Beyond time's limit or what bound soe'er
To circumscribe his being, as he will'd,
Into new natures, like unto himself,
Eternal Love unfolded. Nor before,
As if in dull inaction torpid lay.
For not in process of before or aft
Upon these waters mov'd the Spirit of God.
Simple and mix'd, both form and substance, forth
To perfect being started, like three darts
Shot from a bow three-corded. And as ray
In crystal, glass, and amber, shines entire,
E'en at the moment of its issuing; thus
Did, from th' eternal Sovran, beam entire
His threefold operation, at one act
Produc'd coeval. Yet in order each
Created his due station knew: those highest,
Who pure intelligence were made: mere power
The lowest: in the midst, bound with strict league,
Intelligence and power, unsever'd bond.
Long tract of ages by the angels past,
Ere the creating of another world,
Describ'd on Jerome's pages thou hast seen.
But that what I disclose to thee is true,
Those penmen, whom the Holy Spirit mov'd
In many a passage of their sacred book
Attest; as thou by diligent search shalt find
And reason in some sort discerns the same,
Who scarce would grant the heav'nly ministers
Of their perfection void, so long a space.
Thus when and where these spirits of love were made,
Thou know'st, and how: and knowing hast allay'd
Thy thirst, which from the triple question rose.
Ere one had reckon'd twenty, e'en so soon
Part of the angels fell: and in their fall
Confusion to your elements ensued.
The others kept their station: and this task,
Whereon thou lookst, began with such delight,
That they surcease not ever, day nor night,
Their circling. Of that fatal lapse the cause
Was the curst pride of him, whom thou hast seen
Pent with the world's incumbrance. Those, whom here
Thou seest, were lowly to confess themselves
Of his free bounty, who had made them apt
For ministries so high: therefore their views
Were by enlight'ning grace and their own merit
Exalted; so that in their will confirm'd
They stand, nor feel to fall. For do not doubt,
But to receive the grace, which heav'n vouchsafes,
Is meritorious, even as the soul

341

The Divine Comedy

With prompt affection welcometh the guest.
Now, without further help, if with good heed
My words thy mind have treasur'd, thou henceforth
This consistory round about mayst scan,
And gaze thy fill. But since thou hast on earth
Heard vain disputers, reasoners in the schools,
Canvas the' angelic nature, and dispute
Its powers of apprehension, memory, choice;
Therefore, 't is well thou take from me the truth,
Pure and without disguise, which they below,
Equivocating, darken and perplex.

    "Know thou, that, from the first, these substances,
Rejoicing in the countenance of God,
Have held unceasingly their view, intent
Upon the glorious vision, from the which
Naught absent is nor hid: where then no change
Of newness with succession interrupts,
Remembrance there needs none to gather up
Divided thought and images remote

    "So that men, thus at variance with the truth
Dream, though their eyes be open; reckless some
Of error; others well aware they err,
To whom more guilt and shame are justly due.
Each the known track of sage philosophy
Deserts, and has a byway of his own:
So much the restless eagerness to shine
And love of singularity prevail.
Yet this, offensive as it is, provokes
Heav'n's anger less, than when the book of God
Is forc'd to yield to man's authority,
Or from its straightness warp'd: no reck'ning made
What blood the sowing of it in the world
Has cost; what favour for himself he wins,
Who meekly clings to it. The aim of all
Is how to shine: e'en they, whose office is
To preach the Gospel, let the gospel sleep,
And pass their own inventions off instead.
One tells, how at Christ's suffering the wan moon
Bent back her steps, and shadow'd o'er the sun
With intervenient disk, as she withdrew:
Another, how the light shrouded itself
Within its tabernacle, and left dark
The Spaniard and the Indian, with the Jew.
Such fables Florence in her pulpit hears,
Bandied about more frequent, than the names
Of Bindi and of Lapi in her streets.
The sheep, meanwhile, poor witless ones, return
From pasture, fed with wind: and what avails
For their excuse, they do not see their harm?
Christ said not to his first conventicle,

'Go forth and preach impostures to the world,'
But gave them truth to build on; and the sound
Was mighty on their lips; nor needed they,
Beside the gospel, other spear or shield,
To aid them in their warfare for the faith.
The preacher now provides himself with store
Of jests and gibes; and, so there be no lack
Of laughter, while he vents them, his big cowl
Distends, and he has won the meed he sought:
Could but the vulgar catch a glimpse the while
Of that dark bird which nestles in his hood,
They scarce would wait to hear the blessing said.
Which now the dotards hold in such esteem,
That every counterfeit, who spreads abroad
The hands of holy promise, finds a throng
Of credulous fools beneath. Saint Anthony
Fattens with this his swine, and others worse
Than swine, who diet at his lazy board,
Paying with unstamp'd metal for their fare.
      "But (for we far have wander'd) let us seek
The forward path again; so as the way
Be shorten'd with the time. No mortal tongue
Nor thought of man hath ever reach'd so far,
That of these natures he might count the tribes.
What Daniel of their thousands hath reveal'd
With finite number infinite conceals.
The fountain at whose source these drink their beams,
With light supplies them in as many modes,
As there are splendours, that it shines on: each
According to the virtue it conceives,
Differing in love and sweet affection.
Look then how lofty and how huge in breadth
The' eternal might, which, broken and dispers'd
Over such countless mirrors, yet remains
Whole in itself and one, as at the first."

CANTO XXX

Noon's fervid hour perchance six thousand miles
From hence is distant; and the shadowy cone
Almost to level on our earth declines;
When from the midmost of this blue abyss
By turns some star is to our vision lost.
And straightway as the handmaid of the sun
Puts forth her radiant brow, all, light by light,
Fade, and the spangled firmament shuts in,
E'en to the loveliest of the glittering throng.
Thus vanish'd gradually from my sight
The triumph, which plays ever round the point,

That overcame me, seeming (for it did)
Engirt by that it girdeth. Wherefore love,
With loss of other object, forc'd me bend
Mine eyes on Beatrice once again.

    If all, that hitherto is told of her,
Were in one praise concluded, 't were too weak
To furnish out this turn. Mine eyes did look
On beauty, such, as I believe in sooth,
Not merely to exceed our human, but,
That save its Maker, none can to the full
Enjoy it. At this point o'erpower'd I fail,
Unequal to my theme, as never bard
Of buskin or of sock hath fail'd before.
For, as the sun doth to the feeblest sight,
E'en so remembrance of that witching smile
Hath dispossess my spirit of itself.
Not from that day, when on this earth I first
Beheld her charms, up to that view of them,
Have I with song applausive ever ceas'd
To follow, but not follow them no more;
My course here bounded, as each artist's is,
When it doth touch the limit of his skill.

    She (such as I bequeath her to the bruit
Of louder trump than mine, which hasteneth on,
Urging its arduous matter to the close),
Her words resum'd, in gesture and in voice
Resembling one accustom'd to command:
"Forth from the last corporeal are we come
Into the heav'n, that is unbodied light,
Light intellectual replete with love,
Love of true happiness replete with joy,
Joy, that transcends all sweetness of delight.
Here shalt thou look on either mighty host
Of Paradise; and one in that array,
Which in the final judgment thou shalt see."

    As when the lightning, in a sudden spleen
Unfolded, dashes from the blinding eyes
The visive spirits dazzled and bedimm'd;
So, round about me, fulminating streams
Of living radiance play'd, and left me swath'd
And veil'd in dense impenetrable blaze.
Such weal is in the love, that stills this heav'n;
For its own flame the torch this fitting ever!

    No sooner to my list'ning ear had come
The brief assurance, than I understood
New virtue into me infus'd, and sight
Kindled afresh, with vigour to sustain
Excess of light, however pure. I look'd;
And in the likeness of a river saw
Light flowing, from whose amber-seeming waves

Dante Alighieri

Flash'd up effulgence, as they glided on
'Twixt banks, on either side, painted with spring,
Incredible how fair; and, from the tide,
There ever and anon, outstarting, flew
Sparkles instinct with life; and in the flow'rs
Did set them, like to rubies chas'd in gold;
Then, as if drunk with odors, plung'd again
Into the wondrous flood; from which, as one
Re'enter'd, still another rose. "The thirst
Of knowledge high, whereby thou art inflam'd,
To search the meaning of what here thou seest,
The more it warms thee, pleases me the more.
But first behooves thee of this water drink,
Or ere that longing be allay'd." So spake
The day-star of mine eyes; then thus subjoin'd:
"This stream, and these, forth issuing from its gulf,
And diving back, a living topaz each,
With all this laughter on its bloomy shores,
Are but a preface, shadowy of the truth
They emblem: not that, in themselves, the things
Are crude; but on thy part is the defect,
For that thy views not yet aspire so high."
Never did babe, that had outslept his wont,
Rush, with such eager straining, to the milk,
As I toward the water, bending me,
To make the better mirrors of mine eyes
In the refining wave; and, as the eaves
Of mine eyelids did drink of it, forthwith
Seem'd it unto me turn'd from length to round,
Then as a troop of maskers, when they put
Their vizors off, look other than before,
The counterfeited semblance thrown aside;
So into greater jubilee were chang'd
Those flowers and sparkles, and distinct I saw
Before me either court of heav'n displac'd.

    O prime enlightener! thou who crav'st me strength
On the high triumph of thy realm to gaze!
Grant virtue now to utter what I kenn'd,
   There is in heav'n a light, whose goodly shine
Makes the Creator visible to all
Created, that in seeing him alone
Have peace; and in a circle spreads so far,
That the circumference were too loose a zone
To girdle in the sun. All is one beam,
Reflected from the summit of the first,
That moves, which being hence and vigour takes,
And as some cliff, that from the bottom eyes
Its image mirror'd in the crystal flood,
As if 't admire its brave appareling
Of verdure and of flowers: so, round about,

Eyeing the light, on more than million thrones,
Stood, eminent, whatever from our earth
Has to the skies return'd. How wide the leaves
Extended to their utmost of this rose,
Whose lowest step embosoms such a space
Of ample radiance! Yet, nor amplitude
Nor height impeded, but my view with ease
Took in the full dimensions of that joy.
Near or remote, what there avails, where God
Immediate rules, and Nature, awed, suspends
Her sway? Into the yellow of the rose
Perennial, which in bright expansiveness,
Lays forth its gradual blooming, redolent
Of praises to the never-wint'ring sun,
As one, who fain would speak yet holds his peace,
Beatrice led me; and, "Behold," she said,
"This fair assemblage! stoles of snowy white
How numberless! The city, where we dwell,
Behold how vast! and these our seats so throng'd
Few now are wanting here! In that proud stall,
On which, the crown, already o'er its state
Suspended, holds thine eyes--or ere thyself
Mayst at the wedding sup,--shall rest the soul
Of the great Harry, he who, by the world
Augustas hail'd, to Italy must come,
Before her day be ripe. But ye are sick,
And in your tetchy wantonness as blind,
As is the bantling, that of hunger dies,
And drives away the nurse. Nor may it be,
That he, who in the sacred forum sways,
Openly or in secret, shall with him
Accordant walk: Whom God will not endure
I' th' holy office long; but thrust him down
To Simon Magus, where Magna's priest
Will sink beneath him: such will be his meed."

CANTO XXXI

In fashion, as a snow-white rose, lay then
Before my view the saintly multitude,
Which in his own blood Christ espous'd. Meanwhile
That other host, that soar aloft to gaze
And celebrate his glory, whom they love,
Hover'd around; and, like a troop of bees,
Amid the vernal sweets alighting now,
Now, clustering, where their fragrant labour glows,
Flew downward to the mighty flow'r, or rose
From the redundant petals, streaming back
Unto the steadfast dwelling of their joy.

Dante Alighieri

Faces had they of flame, and wings of gold;
The rest was whiter than the driven snow.
And as they flitted down into the flower,
From range to range, fanning their plumy loins,
Whisper'd the peace and ardour, which they won
From that soft winnowing. Shadow none, the vast
Interposition of such numerous flight
Cast, from above, upon the flower, or view
Obstructed aught. For, through the universe,
Wherever merited, celestial light
Glides freely, and no obstacle prevents.
    All there, who reign in safety and in bliss,
Ages long past or new, on one sole mark
Their love and vision fix'd. O trinal beam
Of individual star, that charmst them thus,
Vouchsafe one glance to gild our storm below!
    If the grim brood, from Arctic shores that roam'd,
(Where helice, forever, as she wheels,
Sparkles a mother's fondness on her son)
Stood in mute wonder 'mid the works of Rome,
When to their view the Lateran arose
In greatness more than earthly; I, who then
From human to divine had past, from time
Unto eternity, and out of Florence
To justice and to truth, how might I choose
But marvel too? 'Twixt gladness and amaze,
In sooth no will had I to utter aught,
Or hear. And, as a pilgrim, when he rests
Within the temple of his vow, looks round
In breathless awe, and hopes some time to tell
Of all its goodly state: e'en so mine eyes
Cours'd up and down along the living light,
Now low, and now aloft, and now around,
Visiting every step. Looks I beheld,
Where charity in soft persuasion sat,
Smiles from within and radiance from above,
And in each gesture grace and honour high.
    So rov'd my ken, and its general form
All Paradise survey'd: when round I turn'd
With purpose of my lady to inquire
Once more of things, that held my thought suspense,
But answer found from other than I ween'd;
For, Beatrice, when I thought to see,
I saw instead a senior, at my side,
 Rob'd, as the rest, in glory. Joy benign
Glow'd in his eye, and o'er his cheek diffus'd,
With gestures such as spake a father's love.
And, "Whither is she vanish'd?" straight I ask'd.
    "By Beatrice summon'd," he replied,
"I come to aid thy wish. Looking aloft

The Divine Comedy

To the third circle from the highest, there
Behold her on the throne, wherein her merit
Hath plac'd her." Answering not, mine eyes I rais'd,
And saw her, where aloof she sat, her brow
A wreath reflecting of eternal beams.
Not from the centre of the sea so far
Unto the region of the highest thunder,
As was my ken from hers; and yet the form
Came through that medium down, unmix'd and pure,

"O Lady! thou in whom my hopes have rest!
Who, for my safety, hast not scorn'd, in hell
To leave the traces of thy footsteps mark'd!
For all mine eyes have seen, I, to thy power
And goodness, virtue owe and grace. Of slave,
Thou hast to freedom brought me; and no means,
For my deliverance apt, hast left untried.
Thy liberal bounty still toward me keep.
That, when my spirit, which thou madest whole,
Is loosen'd from this body, it may find
Favour with thee." So I my suit preferr'd:
And she, so distant, as appear'd, look'd down,
And smil'd; then tow'rds th' eternal fountain turn'd.

And thus the senior, holy and rever'd:
"That thou at length mayst happily conclude
Thy voyage (to which end I was dispatch'd,
By supplication mov'd and holy love)
Let thy upsoaring vision range, at large,
This garden through: for so, by ray divine
Kindled, thy ken a higher flight shall mount;
And from heav'n's queen, whom fervent I adore,
All gracious aid befriend us; for that I
Am her own faithful Bernard." Like a wight,
Who haply from Croatia wends to see
Our Veronica, and the while 't is shown,
Hangs over it with never-sated gaze,
And, all that he hath heard revolving, saith
Unto himself in thought: "And didst thou look
E'en thus, O Jesus, my true Lord and God?
And was this semblance thine?" So gaz'd I then
Adoring; for the charity of him,
Who musing, in the world that peace enjoy'd,
Stood lively before me. "Child of grace!"
Thus he began: "thou shalt not knowledge gain
Of this glad being, if thine eyes are held
Still in this depth below. But search around
The circles, to the furthest, till thou spy
Seated in state, the queen, that of this realm
Is sovran." Straight mine eyes I rais'd; and bright,
As, at the birth of morn, the eastern clime
Above th' horizon, where the sun declines;

To mine eyes, that upward, as from vale
To mountain sped, at th' extreme bound, a part
Excell'd in lustre all the front oppos'd.
And as the glow burns ruddiest o'er the wave,
That waits the sloping beam, which Phaeton
Ill knew to guide, and on each part the light
Diminish'd fades, intensest in the midst;
So burn'd the peaceful oriflamb, and slack'd
On every side the living flame decay'd.
And in that midst their sportive pennons wav'd
Thousands of angels; in resplendence each
Distinct, and quaint adornment. At their glee
And carol, smil'd the Lovely One of heav'n,
That joy was in the eyes of all the blest.
   Had I a tongue in eloquence as rich,
As is the colouring in fancy's loom,
'T were all too poor to utter the least part
Of that enchantment. When he saw mine eyes
Intent on her, that charm'd him, Bernard gaz'd
With so exceeding fondness, as infus'd
Ardour into my breast, unfelt before.

CANTO XXXII

Freely the sage, though wrapt in musings high,
Assum'd the teacher's part, and mild began:
"The wound, that Mary clos'd, she open'd first,
Who sits so beautiful at Mary's feet.
The third in order, underneath her, lo!
Rachel with Beatrice. Sarah next,
Judith, Rebecca, and the gleaner maid,
Meek ancestress of him, who sang the songs
Of sore repentance in his sorrowful mood.
All, as I name them, down from deaf to leaf,
Are in gradation throned on the rose.
And from the seventh step, successively,
Adown the breathing tresses of the flow'r
Still doth the file of Hebrew dames proceed.
For these are a partition wall, whereby
The sacred stairs are sever'd, as the faith
In Christ divides them. On this part, where blooms
Each leaf in full maturity, are set
Such as in Christ, or ere he came, believ'd.
On th' other, where an intersected space
Yet shows the semicircle void, abide
All they, who look'd to Christ already come.
And as our Lady on her glorious stool,
And they who on their stools beneath her sit,
This way distinction make: e'en so on his,

The Divine Comedy

The mighty Baptist that way marks the line
(He who endur'd the desert and the pains
Of martyrdom, and for two years of hell,
Yet still continued holy), and beneath,
Augustin, Francis, Benedict, and the rest,
Thus far from round to round. So heav'n's decree
Forecasts, this garden equally to fill.
With faith in either view, past or to come,
Learn too, that downward from the step, which cleaves
Midway the twain compartments, none there are
Who place obtain for merit of their own,
But have through others' merit been advanc'd,
On set conditions: spirits all releas'd,
Ere for themselves they had the power to choose.
And, if thou mark and listen to them well,
Their childish looks and voice declare as much.
     "Here, silent as thou art, I know thy doubt;
And gladly will I loose the knot, wherein
Thy subtle thoughts have bound thee. From this realm
Excluded, chalice no entrance here may find,
No more shall hunger, thirst, or sorrow can.
A law immutable hath establish'd all;
Nor is there aught thou seest, that doth not fit,
Exactly, as the finger to the ring.
It is not therefore without cause, that these,
O'erspeedy comers to immortal life,
Are different in their shares of excellence.
Our Sovran Lord--that settleth this estate
In love and in delight so absolute,
That wish can dare no further--every soul,
Created in his joyous sight to dwell,
With grace at pleasure variously endows.
And for a proof th' effect may well suffice.
And 't is moreover most expressly mark'd
In holy scripture, where the twins are said
To, have struggled in the womb. Therefore, as grace
Inweaves the coronet, so every brow
Weareth its proper hue of orient light.
And merely in respect to his prime gift,
Not in reward of meritorious deed,
Hath each his several degree assign'd.
In early times with their own innocence
More was not wanting, than the parents' faith,
To save them: those first ages past, behoov'd
That circumcision in the males should imp
The flight of innocent wings: but since the day
Of grace hath come, without baptismal rites
In Christ accomplish'd, innocence herself
Must linger yet below. Now raise thy view
Unto the visage most resembling Christ:

Dante Alighieri

For, in her splendour only, shalt thou win
The pow'r to look on him." Forthwith I saw
Such floods of gladness on her visage shower'd,
From holy spirits, winging that profound;
That, whatsoever I had yet beheld,
Had not so much suspended me with wonder,
Or shown me such similitude of God.
And he, who had to her descended, once,
On earth, now hail'd in heav'n; and on pois'd wing.
"Ave, Maria, Gratia Plena," sang:
To whose sweet anthem all the blissful court,
From all parts answ'ring, rang: that holier joy
Brooded the deep serene. "Father rever'd:
Who deign'st, for me, to quit the pleasant place,
Wherein thou sittest, by eternal lot!
Say, who that angel is, that with such glee
Beholds our queen, and so enamour'd glows
Of her high beauty, that all fire he seems."
So I again resorted to the lore
Of my wise teacher, he, whom Mary's charms
Embellish'd, as the sun the morning star;
Who thus in answer spake: "In him are summ'd,
Whatever of buxomness and free delight
May be in Spirit, or in angel, met:
And so beseems: for that he bare the palm
Down unto Mary, when the Son of God
Vouchsaf'd to clothe him in terrestrial weeds.
Now let thine eyes wait heedful on my words,
And note thou of this just and pious realm
The chiefest nobles. Those, highest in bliss,
The twain, on each hand next our empress thron'd,
Are as it were two roots unto this rose.
He to the left, the parent, whose rash taste
Proves bitter to his seed; and, on the right,
That ancient father of the holy church,
Into whose keeping Christ did give the keys
Of this sweet flow'r: near whom behold the seer,
That, ere he died, saw all the grievous times
Of the fair bride, who with the lance and nails
Was won. And, near unto the other, rests
The leader, under whom on manna fed
Th' ungrateful nation, fickle and perverse.
On th' other part, facing to Peter, lo!
Where Anna sits, so well content to look
On her lov'd daughter, that with moveless eye
She chants the loud hosanna: while, oppos'd
To the first father of your mortal kind,
Is Lucia, at whose hest thy lady sped,
When on the edge of ruin clos'd thine eye.

"But (for the vision hasteneth so an end)
Here break we off, as the good workman doth,
That shapes the cloak according to the cloth:
And to the primal love our ken shall rise;
That thou mayst penetrate the brightness, far
As sight can bear thee. Yet, alas! in sooth
Beating thy pennons, thinking to advance,
Thou backward fall'st. Grace then must first be gain'd;
Her grace, whose might can help thee. Thou in prayer
Seek her: and, with affection, whilst I sue,
Attend, and yield me all thy heart." He said,
And thus the saintly orison began.

CANTO XXXIII

"O virgin mother, daughter of thy Son,
Created beings all in lowliness
Surpassing, as in height, above them all,
Term by th' eternal counsel pre-ordain'd,
Ennobler of thy nature, so advanc'd
In thee, that its great Maker did not scorn,
Himself, in his own work enclos'd to dwell!
For in thy womb rekindling shone the love
Reveal'd, whose genial influence makes now
This flower to germin in eternal peace!
Here thou to us, of charity and love,
Art, as the noon-day torch: and art, beneath,
To mortal men, of hope a living spring.
So mighty art thou, lady! and so great,
That he who grace desireth, and comes not
To thee for aidance, fain would have desire
Fly without wings. Nor only him who asks,
Thy bounty succours, but doth freely oft
Forerun the asking. Whatsoe'er may be
Of excellence in creature, pity mild,
Relenting mercy, large munificence,
Are all combin'd in thee. Here kneeleth one,
Who of all spirits hath review'd the state,
From the world's lowest gap unto this height.
Suppliant to thee he kneels, imploring grace
For virtue, yet more high to lift his ken
Toward the bliss supreme. And I, who ne'er
Coveted sight, more fondly, for myself,
Than now for him, my prayers to thee prefer,
(And pray they be not scant) that thou wouldst drive
Each cloud of his mortality away;
That on the sovran pleasure he may gaze.
This also I entreat of thee, O queen!
Who canst do what thou wilt! that in him thou

Dante Alighieri

Wouldst after all he hath beheld, preserve
Affection sound, and human passions quell.
Lo! Where, with Beatrice, many a saint
Stretch their clasp'd hands, in furtherance of my suit!"
     The eyes, that heav'n with love and awe regards,
Fix'd on the suitor, witness'd, how benign
She looks on pious pray'rs: then fasten'd they
On th' everlasting light, wherein no eye
Of creature, as may well be thought, so far
Can travel inward. I, meanwhile, who drew
Near to the limit, where all wishes end,
The ardour of my wish (for so behooved),
Ended within me. Beck'ning smil'd the sage,
That I should look aloft: but, ere he bade,
Already of myself aloft I look'd;
For visual strength, refining more and more,
Bare me into the ray authentical
Of sovran light. Thenceforward, what I saw,
Was not for words to speak, nor memory's self
To stand against such outrage on her skill.
As one, who from a dream awaken'd, straight,
All he hath seen forgets; yet still retains
Impression of the feeling in his dream;
E'en such am I: for all the vision dies,
As 't were, away; and yet the sense of sweet,
That sprang from it, still trickles in my heart.
Thus in the sun-thaw is the snow unseal'd;
Thus in the winds on flitting leaves was lost
The Sybil's sentence. O eternal beam!
(Whose height what reach of mortal thought may soar?)
Yield me again some little particle
Of what thou then appearedst, give my tongue
Power, but to leave one sparkle of thy glory,
Unto the race to come, that shall not lose
Thy triumph wholly, if thou waken aught
Of memory in me, and endure to hear
The record sound in this unequal strain.
     Such keenness from the living ray I met,
That, if mine eyes had turn'd away, methinks,
I had been lost; but, so embolden'd, on
I pass'd, as I remember, till my view
Hover'd the brink of dread infinitude.
     O grace! unenvying of thy boon! that gav'st
Boldness to fix so earnestly my ken
On th' everlasting splendour, that I look'd,
While sight was unconsum'd, and, in that depth,
Saw in one volume clasp'd of love, whatever
The universe unfolds; all properties
Of substance and of accident, beheld,
Compounded, yet one individual light

The Divine Comedy

The whole. And of such bond methinks I saw
The universal form: for that whenever
I do but speak of it, my soul dilates
Beyond her proper self; and, till I speak,
One moment seems a longer lethargy,
Than five-and-twenty ages had appear'd
To that emprize, that first made Neptune wonder
At Argo's shadow darkening on his flood.

    With fixed heed, suspense and motionless,
Wond'ring I gaz'd; and admiration still
Was kindled, as I gaz'd. It may not be,
That one, who looks upon that light, can turn
To other object, willingly, his view.
For all the good, that will may covet, there
Is summ'd; and all, elsewhere defective found,
Complete. My tongue shall utter now, no more
E'en what remembrance keeps, than could the babe's
That yet is moisten'd at his mother's breast.
Not that the semblance of the living light
Was chang'd (that ever as at first remain'd)
But that my vision quickening, in that sole
Appearance, still new miracles descry'd,
And toil'd me with the change. In that abyss
Of radiance, clear and lofty, seem'd methought,
Three orbs of triple hue clipt in one bound:
And, from another, one reflected seem'd,
As rainbow is from rainbow: and the third
Seem'd fire, breath'd equally from both. Oh speech
How feeble and how faint art thou, to give
Conception birth! Yet this to what I saw
Is less than little. Oh eternal light!
Sole in thyself that dwellst; and of thyself
Sole understood, past, present, or to come!
Thou smiledst; on that circling, which in thee
Seem'd as reflected splendour, while I mus'd;
For I therein, methought, in its own hue
Beheld our image painted: steadfastly
I therefore por'd upon the view. As one
Who vers'd in geometric lore, would fain
Measure the circle; and, though pondering long
And deeply, that beginning, which he needs,
Finds not; e'en such was I, intent to scan
The novel wonder, and trace out the form,
How to the circle fitted, and therein
How plac'd: but the flight was not for my wing;
Had not a flash darted athwart my mind,
And in the spleen unfolded what it sought.

Dante Alighieri

    Here vigour fail'd the tow'ring fantasy:
But yet the will roll'd onward, like a wheel
In even motion, by the Love impell'd,
That moves the sun in heav'n and all the stars.

NOTES TO PARADISE

CANTO 1

Verse 12. Benign Apollo.] Chaucer has imitated this invention very closely at the beginning of the Third Booke of Fame. If, divine vertue, thou Wilt helpe me to shewe now That in my head ymarked is, * * * * * Thou shalt see me go as blive Unto the next laurer I see, And kisse it for it is thy tree Now entre thou my breast anone.

v. 15. Thus for.] He appears to mean nothing more than that this part of his poem will require a greater exertion of his powers than the former.

v. 19. Marsyas.] Ovid, Met. 1. vi. fab. 7. Compare Boccaccio, II Filocopo, 1. 5. p. 25. v. ii. Ediz. Fir. 1723. "Egli nel mio petto entri," &c. - "May he enter my bosom, and let my voice sound like his own, when he made that daring mortal deserve to come forth unsheathed from his limbs. "

v. 29. Caesar, or bard.] So Petrarch, Son. Par. Prima. Arbor vittoriosa e trionfale, Onor d'imperadori e di poeti. And Spenser, F. Q. b. i. c. 1. st. 9, The laurel, meed of mighty conquerours And poets sage.

v. 37. Through that.] "Where the four circles, the horizon, the zodiac, the equator, and the equinoctial colure, join; the last three intersecting each other so as to form three crosses, as may be seen in the armillary sphere."

v. 39. In happiest constellation.] Aries. Some understand the planet Venus by the "miglior stella "

v. 44. To the left.]
Being in the opposite hemisphere to ours, Beatrice that she may behold the rising sun, turns herself to the left.

v. 47. As from the first a second beam.]
"Like a reflected sunbeam," which he compares to a pilgrim hastening homewards.

Ne simil tanto mal raggio secondo Dal primo usci. Filicaja, canz. 15. st. 4.

v. 58. As iron that comes boiling from the fire.]
So Milton, P. L. b. iii.

594. --As glowing iron with fire.

v. 69. Upon the day appear'd.

--If the heaven had ywonne, All new of God another sunne. Chaucer, First Booke of Fame

E par ch' agginuga un altro sole al cielo. Ariosto, O F. c. x. st. 109.

Ed ecco un lustro lampeggiar d' intorno Che sole a sole aggiunse e giorno a giorno. Manno, Adone.

c. xi. st. 27.

Quando a paro col sol ma piu lucente L'angelo gli appari sull; oriente Tasso, G. L. c. i.

-Seems another morn Ris'n on mid-noon. Milton, P. L. b. v. 311.

Compare Euripides, Ion. 1550.

[GREEK HERE] 66. as Glaucus.] Ovid, Met. 1. Xiii. Fab. 9

v. 71. If.] "Thou O divine Spirit, knowest whether I had not risen above my human nature, and were not merely such as thou hadst then, formed me."

v. 125. Through sluggishness.] Perch' a risponder la materia e sorda.
So Filicaja, canz.

vi. st 9. Perche a risponder la discordia e sorda

"The workman hath in his heart a purpose, he carrieth in mind the whole form which his work should have; there wanteth not him skill and desire to bring his labour to the best effect, only the matter, which he hath to work on is unframeable." Hooker's Eccl. Polity, b. 5. 9.

CANTO II

v. 1. In small bark.]
Con la barchetta mia cantando in rima Pulci, Morg. Magg. c. xxviii.

Io me n'andro con la barchetta mia, Quanto l'acqua comporta un picciol legno Ibid.

v. 30. This first star.] the moon

v. 46. E'en as the truth.] Like a truth that does not need demonstration, but is self-evident."

v. 52. Cain.] Compare Hell, Canto XX. 123. And Note

v. 65. Numberless lights.] The fixed stars, which differ both in bulk and splendor.

v. 71. Save one.]
"Except that principle of rarity and denseness which thou hast assigned."

By "formal principles, "principj formali, are meant constituent or essential causes." Milton, in imitation of this passage, introduces the angel arguing with Adam respecting the causes of the spots on the moon.

But, as a late French translator of the Paradise well remarks, his reasoning is physical; that of Dante partly metaphysical and partly theologic.

v. 111 Within the heaven.]
According to our Poet's system, there are ten heavens; the seven planets, the eighth spheres containing the fixed stars, the primum mobile, and the empyrean.

v. 143. The virtue mingled.]
Virg. Aen. 1. vi 724. Principio coelum, &c.

CANTO III

v. 16. Delusion.]
"An error the contrary to that of Narcissus, because he mistook a shadow for a substance, I a substance for a shadow."

v. 50. Piccarda.]
The sister of Forese whom we have seen in the Purgatory, Canto XXIII.

v. 90. The Lady.] St. Clare, the foundress of the order called after her She was born of opulent and noble parents at Assisi, in 1193, and died in 1253.
See Biogr. Univ. t. 1. p. 598. 8vo. Paris, 1813.

v. 121. Constance.]

Daughter of Ruggieri, king of Sicily, who, being taken by force out of a monastery where she had professed, was married to the Emperor Henry Vl. and by him was mother to Frederick 11. She was fifty years old or more at the time, and "because it was not credited that she could have a child at that age, she was delivered in a pavilion and it was given out, that any lady, who pleased, was at liberty to see her.

Many came, and saw her, and the suspicion ceased."

Ricordano Malaspina in Muratori, Rer. It. Script. t. viii.

p. 939; and G. Villani, in the same words, Hist. I v. c. 16

The French translator above mentored speaks of her having poisoned her husband.

The death of Henry Vl. is recorded in the Chronicon Siciliae, by an anonymous writer, (Muratori, t. x.) but not a word of his having been poisoned by Constance, and Ricordano Malaspina even mentions her decease as happening before that of her husband, Henry V., for so this author, with some others, terms him. v. 122.

The second.]

Henry Vl. son of Frederick I was the second emperor of the house of Saab; and his son Frederick II "the third and last."

CANTO IV

v. 6. Between two deer]

Tigris ut auditis, diversa valle duorum Extimulata fame, mugitibus armentorum Neseit utro potius ruat, et ruere ardet utroque. Ovid, Metam. 1. v. 166

v. 13. Daniel.] See Daniel, c. ii.

v. 24. Plato.]

[GREEK HERE]

Plato Timaeus v. ix. p. 326. Edit. Bip.

"The Creator, when he had framed the universe, distributed to the stars an equal number of souls, appointing to each soul its several star."

v. 27. Of that.] Plato's opinion.

v. 34. The first circle.] The empyrean.

v. 48. Him who made Tobias whole.]

Raphael, the sociable spirit, that deign'd To travel with Tobias, and secur'd His marriage with the sev'n times wedded maid, Milton, P. L. b. v. 223.

v. 67. That to the eye of man.]

"That the ways of divine justice are often inscrutable to man, ought rather to be a motive to faith than an inducement to heresy." Such appears to me the most satisfactory explanation of the passage.

v. 82. Laurence.]

Who suffered martyrdom in the third century.

v. 82. Scaevola.] See Liv. Hist. D. 1. 1. ii. 12.

v. 100. Alcmaeon.] Ovid, Met. 1. ix. f. 10.

--Ultusque parente parentem Natus, erit facto pius et sceleratus eodem.

v. 107. Of will.]

"What Piccarda asserts of Constance, that she retained her affection to the monastic life, is said absolutely and without relation to circumstances; and that which I affirm is spoken of the will conditionally and respectively: so that our apparent difference is without any disagreement."

v. 119. That truth.] The light of divine truth.

CANTO V

v. 43. Two things.]
The one, the substance of the vow; the other, the compact, or form of it.

v. 48. It was enjoin'd the Israelites.]
See Lev. e. xii, and xxvii.

v. 56. Either key.]
Purgatory, Canto IX. 108.

v. 86. That region.]
As some explain it, the east, according to others the equinoctial line.

v. 124. This sphere.]
The planet Mercury, which, being nearest to the sun, is oftenest hidden by that luminary

CANTO VI

v. 1. After that Constantine the eagle turn'd.]
Constantine, in transferring the seat of empire from Rome to Byzantium, carried the eagle, the Imperial ensign, from the west to the east. Aeneas, on the contrary had moved along with the sun's course, when he passed from Troy to Italy.

v. 5. A hundred years twice told and more.]
The Emperor Constantine entered Byzantium in 324, and Justinian began his reign in 527.

v. 6. At Europe's extreme point.]
Constantinople being situated at the extreme of Europe, and on the borders of Asia, near those mountains in the neighbourhood of Troy, from whence the first founders of Rome had emigrated.

v. 13. To clear th' incumber'd laws.]
The code of laws was abridged and reformed by Justinian.

v. 15. Christ's nature merely human.]
Justinian is said to have been a follower of the heretical Opinions held by Eutyches," who taught that in Christ there was but one nature, viz. that of the incarnate word." Maclaine's Mosheim, t. ii. Cent. v. p. ii. c. v. 13.

v. 16. Agapete.]
Agapetus, Bishop of Rome, whose Scheda Regia, addressed to the Emperor Justinian, procured him a place among the wisest and most judicious writers of this century." Ibid. Cent. vi. p. ii c. ii. 8.

v. 33. Who pretend its power.]
The Ghibellines.

v. 33. And who oppose]
The Guelphs.

v. 34. Pallas died.]
See Virgil, Aen. 1. X.

v. 39. The rival three.]
The Horatii and Curiatii.

v. 41. Down.]
"From the rape of the Sabine women to the violation of Lucretia."

v. 47. Quintius.] Quintius Cincinnatus.

E Cincinnato dall' inculta chioma. Petrarca.

v. 50. Arab hordes.]
The Arabians seem to be put for the barbarians in general.

v. 54. That hill.]
The city of Fesulae, which was sacked by the Romans after the defeat of Cataline.

v. 56. Near the hour.]
Near the time of our Saviour's birth.

v. 59. What then it wrought.]
In the following fifteen lines the Poet has comprised the exploits of Julius Caesar.

v. 75. In its next bearer's gripe.] With Augustus Caesar.

v. 89. The third Caesar.]
"Tiberius the third of the Caesars, had it in his power to surpass the glory of all who either preceded or came after him, by destroying the city of Jerusalem, as Titus afterwards did, and thus revenging the cause of God himself on the Jews."

v. 95. Vengeance for vengeance]
This will be afterwards explained by the Poet himself.

v. 98. Charlemagne.]
Dante could not be ignorant that the reign of Justinian was long prior to that of Charlemagne; but the spirit of the former emperor is represented, both in this instance and in what follows, as conscious of the events that had taken place after his own time.

v. 104. The yellow lilies.]
The French ensign.

v. 110. Charles.]
The commentators explain this to mean Charles II, king of Naples and Sicily. Is it not more likely to allude to Charles of Valois, son of Philip III of France, who was sent for, about this time, into Italy by Pope Boniface, with the promise of being made emperor? See G. Villani, 1. viii. c. 42.

v. 131. Romeo's light.]
The story of Romeo is involved in some uncertainty.

The French writers assert the continuance of his ministerial office even after the decease of his soverign Raymond Berenger, count of Provence: and they rest this assertion chiefly on the fact of a certain Romieu de Villeneuve, who was the contemporary of that prince, having left large possessions behind him, as appears by his will, preserved in the archives of the bishopric of Venice.

There might however have been more than one person of the name of Romieu, or Romeo which answers to that of Palmer in our language.

Nor is it probable that the Italians, who lived so near the time, were misinformed in an occurrence of such notoriety. According to them, after he had long been a faithful steward to Raymond, when an account was required from him of the revenues whichhe had carefully husbanded, and his master as lavishly disbursed, "He demanded the little mule, the staff, and the scrip, with which he had first entered into the count's service, a stranger pilgrim from the shrine of St. James in Galicia, and parted as he came; nor was it ever known whence he was or wither he went." G. Villani, 1. vi. c. 92.

v. 135. Four daughters.]
Of the four daughters of Raymond Berenger, Margaret, the eldest, was married to Louis IX of France; Eleanor; the next, to Henry III, of England; Sancha, the third, to Richard, Henry's brother, and King of the Romans; and the youngest, Beatrice, to Charles I, King of Naples and Sicily, and brother to Louis.

v. 136. Raymond Berenger.]
This prince, the last of the house of Barcelona, who was count of Provence, died in 1245.

He is in the list of Provencal poets.
See Millot, Hist, Litt des Troubadours, t. ii. P. 112.

CANTO VII
v. 3. Malahoth.]
A Hebrew word, signifying "kingdoms."
v. 4. That substance bright.] Justinian.
v. 17. As might have made one blest amid the flames.] So Giusto de' Conti, Bella Mano. "Qual salamandra."
Che puommi nelle fiammi far beato.
v. 23. That man who was unborn.]
Adam.
v. 61. What distils.]
"That which proceeds immediately from God, and without intervention of secondary causes, in immortal."
v. 140. Our resurrection certain.]
"Venturi appears to mistake the Poet's reasoning, when he observes:
"Wretched for us, if we had not arguments more convincing, and of a higher kind, to assure us of the truth of our resurrection."

It is here intended, I think, that the whole of God's dispensations to man should be considered as a proof of our resurrection.

The conclusion is that as before sin man was immortal, so being restored to the favor of heaven by the expiation made for sin, he necessarily recovers his claim to immortality.

There is much in this poem to justify the encomium which the learned Salvini has passed on it, when, in an epistle to Redi, imitating what Horace had said of Homer, that the duties of life might be better learnt from the Grecian bard than from the teachers of the porch or the academy, he says--

And dost thou ask, what themes my mind engage? The lonely hours I give to Dante's page; And meet more sacred learning in his lines Than I had gain'd from all the school divines.

Se volete saper la vita mia, Studiando io sto lungi da tutti gli nomini Ed ho irnparato piu teologia In questi giorni, che ho riletto Dante, Che nelle scuole fattto io non avria.

CANTO VIII
v. 4. Epicycle,]
"In sul dosso di questo cerchio," &c. Convito di Dante, Opere, t. i. p. 48, ed. Ven. 1793. "Upon the back of this circle, in the heaven of Venus, whereof

The Divine Comedy

we are now treating, is a little sphere, which has in that heaven a revolution of its own: whose circle the astronomers term epicycle."

v. 11. To sit in Dido's bosom.]
Virgil. Aen. 1. i. 718,

v. 40. 'O ye whose intellectual ministry.] Voi ch' intendendo il terzo ciel movete. The first line in our Poet" first canzone.

See his Convito, Ibid. p. 40.

v. 53. had the time been more.]

The spirit now speaking is Charles Martel crowned king of Hungary, and son of Charles 11 king of Naples and Sicily, to which dominions dying in his father's lifetime, he did not succeed.

v. 57. Thou lov'dst me well.]

Charles Martel might have been known to our poet at Florence whither he came to meet his father in 1295, the year of his death.

The retinue and the habiliments of the young monarch are minutely described by G. Villani, who adds, that "he remained more than twenty days in Florence, waiting for his father King Charles and his brothers during which time great honour was done him by the, Florentines and he showed no less love towards them, and he was much in favour with all." 1.

viii. c. 13. His brother Robert, king of Naples, was the friend of Petrarch.

v. 60. The left bank.]
Provence.

v. 62. That horn Of fair Ausonia.] The kingdom of Naples.

v. 68. The land.]
Hungary.

v. 73. The beautiful Trinaeria.]

Sicily, so called from its three promontories, of which Pachynus and Pelorus, here mentioned, are two.

v. 14 'Typhaeus.]

The giant whom Jupiter is fabled to have overwhelmed under the mountain Aetna from whence he vomits forth smoke and flame.

v. 77. Sprang through me from Charles and Rodolph.]

"Sicily would be still ruled by a race of monarchs, descended through me from Charles I and Rodolph I the former my grandfather king of Naples and Sicily; the latter emperor of Germany, my father-in-law; "both celebrated in the Purgatory Canto, Vll.

v. 78. Had not ill lording.]

"If the ill conduct of our governors in Sicily had not excited the resentment and hatred of the people and stimulated them to that dreadful massacre at the Sicilian vespers;" in consequence of which the kingdom fell into the hands of Peter III of Arragon, in 1282

v. 81. My brother's foresight.]

He seems to tax his brother Robert with employing necessitous and greedy Catalonians to administer the affairs of his kingdom.

v. 99. How bitter can spring up.]

"How a covetous son can spring from a liberal father."

Yet that father has himself been accused of avarice in the Purgatory Canto XX. v. 78; though his general character was that of a bounteous prince.

v. 125. Consult your teacher.]
Aristole.

[GREEK HERE] De Rep. 1. iii. c. 4. "Since a state is made up of members differing from one another, (for even as an animal, in the first instance, consists of soul and body, and the soul, of reason and desire; and a family, of man and woman, and property of master and slave; in like manner a state consists both of all these and besides these of other dissimilar kinds,)

it necessarily follows that the excellence of all the members of the state cannot be one and the same."

v. 136. Esau.]
Genesis c. xxv. 22.
v. 137. Quirinus.]
Romulus, born of so obscure a father, that his parentage was attributed to Mars.

CANTO IX

v. 2. O fair Clemenza.] Daughter of Charles Martel, and second wife of Louis X. of France.

v. 2. The treachery.]
He alludes to the occupation of the kingdom of Sicily by Robert, in exclusion of his brother s son Carobert, or Charles. Robert, the rightful heir.
See G. Villani, 1. viii. c. 112.

v. 7. That saintly light.]
Charles Martel.

v. 25. In that part.]
Between Rialto and the Venetian territory, and the sources of the rivers Brenta and Piava is situated a castle called Romano, the birth-place of the famous tyrant Ezzolino or Azzolino, the brother of Cunizza, who is now speaking. The tyrant we have seen in "the river of blood."
Hell, Canto XII. v. 110.

v. 32. Cunizza.]
The adventures of Cunizza, overcome by the influence of her star, are related by the chronicler Rolandino of Padua, 1. i. c. 3, in Muratori Rer. It. Script. t. viii. p. 173. She eloped from her first husband, Richard of St. Boniface, in the company of Sordello, (see Purgatory, Canto VI. and VII.) with whom she is supposed to have cohabited before her marriage: then lived with a soldier of Trevigi, whose wife was living at the same time in the same city, and on his being murdered by her brother the tyrant, was by her brother married to a nobleman of Braganzo, lastly when he also had fallen by the same hand she, after her brother's death, was again wedded in Verona.

v. 37. This.]
Folco of Genoa, a celebrated Provencal poet, commonly termed Folques of Marseilles, of which place he was perhaps bishop. Many errors of Nostradamus, regarding him, which have been followed by Crescimbeni, Quadrio, and Millot, are detected by the diligence of Tiraboschi.
Mr. Matthias's ed. v. 1. P. 18.

All that appears certain, is what we are told in this Canto, that he was of Genoa, and by Petrarch in the Triumph of Love, c. iv.

that he was better known by the appellation he derived from Marseilles, and at last resumed the religious habit. One of his verses is cited by Dante, De Vulg. Eloq. 1. ii. c. 6.

v. 40. Five times.]

The five hundred years are elapsed: and unless the Provencal MSS. should be brought to light the poetical reputation of Folco must rest on the mention made of him by the more fortunate Italians.

v. 43 The crowd.]

The people who inhabited the tract of country bounded by the river Tagliamento to the east, and Adice to the west.

v. 45. The hour is near.]

Cunizza foretells the defeat of Giacopo da Carrara, Lord of Padua by Can Grande, at Vicenza, on the 18th September 1314.

See G. Villani, 1. ix. c. 62.

v. 48. One.]

She predicts also the fate of Ricciardo da Camino, who is said to have been murdered at Trevigi, where the rivers (Sile and Cagnano meet) while he was engaged in playing at chess.

v. 50. The web.]

The net or snare into, which he is destined to fall.

v. 50. Feltro.]

The Bishop of Felto having received a number of fugitives from Ferrara, who were in opposition to the Pope, under a promise of protection, afterwards gave them up, so that they were reconducted to that city, and the greater part of them there put to death.

v. 53. Malta's.]

A tower, either in the citadel of Padua, which under the tyranny of Ezzolino, had been "with many a foul and midnight murder fed," or (as some say) near a river of the same name, that falls into the lake of Bolsena, in which the Pope was accustomed to imprison such as had been guilty of an irremissible sin.

v. 56 This priest.]

The bishop, who, to show himself a zealous partisan of the Pope, had committed the above-mentioned act of treachery.

v. 58. We descry.]

"We behold the things that we predict, in the mirrors of eternal truth."

v. 64. That other joyance.]

Folco.

v. 76. Six shadowing wings.]

"Above it stood the seraphims: each one had six wings." Isaiah, c. vi. 2.

v. 80. The valley of waters.]

The Mediterranean sea.

v. 80. That.]

The great ocean.

v. 82. Discordant shores.]

Europe and Africa.

v. 83. Meridian.]

Extending to the east, the Mediterranean at last reaches the coast of Palestine, which is on its horizon when it enters the straits of Gibraltar. "Wherever a man is," says Vellutello, "there he has, above his head, his own particular meridian circle."

v. 85. --'Twixt Ebro's stream And Macra's.] Eora, a river to the west, and Macra, to the east of Genoa, where Folco was born.

v. 88. Begga.]
A place in Africa, nearly opposite to Genoa.

v. 89. Whose haven.]
Alluding to the terrible slaughter of the Genoese made by the Saracens in 936, for which event Vellutello refers to the history of Augustino Giustiniani.

v. 91. This heav'n.]
The planet Venus.

v. 93. Belus' daughter.]
Dido.

v. 96. She of Rhodope.]
Phyllis.

v. 98. Jove's son.]
Hercules.

v. 112. Rahab.]
Heb. c. xi. 31.

v. 120. With either palm.]
"By the crucifixion of Christ"

v. 126. The cursed flower.]
The coin of Florence, called the florin.

v. 130. The decretals.]
The canon law.

v. 134. The Vatican.]
He alludes either to the death of Pope Boniface VIII. or, as Venturi supposes, to the coming of the Emperor Henry VII. into Italy, or else, according to the yet more probable conjecture of Lombardi, to the transfer of the holy see from Rome to Avignon, which took place in the pontificate of Clement V.

CANTO X

v. 7. The point.]
"To that part of heaven," as Venturi explains it, "in which the equinoctial circle and the Zodiac intersect each other, where the common motion of the heavens from east to west may be said to strike with greatest force against the motion proper to the planets; and this repercussion, as it were, is here the strongest, because the velocity of each is increased to the utmost by their respective distance from the poles. Such at least is the system of Dante."

v. 11. Oblique.]
The zodiac.

v. 25. The part.]
The above-mentioned intersection of the equinoctial circle and the zodiac.

v. 26. Minister.]
The sun.

v. 30. Where.]
In which the sun rises every day earlier after the vernal equinox.

v. 45. Fourth family.]
The inhabitants of the sun, the fourth planet.

v. 46. Of his spirit and of his offspring.]
The procession of the third, and the generation of the second person in the Trinity.

v. 70. Such was the song.]
"The song of these spirits was ineffable.

v. 86. No less constrained.]
"The rivers might as easily cease to flow towards the sea, as we could deny thee thy request."

v. 91. I then.]
"I was of the Dominican order."

v. 95. Albert of Cologne.]
Albertus Magnus was born at Laugingen, in Thuringia, in 1193, and studied at Paris and at Padua, at the latter of which places he entered into the Dominican order.

He then taught theology in various parts of Germany, and particularly at Cologne. Thomas Aquinas was his favourite pupil.

In 1260, he reluctantly accepted the bishopric of Ratisbon, and in two years after resigned it, and returned to his cell in Cologne, where the remainder of his life was passed in superintending the school, and in composing his voluminous works on divinity and natural science.

He died in 1280.

The absurd imputation of his having dealt in the magical art is well known; and his biographers take some pains to clear him of it.

Scriptores Ordinis Praedicatorum, by Quetif and Echard, Lut. Par. 1719. fol. t. 1. p. 162.

v. 96. Of Aquinum, Thomas.]
Thomas Aquinas, of whom Bucer is reported to have said, "Take but Thomas away, and I will overturn the church of Rome," and whom Hooker terms "the greatest among the school divines," (Eccl. Pol. b. 3. 9), was born of noble parents, who anxiously, but vainly, endeavoured to divert him from a life of celibacy and study; and died in 1274, at the age of forty-seven. Echard and Quetif, ibid. p. 271. See also Purgatory Canto XX. v. 67.

v. 101. Gratian.]
"Gratian, a Benedictine monk belonging to the convent of St. Felix and Nabor, at Bologna, and by birth a Tuscan, composed, about the year 1130, for the use of the schools, an abridgment or epitome of canon law, drawn from the letters of the pontiffs, the decrees of councils, and the writings of the ancient doctors." Maclaine's Mosheim, v. iii. cent. 12. part 2. c. i. 6.

v. 101. To either forum.]
"By reconciling," as Venturi explains it "the civil with the canon law."

v. 104. Peter.]
"Pietro Lombardo was of obscure origin, nor is the place of his birth in Lombardy ascertained.

With a recommendation from the bishop of Lucca to St. Bernard, he went into France to continue his studies, and for that purpose remained some time at Rheims, whence he afterwards proceeded to Paris.

Here his reputation was so great that Philip, brother of Louis VII., being chosen bishop of Paris, resigned that dignity to Pietro, whose pupil he had been. He held his bishopric only one year, and died in 1160.

His Liber Sententiarum is highly esteemed.

It contains a system of scholastic theology, so much more complete than any which had been yet seen, that it may be deemed an original work."

Tiraboschi, Storia della Lett. Ital. t. iii. 1. 4. c. 2.

v. 104. Who with the widow gave.]
This alludes to the beginning of the Liber Sententiarum, where Peter says: "Cupiens aliquid de penuria ac tenuitate nostra cum paupercula in gazophylacium domini mittere,"

v. 105. The fifth light.]
Solomon.

v. 112. That taper's radiance.]
St. Dionysius the Areopagite. "The famous Grecian fanatic, who gave himself out for Dionysius the Areopagite, disciple of St. Paul, and who, under the protection of this venerable name, gave laws and instructions to those that were desirous of raising their souls above all human things in order to unite them to their great source by sublime contemplation, lived most probably in this century (the fourth), though some place him before, others after, the present period." Maclaine's Mosheim, v. i. cent. iv. p. 2. c. 3. 12.

v. 116. That pleader.]
In the fifth century, Paulus Orosius, "acquired a considerable degree of reputation by the History he wrote to refute the cavils of the Pagans against Christianity, and by his books against the Pelagians and Priscillianists." Ibid. v. ii. cent. v. p. 2. c. 2. 11.

A similar train of argument was pursued by
Augustine, in his book De Civitate Dei. Orosius is classed by Dante, in his treatise De Vulg. Eloq.

l ii c. 6. as one of his favourite authors, among those "qui usi sunt altissimas prosas,"--" who have written prose with the greatest loftiness of style."

v. 119. The eighth.]
Boetius, whose book De Consolatione Philosophiae excited so much attention during the middle ages, was born, as
Tiraboschi conjectures, about 470.
"In 524 he was cruelly put to death by command of Theodoric, either on real or pretended suspicion of his being engaged in a conspiracy." Della Lett. Ital. t. iii. 1. i. c. 4.

v. 124. Cieldauro.]
Boetius was buried at Pavia, in the monastery of St. Pietro in Ciel d'oro.

v. 126. Isidore.]
He was Archbishop of Seville during forty years, and died in 635.
See Mariana, Hist. 1.

vi. c. 7. Mosheim, whose critical opinions in general must be taken with some allowance, observes that "his grammatical theological, and historical productions, discover more learning and pedantry, than judgment and taste."

v. 127. Bede.]
Bede, whose virtues obtained him the appellation of the Venerable, was born in 672 at Wearmouth and Jarrow, in the bishopric of Durham, and died in 735.

Invited to Rome by Pope Sergius I., he preferred passing almost the whole of his life in the seclusion of a monastery.

A catalogue of his numerous writings may be seen in Kippis's Biographia Britannica, v. ii.

v. 127. Richard.]
Richard of St. Victor, a native either of Scotland or Ireland, was canon and prior of the monastery of that name at Paris and died in 1173.

"He was at the head of the Mystics in this century and his treatise, entitled the Mystical Ark, which contains as it were the marrow of this kind of theology, was received with the greatest avidity."

Maclaine's Mosheim, v. iii. cent. xii. p. 2. c. 2. 23.

v. 132. Sigebert.]
"A monk of the abbey of Gemblours who was in high repute at the end of the eleventh, and beginning of the twelfth century." Dict. de Moreri.

v. 131. The straw-litter'd street.]
The name of a street in Paris: the "Rue du Fouarre."

v. 136. The spouse of God.]
The church.

CANTO XI

v. 1. O fond anxiety of mortal men.]
Lucretius, 1. ii. 14
O miseras hominum mentes ! O pectora caeca Qualibus in tenebris vitae quantisque periclis Degitur hoc aevi quodcunque est!

v. 4. Aphorisms,]
The study of medicine.

v. 17. 'The lustre.]
The spirit of Thomas Aquinas

v. 29. She.]
The church.

v. 34. One.]
Saint Francis.

v. 36. The other.]
Saint Dominic.

v. 40. Tupino.]
A rivulet near Assisi, or Ascesi where Francis was born in 1182.

v. 40. The wave.]
Chiascio, a stream that rises in a mountain near Agobbio, chosen by St. Ubaldo for the place of his retirement.

v. 42. Heat and cold.]
Cold from the snow, and heat from the reflection of the sun.

v. 45. Yoke.]
Vellutello understands this of the vicinity of the mountain to Nocera and Gualdo; and Venturi (as I have taken it) of the heavy impositions laid on those places by the Perugians. For GIOGO, like the Latin JUGUM, will admit of either sense.

v. 50. The east.]
This is the east, and Juliet is the sun. Shakespeare.

v. 55. Gainst his father's will.]
In opposition to the wishes of his natural father

v. 58. In his father's sight.]
The spiritual father, or bishop, in whose presence he made a profession of poverty.

v. 60. Her first husband.]
Christ.

v. 63. Amyclas.]
Lucan makes Caesar exclaim, on witnessing the secure poverty of the fisherman Amyclas:

--O vite tuta facultas Pauperis, angustique lares!
O munera nondum Intellecta deum!
quibus hoc contingere templis, Aut potuit muris, nullo trepidare tumultu, Caesarea pulsante manu? Lucan Phars. 1. v. 531.

v. 72. Bernard.]
One of the first followers of the saint.

v. 76. Egidius.]
The third of his disciples, who died in 1262. His work, entitled Verba Aurea, was published in 1534, at Antwerp See Lucas Waddingus, Annales Ordinis Minoris, p. 5.

v. 76. Sylvester.]
Another of his earliest associates.

v. 83. Pietro Bernardone.]
A man in an humble station of life at Assisi.

v. 86. Innocent.]
Pope Innocent III.

v. 90. Honorius.]
His successor Honorius III who granted certain privileges to the Franciscans.

v. 93. On the hard rock.]
The mountain Alverna in the Apennine.

v. 100. The last signet.]
Alluding to the stigmata, or marks resembling the wounds of Christ, said to have been found on the saint's body.

v. 106. His dearest lady.]
Poverty.

v. 113. Our Patriarch]
Saint Dominic.

v. 316. His flock] The Dominicans.

v. 127. The planet from whence they split.]
"The rule of their order, which the Dominicans neglect to observe."

CANTO XII

v. 1. The blessed flame.]
Thomas Aquinas

v. 12. That voice.]
The nymph Echo, transformed into the repercussion of the voice.

v. 25. One.]
Saint Buonaventura, general of the Franciscan order, in which he effected some reformation, and one of the most profound divines of his age.

"He refused the archbishopric of York, which was offered him by Clement IV, but afterwards was prevailed on to accept the bishopric of Albano and a cardinal's hat.

He was born at Bagnoregio or Bagnorea, in Tuscany, A.D. 1221, and died in 1274."

Dict. Histor. par Chaudon et Delandine. Ed. Lyon. 1804.

v. 28. The love.]

By an act of mutual courtesy, Buonaventura, a Franciscan, is made to proclaim the praises of St. Dominic, as Thomas Aquinas, a Dominican, has celebrated those of St. Francis.

v. 42. In that clime.]

Spain.

v. 48. Callaroga.]

Between Osma and Aranda, in Old Castile, designated by the royal coat of arms.

v. 51. The loving minion of the Christian faith.]

Dominic was born April 5, 1170, and died August 6, 1221.

His birthplace, Callaroga; his father and mother's names, Felix and Joanna, his mother's dream; his name of Dominic, given him in consequence of a vision by a noble matron, who stood sponsor to him, are all told in an anonymous life of the saint, said to be written in the thirteenth century, and published by Quetif and Echard, Scriptores Ordinis Praedicatorum.

Par. 1719. fol. t 1.

p. 25. These writers deny his having been an inquisitor, and indeed the establishment of the inquisition itself before the fourth Lateran council.

Ibid. p. 88.

v. 55. In the mother's womb.]

His mother, when pregnant with him, is said to have dreamt that she should bring forth a white and black dog, with a lighted torch in its mouth.

v. 59. The dame.]

His godmother's dream was, that he had one star in his forehead, and another in the nape of his neck, from which he communicated light to the east and the west.

v. 73. Felix.]

Felix Gusman.

v. 75. As men interpret it.]

Grace or gift of the Lord.

v. 77. Ostiense.]

A cardinal, who explained the decretals.

v. 77. Taddeo.]

A physician, of Florence.

v. 82. The see.]

"The apostolic see, which no longer continues its wonted liberality towards the indigent and deserving; not indeed

through its own fault, as its doctrines are still the same, but through the fault of the pontiff, who is seated in it."

v. 85. No dispensation.]

Dominic did not ask license to compound for the use of unjust acquisitions, by dedicating a part of them to pious purposes.

v. 89. In favour of that seed.]

"For that seed of the divine word, from which have sprung up these four-and-twenty plants, that now environ thee."

v. 101. But the track.]
"But the rule of St. Francis is already deserted and the lees of the wine are turned into mouldiness."

v. 110. Tares.]
He adverts to the parable of the taxes and the wheat.

v. 111. I question not.]
"Some indeed might be found, who still observe the rule of the order, but such would come neither from Casale nor Acquasparta:" of the former of which places was Uberto, one master general, by whom the discipline had been relaxed; and of the latter, Matteo, another, who had enforced it with unnecessary rigour.

v. 121. -Illuminato here, And Agostino.] Two among the earliest followers of St. Francis.

v. 125. Hugues of St. Victor.]
A Saxon of the monastery of Saint
Victor at Paris, who fed ill 1142 at the age of forty-four.
"A man distinguished by the fecundity of his genius, who treated in his writings of all the branches of sacred and profane erudition that were known in his time, and who composed several dissertations that are not destitute of merit." Maclaine's Mosheim, Eccl. Hist. v. iii . cent. xii. p. 2. 2. 23. I have looked into his writings, and found some reason for this high eulogium.

v. 125. Piatro Mangiadore.]
"Petrus Comestor, or the Eater, born at Troyes, was canon and dean of that church, and afterwards chancellor of the church of Paris.
He relinquished these benefices to become a regular canon of St. Victor at Paris, where he died in 1198.
Chaudon et Delandine Dict. Hist. Ed. Lyon. 1804. The work by which he is best known, is his Historia Scolastica, which I shall have occasion to cite in the Notes to Canto XXVI.

v. 126. He of Spain.]
"To Pope Adrian V succeeded John XXI a native of Lisbon a man of great genius and extraordinary acquirements, especially in logic and in medicine, as his books, written in the name of Peter of Spain (by which he was known before he became Pope), may testify.
His life was not much longer than that of his predecessors, for he was killed at Viterbo, by the falling in of the roof of his chamber, after he had been pontiff only eight months and as many days. A.D. 1277.
Mariana, Hist. de Esp. l. xiv. c. 2.

v. 128. Chrysostom.]
The eloquent patriarch of Constantinople.

v. 128. Anselmo.]
"Anselm, Archbishop of Canterbury, was born at Aosta, about 1034, and studied under Lanfrane at the monastery of Bec, in Normandy, where he afterwards devoted himself to a religious life, in his twenty-seventh year.
In three years he was made prior, and then abbot of that monastery!
from whence he was taken, in 1093, to succeed to the archbishopric, vacant by the death of Lanfrane. He enjoyed this dignity till his death, in 1109, though it was disturbed by many dissentions with William II and Henry I respecting the immunities and investitures.

There is much depth and precisian in his theological works." Tiraboschi, Stor. della Lett. Ital. t. iii. 1. iv. c. 2. Ibid. c. v.

"It is an observation made by many modern writers, that the demonstration of the existence of God, taken from the idea of a Supreme Being, of which Des Cartes is thought to be the author, was so many ages back discovered and brought to light by Anselm.

Leibnitz himself makes the remark, vol. v. Oper. p. 570. Edit. Genev. 1768."

v. 129. Donatus.]

Aelius Donatus, the grammarian, in the fourth century, one of the preceptors of St. Jerome.

v. 130. Raban.]

"Rabanus Maurus, Archbishop of Mentz, is deservedly placed at the head of the Latin writers of this age." Mosheim, v. ii. cent. ix. p. 2 c. 2. 14.

v. 131. Joachim.]

Abbot of Flora in Calabria; "whom the multitude revered as a person divinely inspired and equal to the most illustrious prophets of ancient times."

Ibid. v. iii. cent. xiii. p. 2. c. 2. 33.

v. 134. A peer.]

St. Dominic.

CANTO XIII

v. 1. Let him.]

"Whoever would conceive the sight that now presented itself to me, must imagine to himself fifteen of the brightest stars in heaven, together with seven stars of Arcturus Major and two of Arcturus Minor, ranged in two circles, one within the other, each resembling the crown of Ariadne, and moving round m opposite directions."

v. 21. The Chiava.]

See Hell, Canto XXIX. 45.

v. 29. That luminary.]

Thomas Aquinas.

v. 31. One ear.]

"Having solved one of thy questions, I proceed to answer the other.

Thou thinkest, then, that Adam and Christ were both endued with all the perfection of which the human nature is capable and therefore wonderest at what has been said concerning Solomon"

v. 48. That.]

"Things corruptible and incorruptible, are only emanations from the archetypal idea residing in the Divine mind."

v. 52. His brightness.]

The Word: the Son of God.

v. 53. His love triune with them.]

The Holy Ghost.

v. 55. New existences.]

Angels and human souls.

v. 57. The lowest powers.]

Irrational life and brute matter.

v. 62. Their wax and that which moulds it.]
Matter, and the virtue or energy that acts on it.
v. 68. The heav'n.]
The influence of the planetary bodies.
v. 77. The clay.]
Adam.
v. 88. Who ask'd.]
"He did not desire to know the number of the stars, or to pry into the subtleties of metaphysical and mathematical science: but asked for that wisdom which might fit him for his kingly office."

v. 120. --Parmenides Melissus Bryso.] For the singular opinions entertained by the two former of these heathen philosophers, see Diogenes Laertius, 1. ix. and Aristot. de Caelo, 1. iii. c. 1 and Phys. l. i. c. 2. The last is also twice adduced by 2. Aristotle (Anal Post. 1. i. c. 9. and Rhet. 1. iii. c. 2.) as 3. affording instances of false reasoning.

v. 123. Sabellius, Arius.]
Well-known heretics.

v. 124. Scymitars.] A passage in the travels of Bertradon de la Brocquiere, translated by Mr. Johnes, will explain this allusion, which has given some trouble to the commentators.

That traveler, who wrote before Dante, informs us, p. 138, that the wandering Arabs used their scymitars as mirrors.

v. 126. Let not.]
"Let not short-sighted mortals presume to decide on the future doom of any man, from a consideration of his present character and actions."

CANTO XIV

v. 5. Such was the image.]
The voice of Thomas Aquinas proceeding, from the circle to the centre and that of Beatrice from the centre to the circle.

v. 26. Him.]
Literally translated by Chaucer, Troilus and Cresseide.
Thou one two, and three eterne on live That raignest aie in three, two and one Uncircumscript, and all maist circonscrive,

v. 81. The goodliest light.]
Solomon.

v. 78. To more lofty bliss.]
To the planet Mars.

v. 94. The venerable sign.]
The cross.

v. 125. He.]
"He who considers that the eyes of Beatrice became more radiant the higher we ascended, must not wonder that I do not except even them as I had not yet beheld them since our entrance into this planet."

The Divine Comedy
CANTO XV

v. 24. Our greater Muse.]
Virgil Aen.
1. vi. 684.
v. 84. I am thy root.]
Cacciaguida, father to Alighieri, of whom our Poet was the great-grandson.
v. 89. The mountain.]
Purgatory.
v. 92. Florence.]
See G. Villani, l. iii. c. 2.
v. 93. Which calls her still.]
The public clock being still within the circuit of the ancient walls.
v. 98. When.]
When the women were not married at too early an age, and did not expect too large a portion.
v. 101. Void.]
Through the civil wars.
v. 102 Sardanapalus.]
The luxurious monarch of Assyria Juvenal is here imitated, who uses his name for an instance of effeminacy.
Sat.
v. 103. Montemalo] Either an elevated spot between Rome and Viterbo, or Monte Mario, the site of the villa Mellini, commanding a view of Rome.
v. 101. Our suburban turret.]
Uccellatojo, near Florence, from whence that city was discovered.
v. 103. Bellincion Berti.]
Hell, Canto XVI. 38. nd Notes. There is a curious description of the simple manner in which the earlier Florentines dressed themselves in G. Villani, l vi. c. 71.
v. 110. Of Nerli and of Vecchio.]
Two of the most opulent families in Florence.
v. 113. Each.]
"None fearful either of dying in banishment, or of being deserted by her husband on a scheme of battle in France.
v. 120. A Salterello and Cianghella.]
The latter a shameless woman of the family of Tosa, married to Lito degli Alidosi of Imola: the former Lapo Salterello, a lawyer, with whom Dante was at variance.
v. 125. Mary.]
The Virgin was involved in the pains of child-birth Purgatory, Canto XX. 21.
v. 130 Valdipado.]
Cacciaguida's wife, whose family name was Aldighieri; came from Ferrara, called Val di Pado, from its being watered by the Po.
v. 131. Conrad.]
The Emperor Conrad III who died in 1152. See G. Villani, l. iv. 34.
v. 136. Whose people.] The Mahometans, who were left in possession of the Holy Land, through the supineness of the Pope.

CANTO XVI

v. 10. With greeting.]
The Poet, who had addressed the spirit, not knowing him to be his ancestor, with a plain "Thou," now uses more ceremony, and calls him "You," according to a custom introduced among the Romans in the latter times of the empire.

v. 15. Guinever.]
Beatrice's smile encouraged him to proceed just as the cough of Ginevra's female servant gave her mistress assurance to admit the freedoms of Lancelot.
See Hell, Canto V. 124.

v. 23. The fold.]
Florence, of which John the Baptist was the patron saint.

v. 31. From the day.]
From the Incarnation to the birth of Cacciaguida, the planet Mars had returned five hundred and fifty-three times to the constellation of Leo, with which it is supposed to have a congenial influence.
His birth may, therefore, be placed about 1106.

v. 38. The last.]
The city was divided into four compartments. The Elisei, the ancestors of Dante, resided near the entrance of that named from the Porta S. Piero, which was the last reached by the competitor in the annual race at Florence.
See G. Villani, 1. iv. c. 10.

v. 44. From Mars.]
"Both in the times of heathenish and of Christianity."
Hell, Canto XIII. 144.

v. 48. Campi and Certaldo and Fighine.]
Country places near Florence.

v. 50. That these people.]
That the inhabitants of the above- mentioned places had not been mixed with the citizens: nor the limits of Florence extended beyond Galluzzo and Trespiano."

v. 54. Aguglione's hind and Signa's.]
Baldo of Aguglione, and Bonifazio of Signa.

v. 56. Had not the people.]
If Rome had continued in her allegiance to the emperor, and the Guelph and Ghibelline factions had thus been prevented, Florence would not have been polluted by a race of upstarts, nor lost the most respectable of her ancient families.

v. 61. Simifonte.]
A castle dismantled by the Florentines.
G. Villani, 1. v. c. 30.
The individual here alluded to is no longer known.

v. 69. The blind bull.]
So Chaucer, Troilus and Cresseide. b. 2.
For swifter course cometh thing that is of wight When it descendeth than done things light.
Compare Aristotle, Ethic. Nic. l. vi. c. 13.
[GREEK HERE]

v. 72. Luni, Urbisaglia.]
Cities formerly of importance, but then fallen to decay.

v. 74. Chiusi and Sinigaglia.]
The same.

v. 80. As the moon.]
"The fortune of us, that are the moon's men doth ebb and flow like the sea."
Shakespeare, 1 Henry IV. a. i. s. 2.

v. 86. The Ughi.]
Whoever is curious to know the habitations of these and the other ancient Florentines, may consult G. Villani, l. iv.

v. 91. At the poop.]
Many editions read porta, "gate." -The same metaphor is found in Aeschylus, Supp. 356, and is there also scarce understood by the critics. [GREEK HERE] Respect these wreaths, that crown your city's poop.

v. 99. The gilded hilt and pommel.]
The symbols of knighthood

v. 100. The column cloth'd with verrey.]
The arms of the Pigli.

v. 103. With them.]
Either the Chiaramontesi, or the Tosinghi one of which had committed a fraud in measuring out the wheat from the public granary.
See Purgatory, Canto XII. 99

v. 109. The bullets of bright gold.]
The arms of the Abbati, as it is conjectured.

v. 110. The sires of those.]
"Of the Visdomini, the Tosinghi and the Cortigiani, who, being sprung from the founders of the bishopric of Florence are the curators of its revenues, which they do not spare, whenever it becomes vacant."

v. 113. Th' o'erweening brood.]
The Adimari.
This family was so little esteemed, that Ubertino Donato, who had married a daughter of Bellincion Berti, himself indeed derived from the same stock (see Note to Hell Canto XVI. 38.) was offended with his father-in-law, for giving another of his daughters in marriage to one of them.

v. 124. The gateway.]
Landino refers this to the smallness of the city: Vellutello, with less probability, to the simplicity of the people in naming one of the gates after a private family.

v. 127. The great baron.]
The Marchese Ugo, who resided at Florence as lieutenant of the Emperor Otho III, gave many of the chief families license to bear his arms.
See G. Villani, 1.
iv. c. 2., where the vision is related, in consequence of which he sold all his possessions in Germany, and founded seven abbeys, in one whereof his memory was celebrated at Florence on St. Thomas's day.

v. 130. One.]
Giano della Bella, belonging to one of the families thus distinguished, who no longer retained his place among the nobility, and had yet added to his arms a bordure or. See Macchiavelli, 1st.
Fior. 1. ii. p. 86. Ediz. Giolito.

v. 132. -Gualterotti dwelt And Importuni.] Two families in the compartment of the city called Borgo.

v. 135. The house.]
Of Amidei.
See Notes to Canto XXVIII. of Hell. v. 102.

v. 142. To Ema.]
"It had been well for the city, if thy ancestor had been drowned in the Ema, when he crossed that stream on his way from Montebuono to Florence."

v. 144. On that maim'd stone.]
See Hell, Canto XIII. 144. Near the remains of the statue of Mars.
Buondelmonti was slain, as if he had been a victim to the god; and Florence had not since known the blessing of peace.

v. 150. The lily.]
"The arms of Florence had never hung reversed on the spear of her enemies, in token of her defeat; nor been changed from argent to gules;" as they afterwards were, when the Guelfi gained the predominance.

CANTO XVII

v. 1. The youth.]
Phaeton, who came to his mother Clymene, to inquire of her if he were indeed the son of Apollo.
See Ovid, Met. 1. i. ad finem.

v. 6. That saintly lamp.]
Cacciaguida.

v. 12. To own thy thirst.]
"That thou mayst obtain from others a solution of any doubt that may occur to thee."

v. 15. Thou seest as clear.]
"Thou beholdest future events, with the same clearness of evidence, that we discern the simplest mathematical demonstrations."

v. 19. The point.]
The divine nature.

v. 27. The arrow.] Nam praevisa minus laedere tela solent. Ovid.
Che piaga antiveduta assai men duole. Petrarca, Trionfo del Tempo

v. 38. Contingency.]
"The evidence with which we see the future portrayed in the source of all truth, no more necessitates that future than does the image, reflected in the sight by a ship sailing down a stream, necessitate the motion of the vessel."

v. 43. From thence.]
"From the eternal sight; the view of the Deity.

v. 49. There.]
At Rome, where the expulsion of Dante's party from Florence was then plotting, in 1300.

v. 65. Theirs.]
"They shall be ashamed of the part they have taken aga'nst thee."

v. 69. The great Lombard.]
Either Alberto della Scala, or Bartolommeo his eldest son.
Their coat of arms was a ladder and an eagle.

v. 75. That mortal.]
Can Grande della Scala, born under the influence of Mars, but at this time only nine years old

v. 80. The Gascon.]
Pope Clement V.

v. 80. Great Harry.]
The Emperor Henry VII.

v. 127. The cry thou raisest.]
"Thou shalt stigmatize the faults of those who are most eminent and powerful."

CANTO XVIII

v. 3. Temp'ring the sweet with bitter.] Chewing the end of sweet and bitter fancy. Shakespeare, As you Like it, a. 3. s. 3.

v. 26. On this fifth lodgment of the tree.]
Mars, the fifth ot the @

v. 37. The great Maccabee.]
Judas Maccabeus.

v. 39. Charlemagne.]
L. Pulci commends Dante for placing Charlemagne and Orlando here: Io mi confido ancor molto qui a Dante Che non sanza cagion nel ciel su misse Carlo ed Orlando in quelle croci sante, Che come diligente intese e scrisse. Morg. Magg. c. 28.

v. 43. William and Renard.]
Probably not, as the commentators have imagined, William II of Orange, and his kinsman Raimbaud, two of the crusaders under Godfrey of Bouillon, (Maimbourg, Hist. des Croisades, ed. Par. 1682. 12mo. t. i. p. 96.) but rather the two more celebrated heroes in the age of Charlemagne.

The former, William l. of Orange, supposed to have been the founder of the present illustrious family of that name, died about 808, according to Joseph de la Piser, Tableau de l'Hist. des Princes et Principante d'Orange. Our countryman, Ordericus Vitalis, professes to give his true life, which had been misrepresented in the songs of the itinerant bards."

Vulgo canitur a joculatoribus de illo, cantilena; sed jure praeferenda est relatio authentica." Eccl. Hist. in Duchesne, Hist. Normann Script. p. 508. The latter is better known by having been celebrated by Ariosto, under the name of Rinaldo.

v. 43. Duke Godfey.]
Godfrey of Bouillon.

v. 46. Robert Guiscard.]
See Hell, Canto XXVIII. v. 12.

v. 81. The characters.]
Diligite justitiam qui judicatis terrarm. "Love righteousness, ye that be judges of the earth " Wisdom of
Solomon, c. i. 1.

v. 116. That once more.]
"That he may again drive out those who buy and sell in the temple."

v. 124. Taking the bread away.]
"Excommunication, or the interdiction of the Eucharist, is now employed as a weapon of warfare."

v. 126. That writest but to cancel.]
"And thou, Pope Boniface, who writest thy ecclesiastical censures for no other purpose than to be
paid for revoking them."

v. 130. To him.]
The coin of Florence was stamped with the impression of John the Baptist.

CANTO XIX
v. 38. Who turn'd his compass.]
Compare Proverbs, c. viii.
27. And Milton, P. L. b. vii 224.

v. 42. The Word]
"The divine nature still remained incomprehensible. Of this Lucifer was a proof; for had he thoroughly comprehended it, he would not have fallen."

v. 108. The Ethiop.]
Matt. c. xii. 41.

v. 112. That volume.]
Rev. c. xx. 12.

v. 114. Albert.]
Purgatory, Canto VI.
v. 98.

v. 116. Prague.]
The eagle predicts the devastation of Bohemia by Albert, which happened soon after this time, when that Emperor obtained the kingdom for his eldest son Rodolph.

See Coxe's House of Austria, 4to. ed. v. i. part 1. p. 87

v. 117. He.]
Philip IV of France, after the battle of Courtrai, 1302, in which the French were defeated by the Flemings, raised the nominal value of the coin.

This king died in consequence of his horse being thrown to the ground by a wild boar, in 1314

v. 121. The English and Scot.]
He adverts to the disputes between John Baliol and Edward I, the latter of whom is commended in the Purgatory, Canto VII. v. 130.

v. 122. The Spaniard's luxury.]
The commentators refer this to Alonzo X of Spain.

It seems probable that the allusion is to Ferdinand IV who came to the crown in 1295, and died in 1312, at the age of twenty four, in consequence, as it was supposed, of his extreme intemperance. See Mariana, Hist I. xv. c. 11.

v. 123. The Bohemian.]
Winceslaus II.
Purgatory, Canto VII. v.

v. 125. The halter of Jerusalem.]
Charles II of Naples and Jerusalem who was lame.
See note to Purgatory, Canto VII.
v. 122, and XX. v. 78.

v. 127. He.]

Frederick of Sicily son of Peter III of Arragon. Purgatory, Canto VII. v. 117. The isle of fire is Sicily, where was the tomb of Anchises.

v. 133. His uncle.]

James, king of Majorca and Minorca, brother to Peter III.

v. 133. His brother.]

James II of Arragon, who died in 1327. See Purgatory, Canto VII. v. 117.

v. 135. Of Portugal.]

In the time of Dante, Dionysius was king of Portugal.

He died in 1328, after a reign of near forty-six years, and does not seem to have deserved the stigma here fastened on him. See Mariana. and 1. xv. c. 18.

Perhaps the rebellious son of Dionysius may be alluded to.

v. 136. Norway.]

Haquin, king of Norway, is probably meant; who, having given refuge to the murderers of Eric VII king of Denmark, A D. 1288, commenced a war against his successor, Erie VIII, "which continued for nine years, almost to the utter ruin and destruction of both kingdoms."

Modern Univ. Hist. v. xxxii p. 215.

v. 136. -Him Of Ratza.] One of the dynasty of the house of Nemagna, which ruled the kingdom of Rassia, or Ratza, in Sclavonia, from 1161 to 1371, and whose history may be found in Mauro Orbino, Regno degli Slavi, Ediz. Pesaro. 1601. Uladislaus appears to have been the sovereign in Dante's time, but the disgraceful forgery adverted to in the text, is not recorded by the historian

v. 138. Hungary.]

The kingdom of Hungary was about this time disputed by Carobert, son of Charles Martel, and Winceslaus, prince of Bohemia, son of Winceslaus II.

See Coxe's House of Austria, vol. i. p. 1. p. 86. 4to edit.

v. 140. Navarre.]

Navarre was now under the yoke of France.

It soon after (in 1328) followed the advice of Dante and had a monarch of its own.

Mariana, 1. xv. c. 19.

v. 141. Mountainous girdle.]

The Pyrenees.

v. 143. -Famagosta's streets And Nicosia's.]

Cities in the kingdom of Cyprus, at that time ruled by Henry II a pusillanimous prince. Vertot.

Hist. des Chev.

de Malte, 1. iii. iv. The meaning appears to be, that the complaints made by those cities of their weak and worthless governor, may be regarded as an earnest of his condemnation at the last doom.

CANTO XX

v. 6. Wherein one shines.]

The light of the sun, whence he supposes the other celestial bodies to derive their light

v. 8. The great sign.]

The eagle, the Imperial ensign.

v. 34. Who.]
David.
v. 39. He.]
Trajan.
See Purgatory, Canto X. 68.
v. 44. He next.]
Hezekiah.
v. 50. 'The other following.]
Constantine.

There is no passage in which Dante's opinion of the evil; that had arisen from the mixture of the civil with the ecclesiastical power, is more unequivocally declared.

v. 57. William.]
William II, king of Sicily, at the latter part of
the twelfth century He was of the Norman line of sovereigns, and obtained the appellation of "the Good" and, as the poet says his loss was as much the subject of regret in his dominions, as the presence of Charles I of Anjou and Frederick of Arragon, was of sorrow and complaint.

v. 62. Trojan Ripheus.] Ripheus, justissimus unus Qui fuit in Teneris, et servantissimus aequi. Virg. Aen. 1. ii. 4--.

v. 97. This.]
Ripheus.
v. 98. That.]
Trajan.
v. 103. The prayers,] The prayers of St. Gregory
v. 119. The three nymphs.]
Faith, Hope, and Charity. Purgatory, Canto XXIX. 116.
v. 138. The pair.]
Ripheus and Trajan.

CANTO XXI

v. 12. The seventh splendour.]
The planet Saturn
v. 13. The burning lion's breast.]
The constellation Leo.
v. 21. In equal balance.]
"My pleasure was as great in complying with her will as in beholding her countenance."
v. 24. Of that lov'd monarch.]
Saturn.
Compare Hell, Canto XIV. 91.
v. 56. What forbade the smile.]
"Because it would have overcome thee."
v. 61. There aloft.]
Where the other souls were.
v. 97. A stony ridge.]
The Apennine.

v. 112. Pietro Damiano.]

"S. Pietro Damiano obtained a great and well-merited reputation, by the pains he took to correct the abuses among the clergy.

Ravenna is supposed to have been the place of his birth, about 1007.

He was employed in several important missions, and rewarded by Stephen IX with the dignity of cardinal, and the bishopric of Ostia, to which, however, he preferred his former retreat in the monastery of Fonte Aveliana, and prevailed on Alexander II to permit him to retire thither. Yet he did not long continue in this seclusion, before he was sent on other embassies.

He died at Faenza in 1072.

His letters throw much light on the obscure history of these times. Besides them, he has left several treatises on sacred and ecclesiastical subjects. His eloquence is worthy of a better age."

Tiraboschi, Storia della Lett Ital. t. iii. 1. iv. c. 2.

v. 114. Beside the Adriatic.]

At Ravenna.

Some editions have FU instead of FUI, according to which reading, Pietro distinguishes himself from another Pietro, who was termed "Peccator," the sinner.

v. 117. The hat.]

The cardinal's hat.

v. 118. Cephas.]

St. Peter.

v. 119 The Holy Spirit's vessel.]

St. Paul. See Hell, Canto II. 30.

v. 130. Round this.]

Round the spirit of Pietro Damiano.

CANTO XXII

v. 14. The vengeance.]

Beatrice, it is supposed, intimates the approaching fate of Boniface VIII. See Purgatory, Canto XX. 86.

v. 36. Cassino.]

A castle in the Terra di Lavoro.

v. 38. I it was.]

"A new order of monks, which in a manner absorbed all the others that were established in the west, was instituted, A.D. 529, by Benedict of Nursis, a man of piety and reputation for the age he lived in."

Maclaine's Mosheim, Eccles. Hist. v. ii. cent. vi. p. 2. ch. 2 - 6.

v. 48. Macarius.]

There are two of this name enumerated by Mosheim among the Greek theologians of the fourth century, v. i. cent. iv p. 11 ch. 2 - 9.

In the following chapter, 10, it is said, "Macarius, an Egyptian monk, undoubtedly deserves the first rank among the practical matters of this time, as his works displayed, some few things excepted, the brightest and most lovely portraiture of sanctity and virtue."

v. 48. Romoaldo.]

S. Romoaldo, a native of Ravenna, and the founder of the order of Camaldoli, died in 1027.

He was the author of a commentary on the Psalms.

v. 70. The patriarch Jacob.]
So Milton, P. L. b. iii. 510: The stairs were such, as whereon Jacob saw Angels ascending and descending, bands Of guardians bright.

v. 107. The sign.]
The constellation of Gemini.

v. 130. This globe.]
So Chaucer, Troilus and Cresseide, b. v,

And down from thence fast he gan avise This little spot of earth, that with the sea Embraced is, and fully gan despite This wretched world.

Compare Cicero, Somn. Scip.
"Jam ipsa terra ita mihi parva visa est." &c.
Lucan, Phar 1. ix. 11; and Tasso, G. L. c. xiv. st, 9, 10, 11.

v. 140. Maia and Dione.]
The planets Mercury and Venus.

CANTO XXIII

v. 11. That region.]
Towards the south, where the course of the sun appears less rapid, than, when he is in the east or the west.

v. 26. Trivia.]
A name of Diana.

v. 26. Th' eternal nymphs.]
The stars.

v. 36. The Might.]
Our Saviour

v. 71. The rose.]
The Virgin Mary.

v. 73. The lilies.]
The apostles.

v. 84. Thou didst exalt thy glory.]
The diving light retired upwards, to render the eyes of Dante more capable of enduring the spectacle
which now presented itself.

v. 86. The name of that fair flower.]
The name of the Virgin.

v. 92. A cresset.]
The angel Gabriel.

v. 98. That lyre.]
By synecdoche, the lyre is put for the angel

v. 99. The goodliest sapphire.]
The Virgin

v. 126. Those rich-laden coffers.]
Those spirits who, having sown the seed of good works on earth, now contain the fruit of their pious endeavours.

v. 129. In the Babylonian exile.]
During their abode in this world.

v. 133. He.]
St. Peter, with the other holy men of the Old and New testament.

The Divine Comedy
CANTO XXIV

v. 28. Such folds.]
Pindar has the same bold image: [GREEK HERE?] On which Hayne strangely remarks:
Ad ambitus stropharum vldetur

v. 65. Faith.]
Hebrews, c. xi. 1.
So Marino, in one of his sonnets, which calls Divozioni:
Fede e sustanza di sperate cose, E delle non visioili argomento.

v. 82. Current.]
"The answer thou hast made is right; but let me know if thy inward persuasion is conformable to thy profession."

v. 91. The ancient bond and new.]
The Old and New Testament.

v. 114. That Worthy.]
Quel Baron. In the next Canto, St. James is called "Barone."
So in Boccaccio, G. vi. N. 10, we find "Baron Messer Santo Antonio."

v. 124. As to outstrip.]
Venturi insists that the Poet has here, "made a slip;" for that John came first to the sepulchre, though Peter was the first to enter it.
But let Dante have leave to explain his own meaning, in a passage from his third book De Monarchia:
"Dicit etiam Johannes ipsum (scilicet Petrum) introiisse SUBITO, cum venit in monumentum, videns allum discipulum cunctantem ad ostium." Opere de Dante, Ven. 1793. T. ii. P. 146.

CANTO XXV

v. 6. The fair sheep-fold.]
Florence, whence he was banished.

v. 13. For its sake.]
For the sake of that faith.

v. 20. Galicia throng'd with visitants.] See Mariana, Hist. 1. xi. v. 13.
"En el tiempo," &c.
"At the time that the sepulchre of the apostle St. James was discovered, the devotion for that place extended itself not only over all Spain, but even round about to foreign nations. Multitudes from all parts of the world came to visit it.
Many others were deterred by the difficulty for the journey, by the roughness and barrenness of those parts, and by the incursions of the Moors, who made captives many of the pilgrims.
The canons of St. Eloy afterwards (the precise time is not known), with a desire of remedying these evils, built, in many places, along the whole read, which reached as far as to France, hospitals for the reception of the pilgrims."

v. 31. Who.]
The Epistle of St. James is here attributed to the elder apostle of that name, whose shrine was at Compostella, in Galicia.
Which of the two was the author of it is yet doubtful. The learned and candid Michaelis contends very forcibly for its having been written by James the Elder.

Lardner rejects that opinion as absurd; while Benson argues against it, but is well answered by Michaelis, who after all, is obliged to leave the question undecided.

See his Introduction to the New Testament, translated by Dr. Marsh, ed. Cambridge, 1793. V. iv. c. 26. - 1, 2, 3.

v. 35. As Jesus.]
In the transfiguration on Mount Tabor.

v. 39. The second flame.]
St. James.

v. 40. I lifted up.]
"I will lift up mine eyes unto the hills, from whence cometh my help." Ps. Cxxi. 1.

v. 59. From Egypt to Jerusalem.]
From the lower world to heaven.

v. 67. Hope.]
This is from the Sentences of Petrus Lombardus. "Est autem spes virtus, qua spiritualia et aeterna bona speratam, id est, beatitudinem aeternam.

Sine meritis enim aliquid sperare non spes, sed praesumptio, dici potest."
Pet. Lomb. Sent. 1. Iii. Dist. 26. Ed. Bas. 1486. Fol.

v. 74. His anthem.]
Psalm ix. 10.

v. 90. Isaias]
Chap. lxi. 10.

v. 94. Thy brother.]
St. John in the Revelation, c. vii. 9.

v. 101. Winter's month.]
"If a luminary, like that which now appeared, were to shine throughout the month following the winter solstice during which the constellation Cancer appears in the east at the setting of the sun, there would be no interruption to the light, but the whole month would be as a single day."

v. 112. This.]
St. John, who reclined on the bosom of our Saviour, and to whose charge Jesus recommended his mother.

v. 121. So I.]
He looked so earnestly, to descry whether St. John were present there in body, or in spirit only, having had his doubts raised by that saying of our Saviour's:

"If I will, that he tarry till I come what is that to thee."

v. 127. The two.]
Christ and Mary, whom he has described, in the last Canto but one, as rising above his sight

CANTO XXVI

v. 2. The beamy flame.]
St. John.

v. 13. Ananias' hand.]
Who, by putting his hand on St. Paul, restored his sight.
Acts, c. ix. 17.

v. 36. From him.]
Some suppose that Plato is here meant, who, in his Banquet, makes Phaedrus say:
"Love is confessedly amongst the eldest of beings, and, being the eldest, is the cause to us of the greatest goods " Plat. Op. t. x. p. 177. Bip. ed. Others have understood it of Aristotle, and others, of the writer who goes by the name of Dionysius the Areopagite, referred to in the twenty-eighth Canto.

v. 40. I will make.]
Exodus, c. xxxiii. 19.

v. 42. At the outset.]
John, c. i. 1. &c.

v. 51. The eagle of our Lord.]
St. John

v. 62. The leaves.]
Created beings.

v. 82. The first living soul.]
Adam.

v. 107. Parhelion.]
Who enlightens and comprehends all things; but is himself enlightened and comprehended by none.

v. 117. Whence.]
That is, from Limbo.
See Hell, Canto II.
53. Adam says that 5232 years elapsed from his creation to the time of his deliverance, which followed the death of Christ.

v. 133. EL]
Some read UN, "One," instead of EL: but the latter of these readings is confirmed by a passage from Dante's Treatise De Vulg. Eloq. 1. i. cap. 4. "Quod prius vox primi loquentis sonaverit, viro sanae mentis in promptu esse non dubito ipsum fuisse quod Deus est, videlicet El."
St. Isidore in the Origines, 1.
vii. c. 1. had said, "Primum apud Hebraeos Dei nomen El dicitur."

v. 135. Use.]
From Horace, Ars. Poet. 62.

v. 138. All my life.]
"I remained in the terrestrial Paradise only tothe seventh hour."
In the Historia Scolastica of Petrus Comestor, it is said of our first parents: Quidam tradunt eos fuisse in Paradiso septem horae."
I. 9. ed. Par. 1513. 4to.

CANTO XXVII

v. 1. Four torches.]
St. Peter, St. James, St. John, and Adam.

v. 11. That.]
St. Peter' who looked as the planet Jupiter would, if it assumed the sanguine appearance of liars.

v. 20. He.]
Boniface VIII.

v. 26. such colour.] Qui color infectis adversi solis ab ietu Nubibus esse solet; aut purpureae Aurorae. Ovid, Met. 1. iii. 184.

v. 37. Of Linus and of Cletus.]
Bishops of Rome in the first century.

v. 40. Did Sextus, Pius, and Callixtus bleed And Urban.] The former two, bishops of the same see, in the second; and the others, in the fourth century.

v. 42. No purpose was of ours.]
"We did not intend that our successors should take any part in the political divisions among Christians, or that my figure (the seal of St. Peter) should serve as a mark to authorize iniquitous grants and privileges."

v. 51. Wolves.]
Compare Milton, P. L. b. xii. 508, &c.

v. 53. Cahorsines and Gascons.]
He alludes to Jacques d'Ossa, a native of Cahors, who filled the papal chair in 1316, after it had been two years vacant, and assumed the name of John XXII., and to Clement V, a Gascon, of whom see Hell, Canto XIX. 86, and Note.

v. 63. The she-goat.]
When the sun is in Capricorn.

v. 72. From the hour.]
Since he had last looked (see Canto XXII.) he perceived that he had passed from the meridian circle to the eastern horizon, the half of our hemisphere, and a quarter of the heaven.

v. 76. From Gades.]
See Hell, Canto XXVI. 106

v. 78. The shore.]
Phoenicia, where Europa, the daughter of Agenor mounted on the back of Jupiter, in his shape of a bull.

v. 80. The sun.]
Dante was in the constellation Gemini, and the sun in Aries.
There was, therefore, part of those two constellations, and the whole of Taurus, between them.

v. 93. The fair nest of Leda.]
"From the Gemini;" thus called, because Leda was the mother of the twins, Castor and Pollux

v. 112. Time's roots.]
"Here," says Beatrice, "are the roots, from whence time springs: for the parts, into which it is divided, the other heavens must be considered."
And she then breaks out into an exclamation on the degeneracy of human nature, which does not lift itself to the contemplation of divine things.

v. 126. The fair child of him.]
So she calls human nature. Pindar by a more easy figure, terms the day, "child of the sun."

v. 129. None.]
Because, as has been before said, the shepherds are become wolves.

v. 131. Before the date.]
"Before many ages are past, before those fractions, which are drops in the reckoning of every year, shall amount to so large a portion of time, that January shall be no more a winter month." By this periphrasis is meant " in a short

time," as we say familiarly, such a thing will happen before a thousand years are over when we mean, it will happen soon.

v. 135. Fortune shall be fain.]
The commentators in general suppose that our Poet here augurs that great reform, which he vainly hoped would follow on the arrival of the Emperor Henry VII. in Italy. Lombardi refers the prognostication to Can Grande della Scala: and, when we consider that this Canto was not finished till after the death of

Henry, as appears from the mention that is made of John XXII, it cannot be denied but the conjecture is probable.

CANTO XXVIII

v. 36. Heav'n, and all nature, hangs upon that point.]
[GREEK HERE] Aristot. Metaph. 1. xii. c. 7.
"From that beginning depend heaven and nature."

v. 43. Such diff'rence.]
The material world and the intelligential (the copy and the pattern) appear to Dante to differ in this respect, that the orbits of the latter are more swift, the nearer they are to the centre, whereas the contrary is the case with the orbits of the former. The seeming contradiction is thus accounted for by Beatrice.

In the material world, the more ample the body is, the greater is the good of which itis capable supposing all the parts to be equally perfect. But in the intelligential world, the circles are more excellent and powerful, the more they approximate to the central point, which is God.

Thus the first circle, that of the seraphim, corresponds to the ninth sphere, or primum mobile, the second, that of the cherubim, to the eighth sphere, or heaven of fixed stars; the third, or circle of thrones, to the seventh sphere, or planet of Saturn; and in like manner throughout the two other trines of circles and spheres.

In orbs Of circuit inexpressible they stood, Orb within orb Milton, P. L. b. v. 596.

v. 70. The sturdy north.]
Compare Homer, II. b. v. 524.

v. 82. In number.]
The sparkles exceeded the number which would be produced by the sixty-four squares of a chess-board, if for the first we reckoned one, for the next, two; for the third, four; and so went on doubling to the end of the account.

v. 106. Fearless of bruising from the nightly ram.]
Not injured, like the productions of our spring, by the influence of autumn, when the constellation Aries rises at sunset.

v. 110. Dominations.] Hear all ye angels, progeny of light, Thrones, domination's, princedoms, virtues, powers. Milton, P. L. b. v. 601.

v. 119. Dionysius.]
The Areopagite, in his book De Caelesti Hierarchia.

v. 124. Gregory.]
Gregory the Great.

"Novem vero angelorum ordines diximus, quia videlicet esse, testante sacro eloquio, scimus: Angelos, archangelos, virtutes, potestates, principatus, dominationae, thronos, cherubin atque seraphin."

Divi Gregorii, Hom. xxxiv. f. 125. ed. Par. 1518. fol.

v. 126. He had learnt.]
Dionysius, he says, had learnt from St. Paul. It is almost unnecessary to add, that the book, above referred to, which goes under his name, was the production of a later age.

CANTO XXIX

v. 1. No longer.]
As short a space, as the sun and moon are in changing hemispheres, when they are opposite to one another, the one under the sign of Aries, and the other under that of Libra, and both hang for a moment, noised as it were in the hand of the zenith.

v. 22. For, not in process of before or aft.]
There was neither "before nor after," no distinction, that is, of time, till the creation of the world.

v. 30. His threefold operation.]
He seems to mean that spiritual beings, brute matter, and the intermediate part of the creation, which participates both of spirit and matter, were produced at once.

v. 38. On Jerome's pages.]
St. Jerome had described the angels as created before the rest of the universe: an opinion which Thomas
Aquinas controverted; and the latter, as Dante thinks, had Scripture on his side.

v. 51. Pent.]
See Hell, Canto XXXIV. 105.

v. 111. Of Bindi and of Lapi.]
Common names of men at Florence

v. 112. The sheep.]
So Milton, Lycidas. The hungry sheep look up and are not fed, But, swoln with wind and the rank mist they draw, Rot inwardly.

v. 121. The preacher.] Thus Cowper, Task, b. ii.
'Tis pitiful To court a grin, when you should woo a soul, &c.

v. 131. Saint Anthony. Fattens with this his swine.] On the sale of these blessings, the brothers of St. Anthony supported themselves and their paramours.
From behind the swine of St. Anthony, our Poet levels a blow at the object of his inveterate enmity, Boniface VIII, from whom, "in 1297, they obtained the dignity and privileges of an independent congregation."
See Mosheim's Eccles. History in Dr. Maclaine's Translation, v. ii. cent. xi. p. 2. c. 2. - 28.

v. 140. Daniel.]
"Thousand thousands ministered unto him, and ten thousand times ten thousand stood before him."
Dan. c. vii. 10.

The Divine Comedy
CANTO XXX

v. 1. Six thousand miles.]
He compares the vanishing of the vision to the fading away of the stars at dawn, when it is noon-day six thousand miles off, and the shadow, formed by the earth over the part of it inhabited by the Poet, is about to disappear.

v. 13. Engirt.]
" ppearing to be encompassed by these angelic bands, which are in reality encompassed by it."

v. 18. This turn.]
Questa vice. Hence perhaps Milton, P. L. b. viii. 491. This turn hath made amends.

v. 39. Forth.]
From the ninth sphere to the empyrean, which is more light.

v. 44. Either mighty host.]
Of angels, that remained faithful, and of beatified souls, the latter in that form which they will have at the last day.

v. 61. Light flowing.]
"And he showed me a pure river of water of life, clear as crystal, proceeding out of the throne of God and of the Lamb." Rev. cxxii. I.
--underneath a bright sea flow'd Of jasper, or of liquid pearl. Milton, P. L. b. iii. 518.

v. 80. Shadowy of the truth.] Son di lor vero ombriferi prefazii. So Mr. Coleridge, in his Religious Musings, v. 406. Life is a vision shadowy of truth.

v. 88. --the eves Of mine eyelids.] Thus Shakespeare calls the eyelids "penthouse lids." Macbeth, a, 1. s, 3.

v. 108. As some cliff.] A lake That to the fringed bank with myrtle crown'd Her crystal mirror holds. Milton, P. L. b. iv. 263.

v. 118. My view with ease.] Far and wide his eye commands For sight no obstacle found here, nor shade, But all sunshine. Milton, P. l. b. iii. 616.

v. 135. Of the great Harry.]
The Emperor Henry VII, who died in 1313.

v. 141. He.]
Pope Clement V. See Canto XXVII. 53.

v. 145. Alagna's priest.]
Pope Boniface VIII. Hell, Canto XIX. 79.

CANTO XXXI

v. 6. Bees.]
Compare Homer, Iliad, ii. 87. Virg. Aen. I. 430, and Milton, P. L. b. 1. 768.

v. 29. Helice.]
Callisto, and her son Arcas, changed into the constellations of the Greater Bear and Arctophylax, or Bootes. See Ovid, Met. l. ii. fab. v. vi.

v. 93. Bernard.]
St. Bernard, the venerable abbot of Clairvaux, and the great promoter of the second crusade, who died A.D. 1153, in his sixty-third year.
His sermons are called by Henault, "chefs~d'oeuvres de sentiment et de force."

Abrege Chron. de l'Hist. de Fr. 1145. They have even been preferred to all the productions of the ancients, and the author has been termed the last of the fathers of the church. It is uncertain whether they were not delivered originally in the French tongue.

That the part he acts in the present Poem should be assigned to him. appears somewhat remarkable, when we consider that he severely censured the new festival established in honour of the Immaculate Conception of the virgin, and opposed the doctrine itself with the greatest vigour, as it supposed her being honoured with a privilegewhich belonged to Christ Alone Dr. Maclaine's Mosheim, v. iii. cent. xii. p. ii. c. 3 - 19.

v. 95. Our Veronica] The holy handkerchief, then preserved at Rome, on which the countenance of our Saviour was supposed to have been imprest.

v. 101. Him.]
St. Bernard.
v. 108. The queen.]
The Virgin Mary.
v. 119. Oriflamb.]
Menage on this word quotes the Roman des Royau -Iignages of Guillaume Ghyart. Oriflamme est une banniere De cendal roujoyant et simple Sans portraiture d'autre affaire,

CANTO XXXII

v. 3. She.]
Eve.
v. 8. Ancestress.]
Ruth, the ancestress of David.
v. 60. In holy scripture.]
Gen. c. xxv. 22.
v. 123. Lucia.]
See Hell, Canto II. 97.

CANTO XXXIII

v. 63. The Sybil's sentence.]
Virg. Aen. iii. 445.
v. 89. One moment.]
"A moment seems to me more tedious, than five-and-twenty ages would have appeared to the Argonauts, when they had resolved on their expedition.

v. 92. Argo's shadow] Quae simul ac rostro ventosnm proscidit aequor, Tortaque remigio spumis incanduit unda, Emersere feri candenti e gurgite vultus Aequoreae monstrum Nereides admirantes. Catullus, De Nupt. Pel. et Thet. 15.

v. 109. Three orbs of triple hue, clipt in one bound.]
The Trinity.

The Divine Comedy

v. 118. That circling.]
The second of the circles, "Light of Light," in which he dimly beheld the mystery of the incarnation.

End Paradise.

A CHRONOLOGICAL VIEW OF THE AGE OF DANTE

A. D.
1265.
Dante, son of Alighieri degli Alighieri and Bella, is born at Florence. Of his own ancestry he speaks in the Paradise, Canto XV. and XVI.

In the same year, Manfredi, king of Naples and Sicily, is defeated and slain by Charles of Anjou.

Hell, C. XXVIII. 13. And Purgatory, C. III. 110.

Guido Novello of Polenta obtains the sovereignty of Ravenna. H. C. XXVII. 38.

1266.
Two of the Frati Godenti chosen arbitrators of the differences at Florence. H. C. XXIII. 104. Gianni de' Soldanieri heads the populace in that city. H. C. XXXII. 118.

1268.
Charles of Anjou puts Conradine to death, and becomes King of Naples. H. C. XXVIII. 16 and Purg C. XX. 66.

1272.
Henry III. of England is succeeded by Edward I. Purg. C. VII. 129.

1274.
Our Poet first sees Beatrice, daughter of Folco Portinari.
Fra. Guittone d'Arezzo, the poet, dies.
Purg. C. XXIV. 56. Thomas Aquinas dies.
Purg. C. XX. 67.
and Par. C. X. 96. Buonaventura dies.
Par. C. XII. 25.

1275.
Pierre de la Brosse, secretary to Philip III. of France, executed.
Purg. C. VI. 23.

1276.
Giotto, the painter, is born.
Purg. C. XI. 95.
Pope Adrian V. dies.
Purg. C. XIX. 97. Guido Guinicelli, the poet, dies.
Purg. C. XI. 96. and C. XXVI. 83.

1277.
Pope John XXI.
dies.
Par. C. XII. 126.

1278.
Ottocar, king of Bohemia, dies.

The Divine Comedy

Purg. C. VII. 97.
1279.
Dionysius succeeds to the throne of Portugal.
Par. C. XIX. 135.
1280.
Albertus Magnus dies.
Par. C. X. 95.
1281.
Pope Nicholas III. dies.
H. C. XIX 71. Dante studies at the universities of Bologna and Padua.
1282.
The Sicilian vespers.
Par. C. VIII. 80. The French defeated by the people of Forli.
H. C. XXVII. 41. Tribaldello de' Manfredi betrays the city of Faenza.
H. C. XXXII. 119.
1284.
Prince Charles of Anjou is defeated and made prisoner by Rugiez de Lauria, admiral to Peter III. of Arragon.
Purg. C. XX. 78. Charles I.
king of Naples, dies.
Purg. C. VII. 111.
1285.
Pope Martin IV.
dies.
Purg. C. XXIV. 23. Philip III.
of France, and Peter III.
of Arragon, die. Purg. C. VII. 101 and 110. Henry II. king of Cyprus, comes to the throne.
Par. C. XIX. 144.
1287.
Guido dalle Colonne (mentioned by Dante in his De Vulgari Eloquio) writes "The War of Troy."
1288.
Haquin, king of Norway, makes war on Denmark.
Par. C. XIX. 135. Count Ugolino de' Gherardeschi dies of famine.
H. C. XXXIII. 14.
1289.
Dante is in the battle of Campaldino, where the Florentines defeat the people of Arezzo, June 11. Purg. C. V. 90.
1290.
Beatrice dies.
Purg. C. XXXII. 2. He serves in the war waged by the Florentines upon the Pisans, and is present at the surrender of Caprona in the autumn.
H. C. XXI. 92.
1291.
He marries Gemma de' Donati, with whom he lives unhappily.
By this marriage he had five sons and a daughter. Can Grande della Scala is born, March 9.
H. C. I. 98. Purg. C. XX. 16.

Par. C. XVII. 75. and XXVII. 135. The renegade Christians assist the Saracens to recover St. John D'Acre.

H. C. XXVII. 84. The Emperor Rodolph dies.

Purg. C. VI. 104. and VII. 91. Alonzo III.

of Arragon dies, and is succeeded by James II. Purg. C. VII. 113. and Par. C. XIX. 133.

1294.

Clement V.

abdicates the papal chair.

H. C. III. 56. Dante writes his Vita Nuova.

1295.

His preceptor, Brunetto Latini, dies.

H.

C. XV. 28. Charles Martel, king of Hungary, visits Florence, Par.

C. VIII. 57. and dies in the same year. Frederick, son of Peter III. of Arragon, becomes king of Sicily. Purg. C. VII. 117. and Par. C. XIX. 127.

1296.

Forese, the companion of Dante, dies. Purg. C. XXXIII. 44.

1300.

The Bianca and Nera parties take their rise in Pistoia. H. C. XXXII. 60. This is the year in which he supposes himself to see his Vision. H. C. I. 1. and XXI. 109. He is chosen chief magistrate, or first of the Priors of Florence; and continues in office from June 15 to August 15. Cimabue, the painter, dies.

Purg. C. XI. 93. Guido Cavalcanti, the most beloved of our Poet's friends, dies. H. C. X. 59. and Purg

C. XI. 96.

1301.

The Bianca party expels the Nera from Pistoia.

H. C. XXIV. 142.

1302.

January 27.

During his absence at Rome, Dante is mulcted by his fellow-citizens in the sum of 8000 lire, and condemned to two years' banishment. March 10.

He is sentenced, if taken, to be burned. Fulcieri de' Calboli commits great atrocities on certain of the Ghibelline party.

Purg. C. XIV. 61. Carlino de' Pazzi betrays the castle di Piano Travigne, in Valdarno, to the Florentines.

H. C. XXXII. 67. The French vanquished in the battle of Courtrai. Purg. C. XX. 47. James, king of Majorca and Minorca, dies.

Par. C. XIX. 133.

1303.

Pope Boniface VIII.

dies.

H. C. XIX. 55.

Purg.

C. XX. 86.

XXXII. 146. and Par. C. XXVII. 20. The other exiles appoint Dante one of a council of twelve, under Alessandro da Romena. He appears to have been much dissatisfied with his colleagues. Par. C. XVII. 61.

1304.

The Divine Comedy

He joins with the exiles in an unsuccessful attack on the city of Florence. May.

The bridge over the Arno breaks down during a representation of the infernal torments exhibited on that river. H. C. XXVI.

9. July 20.

Petrarch, whose father had been banished two years before from Florence, is born at Arezzo.

1305.

Winceslaus II.

king of Bohemia, dies.

Purg. C. VII. 99. and Par. C. XIX 123. A conflagration happens at Florence.

H. C. XXVI. 9.

1306.

Dante visits Padua.

1307.

He is in Lunigiana with the Marchese Marcello Malaspina. Purg. C. VIII. 133.

and C. XIX. 140. Dolcino, the fanatic, is burned.

H. C. XXVIII. 53.

1308.

The Emperor Albert I.

murdered.

Purg. C. VI. 98. and Par. C. XIX. 114. Corso Donati, Dante's political enemy, slain.

Purg. C. XXIV. 81. He seeks an asylum at Verona, under the roof of the Signori della

Scala.

Par. C. XVII. 69.

He wanders, about this time, over various parts of Italy.

See his Convito.

He is at Paris twice; and, as one of the early commentators reports, at Oxford.

1309.

Charles II. king of Naples, dies.

Par. C. XIX. 125.

1310.

The Order of the Templars abolished.

Purg. C. XX. 94.

1313.

The Emperor Henry of Luxemburg, by whom he had hoped to be restored to Florence, dies.

Par. C. XVII. 80.

and XXX. 135. He takes refuge at Ravenna with Guido Novello da Polenta.

1314.

Pope Clement V. dies.

H. C. XIX. 86.

and Par. C. XXVII. 53.

and XXX. 141. Philip IV.

of France dies.
Purg. C. VII. 108. and Par. C. XIX. 117. Ferdinand IV.
of Spain, dies.
Par.
C.
XIX.
122. Giacopo da Carrara defeated by Can Grande.
Par. C. IX. 45.
1316.
John XXII. elected Pope.
Par. C. XXVII. 53.
1321.
July.
Dante dies at Ravenna, of a complaint brought on by disappointment at his failure in a negotiation which he had been conducting with the Venetians, for his patron Guido Novello da Polenta. His obsequies are sumptuously performed at Ravenna by Guido, who himself died in the ensuing year.

www.ingramcontent.com/pod-product-compliance
Lightning Source LLC
Chambersburg PA
CBHW071949070526
44583CB00015B/1121